INDIVIDUAL COUNTY CHRONOLOGIES, MAPS, AND AREAS presents boundary changes of a particular county complete with dates of recorded change, a summary of changes, and the resulting area in square miles. When changes cannot be mapped, explanations are provided.

Locator maps identify the county within its state, showing current county configuration. For counties now in other states, the locator map will include appropriate areas.

Numbers in black circles link the maps to the entries in the table.

Map headings show the range of dates for which changes are valid; where more than one range of dates appears, the county was later restored to this configuration.

Heavy lines depict the county boundary during the indicated range of dates.

Underlying map is standard base map drawn by the U.S. Geological Survey.

A standard scale is used throughout unless specifically noted.

When smaller scales are necessary, the alternate scale appears directly beneath small-scale maps.

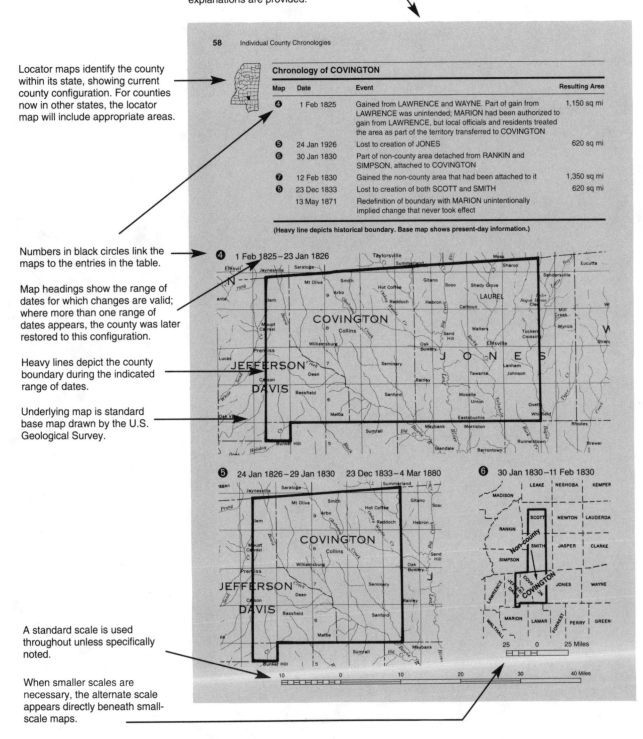

58   Individual County Chronologies

Chronology of COVINGTON

Map	Date	Event	Resulting Area
④	1 Feb 1825	Gained from LAWRENCE and WAYNE. Part of gain from LAWRENCE was unintended; MARION had been authorized to gain from LAWRENCE, but local officials and residents treated the area as part of the territory transferred to COVINGTON	1,150 sq mi
⑤	24 Jan 1926	Lost to creation of JONES	620 sq mi
⑥	30 Jan 1830	Part of non-county area detached from RANKIN and SIMPSON, attached to COVINGTON	
⑦	12 Feb 1830	Gained the non-county area that had been attached to it	1,350 sq mi
⑤	23 Dec 1833	Lost to creation of both SCOTT and SMITH	620 sq mi
	13 May 1871	Redefinition of boundary with MARION unintentionally implied change that never took effect	

(Heavy line depicts historical boundary. Base map shows present-day information.)

④ 1 Feb 1825 – 23 Jan 1826

⑤ 24 Jan 1826 – 29 Jan 1830   23 Dec 1833 – 4 Mar 1880

⑥ 30 Jan 1830 – 11 Feb 1830

CONNECTICUT
MAINE
MASSACHUSETTS
RHODE ISLAND

This atlas has been supported by a grant from the
National Endowment for the Humanities, an independent federal agency.

CONNECTICUT
MAINE
MASSACHUSETTS
RHODE ISLAND

Atlas of Historical County Boundaries

John H. Long, Editor

CONNECTICUT
Compiled by Gordon DenBoer

MAINE, MASSACHUSETTS, and RHODE ISLAND
Compiled by John H. Long

A Project of the
Dr. William M. Scholl Center for Family and Community History
The Newberry Library

Simon & Schuster
A Paramount Communications Company
New York London Toronto Sydney Tokyo Singapore

Simon & Schuster
Academic Reference Division
15 Columbus Circle
New York, New York 10023

Printed in the United States of America

printing number

1 2 3 4 5 6 7 8 9 10

Library of Congress Cataloging-in-Publication Data

Atlas of historical county boundaries. Connecticut, Maine,
   Massachusetts, Rhode Island / John H. Long, editor; Connecticut
   compiled by Gordon DenBoer; Maine, Massachusetts, and Rhode Island
   compiled by John H. Long.
      p.   cm.
   Includes bibliographical references.
   ISBN 0-13-051947-2
   1. Connecticut—Administrative and political divisions—Maps.
2. Maine—Administrative and political divisions—Maps.
3. Massachusetts—Administrative and political divisions—Maps.
4. Rhode Island—Administrative and political divisions—Maps.
5. Connecticut—Historical geography —Maps.   6. Maine—Historical
geography —Maps.   7. Massachusetts—Historical geography —Maps.
8. Rhode Island—Historical geography —Maps.   9. Connecticut—
History   10. Maine—History   11. Massachusetts—History
12. Rhode Island—History   I. Long, John Hamilton.   II. DenBoer,
Gordon.   III. Title: Connecticut, Maine, Massachusetts, Rhode Island
G1201.F7A8   1993 Conn. <G&M>
911'.74—dc20   94-2053
                                                  CIP
                                                  MAP

*This paper meets the requirements of ANSI/NISO
Z39.48–1992 (Permanence of Paper).*

Contents

Connecticut

Maine

Massachusetts

Rhode Island

Preface and Acknowledgments

In 1933 the distinguished historian Frederick Merk lamented the lack of "a set of maps tracing the county divisions of the United States," because such maps "would have been of inestimable service to scholars in various fields" (*New England Quarterly*, 6:622). Merk was concerned primarily with outline maps for the plotting of statistics and, knowing that the federal government had published such maps for the census years 1840 to 1900, he was particularly interested in the earlier censuses, 1790 to 1830. This atlas is an attempt not only to satisfy that longstanding need, but also to provide complete and comprehensive information on all changes in all counties, individually and in aggregate.

A single question has focused the preparation of this atlas: at any time in history, what was the legal, effective arrangement of American county jurisdiction? A great number of people seek answers to that question, and, as Merk knew, their fields vary—demography, economics, genealogy, geography, history, law, political science, and other disciplines—and their interests cover a wide spectrum of place and time, from the national level to the local and from the colonial era to the present. The combined needs of this diverse audience shaped the primary goal of this atlas and determined its scope, its content, and its forms.

The geographic scope of the atlas encompasses the historical territory of the forty-eight contiguous states and Hawaii, and the chronological coverage extends to 1990 from the 1630s when the earliest colonial counties were created. The content is not limited strictly to boundary changes, but also includes such other facets of the jurisdictional issue as unsuccessful authorizations for change and attachments of unorganized counties and non-county areas to operational counties. Data on the many changes in American counties are presented in both text (consolidated and individual county chronologies) and maps (detailed maps of individual counties and outline maps of the entire state's county network). Unlike the offerings of most reference works, these data come not from a synthesis of existing knowledge but are the fruits of original research in primary sources.

The consolidated chronology should be the starting point for readers concerned with a specific period or date, while those interested in particular counties can quickly find their subjects in the section of individual county chronologies and maps. The table of censuses and the set of census outline maps, which cover colonial, territorial, and state enumerations or equivalents, in addition to federal censuses, are designed to serve readers interested in statistical analysis and mapping.

The Newberry Library, Chicago, has been both headquarters and institutional sponsor for this atlas; its rich holdings in old maps and in state and local history, its commitment to scholarship, and its knowledgeable and dedicated staff make it the ideal place to conduct this sort of project. Special thanks are due David Buisseret, Director of the library's Hermon Dunlap Smith Center for the History of Cartography, for his contribution to the continuation of the project, and Richard H. Brown, Academic Vice President, for his stalwart support of the project and his role in bringing the work to fruition. Newberry volunteer Don Burke assisted with measuring county areas and proofreading, and Louise Alcorn and Elizabeth Worzalla, Student Fellows of the Newberry Library–Associated Colleges of the Midwest/ Great Lakes Colleges Association Humanities Seminar, carefully checked many citations. Research Associate Peggy Tuck Sinko compiled all the data on the censuses.

Editorial assistants Karen Lewak and David Strass merit special recognition. Not only did they format and type (and retype) the chronologies and text, they also maintained the master bibliography of nearly two thousand items. In addition, their editing, proofreading, and checking of the bibliography and citations contributed greatly to the accuracy and readability of the information presented here.

Because the Newberry Library lacks the resources of a full-fledged law library, the atlas staff made frequent use of the Northwestern University Law Library and the Cook County Law Library, which generously facilitated use of their collections. Marsha Selmer, Curator of Maps at the University of Illinois at Chicago, rendered valuable assistance with large-scale topographic maps, both new and old.

Thanks are also due the many town, county, and state officials, local historians, and librarians who answered questions and furnished documents. Special thanks go to the following in Connecticut: James W. Campbell, New Haven Colony Historical Society; Malyn Rogers Kamenoff, Sherman Historical Society; Carolyn M. Picciano and Richard C. Roberts, Connecticut State Library; John Pillis, Watertown Historical Society; Joan Quarto, Mansfield; and Alesandra M. Schmidt, Connecticut Historical Society. Special thanks for assistance also go to Elanor Berry and R. W. Swank of Lincoln County, Maine, to the staff of the Maine State Law Library, and to Mary Ann Neary and Bette L. Siegel of the Massachusetts State Library. In Rhode Island special assistance was provided by: Thomas R. Evans, Rhode Island State Library; Howard T. Senzel, Rhode Island Historical Society; and Timothy A. Slavin, Rhode Island State Archivist.

These acknowledgments would be woefully incomplete without special recognition of the important part played by the Reference Materials/Tools program of the National Endowment for the Humanities, an independent federal agency, whose grants have substantially supported the compilation of this atlas.

Introduction

Counties in the United States are, with few exceptions, administrative subdivisions of their states, not self-governing municipalities, such as cities, towns, and boroughs. Their historical significance lies in their important functions, their nearly universal distribution, and their protean nature. United States counties and their equivalents (i.e., parishes in Louisiana and independent cities in Maryland, Missouri, Nevada, and Virginia) today number more than three thousand and embrace within their bounds every part of the forty-eight conterminous states and Hawaii. (Connecticut abolished its counties as operational institutions in 1960 but retained them as geographical units; Alaska is the only state never to have counties.) County functions vary from state to state, and there is no standard system of operation. Nonetheless, counties everywhere provide judicial administration, and in most states they are responsible for a number of other important functions and services as well. The county's role is smallest in New England, larger in the Middle Atlantic and North Central states, and greatest in the South and West.

The county system was transplanted to North America by early colonists from England. Following the practice in the home country, colonial laws and policies were administered through a network of county courts by sheriffs, judges, and justices of the peace. The county's judicial functions grew from law enforcement and simple legal proceedings to probating wills and handling a variety of legal instruments, like deeds and certificates of marriage. The recording of births and deaths was a natural addition, and eventually much of the work of census taking was organized around the county. The courthouse, therefore, became both the local seat of justice and the repository of official information concerning every individual within the county's jurisdiction.

Counties also acquired many of the attributes of local government. Welfare administration, road and bridge maintenance, property evaluation and tax collection, and numerous other tasks all became county responsibilities. Although not a product of voluntary action by local inhabitants, the county eventually came under the control of elected officials answerable only to a local constituency. Outside the limits of densely settled urban areas, counties were the obvious geographical units for organizing representation in the provincial, territorial, and state legislatures and for building congressional districts. One result of these developments was that, in the nineteenth century, counties became the grassroots centers for political parties.

Following close on the heels of independence from Great Britain, American settlers began pushing westward onto land formerly occupied only by Indians, and state and territorial governments laid out counties ahead of them. Such acts were more than posturing claims of jurisdiction or fortuitous arrangements; those states and territories were trying to attract settlers with a promise of the orderly provision of governmental services. Unfortunately, a frontier county created in advance of settlement was usually little more than a name and a boundary description in the laws; frequently it was not technically organized and nearly as often was attached to a fully operational county for services and record keeping. Some of these counties remained attached and dependent for years, while others experienced such rapid population growth that they were soon organized and separated from their hosts. This atlas shows not only the territory within each county's prescribed boundaries but also maps the arrangement of any temporary attachments. Attachments are not included in calculations of the host county's area.

The functional importance of counties is not matched by a comparable geographic stability. Few, indeed, are the counties that today have their original shapes and areas. Some boundaries change when existing counties are divided to make new ones; other changes may be intended by legislators to serve the convenience of constituents or to raise the efficiency of government, or sometimes for less admirable purposes. The original counties of any state are few in number and may not even cover all of the state's territory. As population increases and spreads, as industry, agriculture, and transportation grow, so do the counties. Before long no place is outside the jurisdiction of one county or another. County lines form a network that divides the land in numerous ways, sometimes along prominent physical features or sometimes into areas whose sizes and shapes have been designed to optimize travel to the county seat or to facilitate control of the electorate. Most important, regardless of design, is the simple fact of change.

These changes in county shapes and sizes make it difficult to interpret county-level historical data. Did the size of the county's population really change or did the county merely gain or lose territory between census enumerations—or both? Could politicians have gerrymandered the state legislature or congressional delegation without explicitly changing the electoral laws, possibly by unobtrusively rearranging the county lines that underlay the system of electoral districts? There are many issues besides statistical shifts that draw researchers to counties. Genealogists, family historians, and attorneys, among others, often need evidence of specific events at particular locations and times—perhaps the initial gathering of a church, a land sale, a death, or a marriage. Knowing a locality's current county may not be adequate, and discovering which county had jurisdiction in the past may be the key to finding old records. State and local agencies may need to examine past attempts at judicial or administrative reorganization and reform. Nearly everyone concerned with local, state, and national politics of the past needs to know what happened to the county configurations in order to judge the significance, and perhaps the causes, of changes in electoral behavior.

The practice of temporarily attaching some sparsely settled counties and non-county areas to fully operational and self-sustaining counties implies some interesting questions concerning the conduct of research in county records, the administration of county services, the organization of census data, and a number of other issues. For example, how extensive a region did a sheriff have to cover when his county became responsible for one or more attached counties? Researchers investigating an event in county A at the time it was attached to county B may find the records still in the archives of B.

Working with county-based information, especially statistics, has often meant an abundance of topical data and a dearth of information about the configurations of the counties. One can only guess how many researchers have had to interrupt their thematic analyses to piece together the boundary changes of pertinent counties, or how many have revised or abandoned particular projects because compiling the boundary changes loomed as too formidable an obstacle.

History of This Atlas

The impetus for this endeavor came early in the 1970s during the creation of the *Atlas of Early American History: The Revolutionary Era, 1760–1790* (1976) by a team of historians and cartographers, led by editor-in-chief Lester J. Cappon, in Chicago at the Newberry Library. When the staff compiled reference maps of the British North American colonies in 1775, they discovered that, contrary to expectations, there was no authoritative reference source for the historical county lines. There are, instead, a number of separate compilations covering some but not all of the original thirteen states. The quality of those works ranges from superb to unreliable, and they lack anything approaching a common standard or format.

The *Atlas of Early American History* was succeeded by a project to compile the much needed reference work on county development. That original project was conceived as an experiment that would bypass conventional publication by creating a computerized, historical, cartographic data file, thereby making the boundary information available exclusively in a new and flexible format at supposedly reduced costs. The project succeeded in compiling and encoding the data for fourteen eastern and central states, and the data file is distributed by the Inter-university Consortium for Political and Social Research, Ann Arbor, Michigan. The original dissemination plan was broadened to include printing the data in maps and text (e.g., chronology, county code lists), thus providing in addition to the data file both a printed guide for those who had access to computer facilities and a conventional atlas for those without such equipment. The resulting work, the *Historical Atlas and Chronology of County Boundaries, 1788–1980*, edited by John H. Long, was published in five volumes by G. K. Hall in 1984. In the current project that five-volume work has been treated as any other secondary compilation of county creations and changes (see Sources, below). Except for republication of the data file codes in the appropriate state volumes (as an aid to potential users of the cartographic data file), this *Atlas of Historical County Boundaries*—a projected forty-volume reference—is a thoroughly new atlas with a broader range of subject matter than the 1984 work, as well as a different format and completely new maps and text.

Also in 1984, Thomas D. Rabenhorst and Carville V. Earle of the Geography Department at the University of Maryland, Baltimore County, produced the *Historical U.S. County Outline Map Collection, 1840–1980*, an expanded set of fifteen unbound maps derived from county outline maps for the federal census years 1840 to 1900 published in the early twentieth century by the U.S. Department of Agriculture. By the 1980s, those federal maps had been so long out of print that they had become virtually unknown. In 1987 William Thorndale and William Dollarhide published their *Map Guide to the U.S. Federal Censuses, 1790–1920*, which provides well-designed state outline maps of both modern and historical counties and gives sources and a description of the authors' methodology. Both of these publications provide only small-scale outline maps for a limited number of dates, leaving the need for a comprehensive and detailed reference unfilled.

This atlas has been designed to leave no gaps. The chronological range for each state extends back to its earliest county, at least, and runs up to 1990. Geographically the range includes all territory within each state's bounds in 1990, plus (for the relevant historical period) any other territory over which its jurisdiction extended at an earlier time. Massachusetts, for example, had jurisdiction at one time or another over some or all of present Maine and New Hampshire. The table of contents lists all counties included in the volume, identifying those created by another state or now located beyond the state's boundaries; cross-references are provided for counties that have been renamed.

A secondary goal of this atlas is to provide a frame of reference for understanding boundary changes. The maps and chronologies in the volumes of this atlas answer questions of what, when, and where. Venturing to explain why and how changes occurred requires more information and a different focus for the research. It is hoped some readers will undertake this line of inquiry and will find value in the information and references provided here.

While the strictly defined purpose and scope of this project preclude additional research and writing for analytical monographs and narrative histories, compilers uncover more information than is needed to draw the maps and describe the boundary changes. None of this information has been ignored. The bibliographies list a wide range of materials that were useful in compiling the changes and drawing the maps. The chronologies cover more than boundary changes alone, including county name changes, unsuccessful authorizations for new counties, and redefinitions and clarifications of existing lines. Line shifts too small to map at the scales employed here are also regularly identified.

The structural heart of this atlas for each state, the component on which all others depend, is the *consolidated chronology* in which all boundary changes and related events for the state are brought together in a single chronological list. The entries not only tell what happened but refer readers to the sources for each event. Following the consolidated chronology is a section that presents the counties one by one. Here the reader will find *individual county chronologies* and complementary sets of *individual county maps* that depict the various configurations of every county. As an aid to readers concerned with statistical densities and other areal data, figures for *county areas* (not including temporary attachments) accompany the individual county chronologies. A final topical section covers all censuses in the state's history, including state and colonial or territorial censuses or equivalents (e.g., tax or poll lists), in addition to the more familiar federal enumerations. In this section the reader will find a *table of censuses* describing the available data and a matching series of *census outline maps*.

The maps are arranged in two series, as indicated above, to serve different purposes. The first series of maps is designed to show the historical jurisdictions of individual counties. With few exceptions there is a separate map for each different configuration of the county lines, so readers can easily see the exact jurisdictional area of the county and the places it encompassed at any time. Most of these maps are derived from the U.S. Geological Survey's State Base series at the scale of 1:500,000 or about eight miles per inch (this atlas's standard base for individual counties), and those maps display considerable detail: water features, cities and towns, state and county boundaries, and, when available, the lines of the federal land survey. Drawing the historical boundary lines on these modern base maps permits a clear comparison of old and new and affords the reader a familiar context and a dependable reference system with which he or she can study the historical boundaries. In most cases, for counties too large to fit on a single page at the standard scale, a small-scale map (1:2,500,000—about one fifth the scale of the standard maps) is used instead. Small-scale maps are also used to show how unorganized counties and non-county areas were temporarily attached to fully functioning host counties.

A second series of maps presents small-scale outline maps that match available census data. Some maps cover more than one census because during the intervening period either there were no territorial changes or changes were too small to show on these maps. Readers should consult the individual county maps for small changes.

Sources

The principal sources for historical county boundary lines in the United States are colonial, territorial, and state laws. Occasionally, in the earliest days of a proprietary colony or a territory, counties were created or changed by executive proclamation; in the nineteenth century a few counties were created by new state constitutions. Courts or special arbitrators sometimes settled jurisdictional disputes at the international, state, and county levels. The number of changes produced outside the legislative process does not, however, represent a large proportion of the total changes for any state.

The compilers have relied upon the provincial, territorial, and state laws because counties are the creatures of their states, created and for the most part controlled by the state legislatures. State laws are authoritative and convenient, relatively compact and coherent as a corpus, and available throughout the country. Session laws are the immediate, official products of each session of the legislature. Sets of statutes at large are authoritative and convenient, though not available for all states or for all periods. Rationalized sets of state laws, usually termed revised codes, pass through the same legislative process as individual session laws and are equally authoritative. Apparent alterations wrought by codifying a state's laws are infrequent and usually accidental.

Before codification became a regular feature of the legislative process, a few individuals compiled and published collections of state laws. The most famous is William W. Hening, whose thirteen volumes of *Statutes at Large; Being a Collection of All the Laws of Virginia, from the First Session of the Legislature in the Year 1619 [to 1792]*, published in Richmond, Va., 1819–1823, have become a classic and a standard. Some of these works were commissioned or at least sanctioned by the legislatures, but in all cases they are recognized and accepted as reliable and authoritative.

Collections of pertinent sections of county boundary laws, such as the Historical Records Survey of Mississippi's *State and County Boundaries of Mississippi* (Jackson, Miss., 1942) are convenient but demand caution. There is a potential for error in transcription, as well as the possibility that valuable information (e.g., an effective date) may be lost in the editorial process of excerpting the selected passages. Such a compilation can be a marvelous convenience for the researcher, once it has been checked against the session laws and has been found reliable. There are compilations of county creations and changes for a number of states, but they vary greatly in content and in accuracy. It is virtually impossible to judge their reliability until much of the work has been replicated. These secondary sources, therefore, are useful chiefly as guides to the primary laws, proclamations, and decisions.

The histories of United States international and state boundaries, unlike those of county lines, have been thoroughly described and documented in a number of publications. Without the need for further original research at these levels, staff historians have relied heavily upon secondary sources for changes in national, colonial, territorial, and state lines.

Among the most useful modern sources are the large-scale, up-to-date county maps usually published by state departments of transportation or by the individual counties. Used regularly for a number of different purposes, both official and unofficial, such maps normally are extremely reliable compilations of the details of boundaries, roads, natural features, and other landmarks.

Although historical maps are very useful for interpreting boundary descriptions in these four New England states, especially when the county lines depend upon municipal boundaries, in most other states they are useful primarily for lost landmarks and names no longer in use. Throughout the seventeenth and eighteenth centuries, map makers knew little about the lay of the land and had to work with relatively inaccurate instruments and data. During the nineteenth century, maps improved with the surveying of the land and advancements in cartography, but maps from the late nineteenth century may have limited research value because boundary landmarks employed at that time often survive on our modern maps. In any case, it is important to remember that a map is, by its nature, more like a secondary work than a primary source.

Sometimes errors on old maps can benefit research. When a boundary description cannot be plotted on a modern base map or does not seem to make sense, the flaw may lie not in the description but in the geographic notions upon which it was based. If the errors on an old map accurately reflect accepted ideas and knowledge, however mistaken they may have been, that map may be the key to the true meaning of contemporaneous boundary descriptions.

For example, if the line established in 1790 between Hancock and Lincoln counties in Maine is drawn as described in the law, it will appear about nine miles east of where it actually ran. Plotting it that way would also render a half dozen subsequent boundary laws meaningless or impossible because each of them was meant to alter that 1790 line. If, however, that line is drawn as depicted on Osgood Carleton's 1802 *Map of the District of Maine, Massachusetts, Compiled from Actual Surveys Made by Order of the General Court and under the Inspection of Agents of Their Appointment,* and on other maps of the period, everything fits together and works. Accordingly, in this atlas the line is drawn according to those old maps. All evidence points to the Carleton map as an accurate guide to the contemporaneous understanding of the Hancock-Lincoln boundary line. (See the section on Special Topics, below, for more about this line and about the problems encountered using old maps as sources.)

The table of censuses in this atlas does not document the well-known federal enumerations, but it does help readers find extant provincial, territorial, and state statistics and/or records containing the names of individuals, whether in a publication or in an institution. Whenever possible, the citation directs the reader to Henry J. Dubester's widely available *State Censuses: An Annotated Bibliography of Censuses of Population Taken after the Year 1790 by States and Territories of the United States* (1948), rather than to the document (usually a state government publication) in which the data actually appear. For example, for the 1865 Rhode Island state census, the reader is referred simply to page 54 of Dubester, which provides a detailed reference to the *Report upon the Census of Rhode Island, 1865,* where the statistics were published. This approach keeps the citations brief, simple, and clear.

The manner in which sources are described in the bibliography, the citations of the consolidated chronology, and the table of abbreviations is a composite style fashioned from the guidelines set out in the thirteenth edition of the University of Chicago Press's *Chicago Manual of Style for Authors, Editors, and Copywriters* (Chicago, 1982) and, for legal sources, from the fifteenth edition of *Bluebook: A Uniform System of Citation* (Cambridge, Mass., 1991), compiled jointly by the editors of *Columbia Law Review, Harvard Law*

Review, University of Pennsylvania Law Review, and *Yale Law Journal.* So many old maps lack the name of an individual cartographer that some bibliographers attribute those maps to their publishers. In this atlas, such an anonymous map is listed by title, but the publisher is also identified as an aid to readers who use catalogues and lists in which publishers get credit for authorship.

Procedures

There appears to be more than one way to compile the changes in county lines. One attractive approach is starting in the present and working back to the beginning. The most appealing aspect of working from present to past is the apparent logic of the approach—something like following the branches of a family tree back down to its roots or taking down a building brick by brick. But these analogies are misleading. The current array of counties was not constructed by the process of accretion that is at the heart of house-building, nor is it like a genealogical diagram in which changes occur only through the addition of new family members. Trying to dismantle the present to reach the past usually yields little more than frustration or error.

In this project, the compilers map county boundary changes in chronological order, a procedure that provides a built-in checking mechanism. By using a modern map as a base and plotting boundary changes from the past to the present, it is easy to compare the compiler's version of each county's final set of lines with its current configuration. If the two are not the same, there must be an error on the modern map or the compiler has made a mistake, either missing a change or plotting a line incorrectly. Whatever the cause, therefore, a mismatch at the end of research and sketching automatically reveals a problem that must be resolved.

Working directly from originals or photocopies of the verbal boundary descriptions in the laws, the researcher plots the lines on a compilation sheet of tracing paper laid over a base map of the state. These are the graphic equivalents of notes, and the linework is always accompanied by some text, if only the county name, the nature of the change, and the effective date. As each change is plotted, the compiler writes a descriptive entry for the state's boundary chronology and a brief citation to the source of information. Reading straight through the session laws of a state is normally unnecessary, because the titles of acts and the indexes to the laws usually indicate all boundary changes. Occasionally, however, changes in county boundaries are hidden in laws on other topics, as in laws changing the official status of a place from town to borough or providing for the maintenance of roads and bridges. When it becomes clear that a change has been missed, the compiler broadens the search to include enactments on related subjects.

With few exceptions, all boundary changes have been mapped. Occasionally it has been necessary to use an asterisk or similar device to indicate the approximate location, along the existing boundary, of a change too small to draw with lines. Changes of unusual proportions (one dimension small, the other large) cannot be represented at all on the maps used here, for example, a change that straightens slight irregularities in a long boundary or that shifts a boundary from the center of a stream to one bank or the other. Another unmappable exception is any small change whose location cannot be determined, such as an individual farm identified only by the owner's name or a small area identified only by a landmark now lost. Each unmapped change is noted in the chronology.

Areas of counties are calculated by tracing the boundaries on the individual county maps with a digitizer connected to a microcomputer; data from the digitizer are processed by a program that calculates the areas. In order to avoid having the figures appear more precise than is possible, the numbers are rounded to the nearest ten. The county areas published in current reference works commonly are for land area, excluding all bodies of water larger than a certain minimum size. In this atlas figures for present areas normally match those land-only areas; when there is a difference, the number here usually is larger. It is not difficult to avoid counting large water areas by tracing the shorelines of very large lakes and the seacoast, instead of the boundary lines that delineate offshore jurisdiction.

No attempt is made to measure and subtract smaller lakes and ponds, nor to add small islands. Thus, for example, the counties of Minnesota are measured without subtracting any of the state's thousands of lakes, but the state's jurisdiction over the waters of Lake Superior is excluded.

Special Topics and Sources for Connecticut, Maine, Massachusetts, and Rhode Island

Maine's present northern limit is used for events starting in 1763 because that is when it was defined as the Atlantic–St. Lawrence R. watershed. The disputes that flared on and off from then until the final settlement in detail in 1842 concerned the interpretation and implementation of that earlier definition.

Defining counties in terms of municipalities, as so often happened in these four New England states, increases the difficulty of discovering and plotting county boundary changes. Many county boundary alterations are only implicit in changes between adjacent towns or cities that happen to lie in different counties; the counties are not named but their lines necessarily shift with the municipal lines. The only way to be certain of finding all such changes is to identify neighboring towns and cities that could produce a county change and then to search for changes. For Massachusetts that task was eased considerably by the Secretary of the Commonwealth's *Historical Data Relating to Counties, Cities, and Towns in Massachusetts* (1966), a remarkably thorough and accurate listing of jurisdictional changes between municipalities. A similar collection of data for Maine is *Counties, Cities, Towns, and Plantations of Maine: A Handbook of Incorporations, Dissolutions, and Boundary Changes* (1940), originally compiled and published by the Historical Records Survey of that state.

Plotting the town lines, especially the configurations of the colonial period, for which verbal descriptions are often entirely lacking, is also an unusual problem. Old maps that show municipal, as well as county, lines can be a great help. Differences between maps of different dates obviously imply changes during the intervening years. Even if a map is very old and clearly not as precise as today's maps, a comparison with present-day maps will reveal lines that have not changed. Sometimes such lines survive intact on present maps of towns, sometimes even on federal maps. Those long-lived boundaries, the legacy of events possibly centuries past, can be the base for reconstructing the old lines, and they greatly facilitate the work of correct interpolation. The maps of Connecticut and Maine that are listed in the bibliography are especially valuable in this regard.

In Maine it has been necessary to infer the correct lines in two important changes. One case concerns the southern end of the boundary that today separates the towns of Detroit and Palmyra in Somerset County from the towns of Plymouth and Newport in Penobscot County. In 1790 that was the line between Hancock and Lincoln, described above, and it originally ran straight north, cutting through Plymouth, Newport, and a number of other towns stacked in a range north of them. During the 1810s many of those northern towns were placed wholly in one county or another, but there survives no law that adjusted the southern end of the line to its present course. On 29 February 1844 an act apparently confirming a demarcation of the boundary between Detroit and Plymouth stated incidentally that the two towns were in different counties and implied that the county line had effectively run along their common boundary for some time. Lacking other evidence, it appears that before February 1844 official and local residents adopted the town lines as the de facto county lines. In the chronology, the change is dated "by" the time the arrangement was so casually revealed in the laws, an approach described more fully below in the section on Dates.

The second case involves Aroostook County, which was extended across the northern cap of Maine in 1844. The southern limit of that part of the county, the boundary separating it from Piscataquis and Somerset, runs along the line between two rows of towns. The verbal boundary description does not prescribe that particular course for the line; instead it refers to towns laid out farther to the east that are not perfectly aligned with those where the line now runs. A literal interpretation would force the line to cut through a full row of western towns. That misalignment probably is simply the result of a surveying adjustment when the western towns were demarcated. Regardless of problems with the arrangement of the towns, it appears that, as a practical matter, the county line was extended along the town boundaries. This reflected the increasingly common practice of adjusting old lines to make sure towns are not split and lie wholly in one county or another.

Base Maps

This project relies on maps published by the U.S. Geological Survey. Most of the individual county maps show the historical boundary drawn on a special version of the U.S.G.S. State Base map of Connecticut, Massachusetts, and Rhode Island, or the comparable map of Maine, published at the scale of 1:500,000 or eight miles per inch. These special versions of the 1:500,000-scale maps, products of the Geological Survey's custom printing service, are designed to be as uncluttered as possible without losing essential features. The special printing for this atlas has the coastline, rivers, outlines of lakes, and the names of water features, all reduced in blackness by a fifty-percent, bi-angle screen; place names, longitude and latitude lines, state and county boundary lines, and land survey lines (when available) are all in solid black. Omitted from the standard versions of the maps of these New England states, therefore, are contour lines, boundaries of federal reservations and large municipalities, railroads and miscellaneous symbols, and the small circles for place locations.

The small-scale maps used to show counties too large to fit on a single page using the 1:500,000-scale bases are essentially the same as those used to depict both the state's county network for the various censuses and the attachments of unorganized counties and non-county areas. All these maps are redrawings of the pertinent sections of the U.S. Geological Survey's map of the United States at the scale of 1:2,500,000 or about forty miles per inch. This map is dated 1972, and nearly all changes in the county lines since then are too small to show; changes large enough to map have been incorporated into the redrawing.

Errors on federal maps are unusual, but there are two in the representation of Suffolk County in Massachusetts. In both cases, the northwestern and the southern corners, the federal map depicts Suffolk as noticeably less extensive than it is.

All the maps in this atlas have been reduced from their original sizes for publication. Determining distances accurately is made possible by the graphic bar scales provided for the maps. While each small-scale map is accompanied by its own scale bar, the standard maps of individual counties have their graphic scale printed across the bottom of the page.

Dates

Every effort has been made to give the day, month, and year (e.g., 25 February 1785) for all county creations, boundary changes, and other events in this atlas. Occasionally it is impossible to date an event so precisely, but a reasonable estimate is possible. When the precise date is not known or an approximate date is more appropriate, the date is generalized to the month and year (e.g., February 1785) or to the year alone. A lack of evidence may make it impossible to give any date at all for a county's creation, and its occurrence can only be confirmed by the record of a later, related happening, such as the appointment of a sheriff. In such a situation, the date of the later event is used with the simple addition of "by" (e.g., by 25 February 1785) to indicate that the county creation or other event occurred no later than that date and probably earlier.

Several dates may be associated with the creation of a county or a change in county lines. To many individuals the date that makes the most sense is the one when people began to observe the change, but in most cases that date is impossible to ascertain. An alternative is the date on which the law effecting the change passed the legislature or was approved by the governor. The date of passage is an important reference because it helps identify the law; now as in the past, references to a law often include the date of passage. Most other compilations of county changes have adopted the date of passage as their standard for when change occurred, but it is not always sufficient.

The dating standard in this atlas is the legally effective date of change, whether it be for the creation of a new county or for the alteration of lines between existing counties. Through the colonial period and into the nineteenth century, the date a law passed was generally the date it went into effect. As the nineteenth century progressed, legislators recognized the importance of preparing for the establishment of a new county organization or for the shift in jurisdiction that accompanies boundary changes. Some laws, therefore, began to carry two dates: one marking the passage of the law and the other specifying when the line change or new county creation would go into effect. If the date of passage and effective date are different, the law gives both. (Connecticut, however, is an exception. For every county boundary change there before 1820, the date given here usually marks the beginning of the legislative session. The sessions were short, dates of passage were not given in the published records, and the opening date of the session is always available.)

Using effective dates means that many of the dates in this atlas may disagree with dates in other references. As an aid to appreciating how great the differences between the two dates can be and to help correlate the data in this book with other publications, this atlas offers a *table of county creations* that gives both the date of passage and the effective date for all county creations.

Dating events before 1752 is a problem because the calendar then in use is very different from the one in use today. Whereas by 1600 most of Europe had adopted the Gregorian calendar, as the modern system of reckoning the days is called, England observed the Julian calendar until 2 September 1752. For the purposes of this atlas, the chief differences between the two systems are, first, numbering the days and, second, designating the change from one year to the next. There has been no attempt to convert the dates of one system to those of the other. Differences in numbering days, therefore, are effectively ignored; whatever day and month are given in a source are the day and month used here, regardless of whether the document was written in England or some other country, before or after 1752. Under the old, Julian calendar the last day of the year was 24 March and the first day was 25 March, which means that in England and its colonies the day after 24 March 1750 was 25 March 1751. This atlas follows the convention of showing both years for dates that fall within the period from 1 January through 24 March when the different calendars call for different years. Thus, successive dates before England's adoption of the Gregorian calendar would occur as follows: the day after 24 March 1688/1689 would be 25 March 1689; the day after 31 December 1689 would be 1 January 1689/1690. About three months later would come 24 March 1689/1690, and the next day after that would be 25 March 1690.

Abbreviations

Abbreviated References in Citations

Many citations identify works by author or by author and short title, but most employ abbreviations. Authors and titles for abbreviated references are given below; see the bibliography at the back of the atlas for full descriptions of these works.

Conn. Col. Recs.	Connecticut. *Public Records of the Colony of Connecticut.*
Conn. Pub. Acts	Connecticut. *Public Acts.*
Conn. Spec. Acts	Connecticut. *Special Acts.*
Conn. St. Recs.	Connecticut. *Public Records of the State of Connecticut.*
Mass. Acts	Massachusetts. *Acts and Resolves of Massachusetts.*
Mass. Col. Acts	Massachusetts. *Acts and Resolves, Public and Private, of the Province of Massachusetts Bay. . . .*
Mass. Recs.	Massachusetts. *Records of the Governor and Company of the Massachusetts Bay in New England.*
Mass. Sec. Comm.	Massachusetts. Secretary of the Commonwealth. *Historical Data . . . .*
Me. Gov. Proc.	Maine. Governor. Proclamation.
Me. Laws	Maine. *Laws of the State of Maine.* Each volume includes a section of Public Laws (Pub.) and a section of Private and Special Laws (Priv.).
Me. Priv. Acts	Maine. *Private and Special Acts of the State of Maine.*
Me. Pub. Acts	Maine. *Public Acts of the State of Maine.*
N.H. Early Laws	New Hampshire. *Laws of New Hampshire, Including Public and Private Acts and Resolves [1680–1835].*
N.H. State Papers	New Hampshire. *Provincial and State Papers.*
N.Y. Col. Laws	New York. Commissioners of Statutory Revision. *Colonial Laws of New York from the Year 1664 to the Revolution. . . .*
Ply. Laws	New Plymouth Colony. *Book of the General Laws of the Inhabitants of the Jurisdiction of New-Plimouth. . . .*
R.I. Acts & Resolves	Rhode Island. *Acts and Resolves of Rhode Island and Providence Plantations.*
R.I. Recs.	Rhode Island. *Records of the Colony of Rhode Island and Providence Plantations, in New England.*
Terr. Papers U.S.	*Territorial Papers of the United States.*
U.S. Stat.	United States. *Statutes at Large of the United States of America, 1789–1873.*

Abbreviations to Be Found in This Atlas

Except where noted, plurals are formed by adding s.

A.D.	*anno Domini,* in the year of our Lord	arch.	archives
adj.	adjourned	Ariz.	Arizona
Ala.	Alabama	Ark.	Arkansas
ann.	annotated, annual	art.	article
Apr.	April	Aug.	August

bien.	biennial	Me.	Maine
bros.	brothers	mi.	mile
c.	*circa,* about, approximately	Mich.	Michigan
Calif.	California	Minn.	Minnesota
ch.	chapter	misc.	miscellaneous
co.	company, county	Miss.	Mississippi
Col.	colonial	Mo.	Missouri
Colo.	Colorado	Mont.	Montana
comp.	compiler	MS	manuscript
Conn.	Connecticut	Mt.	Mount, Mountain
cr.	creek	n.	north, note
D.C.	District of Columbia	N.C.	North Carolina
Dec.	December	n.d.	no date
Del.	Delaware	N.Dak.	North Dakota
dept.	department	Nebr.	Nebraska
diss.	dissertation	Nev.	Nevada
doc.	document	N.H.	New Hampshire
ed.	edition, editor	N.J.	New Jersey
e.g.	*exempli gratia,* for example	N.Mex.	New Mexico
et al.	*et alii,* and others	no.	number
etc.	*etcetera,* and so forth	Nov.	November
exec.	executive	n.p.	no place
ext.	extra, extraordinary	N.W. Terr.	Northwest Territory
Feb.	February	N.Y.	New York
Fla.	Florida	Oct.	October
Ft.	Fort	Okla.	Oklahoma
Ga.	Georgia	opp.	opposite
gen.	general	Oreg.	Oregon
geneal.	genealogical	p. (plural, pp.)	page
Gov.	governor	Pa.	Pennsylvania
hist.	historical, history	par.	paragraph
HRS	Historical Records Survey	Ph.D.	*Philosophiae Doctor,* Doctor of Philosophy
I. (plural, Is.)	Island	pl.	plate
Id.	Idaho	Ply.	Plymouth
i.e.	*id est,* that is	Priv.	private
Ill.	Illinois	pt.	part
Ind.	Indiana	Pub.	public
Jan.	January	quad.	quadrennial
jour.	journal	quart.	quarter, quarterly
Jr.	junior	R.	River
Jul.	July	rec.	record
Jun.	June	reg.	register, regular
Kans.	Kansas	res.	resolution
Ky.	Kentucky	rev.	revised
La.	Louisiana	R.I.	Rhode Island
loc.	local	rpt.	report
Mar.	March	S.C.	South Carolina
Mass.	Massachusetts	S.Dak.	South Dakota
Md.	Maryland	sec.	section

Sec. State	secretary of State	Tex.	Texas
Sen.	Senate	Univ.	university
Sep.	September	U.S.	United States
ser.	series	U.S.G.S.	United States Geological Survey
sess.	session	v.	versus
spec.	special	Va.	Virginia
sq.	square	vol.	volume
sq. mi.	square miles	Vt.	Vermont
St.	Saint	Wash.	Washington
stat.	statute, statutes	Wis.	Wisconsin
Ste.	Sainte	W.Va.	West Virginia
Tenn.	Tennessee	Wyo.	Wyoming
terr.	territorial, territory		

CONNECTICUT

Connecticut County Creations

County	Source	Dates	
		Authorization	Creation Effective
FAIRFIELD	Conn. Col. Recs., 2:34–35	10 May 1666	same
HARTFORD	Conn. Col. Recs., 2:34–35	10 May 1666	same
LITCHFIELD	Conn. Col. Recs., 10:56–58	9 Oct 1751	same
MIDDLESEX	Conn. St. Recs., 6:10–11	12 May 1785	same
NEW HAVEN	Conn. Col. Recs., 2:34–35	10 May 1666	same
NEW LONDON	Conn. Col. Recs., 2:34–35	10 May 1666	same
TOLLAND	Conn. St. Recs., 6:93	13 Oct 1785	same
WESTMORELAND (extinct)	Conn. St. Recs., 1:7	10 Oct 1776	same
WINDHAM	Conn. Col. Recs., 7:11–13	12 May 1726	same

Counties established by Connecticut beyond its present limits

In Pennsylvania (1776–1782)   WESTMORELAND (1776)

Consolidated Chronology of Connecticut State and County Boundaries

10 April 1606

King James I chartered two Virginia companies, headquartered in different cities, to establish colonies along the coast of North America: the Virginia Company of London, assigned coast between 34 degrees and 41 degrees north latitude; and the Virginia Company of Plymouth, assigned coast between 38 degrees and 45 degrees north latitude, including present Connecticut. Colonies of the two companies were to be at least 100 miles apart, even in area of overlapping grants. (Paullin, pl. 42; Swindler, 10:17–23; Van Zandt, 92)

1613

The Dutch established trading posts on the Hudson R. and claimed jurisdiction between the Connecticut and Delaware rivers, including present western Connecticut. (Van Zandt, 74)

3 November 1620

King James I replaced the charter to the Virginia Company of Plymouth with a charter for a Council for New England to establish colonies in a region between 40 degrees and 48 degrees north latitude and extending from the Atlantic to the Pacific Ocean, including present Connecticut. (Swindler, 5:16–26)

Summer 1624

The Dutch West India Company founded the colony of New Netherland, including the first permanent European settlement in the area of present New York. Over the next two and a half decades conflict developed between the Dutch and the English as settlers from both countries moved into Long Island and the area of present western Connecticut. (Flick, 1:234–235, 238, 2:40–48)

3 March 1636

Initial government of Connecticut organized, signaling the creation of that colony. (Taylor, 8)

Summer 1638

New Haven colony established by immigrants from England, who purchased land from the Indians and set up an independent government. Other settlements were established in present western Connecticut along the coast west of New Haven in 1641 and 1643. (Taylor, 50)

1642

Nathaniel Woodward and Solomon Saffrey officially demarcated the southern limit of Massachusetts, supposedly three miles south of the Charles R., as prescribed in its charter of 1628/1629, implicitly setting the northern limit of Connecticut. (Hooker, 16–17; Van Zandt, 66–67)

1644

Based upon its participation with Connecticut and New Plymouth in the Pequot War (1636–1637), Massachusetts claimed much of the territory formerly controlled by the Pequots, roughly between the Thames and Pawcatuck rivers at the eastern end of present Connecticut, plus Block I. in present Rhode Island. Massachusetts established a settlement (now Pawcatuck, Conn.) near mouth of the Pawcatuck R. (Bowen, *Disputes*, 31)

19 September 1650

In the Hartford Treaty, Connecticut and New Netherland agreed on a boundary, never ratified by England but observed by both sides until war erupted between the English and the Dutch in 1652. This agreement divided Long Island by a line due south from Oyster Bay and, on the mainland, specified a line 20 miles long running due north from Greenwich Bay, but specified no other limits. Conflict over uncertain colonial limits continued until the Duke of York captured New Netherland in 1664. (Bowen, *Disputes*, 17–18; Flick, 2:50–57)

18 September 1658

Commissioners of the United Colonies of New England, a confederation of Connecticut, Massachusetts, New Haven, and Plymouth (1643 – c. 1686), tried to settle the dispute between Connecticut and Massachusetts over the Pequot Country (area in present eastern Connecticut) when it decided the Mystic R. was the boundary between the two colonies, leaving Massachusetts with the territory between the Mystic and Pawcatuck rivers. (Arnold, 1:277–278; Bowen, *Disputes*, 32)

23 April 1662

King Charles II granted Connecticut a charter as a self-governing corporate colony, consolidating Hartford and other settlements on the Connecticut R. with New Haven and other coastal settlements into a single colony. Bounds were the southern Massachusetts line on the north, Narragansett Bay on the east, Long Island Sound on the south, and the Pacific Ocean ("South Sea") on the west. Massachusetts did not concede its claim to territory between the Mystic and Pawcatuck rivers in present eastern Connecticut, but Connecticut quickly took control of that area as well as a part of present Rhode Island lying southwest of Narragansett Bay and then known as the Narragansett Country. (Bowen, *Disputes*, 32; Swindler, 2:135–136)

8 July 1663

King Charles II granted Rhode Island a charter as a self-governing corporate colony. Boundary with Connecticut prescribed as the Pawcatuck R. and a line due north to Massachusetts. This charter also supposedly implemented a 1662 agreement between agents of Connecticut and Rhode Island to establish their boundary along the Pawcatuck, but Connecticut rejected that agreement and pressed for control of the Narragansett Country, including present Rhode Island southwest of Narragansett Bay. (Bowen, *Disputes*, 33; Swindler, 8:368)

12 March 1663/1664

King Charles II granted to the Duke of York all territory between the Connecticut and Delaware rivers, the islands of Long Island, Martha's Vineyard, and Nantucket, and the area between the Kennebec and St. Croix rivers extending inland from the Atlantic coast to the St. Lawrence R. Covered western half of present Connecticut. (Swindler, 4:278–280)

19 October 1664

Massachusetts, faced with new charters for Connecticut and Rhode Island, gave up its claim to the Pequot Country east of the Mystic R. in present eastern Connecticut. (Arnold, 1:308)

1664

Connecticut and New York agreed that New York would have sole jurisdiction over Long Island and that their mutual boundary would run north-northwest from the Mamaroneck R. to the southern line of Massachusetts. Agreement effective locally but never confirmed in England; line never surveyed and not well observed far inland. Town of Rye came under Connecticut's jurisdiction in 1665. (Bowen, *Disputes*, 17, 70–72)

20 March 1664/1665

Royal Commissioners decided the dispute over the Narragansett Country (present southwestern Rhode Island) by dismissing Massachusetts's claim and placing the area directly under royal jurisdiction. They named it King's Province and on 8 April 1665 gave Rhode Island temporary administrative authority over this new province until a royal decision should settle the competing claims of Connecticut and Rhode Island, which did not occur until 1686. (Arnold, 1:315; James, 86–87; Potter, 178, 181)

10 May 1666

Connecticut created four original counties: FAIRFIELD, HARTFORD, NEW HAVEN, and NEW LONDON. (Conn. Col. Recs., 2:34–35)

19 May 1669

Massachusetts created Westfield from Springfield in its HAMPSHIRE County west of the Connecticut R. Part of this town (now Southwick, Mass.) extended into present Connecticut, the result of uncertain geographic knowledge and disagreement over the line between Connecticut and Massachusetts. (Bowen, *Disputes*, 53–58; Mass. Recs., vol. 4, pt. 2:432)

12 May 1670

HARTFORD gained town of Simsbury from non-county area. (Conn. Col. Recs., 2:127)

11 May 1671

NEW HAVEN gained town of Wallingford from non-county area. (Conn. Col. Recs., 2:152)

3 June 1674

Massachusetts created Suffield in its HAMPSHIRE County west of the Connecticut R. This town lay entirely within present Connecticut, the result of uncertain geographic knowledge and disagreement over the line between Connecticut and Massachusetts. (Bowen, *Disputes*, 53–58; Mass. Recs., 5:13)

29 June 1674

Following the Treaty of Westminster (9 Feb. 1673/1674) that restored New York to the English (following rule by the Dutch since Aug. 1673), King Charles II regranted to the Duke of York the territory he had granted on 12 March 1663/1664, including all territory between the Connecticut and Delaware rivers. Covered western portion of Connecticut. (Parry, 13:136; Swindler, 4:282; Williamson, 1:446)

13 May 1675

NEW HAVEN gained town of Derby from non-county area. (Conn. Col. Recs., 2:248–249)

18 May 1675

FAIRFIELD gained town of Woodbury from non-county area. (Conn. Col. Recs., 2:253)

16 May 1683

Massachusetts created Enfield as part of its HAMP-SHIRE County east of the Connecticut R. This town lay almost entirely within present Connecticut, the result of uncertain geographic knowledge and disagreement over the line between Connecticut and Massachusetts. (Bowen, *Disputes*, 53–58; Mass. Recs., 5:410–411)

28 November 1683

Connecticut and New York agreed on a new boundary: starting at mouth of Byram's R., running inland along east side of town of Rye about 8 miles, thence 20 miles in a line roughly parallel to the shore, thence northward in a line more than 20 miles east of the Hudson R. WEST-CHESTER (N.Y.) gained from FAIRFIELD when town of Rye reverted to New York. Agreement was confirmed in England in 1700 and demarcation of the line was completed in 1731; has remained substantially unchanged to the present. (Bowen, *Disputes*, 73–74; Van Zandt, 72–73)

15 May 1686

HARTFORD gained town of Waterbury from non-county area. (Conn. Col. Recs., 3:197)

28 May 1686

The royal governor of the Dominion of New England (a consolidation of older colonies into a single province), proclaimed a provisional government for King's Province in present southwestern Rhode Island and prohibited both Connecticut and Rhode Island from further attempts to exercise authority in the area. (R.I. Recs., 3:197)

13 October 1687

FAIRFIELD gained town of Danbury from non-county area. NEW LONDON gained Preston from non-county area. (Conn. Col. Recs., 3:240)

1 November 1687

The governor of the Dominion of New England formally incorporated Connecticut into the new province, following instructions (27 Jun. 1687) from King James II. No change in counties. (Conn. Col. Recs., 3:248; N.H. Early Laws, 1:171)

9 May 1689

Connecticut reinstated its former government after the fall of the Dominion of New England (18 Apr. 1689). Connecticut and Rhode Island soon resumed their boundary dispute over the Narragansett Country (King's Province) in present southwestern Rhode Island. (Arnold, 1:512; Craven, 225)

15 March 1689/1690

Massachusetts created Woodstock as part of its SUF-FOLK County east of the Connecticut R. This town lay almost entirely on the Connecticut side of the provincial boundary, the result of uncertain geographic knowledge and disagreement over the line between Connecticut and Massachusetts. (Bowen, *Disputes*, 53–58; Bowen, *Woodstock*, 1:31)

10 May 1694

HARTFORD gained town of Windham from non-county area. (Conn. Col. Recs., 4:123–124)

14 October 1697

NEW LONDON gained the Quinesbaug River Valley from non-county area. (Conn. Col. Recs., 4:226)

12 October 1699

NEW LONDON gained town of Colchester from non-county area. (Conn. Col. Recs., 4:298)

10 October 1700

NEW LONDON gained town of Lebanon from non-county area. (Conn. Col. Recs., 4:334)

12 May 1703

Connecticut and Rhode Island settled their dispute over present southwestern Rhode Island (at one time the separate King's Province and also known as the Narragansett Country) substantially along the line agreed by colonial agents in 1662, described in Rhode Island's 1663 charter, and claimed since then by Rhode Island. Boundary was to run up the Pawcatuck R. to its junction with the Ashaway R., thence a straight line to the southwestern corner of the Warwick Purchase, and thence due north to the southern line of Massachusetts. Although not confirmed in London until February 1726/1727, this line appears to have become effective almost immediately, and except for small refinements through surveying, it has remained unchanged to the present. (Potter, 206–211; R.I. Rec., 3:474; Van Zandt, 71)

10 October 1706

NEW HAVEN gained town of New Milford from non-county area. (Conn. Col. Recs., 5:10)

13 May 1708

HARTFORD gained town of Hebron from non-county area. (Conn. Col. Recs., 5:64)

NEW HAVEN gained town of Durham from non-county area. (Conn. Col. Recs., 5:51)

14 October 1708

HARTFORD gained town of Colchester from NEW LONDON. (Conn. Col. Recs., 5:80–81)

13 October 1709

FAIRFIELD gained town of Ridgefield from non-county area. (Conn. Col. Recs., 5:120–122)

8 May 1712

HARTFORD gained town of Coventry from non-county area. (Conn. Col. Recs., 5:321–322)

13 July 1713

Agents of Connecticut and Massachusetts accepted a 1702 survey as the definitive rendition of their mutual chartered limits east of the Connecticut R. (substantially the same as the present line and up to eight miles north of the Woodward-Saffrey line of 1642). They also agreed that Massachusetts would retain its jurisdiction over the border towns of Enfield and Woodstock that it had formed when the 1642 line was believed accurate, even though those towns extended south of the new line into Connecticut's territory. This agreement was accepted by both colonies (13 Feb. 1714) but never confirmed by London. Demarcation of the new line was completed in 1717. [No change.] (Bowen, *Disputes*, 58; Hooker, 20)

13 May 1714

HARTFORD gained from non-county area. (Conn. Col. Recs., 5:427)

14 October 1714

FAIRFIELD gained town of Newtown from non-county area. (Conn. Col. Recs., 5:469–470)

9 May 1717

NEW LONDON gained from non-county area. (Conn. Col. Recs., 6:6–7)

1717

Commissioners from Connecticut and Massachusetts settled their boundary from the Connecticut R. westward to New York. Massachusetts retained its jurisdiction over the border towns of Suffield and Westfield, which it had created earlier and which extended south of the line into Connecticut. (Bowen, *Disputes*, 59)

11 October 1722

HARTFORD gained town of Litchfield from non-county area. NEW HAVEN gained from non-county area. (Conn. Col. Recs., 6:339)

12 May 1726

WINDHAM created from HARTFORD and NEW LONDON. (Conn. Col. Recs., 7:11–13)

9 May 1728

NEW HAVEN gained town of Waterbury from HARTFORD. (Conn. Col. Recs., 7:168)

10 October 1728

FAIRFIELD gained town of New Fairfield from non-county area. (Conn. Col. Recs., 7:214)

14 May 1730

HARTFORD gained towns of Barkhamstead, Colebrook, Hartland, Harwinton, New Hartford, Torrington, and Winchester from NEW HAVEN. (Conn. Col. Recs., 7:272, 387–390, 445–449)

11 May 1738

HARTFORD gained towns of Canaan, Cornwall, Goshen, Kent, and Norfolk from NEW HAVEN. (Conn. Col. Recs., 8:169–171)

May 1749

Connecticut gained the towns of Enfield, Somers (created from Enfield in 1734), and Suffield from HAMPSHIRE (Mass.) and Woodstock from WORCESTER (Mass.) when it responded to the towns' requests for annexation by extending its jurisdiction over all portions of them south of the 1713 provincial line. These towns lay mostly on Connecticut's side of the boundary with Massachusetts, but had been founded by Massachusetts and continued under its government as a result of the 1713 and 1717 agreements. This left jogs in the inter-colonial line along the northern limit of Enfield and where Westfield (now Southwick, Mass.) extended into Connecticut west of Suffield. (Bowen, *Disputes*, 62; Hooker, 22, 26)

12 October 1749

HARTFORD gained towns of Enfield, Somers, and Suffield, and WINDHAM gained Woodstock, in accordance with the May 1749 annexation of those towns from Massachusetts. (Conn. Col. Recs., 9:476)

9 October 1751

LITCHFIELD created from FAIRFIELD, HARTFORD, and NEW HAVEN. (Conn. Col. Recs., 10:56–58)

9 May 1754

FAIRFIELD gained small area from LITCHFIELD. (Conn. Col. Recs., 10:274–275)

10 February 1763

The Treaty of Paris, ending the Seven Years' War between Great Britain (the victor) and France and Spain, implicitly set the Mississippi R. as a new western limit for British colonies, including Connecticut, whose charter bounds had technically extended to the Pacific Ocean. (Cappon, Petchenik, and Long, 1)

12 January 1774

Connecticut created the town of Westmoreland in the northeast corner of present Pennsylvania and put it under the jurisdiction of its LITCHFIELD County, based on the claim that its charter limits extended west of the Delaware R. Boundaries were the Delaware R. on the east, a north-south line 15 miles west of Wyoming (now Wilkes-Barre, Pa.) on the west, and on the north and south the limits of Connecticut as defined by its 1662 charter. It was in this area that the Susquehannah Company had acquired Indian land in 1754, established a colony of settlers (primarily from Connecticut) in 1771, and set up an independent government in 1773. Pennsylvania insisted on its charter claim to the area, but the settlers held control until 1782. (Cappon, Petchenik, and Long, 17, 92; Conn. Col. Recs., 13:427, 14:218)

22 June 1774

King George III approved the Quebec Act, which added to Quebec all territory west of Pennsylvania and north of the Ohio R., implicitly reducing the western extent of Connecticut and other colonies whose charter limits had technically extended to the Pacific Ocean. (Cappon, Petchenik, and Long, 90)

August 1774

New York and Pennsylvania agreed to define their boundary as running up the Delaware R. to the parallel of 42 degrees north latitude. Both colonies were motivated in part by Connecticut's creation (12 Jan. 1774) of the town of Westmoreland in present northeastern Pennsylvania. (Cappon, Petchenik, and Long, 17; Pratt, 1:241–248)

1774

HARTFORD gained from HAMPSHIRE (Mass.) when Connecticut unilaterally took over a small part of the town of Southwick (Mass.), formerly part of Westfield (Mass.), that extended south of the 1713 provincial boundary. (Bowen, *Disputes*, 65; Hooker, 25)

11 May 1775

Connecticut enlarged LITCHFIELD when it extended the western limit of its town of Westmoreland (present northeastern Pa.) to the Fort Stanwix Indian Treaty line. Local settlers loyal to Connecticut continued to maintain control against all efforts by Pennsylvania. (Cappon, Petchenik, and Long, 17, 92; Conn. Col. Recs., 15:13)

14 December 1775

Connecticut reduced LITCHFIELD when it changed the western extent of its town of Westmoreland (present northeastern Pa.) to a straight line running northeastward from a point 15 miles west of the East Branch of the Susquehanna R. on the parallel of 41 degrees north latitude through "the forks of the river Tioga" to the northern limit of the colony. (Cappon, Petchenik, and Long, 17, 92; Conn. Col. Recs., 15:197–198)

4 July 1776

Connecticut became an independent state. (*Declaration of Independence*)

10 October 1776

WESTMORELAND created from LITCHFIELD when Connecticut removed its town of Westmoreland (present northeastern Pa.) from LITCHFIELD and made it also "a distinct County," so that thereafter Westmoreland comprised both a town and a county. (Cappon, Petchenik, and Long, 17, 92; Conn. St. Recs. 1:7)

11 May 1780

LITCHFIELD gained from NEW HAVEN when town of Watertown created from Waterbury. (Conn. St. Recs., 3:73–75)

30 December 1782

A special court of arbitration, established by Congress under the Articles of Confederation, Article IX, decided the dispute over the Connecticut county and town of WESTMORELAND (present northeastern Pennsylvania) in favor of Pennsylvania. WESTMORELAND eliminated. Within a few weeks Pennsylvania was exercising full jurisdiction in the area. (*Susquehannah Co. Papers*, 7:xxxiii, 245)

3 September 1783

Commissioners from Great Britain and the United States signed the Treaty of Paris (ratifications exchanged 12 May 1784) ending the War of the American Revolution and recognizing American independence. (Parry, 48:481–486; Van Zandt, 12)

9 October 1783

NEW LONDON gained town of Colchester from HARTFORD. (Conn. St. Recs., 5:220, 281, 378, 384)

12 May 1785

MIDDLESEX created from HARTFORD and NEW LONDON. (Conn. St. Recs., 6:10–11)

13 October 1785

TOLLAND created from HARTFORD and WINDHAM. (Conn. St. Recs., 6:93)

11 May 1786

TOLLAND gained town of Coventry from WINDHAM. (Conn. St. Recs., 6:154)

14 September 1786

The United States accepted Connecticut's cession of its claim to jurisdiction over lands north and west of Pennsylvania and the Ohio R., except for a tract lying between 41 degrees and 42 degrees, 2 minutes north latitude (the state's northern and southern limits) and extending 120 miles west of Pennsylvania. This tract, lying in the northeast corner of present Ohio, became known as the Connecticut Western Reserve and was not ceded to the federal government until 1800. (*Terr. Papers U.S.*, 2:24 n.62)

8 May 1788

FAIRFIELD gained from LITCHFIELD when town of Brookfield created from Danbury, Newtown, and New Milford. (Conn. St. Recs., 6:410)

14 May 1789

TOLLAND gained from HARTFORD when town of Bolton gained from East Windsor. (Conn. St. Recs., 7:62)

2 May 1796

HARTFORD gained town of Hartland from LITCHFIELD. (Conn. St. Recs., 8:372–373)

NEW HAVEN gained from HARTFORD when town of Wolcott created from Southington and Waterbury. (Conn. St. Recs., 8:373)

31 October 1796

Boundaries of all counties redefined [no change]. (Conn. Pub. Acts 1796, pp. 123–124)

11 October 1798

HARTFORD gained from NEW HAVEN when town of Wallingford gained from Berlin. (Conn. St. Recs., 9: 284–285)

NEW HAVEN gained from LITCHFIELD when town of Oxford created from Derby and Southbury. (Conn. St. Recs., 9:311–313)

9 May 1799

MIDDLESEX gained town of Durham from NEW HAVEN. (Conn. St. Recs., 9:351)

28 April 1800

The United States accepted Connecticut's cession of its jurisdiction over the area in present northeastern Ohio known as the Connecticut Western Reserve. (*Terr. Papers U.S.*, 3:84–86)

13 October 1803

HARTFORD gained from NEW LONDON and TOLLAND when town of Marlborough was created from Colchester, Glastonbury, and Hebron. (Conn. Spec. Acts 1803, 2:1157–1158)

1804

HAMPSHIRE (Mass.) gained from HARTFORD when Massachusetts gained part of the town of Southwick (the "Southwick Jog") that lay south of the Connecticut boundary and that had been annexed from Massachusetts in 1774. (Hooker, 25–26; Van Zandt, 69)

8 May 1806

HARTFORD gained from LITCHFIELD when town of Canton was created from New Hartford and Simsbury. (Conn. Pub. Acts 1806, p. 721)

14 May 1807

NEW HAVEN gained town of Southbury from LITCHFIELD. (Conn. Pub. Acts 1807, p. 771)

8 October 1807

NEW HAVEN gained from LITCHFIELD when town of

Middlebury was created from Southbury, Waterbury, and Woodbury. (Conn. Pub. Acts 1807, p. 800; Conn. Pub. Acts 1808, p. 815)

3 June 1824

NEW LONDON gained town of Lebanon from WINDHAM. (Conn. Pub. Acts 1824, ch. 8/p. 47)

3 November 1826

HAMPDEN (Mass.) and WORCESTER (Mass.) exchanged narrow strips with TOLLAND (Conn.) and WINDHAM (Conn.) when an irregularity in the state boundary was straightened [not mapped]. (Bowen, *Disputes*, 66; Hooker, 28)

25 May 1827

TOLLAND gained towns of Columbia and Mansfield from WINDHAM. (Conn. Pub. Acts 1827, ch. 20–21/pp. 157–158)

26 February 1881

Congress confirmed a redefinition of the boundary between Connecticut and New York over land and through Long Island Sound [no change]. (Van Zandt, 74)

16 March 1881

NEW LONDON gained town of Voluntown from WINDHAM. (Conn. Pub. Acts 1881, ch. 28, sec. 1/p. 16)

22 March 1881

Jurisdiction of FAIRFIELD, NEW HAVEN, MIDDLESEX, and NEW LONDON over waters of Long Island Sound redefined, in accordance with redefinition of the state line that took effect 26 February 1881 [no change]. (Conn. Pub. Acts 1881, ch. 37, sec. 1/p. 19)

7 April 1885

WINDHAM gained from TOLLAND when town of Windham gained from Mansfield. (Conn. Spec. Acts 1885, no. 122, sec. 1/p. 117)

1 October 1960

Connecticut abolished all its counties as operational institutions, their functions performed since this date directly by the state. Counties continue to be used as geographical units. (Conn. Pub. Acts 1959, no. 152/pp. 442–489)

Individual County Chronologies, Maps, and Areas for Connecticut

Chronology of FAIRFIELD

Map	Date	Event	Resulting Area
❶	10 May 1666	Created as one of four original counties	Indefinite
❷	18 May 1675	Gained town of Woodbury from non-county area	Indefinite

(Heavy line depicts historical boundary. Base map shows present-day information.)

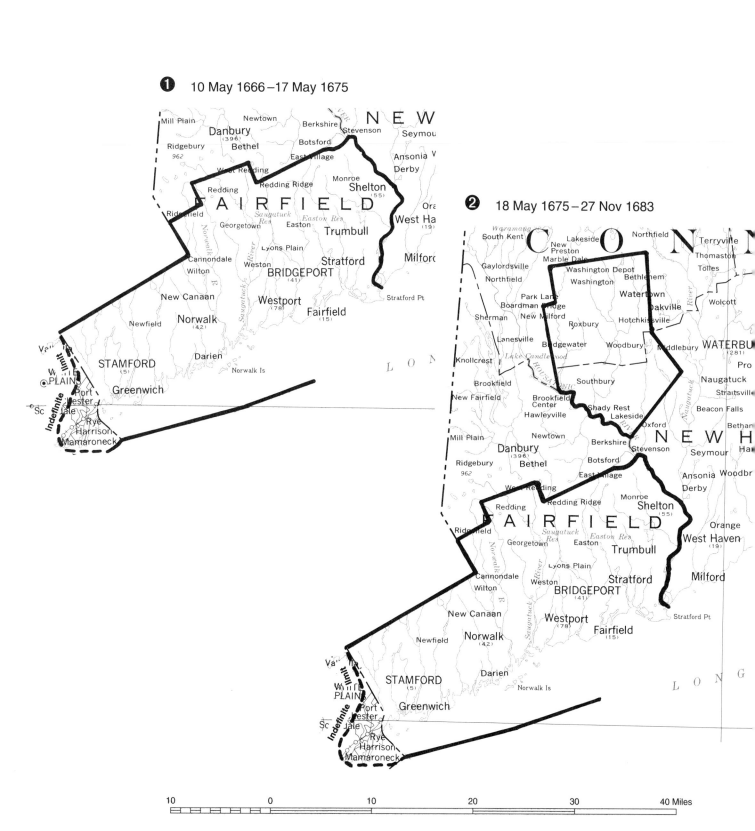

❶ 10 May 1666 – 17 May 1675

❷ 18 May 1675 – 27 Nov 1683

10   0   10   20   30   40 Miles

Chronology of FAIRFIELD

Map	Date	Event	Resulting Area
❸	28 Nov 1683	Lost to WESTCHESTER (N.Y.) when provincial boundary adjusted	580 sq mi

(Heavy line depicts historical boundary. Base map shows present-day information.)

❸   28 Nov 1683–12 Oct 1687

| 10 | 0 | 10 | 20 | 30 | 40 Miles |

Chronology of FAIRFIELD

Map	Date	Event	Resulting Area
❹	13 Oct 1687	Gained town of Danbury from non-county area	630 sq mi

(Heavy line depicts historical boundary. Base map shows present-day information.)

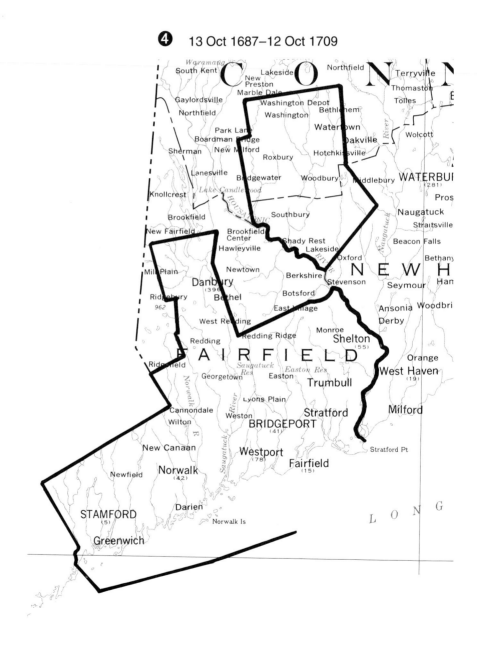

❹ 13 Oct 1687–12 Oct 1709

| 10 | 0 | 10 | 20 | 30 | 40 Miles |

Chronology of FAIRFIELD

Map	Date	Event	Resulting Area
❺	13 Oct 1709	Gained town of Ridgefield from non-county area	670 sq mi

(Heavy line depicts historical boundary. Base map shows present-day information.)

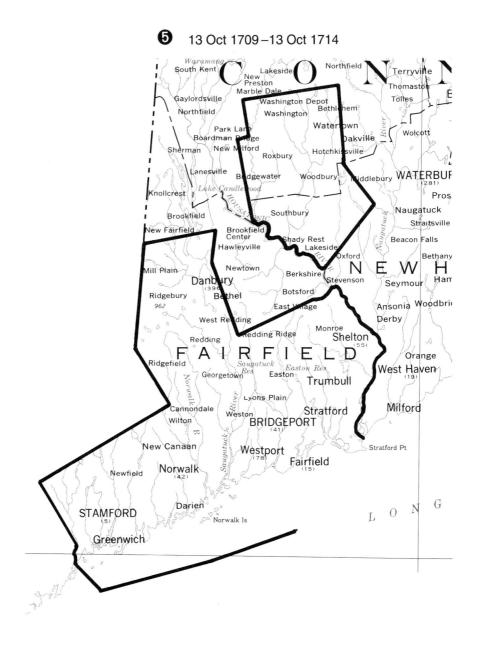

❺   13 Oct 1709 – 13 Oct 1714

10   0   10   20   30   40 Miles

Chronology of FAIRFIELD

Map	Date	Event	Resulting Area
❻	14 Oct 1714	Gained town of Newtown from non-county area	750 sq mi

(Heavy line depicts historical boundary. Base map shows present-day information.)

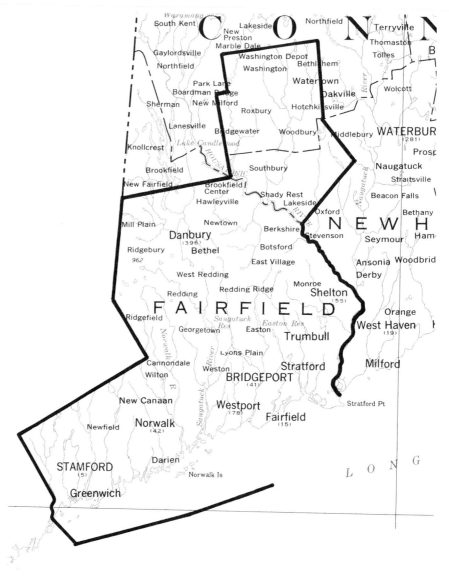

❻   14 Oct 1714 – 9 Oct 1728

```
10        0        10        20        30        40 Miles
```

Chronology of FAIRFIELD

Map	Date	Event	Resulting Area
❼	10 Oct 1728	Gained town of New Fairfield from non-county area	800 sq mi

(Heavy line depicts historical boundary. Base map shows present-day information.)

❼ 10 Oct 1728 – 8 Oct 1751

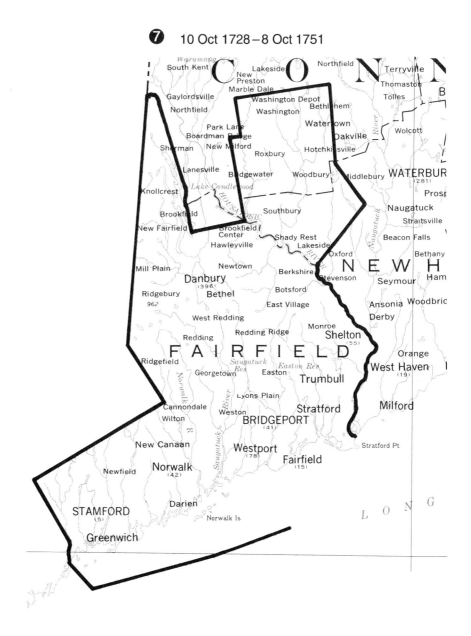

10   0   10   20   30   40 Miles

Chronology of FAIRFIELD

Map	Date	Event	Resulting Area
❽	9 Oct 1751	Lost to creation of LITCHFIELD	640 sq mi
❽	9 May 1754	Gained small area from LITCHFIELD	640 sq mi

(Heavy line depicts historical boundary. Base map shows present-day information.)

❽ 9 Oct 1751–7 May 1788

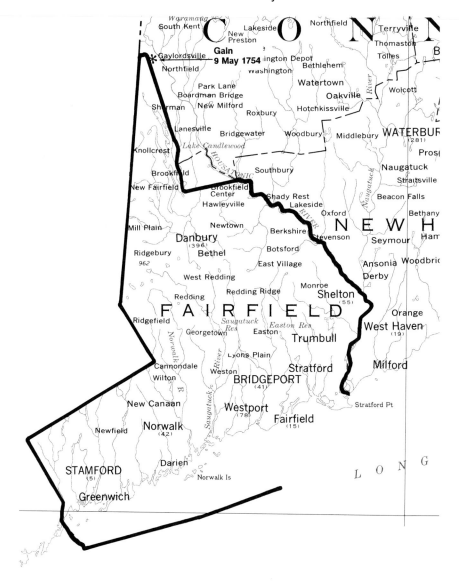

Chronology of FAIRFIELD

Map	Date	Event	Resulting Area
❾	8 May 1788	Gained from LITCHFIELD when town of Brookfield created from Danbury, Newtown, and New Milford	650 sq mi
	22 Mar 1881	Jurisdiction over waters of Long Island Sound redefined [no change]	

(Heavy line depicts historical boundary. Base map shows present-day information.)

❾ 8 May 1788–present

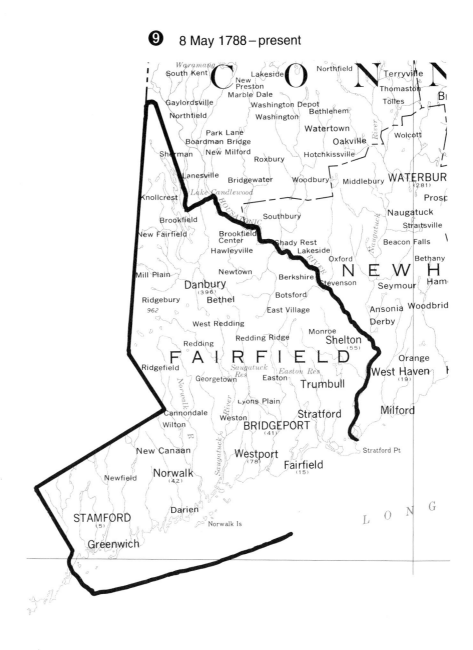

Chronology of HARTFORD

Map	Date	Event	Resulting Area
❶	10 May 1666	Created as one of four original counties	790 sq mi

(Heavy line depicts historical boundary. Base map shows present-day information.)

❶   10 May 1666 – 11 May 1670

Chronology of HARTFORD

Map	Date	Event	Resulting Area
❷	12 May 1670	Gained town of Simsbury from non-county area	900 sq mi

(Heavy line depicts historical boundary. Base map shows present-day information.)

❷   12 May 1670 – 14 May 1686

disfield Granville Southwick E Longmeadow
Feeding Longmeadow Hampden W
Hills
rmington West Hartland Thompsonville
Res
ok East Hartland North Granby W Suffield Scitico Somers Staffor
bertsville Riverton West Granby Suffield Hazardville Stafford
1451 Granby East Granby Enfield West Stafford Stafford
Winsted Barkhamsted Winder Locks Crystal Lake 845 Springs
Res Tariffville Broad Brook
Pleasant Poquonock Scantic Ellington
New Hartford Valley North Canton Shenipsit W Willington
Burrville W Simsbury Simsbury Lake Tolland
Canton Weatogue Windsor Rockville S Willington
Center Bloomfield TOLLAND Mansfi
Bakersville HARTFORD Vernon Center Merrow
Nepaug Canton Avon Wapping Talcottville Storrs Gu
Torrington Res Collinsville Manchester Quarryville Eagleville
595 Burlington West Hartford East Hartford Mansfield
L D Unionville HARTFORD Bolton S Coventry Center
Harwinton Andover River Perkins
1112 Whigville E Hartford Gardens Corner
Farmington Wethersfield Andover Columbia
Terryville Newington Glastonbury 809
N N Plainville E C E. Glastonbury T I C
Thomasto Bristol New Britain S Glastonbury Gilead Hebron Liberty
Tolles Rocky Hill Lebanon
Kensington Berlin Marlborough North Fra
Southington Goodrich Hts
ille Wolcott Cromwell Portland East N Westchester
Plantsville Hampton Colchester
Marion Middle Haddam Ya
dlebury WATERBURY Meriden Middletown NE
(281) (259) Rockfall (51) Haddam Salem
Prospect Middlefield Neck Moodus Oak
Naugatuck Cheshire Higganum Haddam
Straitsville Yalesville Durham MIDDLESEX
Beacon Falls Wallingford East Haddam
Bethany (71) Chesterfield
E W H A V E N Hadlyme
Seymour Hamden Northford Chester
North Haven Deep River Hamburg
Ansonia Woodbridge Winthrop Flanders
Killingworth Essex Ne
Laysville

Chronology of HARTFORD

Map	Date	Event	Resulting Area
❸	15 May 1686	Gained town of Waterbury from non-county area	1,030 sq mi

(Heavy line depicts historical boundary. Base map shows present-day information.)

❸ 15 May 1686 – 9 May 1694

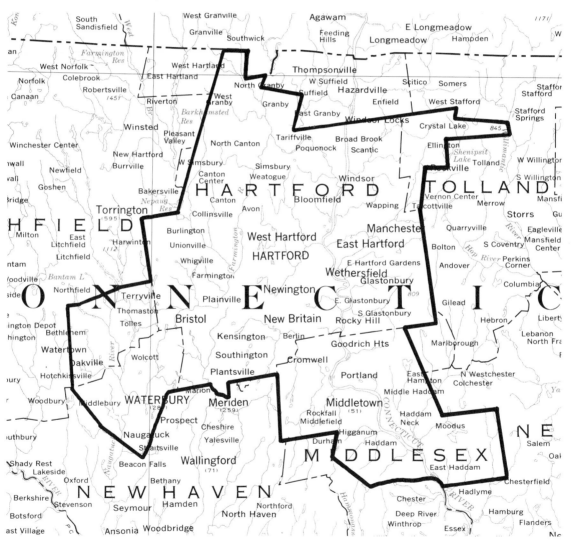

| 10 | | 0 | | 10 | | 20 | | 30 | | 40 Miles |

Chronology of HARTFORD

Map	Date	Event	Resulting Area
❹	10 May 1694	Gained town of Windham from non-county area	1,150 sq mi

(Heavy line depicts historical boundary. Base map shows present-day information.)

❹   10 May 1694 – 12 May 1708

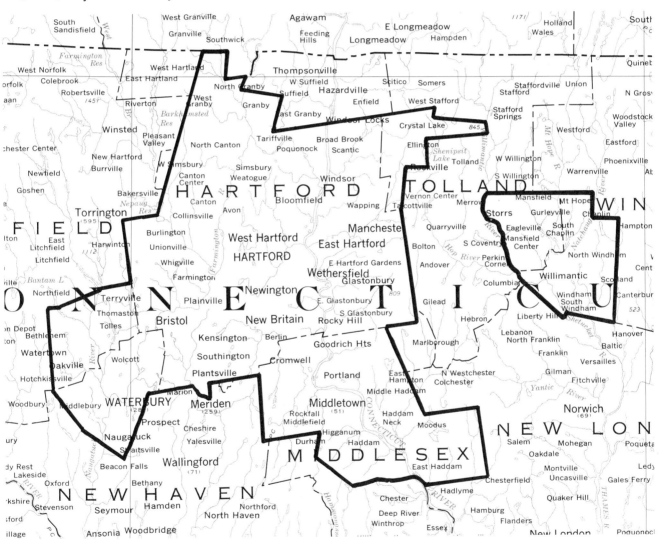

Chronology of HARTFORD

Map	Date	Event	Resulting Area
❺	13 May 1708	Gained town of Hebron from non-county area	1,200 sq mi

(Heavy line depicts historical boundary. Base map shows present-day information.)

❺   13 May 1708 – 13 Oct 1708

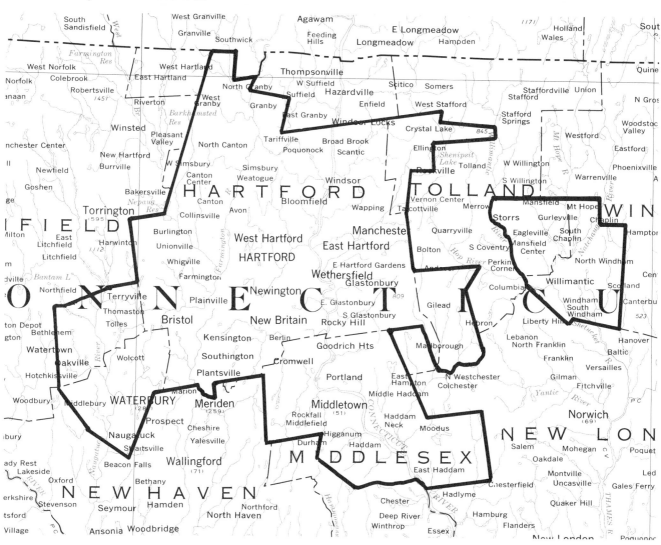

| 10 | 0 | 10 | 20 | 30 | 40 Miles |

Chronology of HARTFORD

Map	Date	Event	Resulting Area
❻	14 Oct 1708	Gained town of Colchester from NEW LONDON	1,270 sq mi

(Heavy line depicts historical boundary. Base map shows present-day information.)

❻   14 Oct 1708 – 7 May 1712

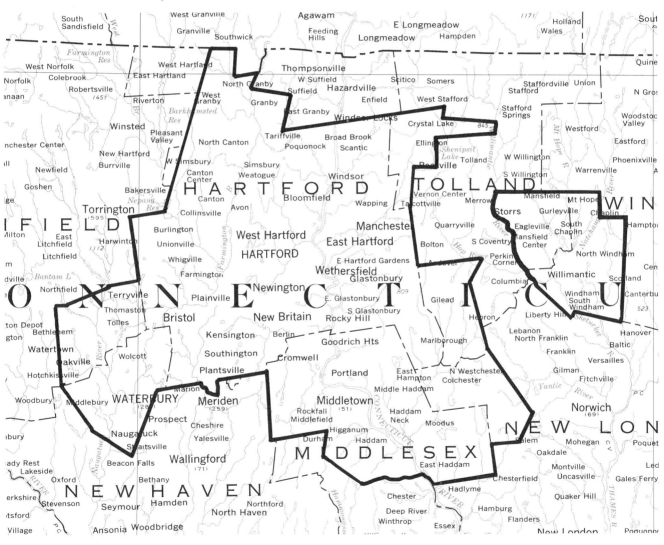

Chronology of HARTFORD

Map	Date	Event	Resulting Area
❼	8 May 1712	Gained town of Coventry from non-county area	1,320 sq mi

(Heavy line depicts historical boundary. Base map shows present-day information.)

❼   **8 May 1712–12 May 1714**

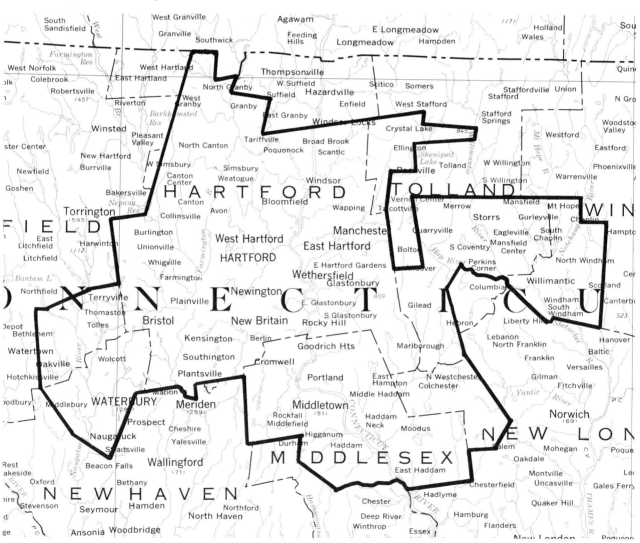

| 10 | 0 | 10 | 20 | 30 | 40 Miles |

Chronology of HARTFORD

Map	Date	Event	Resulting Area
❽	13 May 1714	Gained from non-county area	1,580 sq mi

(Heavy line depicts historical boundary. Base map shows present-day information.)

❽   **13 May 1714–10 Oct 1722**

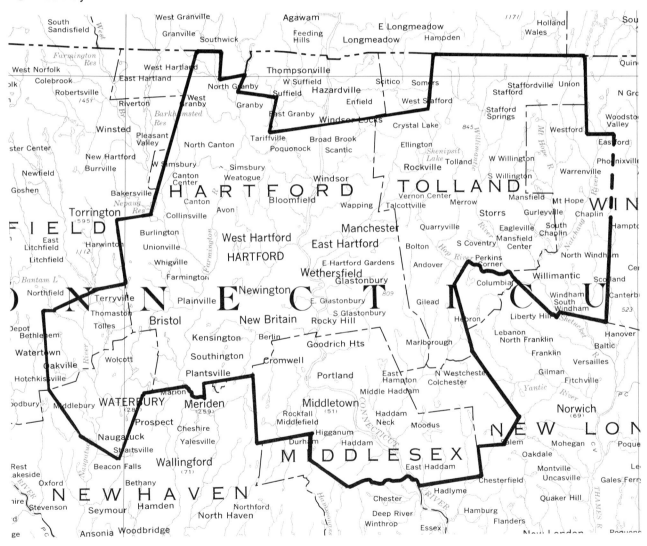

10   0   10   20   30   40 Miles

Chronology of HARTFORD

Map	Date	Event	Resulting Area
❾	11 Oct 1722	Gained town of Litchfield from non-county area	1,660 sq mi

(Heavy line depicts historical boundary. Base map shows present-day information.)

❾   11 Oct 1722 – 11 May 1726

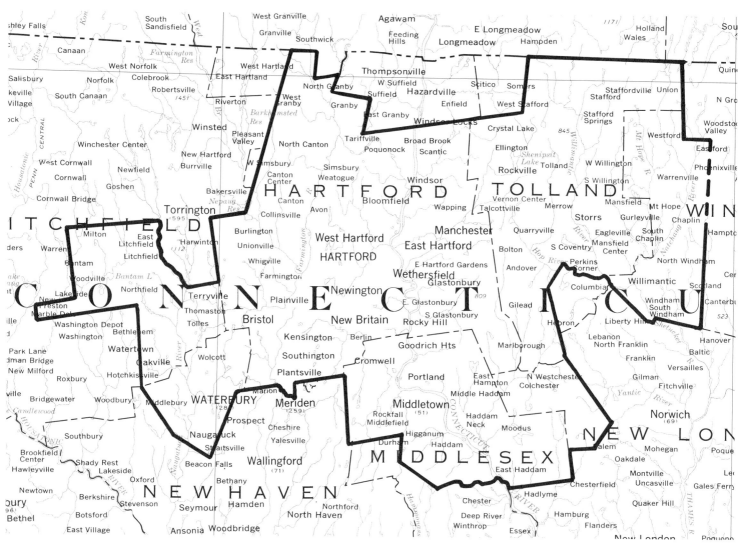

Chronology of HARTFORD

Map	Date	Event	Resulting Area
⑩	12 May 1726	Lost to creation of WINDHAM	1,390 sq mi

(Heavy line depicts historical boundary. Base map shows present-day information.)

⑩   12 May 1726 – 8 May 1728

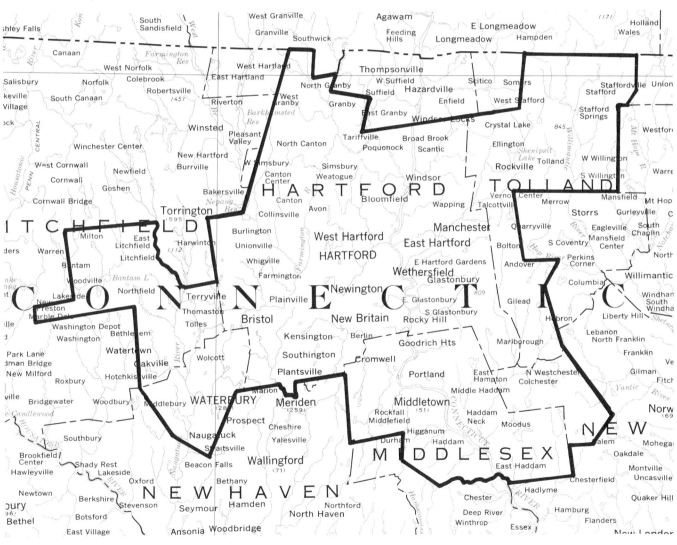

Chronology of HARTFORD

Map	Date	Event	Resulting Area
⓫	9 May 1728	Lost town of Waterbury to NEW HAVEN	1,280 sq mi

(Heavy line depicts historical boundary. Base map shows present-day information.)

⓫　9 May 1728–13 May 1730

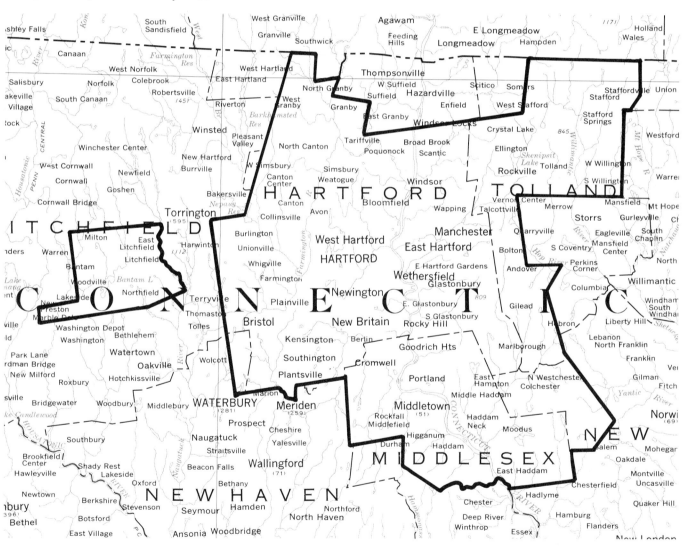

Chronology of HARTFORD

Map	Date	Event	Resulting Area
⑫	14 May 1730	Gained towns of Barkhamstead, Colebrook, Hartland, Harwinton, New Hartford, Torrington, and Winchester from NEW HAVEN	1,530 sq mi

(Heavy line depicts historical boundary. Base map shows present-day information.)

⑫   14 May 1730 – 10 May 1738

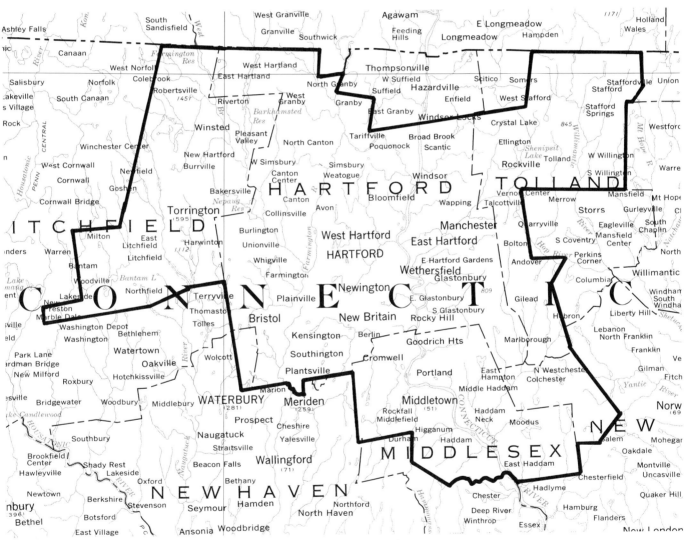

Chronology of HARTFORD

Map	Date	Event	Resulting Area
⑬	11 May 1738	Gained towns of Canaan, Cornwall, Goshen, Kent, and Norfolk from NEW HAVEN	1,830 sq mi

(Heavy line depicts historical boundary. Base map shows present-day information.)

⑬   11 May 1738 – 11 Oct 1749

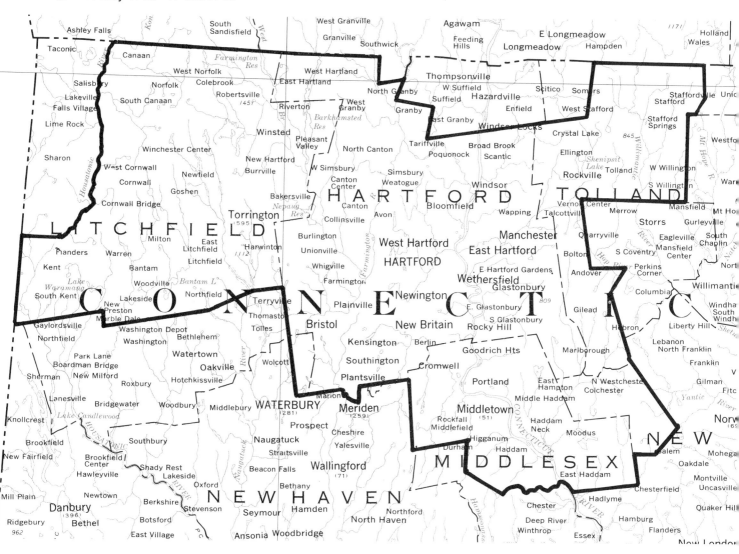

| 10 | 0 | 10 | 20 | 30 | 40 Miles |

Chronology of HARTFORD

Map	Date	Event	Resulting Area
⑭	12 Oct 1749	Gained towns of Enfield, Somers, and Suffield in accordance with May 1749 annexation from Massachusetts	1,940 sq mi

(Heavy line depicts historical boundary. Base map shows present-day information.)

⑭ 12 Oct 1749–8 Oct 1751

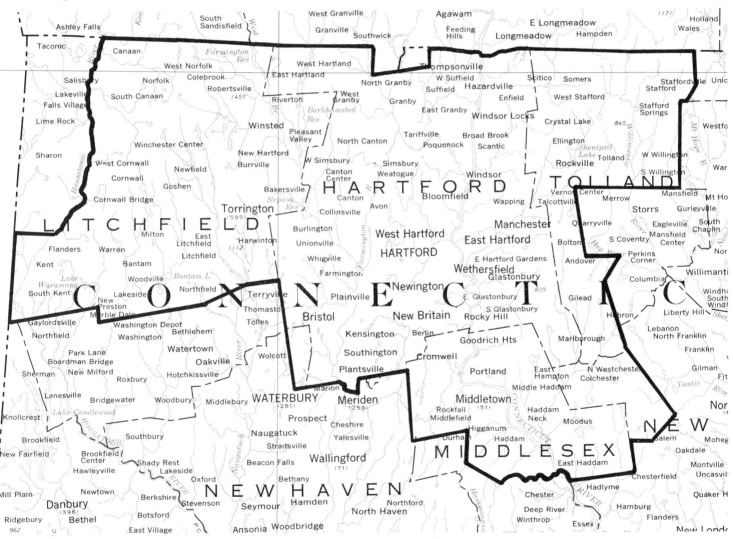

Chronology of HARTFORD

Map	Date	Event	Resulting Area
⑮	9 Oct 1751	Lost to creation of LITCHFIELD	1,300 sq mi

(Heavy line depicts historical boundary. Base map shows present-day information.)

⑮   9 Oct 1751–1774

10   0   10   20   30   40 Miles

Chronology of HARTFORD

Map	Date	Event	Resulting Area
⑯	1774	Gained from HAMPSHIRE (Mass.) when Connecticut annexed part of town of Southwick (Mass.)	1,320 sq mi

(Heavy line depicts historical boundary. Base map shows present-day information.)

⑯ 1774 – 8 Oct 1783

| 10 | 0 | 10 | 20 | 30 | 40 Miles |

Chronology of HARTFORD

Map	Date	Event	Resulting Area
⑰	9 Oct 1783	Lost town of Colchester to NEW LONDON	1,250 sq mi

(Heavy line depicts historical boundary. Base map shows present-day information.)

⑰   9 Oct 1783–11 May 1785

| 10 | 0 | 10 | 20 | 30 | 40 Miles |

Chronology of HARTFORD

Map	Date	Event	Resulting Area
⑱	12 May 1785	Lost to creation of MIDDLESEX	1,010 sq mi

(Heavy line depicts historical boundary. Base map shows present-day information.)

⑱   12 May 1785–12 Oct 1785

| 10 | 0 | 10 | 20 | 30 | 40 Miles |

Chronology of HARTFORD

Map	Date	Event	Resulting Area
⑲	13 Oct 1785	Lost to creation of TOLLAND	730 sq mi

(Heavy line depicts historical boundary. Base map shows present-day information.)

⑲   13 Oct 1785 – 13 May 1789

Chronology of HARTFORD

Map	Date	Event	Resulting Area
㉚	14 May 1789	Lost to TOLLAND when town of Bolton gained from East Windsor	720 sq mi

(Heavy line depicts historical boundary. Base map shows present-day information.)

㉚   14 May 1789 – 1 May 1796

South Sandisfield West Granville Agawam E Longmeadow Granville Southwick Feeding Hills Longmeadow Hampden *Farmington Res* folk West Hartland Thompsonville ebrook East Hartland W Suffield Scitico Somers Robertsville *1451* North Granby Suffield Hazardville Riverton West Granby Granby Enfield West Stafford *Barkhamsted Res* East Granby Windsor Locks Crystal Lake *845* Winsted Pleasant Valley Tariffville Broad Brook Ellington North Canton Poquonock Scantic *Shenipsit Lake* New Hartford W Simsbury Simsbury Rockville Tolland Burrville Weatogue Windsor *Nepaug* Canton Center H A R T F O R D T O L L A Bakersville Canton Bloomfield Vernon Center Merrow *Res* Avon Wapping Talcottville Torrington *1595* Collinsville Quarryville Burlington Manchester ast eld Harwinton *1112* Unionville West Hartford East Hartford Bolton S Cove field Whigville HARTFORD Andover *L* Farmington E Hartford Gardens Wethersfield field N E Newington Glastonbury Terryville Plainville E. Glastonbury *809* Gilead Thomaston S Glastonbury Hebron Tolles Bristol New Britain Rocky Hill em Kensington Berlin Marlborough wn Southington Goodrich Hts)akville Wolcott Cromwell East Hampton N Westchester sville Plantsville Portland Colchester Marion Middle Haddam Middlebury WATERBURY *(281)* Meriden *(259)* Middletown Prospect Rockfall *(51)* Haddam Neck Moodus Cheshire Middlefield Naugatuck Yalesville Higganum Durham Haddam

| 10 | 0 | 10 | 20 | 30 | 40 Miles |

Chronology of HARTFORD

Map	Date	Event	Resulting Area
㉑	2 May 1796	Lost to NEW HAVEN when town of Wolcott created from Southington and Waterbury; gained Hartland from LITCHFIELD	740 sq mi

(Heavy line depicts historical boundary. Base map shows present-day information.)

㉑ 2 May 1796 – 10 Oct 1798

| 10 | 0 | 10 | 20 | 30 | 40 Miles |

Chronology of HARTFORD

Map	Date	Event	Resulting Area
㉒	11 Oct 1798	Gained from NEW HAVEN when town of Wallingford gained from Berlin	740 sq mi

(Heavy line depicts historical boundary. Base map shows present-day information.)

㉒ 11 Oct 1798 – 12 Oct 1803

Chronology of HARTFORD

Map	Date	Event	Resulting Area
㉓	13 Oct 1803	Gained from NEW LONDON and TOLLAND when town of Marlborough created from Colchester, Glastonbury, and Hebron	760 sq mi

(Heavy line depicts historical boundary. Base map shows present-day information.)

㉓   13 Oct 1803–1804

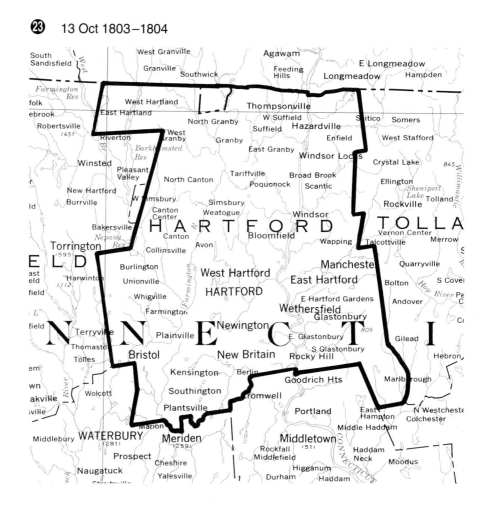

10   0   10   20   30   40 Miles

Chronology of HARTFORD

Map	Date	Event	Resulting Area
㉔	1804	Lost part of town of Southwick (the "Southwick Jog") to HAMPSHIRE (Mass.) when state boundary adjusted	750 sq mi

(Heavy line depicts historical boundary. Base map shows present-day information.)

㉔   1804–7 May 1806

| 10 | 0 | 10 | 20 | 30 | 40 Miles |

Chronology of HARTFORD

Map	Date	Event	Resulting Area
㉕	8 May 1806	Gained from LITCHFIELD when town of Canton created from New Hartford and Simsbury	750 sq mi

(Heavy line depicts historical boundary. Base map shows present-day information.)

㉕   8 May 1806 – present

[map showing Hartford County boundaries with place names including West Granville, Granville, Southwick, Agawam, Feeding Hills, Longmeadow, E Longmeadow, Hampden, South Sandisfield, West Hartland, Thompsonville, West Stafford, Somers, East Hartland, W Suffield, Scitico, Robertsville, Riverton, North Granby, Suffield, Hazardville, West Granby, Granby, Enfield, Winsted, Pleasant Valley, Tariffville, Broad Brook, Crystal Lake, East Granby, Windsor Locks, Ellington, New Hartford, North Canton, Poquonock, Scantic, Tolland, Burrville, W Simsbury, Simsbury, Weatogue, Windsor, Rockville, HARTFORD, TOLLA, Bakersville, Canton Center, Bloomfield, Vernon Center, Merrow, Torrington, Canton, Avon, Wapping, Talcottville, Collinsville, Quarryville, Burlington, West Hartford, Manchester, Bolton, S Cover, Harwinton, Unionville, East Hartford, Andover, Whigville, E Hartford Gardens, Wethersfield, Farmington, Glastonbury, Terryville, Newington, E Glastonbury, Gilead, Plainville, Thomaston, S Glastonbury, Bristol, New Britain, Rocky Hill, Hebron, Tolles, Kensington, Berlin, Goodrich Hts, Marlborough, Wolcott, Southington, Cromwell, Plantsville, Portland, East Hampton, N Westcheste, Colchester, Marion, Middle Haddam, Middlebury, WATERBURY, Meriden, Middletown, Haddam Neck, Prospect, Rockfall, Middlefield, Haddam, Moodus, Naugatuck, Cheshire, Higganum, Yalesville, Durham, Haddam; with NNECTICUT across bottom]

10   0   10   20   30   40 Miles

Chronology of LITCHFIELD

Map	Date	Event	Resulting Area
❶	9 Oct 1751	Created from FAIRFIELD, HARTFORD, and NEW HAVEN	1,010 sq mi
❶	9 May 1754	Lost small area to FAIRFIELD	1,010 sq mi

(Heavy line depicts historical boundary. Base map shows present-day information.)

❶ 9 Oct 1751–11 Jan 1774
10 Oct 1776–10 May 1780

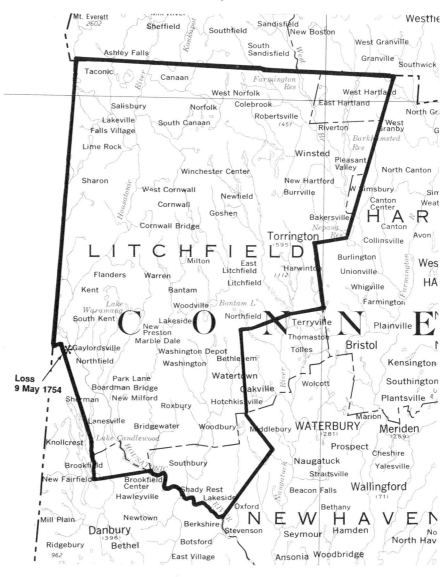

10   0   10   20   30   40 Miles

Chronology of LITCHFIELD

Map	Date	Event	Resulting Area
❷	12 Jan 1774	Gained town of Westmoreland, a town created by Connecticut in northeastern Pennsylvania	6,500 sq mi
❸	11 May 1775	Gained territory in northeastern Pennsylvania when Connecticut enlarged town of Westmoreland	9,700 sq mi

(Heavy line depicts historical boundary. Base map shows present-day information.)

❷ 12 Jan 1774–10 May 1775

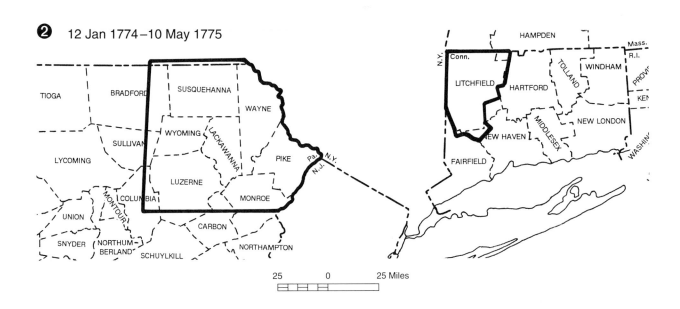

❸ 11 May 1775–13 Dec 1775

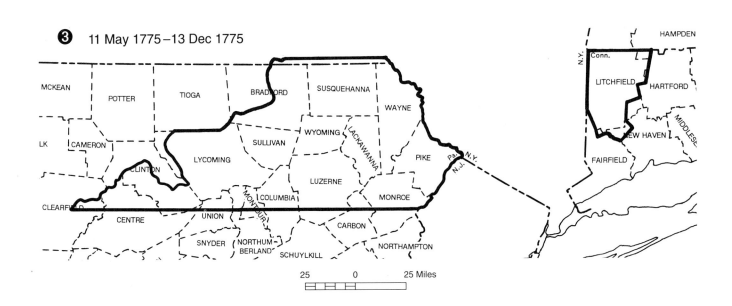

Chronology of LITCHFIELD

Map	Date	Event	Resulting Area
❹	14 Dec 1775	Lost territory in northeastern Pennsylvania when Connecticut reduced town of Westmoreland	7,450 sq mi
❶	10 Oct 1776	Lost to creation of WESTMORELAND in northeastern Pennsylvania	1,010 sq mi

(Heavy line depicts historical boundary. Base map shows present-day information.)

❹ 14 Dec 1775 – 9 Oct 1776

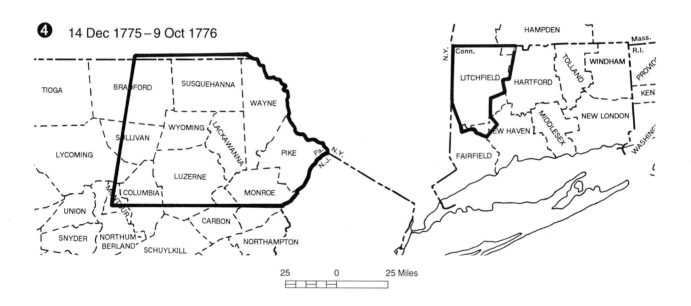

Chronology of LITCHFIELD

Map	Date	Event	Resulting Area
❺	11 May 1780	Gained from NEW HAVEN when town of Watertown created from Waterbury	1,070 sq mi

(Heavy line depicts historical boundary. Base map shows present-day information.)

❺ 11 May 1780 – 7 May 1788

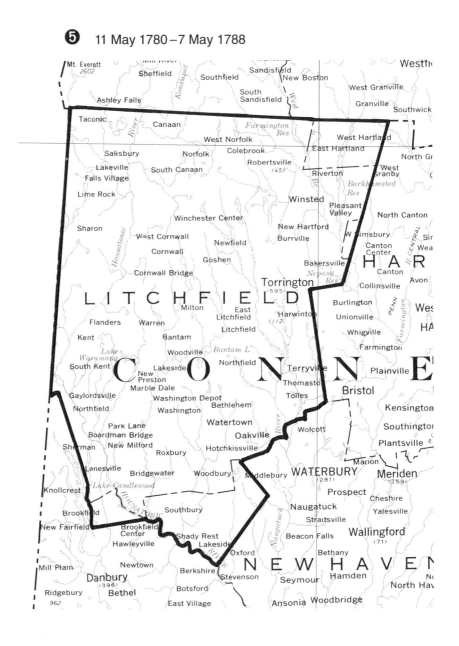

| 10 | 0 | 10 | 20 | 30 | 40 Miles |

Chronology of LITCHFIELD

Map	Date	Event	Resulting Area
❻	8 May 1788	Lost to FAIRFIELD when town of Brookfield created from Danbury, Newtown, and New Milford	1,060 sq mi

(Heavy line depicts historical boundary. Base map shows present-day information.)

❻ 8 May 1788 – 1 May 1796

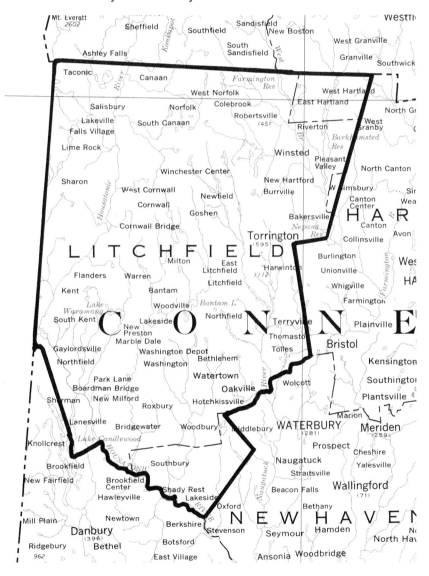

10	0	10	20	30	40 Miles

Chronology of LITCHFIELD

Map	Date	Event	Resulting Area
❼	2 May 1796	Lost town of Hartland to HARTFORD	1,030 sq mi

(Heavy line depicts historical boundary. Base map shows present-day information.)

❼ 2 May 1796 – 10 Oct 1798

Chronology of LITCHFIELD

Map	Date	Event	Resulting Area
❽	11 Oct 1798	Lost to NEW HAVEN when town of Oxford created from Derby and Southbury	1,010 sq mi

(Heavy line depicts historical boundary. Base map shows present-day information.)

❽   11 Oct 1798 – 7 May 1806

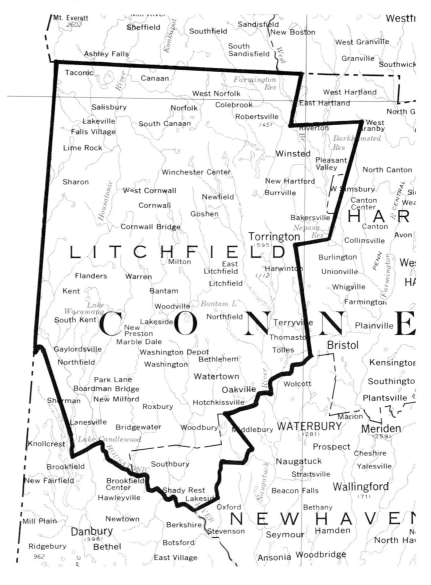

Chronology of LITCHFIELD

Map	Date	Event	Resulting Area
9	8 May 1806	Lost to HARTFORD when town of Canton created from New Hartford and Simsbury	1,010 sq mi

(Heavy line depicts historical boundary. Base map shows present-day information.)

9   8 May 1806 – 13 May 1807

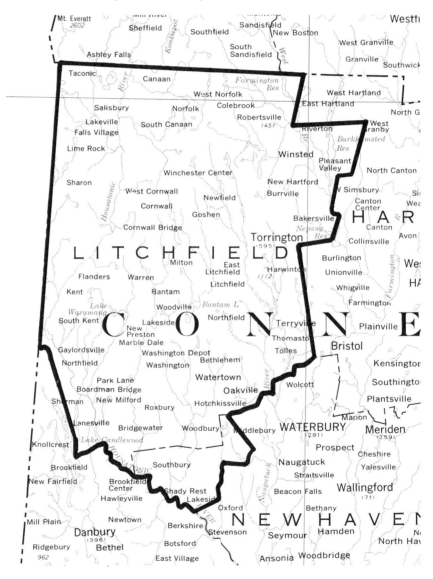

Chronology of LITCHFIELD

Map	Date	Event	Resulting Area
⑩	14 May 1807	Lost town of Southbury to NEW HAVEN	970 sq mi

(Heavy line depicts historical boundary. Base map shows present-day information.)

⑩   14 May 1807–7 Oct 1807

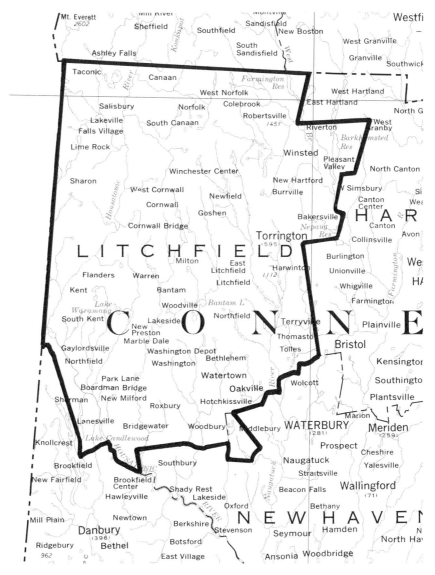

10   0   10   20   30   40 Miles

Chronology of LITCHFIELD

Map	Date	Event	Resulting Area
⑪	8 Oct 1807	Lost to NEW HAVEN when town of Middlebury created from Southbury, Waterbury, and Woodbury	950 sq mi

(Heavy line depicts historical boundary. Base map shows present-day information.)

⑪   8 Oct 1807–present

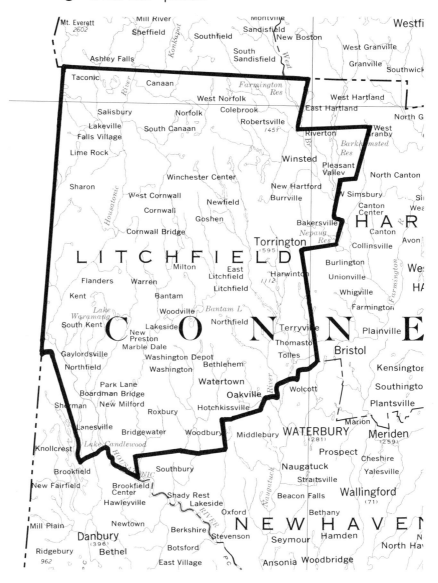

10   0   10   20   30   40 Miles

Chronology of MIDDLESEX

Map	Date	Event	Resulting Area
❶	12 May 1785	Created from HARTFORD and NEW LONDON	360 sq mi
❷	9 May 1799	Gained town of Durham from NEW HAVEN	380 sq mi
	22 Mar 1881	Jurisdiction over waters of Long Island Sound redefined [no change]	

(Heavy line depicts historical boundary. Base map shows present-day information.)

❶ 12 May 1785 – 8 May 1799

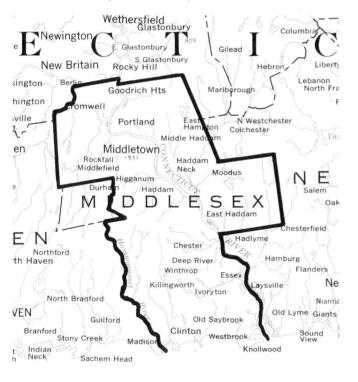

❷ 9 May 1799 – present

Chronology of NEW HAVEN

Map	Date	Event	Resulting Area
❶	10 May 1666	Created as one of four original counties	330 sq mi
❷	11 May 1671	Gained town of Wallingford from non-county area	440 sq mi

(Heavy line depicts historical boundary. Base map shows present-day information.)

❶ 10 May 1666–10 May 1671

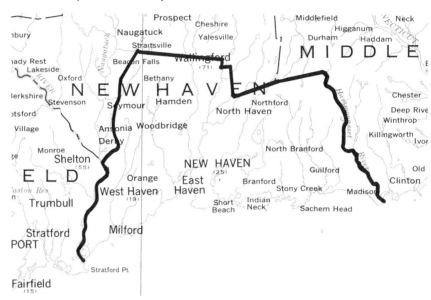

❷ 11 May 1671–12 May 1675

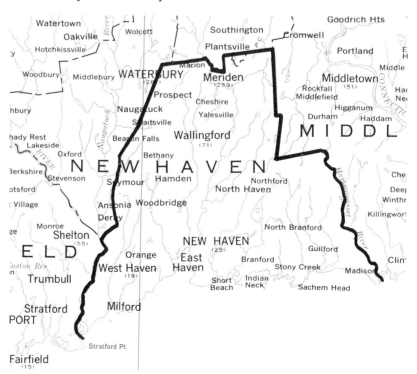

10   0   10   20   30   40 Miles

Chronology of NEW HAVEN

Map	Date	Event	Resulting Area
❸	13 May 1675	Gained town of Derby from non-county area	520 sq mi

(Heavy line depicts historical boundary. Base map shows present-day information.)

❸ 13 May 1675 – 9 Oct 1706

Chronology of NEW HAVEN

Map	Date	Event	Resulting Area
❹	10 Oct 1706	Gained town of New Milford from non-county area	600 sq mi

(Heavy line depicts historical boundary. Base map shows present-day information.)

❹ 10 Oct 1706 – 18 May 1708

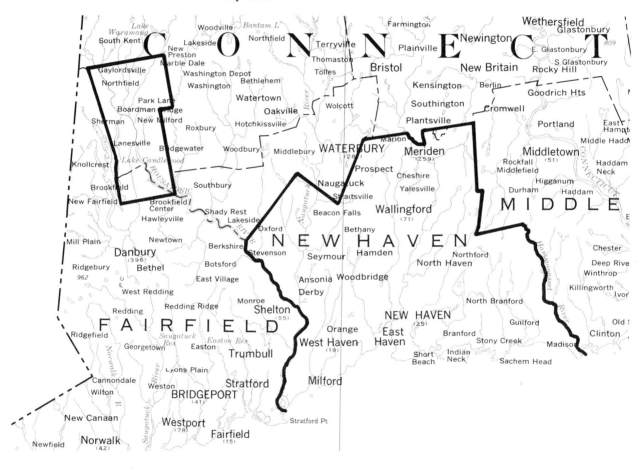

Chronology of NEW HAVEN

Map	Date	Event	Resulting Area
❺	19 May 1708	Gained town of Durham from non-county area	680 sq mi

(Heavy line depicts historical boundary. Base map shows present-day information.)

❺ 19 May 1708–10 Oct 1722

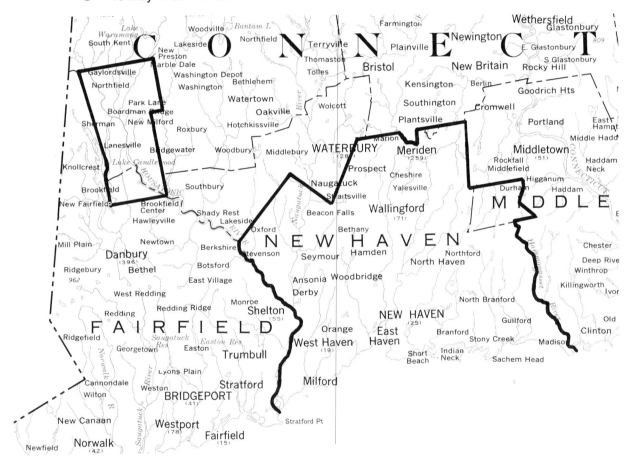

10   0   10   20   30   40 Miles

Chronology of NEW HAVEN

Map	Date	Event	Resulting Area
❻	11 Oct 1722	Gained from non-county area	1,350 sq mi

(Heavy line depicts historical boundary. Base map shows present-day information.)

❻ 11 Oct 1722 – 8 May 1728

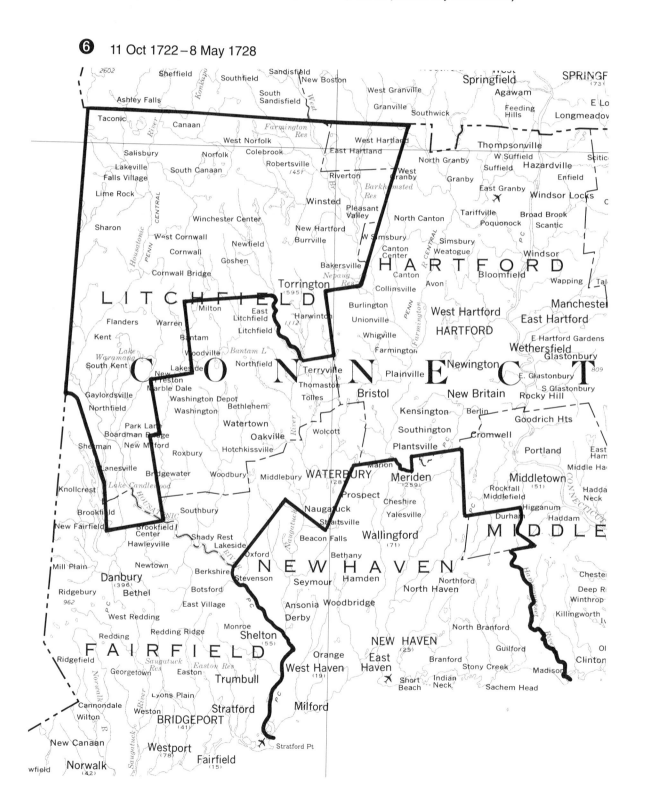

Chronology of NEW HAVEN

Map	Date	Event	Resulting Area
❼	9 May 1728	Gained town of Waterbury from HARTFORD	1,420 sq mi

(Heavy line depicts historical boundary. Base map shows present-day information.)

❼   9 May 1728 – 13 May 1730

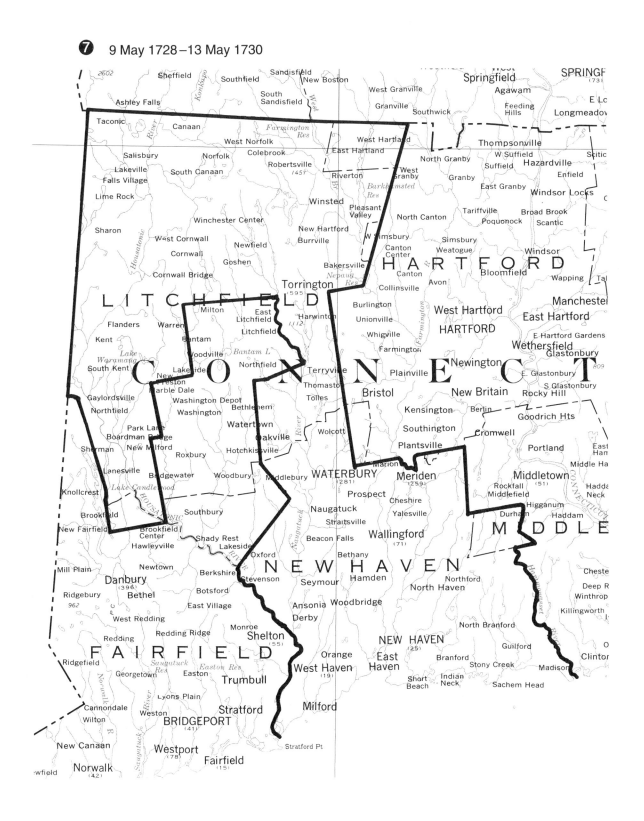

Chronology of NEW HAVEN

Map	Date	Event	Resulting Area
❽	14 May 1730	Lost towns of Barkhamstead, Colebrook, Hartland, Harwinton, New Hartford, Torrington, and Winchester to HARTFORD	1,140 sq mi

(Heavy line depicts historical boundary. Base map shows present-day information.)

❽   14 May 1730–10 May 1738

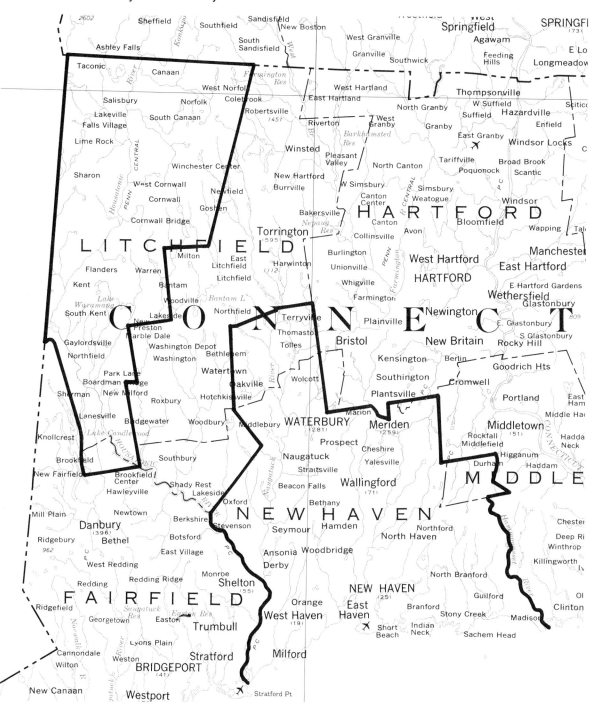

10   0   10   20   30   40 Miles

Chronology of NEW HAVEN

Map	Date	Event	Resulting Area
⑨	11 May 1738	Lost towns of Canaan, Cornwall, Goshen, Kent, and Norfolk to HARTFORD	870 sq mi

(Heavy line depicts historical boundary. Base map shows present-day information.)

⑨ 11 May 1738 – 8 Oct 1751

2602
Sheffield
Southfield
Sandisfield
New Boston
West
SPRINGFI
Springfield (73)
Agawam
E Lo
Ashley Falls
South
Sandisfield
West Granville
Granville
Southwick
Feeding
Hills
Longmeadow
Taconic
Canaan
West Norfolk
Farmington
Res
East Hartland
West Hartland
North Granby
W Suffield
Suffield
Hazardville
Scitico
Salisbury
Norfolk
Colebrook
West
Granby
Granby
Enfield
Lakeville
South Canaan
Robertsville
1451
Riverton
East Granby
Windsor Locks
Falls Village
Lime Rock
Winsted
Barkhamsted
Res
Tariffville
Broad Brook
Poquonock
Scantic
Sharon
Winchester Center
Pleasant
Valley
North Canton
Simsbury
Windsor
West Cornwall
New Hartford
W Simsbury
Weatogue
Wapping
Tal
Newfield
Burrville
Canton
Center
HARTFORD
Cornwall
Goshen
Bakersville
Nepaug
Res
Canton
Bloomfield
Cornwall Bridge
Torrington
595
Collinsville
Avon
Manchester
L I T C H F I E L D
Milton
East
Litchfield
Burlington
West Hartford
East Hartford
Flanders
Warren
Harwinton
1112
Unionville
HARTFORD
Kent
Bantam
Litchfield
Whigville
E Hartford Gardens
Woodville
Farmington
Wethersfield
Glastonbury
Lake
Waramaug
South Kent
Bantam L.
Lakeside
Northfield
C O N N E
Newington
C T
809
New
Preston
Terryville
Plainville
E. Glastonbury
Marble Dale
Thomaston
New Britain
S Glastonbury
Gaylordsville
Washington Depot
Tolles
Bristol
Rocky Hill
Northfield
Washington
Bethlehem
Wolcott
Kensington
Berlin
Goodrich Hts
Park Lane
Watertown
Southington
Cromwell
East
Boardman Bridge
Oakville
Portland
Ham
Sherman
New Milford
Roxbury
Hotchkissville
Plantsville
Middle Ha
Lanesville
Bridgewater
Woodbury
Middlebury
WATERBURY
281
Meriden
259
Middletown
Knollcrest
Lake Candlewood
Prospect
Rockfall
Middlefield
51
Hadda
Neck
Brookfield
Southbury
Naugatuck
Cheshire
Yalesville
Higganum
Haddam
New Fairfield
Brookfield
Center
Straitsville
Durham
M I D D L E
Shady Rest
Lakeside
Beacon Falls
Wallingford
71
Hawleyville
Oxford
Bethany
Mill Plain
Newtown
Berkshire
Stevenson
N E W H A V E N
Cheste
Danbury
396
Seymour
Hamden
Northford
North Haven
Deep R
Ridgebury
Bethel
Botsford
Winthrop
962
East Village
Ansonia
Woodbridge
Killingworth
West Redding
Derby
North Branford
Redding
Redding Ridge
Monroe
Shelton
55
NEW HAVEN
25
Guilford
Clintor
Ridgefield
F A I R F I E L D
Orange
East
Branford
Stony Creek
Madison
Saugatuck
Res
Easton Res
West Haven
19
Haven
Short
Beach
Indian
Neck
Sachem Head
Georgetown
Easton
Trumbull
Milford
Cannondale
Lyons Plain
Weston
Stratford
Wilton
BRIDGEPORT
41
New Canaan
Westport
Stratford Pt

10	0	10	20	30	40 Miles

Chronology of NEW HAVEN

Map	Date	Event	Resulting Area
⑩	9 Oct 1751	Lost to creation of LITCHFIELD	650 sq mi

(Heavy line depicts historical boundary. Base map shows present-day information.)

⑩ 9 Oct 1751–10 May 1780

| 10 | 0 | 10 | 20 | 30 | 40 Miles |

Chronology of NEW HAVEN

Map	Date	Event	Resulting Area
⓫	11 May 1780	Lost to LITCHFIELD when town of Watertown created from Waterbury	590 sq mi

(Heavy line depicts historical boundary. Base map shows present-day information.)

⓫ 11 May 1780 – 1 May 1796

10   0   10   20   30   40 Miles

Chronology of NEW HAVEN

Map	Date	Event	Resulting Area
⑫	2 May 1796	Gained from HARTFORD when town of Wolcott created from Southington and Waterbury	610 sq mi

(Heavy line depicts historical boundary. Base map shows present-day information.)

⑫   2 May 1796–10 Oct 1798

Chronology of NEW HAVEN

Map	Date	Event	Resulting Area
⑬	11 Oct 1798	Gained from LITCHFIELD when town of Oxford created from Derby and Southbury and lost to HARTFORD when Wallingford gained from Berlin	610 sq mi

(Heavy line depicts historical boundary. Base map shows present-day information.)

⑬   11 Oct 1798 – 8 May 1799

Chronology of NEW HAVEN

Map	Date	Event	Resulting Area
⑭	9 May 1799	Lost town of Durham to MIDDLESEX	590 sq mi

(Heavy line depicts historical boundary. Base map shows present-day information.)

⑭ 9 May 1799 – 13 May 1807

Chronology of NEW HAVEN

Map	Date	Event	Resulting Area
⑮	14 May 1807	Gained town of Southbury from LITCHFIELD	630 sq mi

(Heavy line depicts historical boundary. Base map shows present-day information.)

⑮   14 May 1807–7 Oct 1807

10   0   10   20   30   40 Miles

Chronology of NEW HAVEN

Map	Date	Event	Resulting Area
⑯	8 Oct 1807	Gained from LITCHFIELD when town of Middlebury created from Southbury, Waterbury, and Woodbury	640 sq mi
	22 Mar 1881	Jurisdiction over waters of Long Island Sound redefined [no change]	

(Heavy line depicts historical boundary. Base map shows present-day information.)

⑯   8 Oct 1807–present

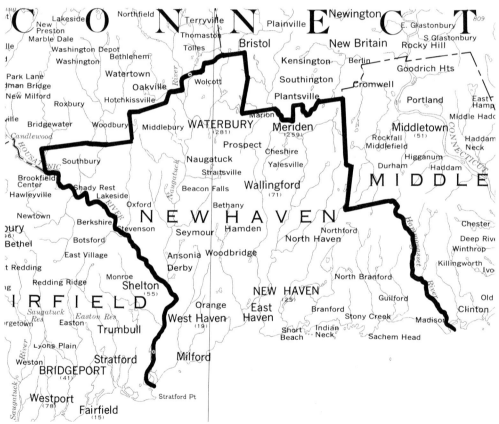

10   0   10   20   30   40 Miles

Chronology of NEW LONDON

Map	Date	Event	Resulting Area
❶	10 May 1666	Created as one of four original counties	610 sq mi
❷	13 Oct 1687	Gained town of Preston from non-county area	700 sq mi

(Heavy line depicts historical boundary. Base map shows present-day information.)

❶ 10 May 1666 – 12 Oct 1687

❷ 13 Oct 1687 – 13 Oct 1697

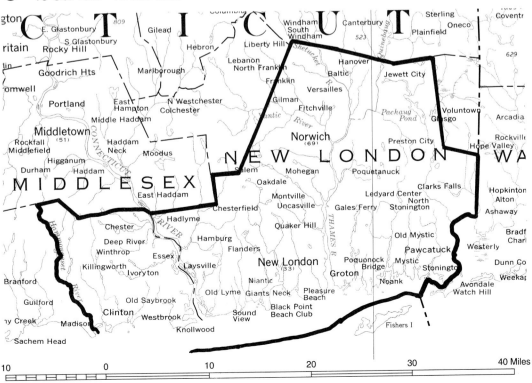

| 10 | 0 | 10 | 20 | 30 | 40 Miles |

Chronology of NEW LONDON

Map	Date	Event	Resulting Area
❸	14 Oct 1697	Gained the Quinesbaug River Valley from non-county area	Indefinite

(Heavy line depicts historical boundary. Base map shows present-day information.)

❸   14 Oct 1697–11 Oct 1699

| 10 | | 0 | | 10 | | 20 | | 30 | | 40 Miles |

Chronology of NEW LONDON

Map	Date	Event	Resulting Area
❹	12 Oct 1699	Gained town of Colchester from non-county area	Indefinite

(Heavy line depicts historical boundary. Base map shows present-day information.)

❹   12 Oct 1699 – 9 Oct 1700

| 10 | | 0 | | 10 | | 20 | | 30 | | 40 Miles |

Chronology of NEW LONDON

Map	Date	Event	Resulting Area
❺	10 Oct 1700	Gained town of Lebanon from non-county area	Indefinite

(Heavy line depicts historical boundary. Base map shows present-day information.)

❺   10 Oct 1700 – 13 Oct 1708

10   0   10   20   30   40 Miles

Chronology of NEW LONDON

Map	Date	Event	Resulting Area
❻	14 Oct 1708	Lost town of Colchester to HARTFORD	Indefinite

(Heavy line depicts historical boundary. Base map shows present-day information.)

❻   14 Oct 1708 – 8 May 1717

Chronology of NEW LONDON

Map	Date	Event	Resulting Area
❼	9 May 1717	Gained from non-county area	1,130 sq mi

(Heavy line depicts historical boundary. Base map shows present-day information.)

❼ 9 May 1717–11 May 1726

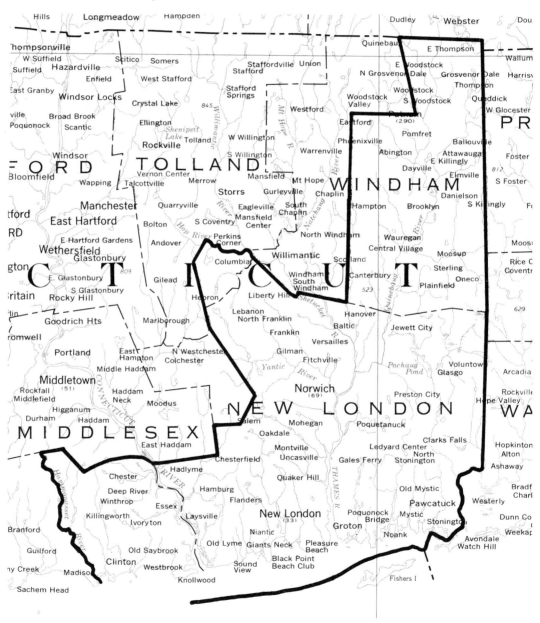

10   0   10   20   30   40 Miles

Chronology of NEW LONDON

Map	Date	Event	Resulting Area
⑧	12 May 1726	Lost to creation of WINDHAM	690 sq mi
⑨	9 Oct 1783	Gained town of Colchester from HARTFORD	770 sq mi

(Heavy line depicts historical boundary. Base map shows present-day information.)

⑧   12 May 1726 – 8 Oct 1783

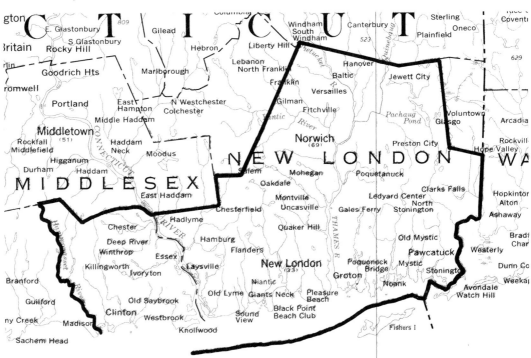

⑨   9 Oct 1783 – 11 May 1785

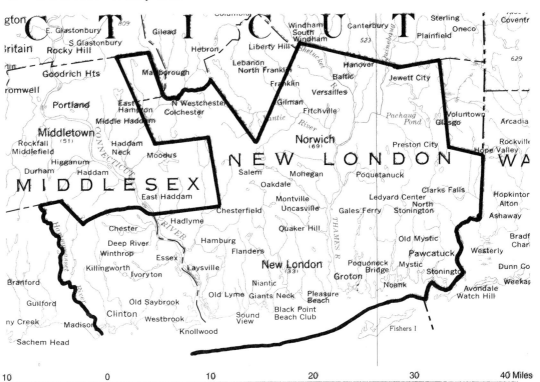

10   0   10   20   30   40 Miles

Chronology of NEW LONDON

Map	Date	Event	Resulting Area
⑩	12 May 1785	Lost to creation of MIDDLESEX	630 sq mi
⑪	13 Oct 1803	Lost to HARTFORD when town of Marlborough created from Colchester and other towns	620 sq mi

(Heavy line depicts historical boundary. Base map shows present-day information.)

⑩   12 May 1785 – 12 Oct 1803

⑪   13 Oct 1803 – 2 Jun 1824

10   0   10   20   30   40 Miles

Chronology of NEW LONDON

Map	Date	Event	Resulting Area
⑫	3 Jun 1824	Gained town of Lebanon from WINDHAM	680 sq mi

(Heavy line depicts historical boundary. Base map shows present-day information.)

⑫ 3 Jun 1824–15 Mar 1881

| 10 | 0 | 10 | 20 | 30 | 40 Miles |

Chronology of NEW LONDON

Map	Date	Event	Resulting Area
⑬	16 Mar 1881	Gained town of Voluntown from WINDHAM	720 sq mi
	22 Mar 1881	Jurisdiction over waters of Long Island Sound redefined [no change]	

(Heavy line depicts historical boundary. Base map shows present-day information.)

⑬   16 Mar 1881–present

10   0   10   20   30   40 Miles

Chronology of TOLLAND

Map	Date	Event	Resulting Area
❶	13 Oct 1785	Created from HARTFORD and WINDHAM	300 sq mi
❷	11 May 1786	Gained town of Coventry from WINDHAM	340 sq mi

(Heavy line depicts historical boundary. Base map shows present-day information.)

❶   13 Oct 1785 – 10 May 1786

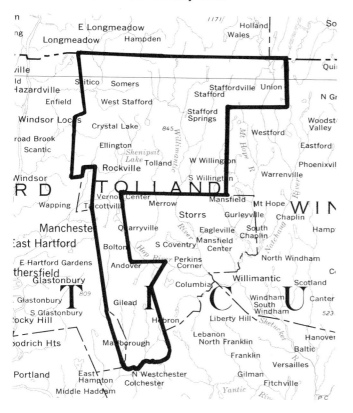

❷   11 May 1786 – 13 May 1789

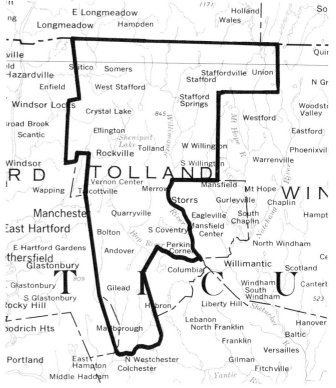

10	0	10	20	30	40 Miles

Chronology of TOLLAND

Map	Date	Event	Resulting Area
❸	14 May 1789	Gained from HARTFORD when town of Bolton gained from East Windsor	350 sq mi
❹	13 Oct 1803	Lost to HARTFORD when town of Marlborough created from Hebron and other towns	340 sq mi
	3 Nov 1826	Exchanged narrow strips with HAMPDEN (Mass.) when state boundary was straightened [not mapped]	

(Heavy line depicts historical boundary. Base map shows present-day information.)

❸   14 May 1789 – 12 Oct 1803

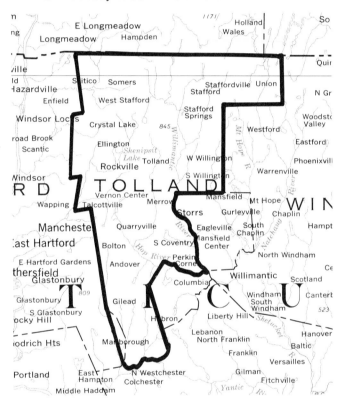

❹   13 Oct 1803 – 24 May 1827

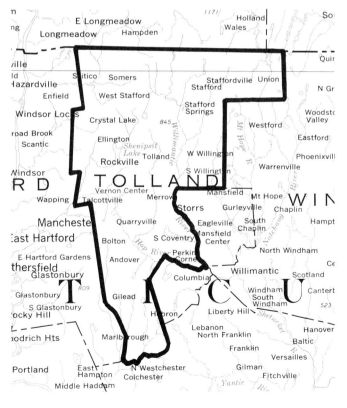

10   0   10   20   30   40 Miles

Chronology of TOLLAND

Map	Date	Event	Resulting Area
❺	25 May 1827	Gained towns of Columbia and Mansfield from WINDHAM	410 sq mi
❻	7 Apr 1885	Lost to WINDHAM when town of Windham gained from Mansfield	410 sq mi

(Heavy line depicts historical boundary. Base map shows present-day information.)

❺ 25 May 1827– 6 Apr 1885

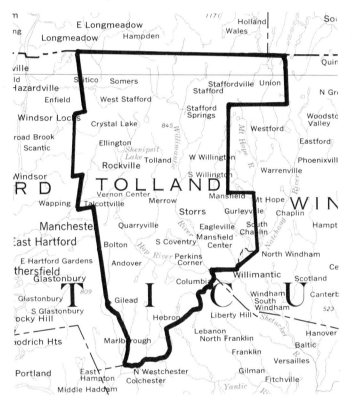

❻ 7 Apr 1885– present

10		0		10	20	30	40 Miles

Chronology of WESTMORELAND (extinct)

Map	Date	Event	Resulting Area
❶	10 Oct 1776	Created in northeastern Pennsylvania from LITCHFIELD	6,400 sq mi
	30 Dec 1782	Eliminated when special congressional court decided its territory belonged to Pennsylvania, not Connecticut	

(Heavy line depicts historical boundary. Base map shows present-day information.)

❶   10 Oct 1776 – 30 Dec 1782

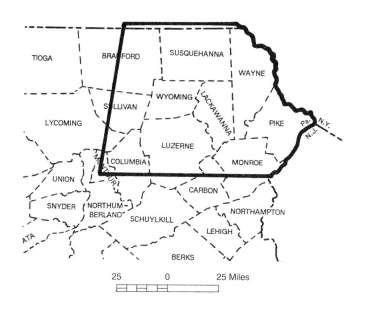

Chronology of WINDHAM

Map	Date	Event	Resulting Area
❶	12 May 1726	Created from HARTFORD and NEW LONDON	700 sq mi

(Heavy line depicts historical boundary. Base map shows present-day information.)

❶   12 May 1726–11 Oct 1749

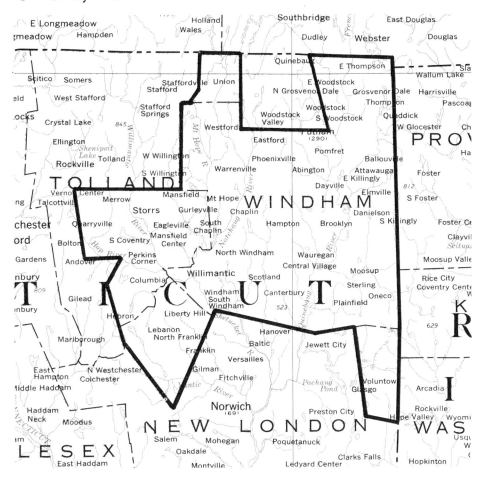

Chronology of WINDHAM

Map	Date	Event	Resulting Area
❷	12 Oct 1749	WINDHAM gained town of Woodstock in accordance with May 1749 annexation from Massachusetts	760 sq mi

(Heavy line depicts historical boundary. Base map shows present-day information.)

❷   12 Oct 1749 – 12 Oct 1785

| 10 | 0 | 10 | 20 | 30 | 40 Miles |

Chronology of WINDHAM

Map	Date	Event	Resulting Area
❸	13 Oct 1785	Lost to creation of TOLLAND	740 sq mi

(Heavy line depicts historical boundary. Base map shows present-day information.)

❸   13 Oct 1785 – 10 May 1786

10	0	10	20	30	40 Miles

Chronology of WINDHAM

Map	Date	Event	Resulting Area
❹	11 May 1786	Lost town of Coventry to TOLLAND	690 sq mi

(Heavy line depicts historical boundary. Base map shows present-day information.)

❹   11 May 1786 – 2 Jun 1824

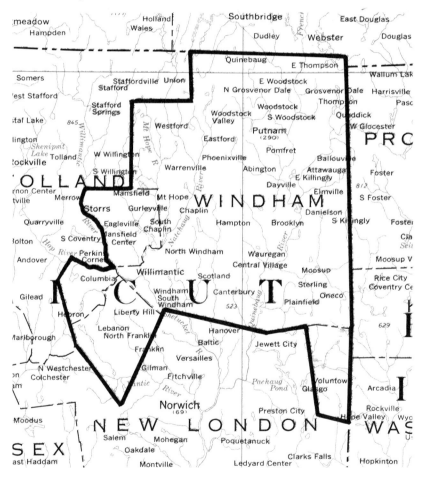

| 10 | 0 | 10 | 20 | 30 | 40 Miles |

Chronology of WINDHAM

Map	Date	Event	Resulting Area
❺	3 Jun 1824	Lost town of Lebanon to NEW LONDON	630 sq mi
	3 Nov 1826	Exchanged narrow strips with HAMPDEN (Mass.) when state boundary was straightened [not mapped]	

(Heavy line depicts historical boundary. Base map shows present-day information.)

❺   3 Jun 1824 – 24 May 1827

Chronology of WINDHAM

Map	Date	Event	Resulting Area
❻	25 May 1827	Lost towns of Columbia and Mansfield to TOLLAND	560 sq mi

(Heavy line depicts historical boundary. Base map shows present-day information.)

❻   25 May 1827–15 Mar 1881

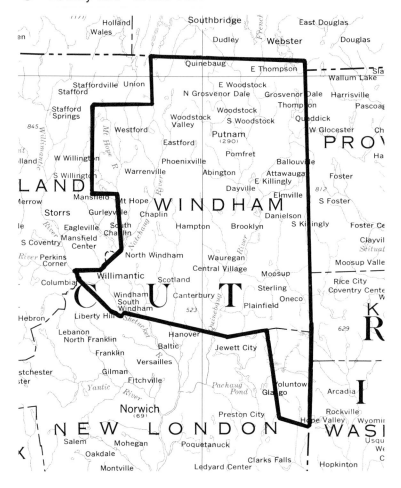

| 10 | 0 | 10 | 20 | 30 | 40 Miles |

Chronology of WINDHAM

Map	Date	Event	Resulting Area
❼	16 Mar 1881	Lost town of Voluntown to NEW LONDON	530 sq mi
❽	7 Apr 1885	Lost to WINDHAM when town of Windham gained from Mansfield	530 sq mi

(Heavy line depicts historical boundary. Base map shows present-day information.)

❼ 16 Mar 1881– 6 Apr 1885

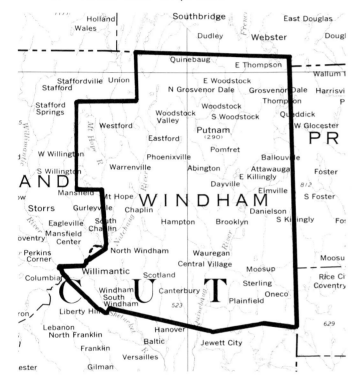

❽ 7 Apr 1885 – present

10   0   10   20   30   40 Miles

Colonial, State, and Federal Censuses in Connecticut

Date	Census
by 15 Apr 1756	Colonial census. Statistics (Conn. Col. Recs., 14:492; Bickford); no names.
1 Jan 1762	Colonial census. Statistics (Bickford); no names.
by May 1774	Colonial census. Statistics (Conn. Col. Recs., 14:484–491; Bickford); no names.
by 1 Sep 1776	Colonial census [authorized in May, completed by Sep; not mapped]. Some statistics; names for town of Newington only (Willard).
1779	State census. Statistics in the Trumbull Papers at Connecticut State Library, Hartford; no names.
1 Feb 1782	State census. Statistics in the Trumbull Papers at Connecticut State Library, Hartford; no names.
2 Aug 1790	Federal census. Statistics and names.
1798	Direct tax of 1798. No statistics; names at Connecticut Historical Society, Hartford.
4 Aug 1800	Federal census. Statistics and names.
6 Aug 1810	Federal census. Statistics and names.
7 Aug 1820	Federal census. Statistics and names.
1 Jun 1830	Federal census. Statistics and names.
1 Jun 1840	Federal census. Statistics and names.
1 Jun 1850	Federal census. Statistics and names.
1 Jun 1860	Federal census. Statistics and names.
1 Jun 1870	Federal census. Statistics and names.
1 Jun 1880	Federal census. Statistics and names.
2 Jun 1890	Federal census. Statistics; no names.
1 Jun 1900	Federal census. Statistics and names.
15 Apr 1910	Federal census. Statistics and names.
1917	State military census. Statistics and names at Connecticut State Library, Hartford.
1 Jan 1920	Federal census. Statistics and names.
1 Apr 1930	Federal census. Statistics; names not available until 2002.
1 Apr 1940	Federal census. Statistics; names not available until 2012.

Date	Census
1 Apr 1950	Federal census. Statistics; names not available until 2022.
1 Apr 1960	Federal census. Statistics; names not available until 2032.
1 Apr 1970	Federal census. Statistics; names not available until 2042.
1 Apr 1980	Federal census. Statistics; names not available until 2052.
1 Apr 1990	Federal census. Statistics; names not available until 2062.

Sources

Bickford, Christopher P. "Lost Connecticut Census of 1762 Found." *Connecticut Historical Society Bulletin* 44 (1979): 33–43.

Connecticut. *Public Records of the Colony of Connecticut.* Vols. 1–3 edited by J. H. Trumbull; vols. 4–15 edited by C. J. Hoadly. Hartford, 1850–1890. Cited as Conn. Col. Recs.

Wells, Robert V. *Population of the British Colonies in America before 1776: A Survey of Census Data.* Princeton, N.J.: Princeton University Press, 1975.

Willard, Josiah. *Census of Newington, Connecticut, Taken According to Households in 1776.* Edited by Edwin Stanley Welles. Hartford: Frederic B. Hartranft, 1909.

Census Outline
Maps for Connecticut

Colonial Censuses 1756, 1762

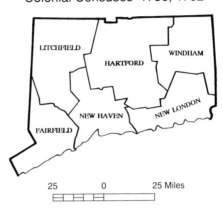

LITCHFIELD

HARTFORD

WINDHAM

NEW HAVEN

NEW LONDON

FAIRFIELD

25   0   25 Miles

Colonial Censuses 1774, 1776

LITCHFIELD

LITCHFIELD

HARTFORD

WINDHAM

NEW HAVEN

NEW LONDON

FAIRFIELD

25   0   25 Miles

State Census 1779

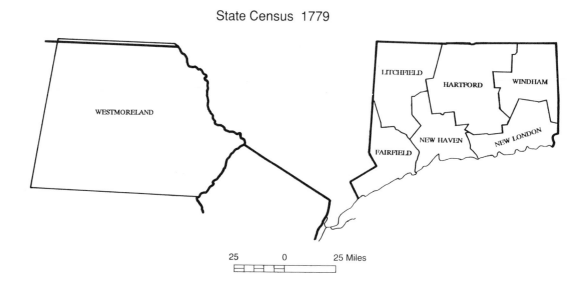

25   0   25 Miles

State Census 1782

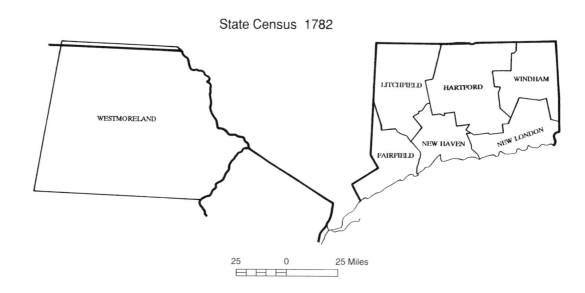

25   0   25 Miles

Federal Census 1790

25   0   25 Miles

State Tax List 1798

25   0   25 Miles

Federal Census 1800

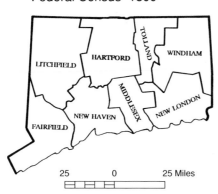

Federal Censuses 1830–1880

Federal Censuses 1810, 1820

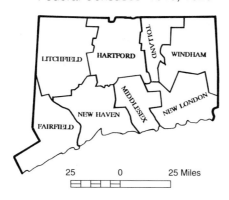

Federal Censuses 1890–1990
State Military Census 1917

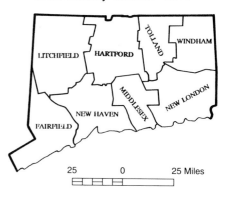

MAINE

Maine County Creations

County	Source	Dates	
		Authorization	**Creation Effective**
ANDROSCOGGIN	Me. Laws 1854, Pub., ch. 60, sec. 1/p. 74	18 Mar 1854	31 Mar. 1854
AROOSTOOK	Me. Pub. Acts 1839, ch. 395, sec. 1/p. 562	16 Mar 1839	1 May 1839
CORNWALL (created by N.Y., extinct)	Williamson, 1:421	5 Sep 1665	same
CUMBERLAND (created by Mass.)	Mass. Col. Acts, vol. 4, ch. 7 [1760–1761], sec. 2/pp. 372–374	21 Jun 1760	1 Nov 1760
DEVONSHIRE (created by Mass., extinct)	Mass. Recs., 5:16	by 7 Oct 1673	same
FRANKLIN	Me. Pub. Acts 1838, ch. 328, sec. 1/p. 476	20 Mar 1838	9 May 1838
HANCOCK (created by Mass.)	Mass. Acts 1789, ch. 25, sec. 1/p. 25	25 Jun 1789	1 May 1790
KENNEBEC (created by Mass.)	Mass. Acts 1799, ch. 23, sec. 1/p. 257	20 Feb 1799	same
KNOX	Me. Acts 1860, Pub., ch. 146, sec. 1/p. 129	9 Mar 1860	1 Apr 1860
LINCOLN (created by Mass.)	Mass. Col. Acts, vol. 4, ch. 7 [1760–1761], sec. 6/p. 372	21 Jun 1760	1 Nov 1760
OXFORD (created by Mass.)	Mass. Acts 1805, ch. 24, secs. 1-2/p. 573–574	4 Mar 1805	same
PENOBSCOT (created by Mass.)	Mass. Acts 1816, ch. 121/p. 156	15 Feb 1816	same
PISCATAQUIS	Me. Pub. Acts 1838, ch. 353, sec. 1/p. 512	23 Mar 1838	30 Apr 1838
SAGADAHOC	Me. Laws 1854, Pub., ch. 70, sec. 1/p. 82	4 Apr 1854	same
SOMERSET (created by Mass.)	Mass. Acts 1809, ch. 62, sec. 1/p. 459	1 Mar 1809	1 Jun 1809
WALDO	Me. Pub. Acts 1827, ch. 354, sec. 1/p. 1109 and ch. 362/p. 1125	7 Feb 1827	3 Jul 1827
WASHINGTON (created by Mass.)	Mass. Acts 1789, ch. 25, sec. 1/p. 25	25 Jun 1789	1 May 1790
YORK (created by Mass. as YORKSHIRE)	Mass. Recs., vol. 4, pt. 1:124	20 Nov 1652	same

Counties established within present Maine by other authorities

By Massachusetts (1652–1820)   CUMBERLAND (1760)

DEVONSHIRE (1673)

HANCOCK (1789)

KENNEBEC (1799)

LINCOLN (1760)

OXFORD (1805)

PENOBSCOT (1816)

SOMERSET (1809)

WASHINGTON (1790)

YORK (1652)

By New York (1665–1687)   CORNWALL (1665)

Consolidated Chronology of Maine State and County Boundaries

10 April 1606

King James I chartered two Virginia Companies, head-quartered in different cities, to establish colonies along the coast of North America: the Virginia Company of London, assigned coast between 34 degrees and 41 degrees north latitude; and the Virginia Company of Plymouth, assigned coast between 38 degrees and 45 degrees north latitude, including present Maine. (Paullin, pl. 42; Swindler, 10:17–23; Van Zandt, 92)

3 November 1620

King James I replaced the charter to the Virginia Company of Plymouth with a charter for a Council for New England to establish colonies in a region between 40 degrees and 48 degrees north latitude and extending from the Atlantic to the Pacific Ocean, including present Maine and Massachusetts. (Swindler, 5:16–26)

20 August 1622

The Council for New England granted to Ferdinando Gorges and John Mason all land along the Atlantic coast between the Merrimack and Sagadahoc (now Kennebec) rivers, to be called the province of Maine. Covered present eastern New Hampshire and southwestern Maine. (Andrews, 1:334; Swindler, 4:264)

4 March 1628/1629

King Charles I chartered the Massachusetts Bay Company to establish a colony in the territory stretching from three miles north of the Merrimack R. ("to the Northward of any and every Parte thereof") to three miles south of the Charles R. and extending westward from the Atlantic coast to the Pacific Ocean, thereby taking a three-mile wide strip of Maine (area south of Kennebec R.) north of the Merrimack R. (Andrews, 1:359; Swindler, 5:32–42)

7 November 1629

After Ferdinando Gorges and John Mason divided their 1622 land grant, the Council for New England granted to Mason the territory lying between the Merrimack and Piscataqua rivers and extending up to 60 miles inland from the coast, to be called New Hampshire. Maine, the remainder of the 1622 grant that lay between the Piscataqua and Kennebec rivers, was left to Gorges. (Swindler, 6:304)

26 June 1630

The Council for New England patented the Province of Lygonia, consisting of a square territory south and west of the Sagadahoc (now Kennebec) R. measuring 40 miles long and 40 miles wide. Overlapped part of Maine (area between the Kennebec and Piscataqua rivers). Patent included "power to make Laws &c." (Farnham, 7:134)

7 June 1635

The Council for New England, faced with competition from Massachusetts and less success than expected in managing its own colonies, tried to protect the interests of its principal members, including Ferdinando Gorges (for Me.) and John Mason (for N.H.), by first distributing all its land among them and then, on this date, surrendering its charter to the crown. Members hoped the king would a) confirm the land grants they had made to themselves, b) abrogate the Massachusetts charter, and c) create a new royal colony for all of New England with Gorges as its governor. Technically, this threw all of former New England, outside Massachusetts, under the direct jurisdiction of the crown, but some earlier grants remained effective. (Preston, 305)

3 April 1639

King Charles I granted Maine to Ferdinando Gorges as a proprietary colony. Territory included the area in present western Maine between the Piscataqua and Kennebec rivers inland (up river) 120 miles from the Atlantic coast, plus two islands south of Cape Cod in present Massachusetts, Martha's Vineyard and Nantucket. Thomas Gorges, a distant relative of Ferdinando Gorges, established a government in 1640, created several "counties" (without specified names or boundaries), and conducted the colony's affairs until annexation by Massachusetts in 1652. (Preston, 321–322, 334, 344; Swindler, 4:269)

14 June 1641

Massachusetts gained all of New Hampshire when the colonists there voluntarily accepted Massachusetts's jurisdiction; there had been no effective government or judicial system there since the dissolution of the Council for New England and the death of John Mason, New Hampshire's principal land holder. (Swindler, 6:319)

March 1645/1646

Lygonia gained from Maine when the English government settled the jurisdictional dispute between the two provinces in favor of Lygonia, effectively reducing Maine to a few settlements between the Piscataqua and Kennebec rivers. (Williamson, 1:302)

26 May 1652

Massachusetts declared an interpretation of its 1628/1629 charter that would make its northern boundary an east-west line through a point three miles north of the most northerly part of the Merrimack R., which it decided later (1 Aug. 1652) was the parallel of 43 degrees, 40 minutes, 12 seconds north latitude, cutting the Atlantic coast near present Casco Bay, Maine. Massachusetts used this interpretation to claim part of Maine. (Van Zandt, 64; Williamson, 1:337)

20 November 1652

Massachusetts, after towns in southern Maine (area between the Kennebec and Piscataqua rivers) acknowledged its jurisdiction, created YORKSHIRE in Maine to cover all territory within the new bounds declared on 26 May 1652. Towns located farther north near Casco Bay gave their allegiance later, the last in 1658, practically eliminating Lygonia. (Farnham, 7:274, 288; Mass. Recs., vol. 4, pt. 1:124; Reid, *Maine*, 21)

12 March 1663/1664

King Charles II granted to the Duke of York the following: all territory between the Connecticut and Delaware rivers; the islands of Long Island, Martha's Vineyard, and Nantucket; and the area between the

Kennebec and St. Croix rivers extending inland from the Atlantic coast to the St. Lawrence R., including most of present Maine and part of Quebec, Canada. (Swindler, 4:278–280)

November 1664

Representatives of the Gorges family rejected Massachusetts's claim and resumed government of Maine (area between the Kennebec and Piscataqua rivers). YORKSHIRE went into abeyance. (York County, 2:5)

23 June 1665

Royal commissioners replaced Gorges's jurisdiction over Maine (between the Kennebec and Piscataqua rivers) with a new government under direct authority of the crown. (Farnham, 7:308)

5 September 1665

New York created the county of CORNWALL to cover all of the Duke of York's territory between the Kennebec and St. Croix rivers in present Maine. (Williamson, 1:421)

21 July 1667

The Peace of Breda, between England and France and the Netherlands, confirmed the English conquest of New York from the Dutch in 1664 and removed Acadia (now Nova Scotia) from English to French control, including a fort on the Penobscot R. in present Maine. Actual transfer of Acadia did not occur until 1670. (Farnham, 7:311, 314; Parry, 10:231)

27 May 1668

Massachusetts reasserted authority over all of Maine west of the Kennebec R., an area that had been put under royal government in June 1665. YORK (formerly called YORKSHIRE) reinstated. (Farnham, 7:317)

1670

The English surrendered to France the forts of Acadia (now Nova Scotia), including one on the Penobscot R. in present Maine. France claimed remainder of territory east of the Kennebec R. in present Maine. (Farnham, 7:312; Hart, 1:511)

by 7 October 1673

Massachusetts, relying on a new survey of its northern limit and responding to the Dutch capture of New York (Aug. 1673), claimed some of the Duke of York's territory east of the Kennebec R. in present Maine, including the Pemaquid settlement, and established a new county there. On 27 May 1674 this county was named DEVONSHIRE. New York's CORNWALL implicitly reduced to area north of the Massachusetts claim. (Mass. Recs., 5:16; Reid, *Maine*, 138; Williamson, 1:443)

29 June 1674

Following the Treaty of Westminster (9 Feb. 1673/1674) that restored New York to the English (following rule by the Dutch since Aug. 1673), King Charles II regranted to the Duke of York the territory he had granted on 12 March 1663/1664, including the area between the Kennebec and St. Croix rivers extending inland from the Atlantic coast to the St. Lawrence R., covering most of present Maine and part of Quebec, Canada. Massachusetts's DEVONSHIRE continued to operate for settlements in present Maine situated east of the Kennebec R., although they were within the formally defined area of jurisdiction of New York's CORNWALL. (Parry, 13:136; Swindler, 4:282; Williamson, 1:446)

Autumn 1675

Outbreak of war between the Abnaki Indians and the English in present Maine apparently eliminated New York's CORNWALL and its rival Massachusetts county DEVONSHIRE. (Williamson, 1:446)

20 July 1677

England's Committee for Trade and Plantations ruled that the 1639 proprietary grant of Maine (area between the Kennebec and Piscataqua rivers) to Ferdinando Gorges was valid and that Massachusetts had exceeded the intent of its charter by extending its jurisdiction more than three miles north of where the Merrimack R. meets the Atlantic coast. YORK continued as a de facto county in present southwestern Maine. (Farnham, 7:339)

15 March 1677/1678

Massachusetts purchased the proprietary rights granted in 1635 to Ferdinando Gorges, an attempt to legitimate the extension of its jurisdiction northeastward to the Kennebec R. in present New Hampshire and Maine. (Farnham, 7:350)

17 March 1679/1680

Massachusetts organized a new government for Maine (area between the Piscataqua and Kennebec rivers) in accordance with terms of Ferdinando Gorges's 1635 grant. YORK eliminated. (Farnham, 7:356; Williamson, 1:556, 563)

1 November 1683

New York re-created CORNWALL to cover all of the Duke of York's grant in area of present Maine and Quebec between the Kennebec and St. Croix rivers and extending from the Atlantic coast to the St. Lawrence R., including the Pemaquid settlement governed since 1674 by Massachusetts. (N.Y. Col. Laws, ch. 4/1:122)

18 June 1684

England's Court of Chancery annulled the Massachusetts charter, technically putting Massachusetts and Maine (area between the Kennebec and Piscataqua rivers) directly under the authority of the crown. Actual transfer of authority occurred when royal governor arrived 17 May 1686. (Farnham, 7:359; Van Zandt, 66)

17 May 1686

Arrival of its first royal governor inaugurated the Dominion of New England, the new single province that King James II created (8 Oct. 1685) by uniting King's Province (present southwestern Rhode Island), Massachusetts, New Hampshire, and Maine (area between New Hampshire and the Kennebec R.). No change in counties. (Farnham, 7:367; Hart, 1:573; N.H. Early Laws, 1:99; Williamson, 1:576)

20 December 1686

New royal governor of the Dominion of New England added the New Plymouth colony and territory of present Maine east of the Kennebec R. ("Country of Pemaquid") to the Dominion, according to his commission (3 Jun. 1686) and royal order (12 Sep. 1686). New York's CORNWALL eliminated from present Maine and Quebec in spring of 1687. (Barnes, 69; N.H. Early Laws, 1:144)

18 April 1689

Upon learning of the Glorious Revolution (replacement of King James II by King William III and Queen Mary II) in England, Bostonians imprisoned the royal governor and others, thereby ending the Dominion of New England. Massachusetts resumed self-government and attempted to re-establish its authority in southern

Maine, but a new war between England and France left the area of present Maine either in turmoil or under French control until the Treaty of Ryswick in 1697. (Craven, 224; Morris and Kelly, pl. 11)

7 October 1691

King William III and Queen Mary II issued a new charter for the province of Massachusetts Bay, including an extension of its boundaries to encompass the New Plymouth colony, the islands of Nantucket and Martha's Vineyard, the former colonies of Maine (area between the Kennebec and Piscataqua rivers) and Acadia (now Nova Scotia), and all remaining territory of present Maine between Acadia and the Kennebec R. Massachusetts reinstated YORK in present southwestern Maine. (Mass. Col. Acts, vol. 1, ch. 27 [1692–1693], sec. 1/p. 63; Swindler, 5:80)

20 September 1697

Acadia (now Nova Scotia) effectively separated from Massachusetts and confirmed to France by the Treaty of Ryswick that ended King William's War between England and France and restored the pre-war empires. No boundaries were specified and France threw jurisdiction of present Maine into doubt by claiming all territory east of the Kennebec R. (Farnham, 8:29; Hart, 2:76–77)

15 April 1713

Following the Treaty of Utrecht (31 Mar. 1713), by which Acadia (now Nova Scotia) was formally transferred from France to Great Britain, Massachusetts lost nominal jurisdiction over Nova Scotia when that area was made a separate province. Limits specified in the treaty ("ancient boundaries") were vague, but from this date Massachusetts held actual control of territory west of the St. Croix R. that is present Maine. (Farnham, 8:33; Gipson, 3:29 n.74, 5:334)

26 June 1716

YORK gained all territory between the Kennebec and St. Croix rivers, that is the remaining area of present Maine south of the 120-mile inland limit set by the charter of 1691. (Mass. Col. Acts, vol. 9, ch. 75 [1716–1717]/p. 485)

5 August 1740

King George II settled the lines between Massachusetts and New Hampshire substantially as they are today. Eastern boundary of New Hampshire with Maine went up the Piscataqua and Salmon Falls rivers and thence on a straight line north to a point 120 miles inland or, if closer, the limit of the colony; has remained unchanged to the present. (Farnham, 8:47; Van Zandt, 59)

12 April 1753

YORK redefined to cover all territory east of New Hampshire that was not specifically part of any other Massachusetts county [no change]. (Mass. Col. Acts, vol. 3, ch. 27 [1752–1753]/p. 656)

1 November 1760

CUMBERLAND and LINCOLN created by Massachusetts from YORK. All three counties were to extend northward to the limit of the province, which was set at 120 miles inland by the 1691 Massachusetts charter. (Mass. Col. Acts, vol. 4, ch. 7 [1760–1761], secs. 1, 2, 6/pp. 372–374)

7 October 1763

King George III, by his Proclamation of 1763, created the new royal province of Quebec in Canada, bounded on the south in part by the watershed between rivers flowing into the St. Lawrence R. and those flowing into the Atlantic Ocean, implicitly setting the northern limit for Maine (then part of Mass.) and its counties of CUMBERLAND, LINCOLN, and YORK, along the watershed. (Cappon, Petchenik, and Long, 1, 77; Shortt and Doughty, 119–120)

4 July 1776

Massachusetts, including Maine, became an independent state. (*Declaration of Independence*)

3 September 1783

Commissioners from Great Britain and the United States signed the Treaty of Paris (ratifications exchanged 12 May 1784) ending the War of the American Revolution, recognizing American independence, and defining northern U.S. boundary around Maine as the St. Croix R. to the Atlantic watershed and thence westward to the parallel of 45 degrees north latitude. Later treaties and surveys settled details of this boundary (and some disputes over them), but there were no later changes in its essential definition. (Parry, 48:481–486; Van Zandt, 12)

3 March 1786

CUMBERLAND gained from YORK. (Mass. Acts 1786, ch. 18, sec. 1/p. 407)

1 May 1790

HANCOCK and WASHINGTON created by Massachusetts from LINCOLN. (Mass. Acts 1789, ch. 25, sec. 1/p. 25)

1 May 1791

LINCOLN gained from HANCOCK. (Mass. Acts 1790, ch. 10, sec. 1/p. 81)

25 October 1798

Commissioners from Great Britain and the United States agreed on the true course of the St. Croix R., fixing part of the U.S.–Canadian boundary in accordance with the Treaty of Paris of 1783 and settling a dispute between Massachusetts and Nova Scotia that dated back to 1764 [no change]. (Van Zandt, 12)

20 February 1799

KENNEBEC created by Massachusetts from LINCOLN. (Mass. Acts 1799, ch. 23, sec. 1/p. 257)

28 February 1799

Boundary between KENNEBEC and HANCOCK clarified [no change]. (Mass. Acts 1799, ch. 39, sec. 1/p. 275)

4 March 1805

OXFORD created by Massachusetts from CUMBERLAND and YORK. KENNEBEC gained from CUMBERLAND. (Mass. Acts 1805, ch. 24, secs. 1–2/pp. 573–574)

8 March 1808

OXFORD gained from KENNEBEC. (Mass. Acts 1808, ch. 97/p. 323)

1 June 1809

SOMERSET created by Massachusetts from KENNEBEC. (Mass. Acts 1809, ch. 62, sec. 1/p. 459)

6 March 1810

Boundary between KENNEBEC and LINCOLN redefined in part when line between towns of Gardiner and Litchfield redefined [no change]. (Mass. Acts 1810, ch. 108/p. 194)

25 February 1811

LINCOLN gained from KENNEBEC. (Mass. Acts 1811, ch. 61/p. 290)

21 June 1811

HANCOCK gained from SOMERSET. (Mass. Acts 1811, ch. 36/p. 430)

29 February 1812

KENNEBEC exchanged with LINCOLN. (Mass. Acts 1812, ch. 160/p. 309)

12 June 1812

HANCOCK gained from SOMERSET. (Mass. Acts 1812, ch. 4/p. 7)

16 February 1813

SOMERSET gained from HANCOCK. (Mass. Acts 1813, ch. 85/p. 157)

26 February 1813

KENNEBEC gained from SOMERSET. (Mass. Acts 1813, ch. 108/p. 179)

28 January 1814

OXFORD gained from KENNEBEC. (Mass. Acts 1814, ch. 79/pp. 316–317)

15 February 1816

PENOBSCOT created by Massachusetts from HANCOCK. (Mass. Acts 1816, ch. 121, sec. 1/p. 156)

17 June 1816

PENOBSCOT gained from HANCOCK when town of Hampden gained from Frankfurt and town of Orrington gained from Buckstown. (Mass. Acts 1816, ch. 13, sec. 1/p. 195 and ch. 14/p. 196)

14 June 1817

PENOBSCOT gained from SOMERSET. (Mass. Acts 1817, ch. 15/p. 398)

24 November 1817

Under authority of the Treaty of Ghent (24 Dec. 1814) commissioners from Great Britain and the United States agreed on the division of the islands in Passamaquoddy Bay: Mouse, Dudley (now Trent), and Frederick (now Dudley) islands assigned to the United States and made part of WASHINGTON [no change]. (Paullin, 59)

2 February 1819

SOMERSET gained from OXFORD. (Mass. Acts 1819, ch. 41, sec. 1/p. 71)

15 March 1820

State of Maine admitted to the Union, separate from Massachusetts, with boundaries same as at present. Consisted of CUMBERLAND, HANCOCK, KENNEBEC, LINCOLN, OXFORD, PENOBSCOT, SOMERSET, WASHINGTON, and YORK. (U.S. Stat., vol. 3, ch. 19 [1820]/p. 544)

5 February 1821

Boundary between CUMBERLAND and OXFORD clarified [no change]. (Me. Priv. Acts 1821, ch. 26/p. 28)

8 February 1821

KENNEBEC gained from OXFORD. (Me. Priv. Acts 1821, ch. 35/p. 36)

28 February 1821

OXFORD gained from CUMBERLAND. (Me. Priv. Acts 1821, ch. 47/p. 45)

8 March 1821

KENNEBEC gained from LINCOLN. (Me. Priv. Acts 1821, ch. 58/p. 58)

17 March 1821

KENNEBEC gained from SOMERSET. (Me. Priv. Acts 1821, ch. 76/p. 83)

31 January 1823

SOMERSET gained from OXFORD. (Me. Priv. Acts 1823, ch. 188/p. 269)

17 February 1824

CUMBERLAND gained from YORK. (Me. Priv. Acts 1824, ch. 276/p. 397)

3 July 1827

WALDO created from HANCOCK, KENNEBEC, LINCOLN, and PENOBSCOT. (Me. Pub. Acts 1827, ch. 354, sec. 1/p. 1109 and ch. 362/p. 1125)

1 July 1829

New Hampshire agreed to new definition of boundary with Maine (Maine had agreed 28 Feb. 1829) [no change]. (Van Zandt, 60)

6 March 1830

KENNEBEC gained from SOMERSET. (Me. Priv. Acts 1830, ch. 71/p. 123)

12 March 1830

CUMBERLAND gained from OXFORD when town of Sebago gained from Denmark. (Me. Priv. Acts 1830, ch. 94/p. 159)

17 March 1830

OXFORD gained from CUMBERLAND when town of Oxford gained from Otisfield. (Me. Priv. Acts 1830, ch. 115/p. 194)

15 March 1831

PENOBSCOT gained from WASHINGTON. (Me. Priv. Acts 1831, ch. 151, sec. 2/p. 244)

17 March 1831

HANCOCK exchanged with WASHINGTON. (Me. Priv. Acts 1831, ch. 154/p. 247)

10 February 1833

PENOBSCOT gained from SOMERSET. (Me. Priv. Acts 1833, ch. 314/p. 488)

10 March 1835

KENNEBEC gained from LINCOLN. (Me. Priv. Acts 1835, ch. 553/p. 817)

PENOBSCOT gained from HANCOCK. (Me. Priv. Acts 1835, ch. 559/p. 826)

10 February 1836

WALDO gained from LINCOLN when town of Camden gained from Warren. (Me. Priv. Acts 1836, ch. 17/p. 18)

15 March 1838

WALDO gained N. Haven I. and Vinalhaven I. from HANCOCK. (Me. Priv. Acts 1838, ch. 451/p. 552)

30 April 1838

PISCATAQUIS created from SOMERSET and PENOB-SCOT. (Me. Pub. Acts 1838, ch. 353, sec. 1/p. 512)

9 May 1838

FRANKLIN created from KENNEBEC, OXFORD, and SOMERSET. (Me. Pub. Acts 1838, ch. 328, sec. 1/p. 476; Me. Gov. Proc. 2:99–100)

1 May 1839

AROOSTOOK created from PENOBSCOT and WASH-INGTON. (Me. Pub. Acts 1839, ch. 395, sec. 1/p. 562)

29 February 1840

SOMERSET gained from KENNEBEC. (Me. Laws 1840, ch. 27, sec. 1/p. 26)

6 March 1840

KENNEBEC gained from LINCOLN. (Me. Laws 1840, ch. 5, sec. 1/p. 5 and ch. 37/p. 39)

18 March 1840

SOMERSET gained small area from FRANKLIN when town of Anson gained from New Vineyard. (Me. Laws 1840, ch. 75/p. 100)

20 February 1841

PENOBSCOT gained from HANCOCK when town of Lowell gained from Page's Mill Settlement. (Me. Laws 1841, ch. 102/p. 296)

27 March 1841

YORK gained small area from CUMBERLAND when town of Saco gained from Scarborough [location unknown, not mapped]. (Me. Laws 1841, ch. 136, sec. 1/p. 330)

6 April 1841

FRANKLIN gained from SOMERSET when town of New Sharon gained from Mercer. (Me. Laws 1841, ch. 148/p. 349)

10 April 1841

PENOBSCOT gained small area from HANCOCK when town of Brewer gained from Bucksport and Dedham. (Me. Laws 1841, ch. 161/p. 357)

7 March 1842

CUMBERLAND gained small area from OXFORD when town of Bridgton gained from Denmark. (Me. Laws 1842, Priv., ch. 16/p. 15)

9 August 1842

Webster–Ashburton Treaty between Great Britain and the United States completed the establishment in detail of the northern boundary of the United States in accordance with the Peace Treaty of 1783, including the U.S.–Canadian boundary around Maine from the head of the St. Croix R., fixing northern limits of AROOSTOOK, FRANKLIN, OXFORD, PENOBSCOT, PISCATAQUIS, and SOMERSET [no change]. (Van Zandt, 17–18)

21 March 1843

AROOSTOOK gained from PENOBSCOT. (Me. Laws 1843, Priv., ch. 15/p. 51)

24 March 1843

LINCOLN gained Matinicus I. from HANCOCK. (Me. Laws 1843, Priv., ch. 118/p. 137)

by 29 February 1844

PENOBSCOT exchanged with SOMERSET, putting line along town boundaries. (Me. Laws 1844, Priv., ch. 148/p. 190)

1 March 1844

KENNEBEC gained from OXFORD. (Me. Laws 1843, Priv., ch. 97, sec. 1/p. 102)

7 March 1844

OXFORD gained small area from CUMBERLAND when town of Hiram gained from Baldwin. (Me. Laws 1844, Priv., ch. 156/p. 194)

12 March 1844

AROOSTOOK gained from SOMERSET and exchanged with PISCATAQUIS. PENOBSCOT gained from WASHINGTON and exchanged with PISCATAQUIS. SOMERSET gained from PISCATAQUIS. Part of line between HANCOCK and WASHINGTON clarified [no change]. (Me. Laws 1844, Pub., ch. 99, secs. 1–5/ pp. 92–94)

2 August 1847

CUMBERLAND gained from OXFORD when town of Bridgton gained from Fryeburg and Denmark. (Me. Laws 1847, Priv., ch. 84, sec. 1/pp. 110–111)

FRANKLIN gained from KENNEBEC when town of Chesterville gained from Vienna. (Me. Laws 1847, Priv., ch. 93/p. 132)

24 July 1849

SOMERSET gained from KENNEBEC when town of Canaan gained from Clinton. (Me. Laws 1849, Priv., ch. 234/p. 334)

8 August 1850

KENNEBEC gained from SOMERSET when town of Clinton gained from Canaan. (Me. Laws 1850, Priv., ch. 351/p. 487)

20 August 1850

PENOBSCOT gained from HANCOCK when town of Orrington gained from Bucksport. (Me. Laws 1850, Priv., ch. 376, sec. 1/p. 519)

9 April 1852

Boundary between KENNEBEC and FRANKLIN redefined [no change]. (Me. Laws 1852, Priv., ch. 566/p. 567)

LINCOLN gained islands from HANCOCK. (Me. Laws 1852, Priv., ch. 578/p. 577)

20 April 1852

LINCOLN gained small area from KENNEBEC when town of Lewiston gained from Greene to accommodate local property owner [location unknown, not mapped]. (Me. Laws 1852, Priv., ch. 617/p. 614)

31 March 1854

ANDROSCOGGIN created from CUMBERLAND, KENNEBEC, LINCOLN, and OXFORD. (Me. Laws 1854, Pub., ch. 60, sec. 1/p. 74)

4 April 1854

SAGADAHOC created from LINCOLN. (Me. Laws 1854, Pub., ch. 70, sec. 1/p. 82)

11 April 1854

LINCOLN gained small area from WALDO when town of Washington gained from Palermo to accommodate local property owners [location unknown, not mapped]. (Me. Laws 1854, Priv., ch. 327/pp. 336–337)

16 March 1855

ANDROSCOGGIN gained from KENNEBEC when town of Wales gained from Monmouth. (Me. Laws 1855, Priv., ch. 526/p. 588)

12 March 1856

ANDROSCOGGIN gained from KENNEBEC when town of Wales gained from Litchfield. (Me. Laws 1856, Priv., ch. 592/p. 650)

15 March 1858

PENOBSCOT gained from HANCOCK. (Me. Laws 1858, Priv., ch. 198/p. 170)

20 March 1858

CUMBERLAND gained from ANDROSCOGGIN when towns of Casco and Otisfield gained from Poland. (Me. Laws 1858, Priv., ch. 220/p. 185 and ch. 222/p. 187)

2 April 1859

KENNEBEC gained small area from ANDROSCOGGIN when town of Wayne gained from Leeds. (Me. Laws 1859, Priv., ch. 344/p. 317)

1 April 1860

KNOX created from LINCOLN and WALDO. (Me. Laws 1860, Pub., ch. 146, sec. 1/p. 129)

14 February 1867

ANDROSCOGGIN gained small area from KENNEBEC when town of Webster gained from Litchfield. (Me. Laws 1867, Priv., ch. 270/p. 226)

26 February 1873

WALDO gained from KENNEBEC when town of Burnham gained from Clinton Gore Plantation. (Me. Laws 1873, Priv., ch. 384, sec. 1/p. 368)

27 February 1873

SOMERSET gained from KENNEBEC when town of Fairfield gained from Benton. (Me. Laws 1873, Priv., ch. 390, sec. 1/p. 378)

13 March 1883

Boundary between SOMERSET and PISCATAQUIS redefined [no change]. (Me. Laws 1883, Pub., ch. 210/p. 173)

27 February 1885

SOMERSET gained small area from PISCATAQUIS when town of Cambridge gained from Wellington. (Me. Laws 1885, Priv., ch. 464/p. 634)

4 March 1885

WASHINGTON gained from AROOSTOOK when town of Danforth gained from Weston. (Me. Laws 1885, Priv., ch. 499/p. 677)

5 March 1889

AROOSTOOK gained from PENOBSCOT when Reed Plantation gained from Drew Plantation. (Me. Laws 1889, Priv., ch. 514/p. 874)

5 February 1891

CUMBERLAND gained from SAGADAHOC. (Me. Laws 1891, Priv., ch. 25/p. 25)

28 March 1903

Boundary between CUMBERLAND and SAGADAHOC redefined [no change]. (Me. Laws 1903, Priv., ch. 415/p. 628)

PENOBSCOT gained from AROOSTOOK when Drew Plantation gained from Reed Plantation. (Me. Laws 1903, Priv., ch. 364/p. 550)

15 March 1905

Boundary between CUMBERLAND and SAGADAHOC redefined [no change]. (Me. Laws 1905, Priv., ch. 200/p. 231)

21 February 1907

LINCOLN gained from KENNEBEC when town of Whitefield gained from Windsor. (Me. Laws 1907, Priv., ch. 96/p. 316)

21 May 1910

Great Britain and the United States refined the U.S.–Canadian boundary through Passamaquoddy Bay between Maine and New Brunswick [not mapped]. (Van Zandt, 20)

12 March 1913

KNOX gained Isle au Haut from HANCOCK. (Me. Laws 1913, Priv., ch. 83/p. 425)

19 March 1917

Boundary between CUMBERLAND and SAGADAHOC redefined [no change]. (Me. Laws 1917, Priv., ch. 68/p. 501)

Individual County Chronologies, Maps, and Areas for Maine

Chronology of ANDROSCOGGIN

Map	Date	Event	Resulting Area
❶	31 Mar 1854	Created from CUMBERLAND, KENNEBEC, LINCOLN, and OXFORD	520 sq mi
❶	16 Mar 1855	Gained from KENNEBEC when town of Wales gained from Monmouth	520 sq mi
❶	12 Mar 1856	Gained from KENNEBEC when town of Wales gained from Litchfield	520 sq mi
❶	20 Mar 1858	Lost to CUMBERLAND when towns of Casco and Otisfield gained from Poland	520 sq mi
❷	2 Apr 1859	Lost to KENNEBEC when town of Wayne gained from Leeds	520 sq mi
❷	14 Feb 1867	Gained small area from KENNEBEC when town of Webster gained from Litchfield	520 sq mi

(Heavy line depicts historical boundary. Base map shows present-day information.)

❶   31 Mar 1854 – 1 Apr 1859   ❷   2 Apr 1859 – present

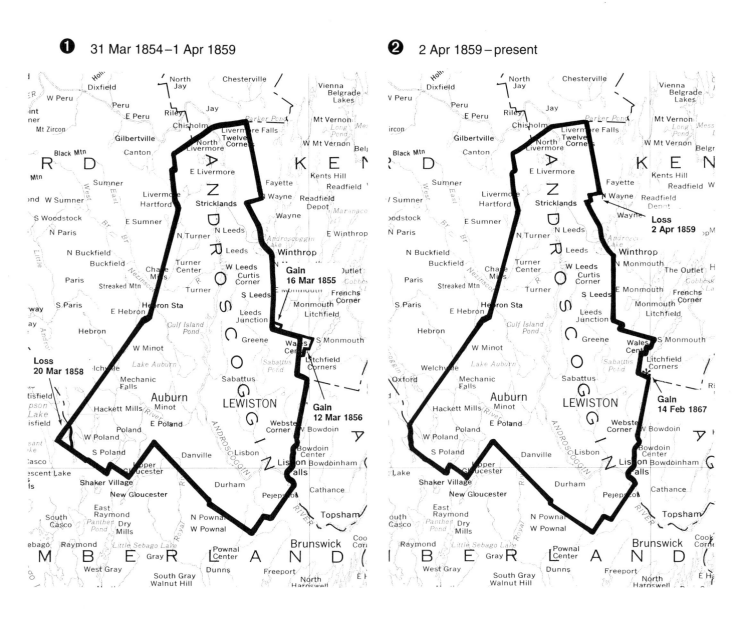

Chronology of AROOSTOOK

Map	Date	Event	Resulting Area
❶	1 May 1839	Created from PENOBSCOT and WASHINGTON	3,520 sq mi
	9 August 1842	Webster–Ashburton Treaty between Great Britain and the United States settled the U.S.–Canadian boundary, fixing northern limits of AROOSTOOK [no change]	
❷	21 Mar 1843	Gained from PENOBSCOT	4,740 sq mi
❸	12 Mar 1844	Gained from SOMERSET and exchanged with PISCATAQUIS [For full-scale details of northern parts, see maps 4 and 5.]	6,980 sq mi

(Heavy line depicts historical boundary. Base map shows present-day information.)

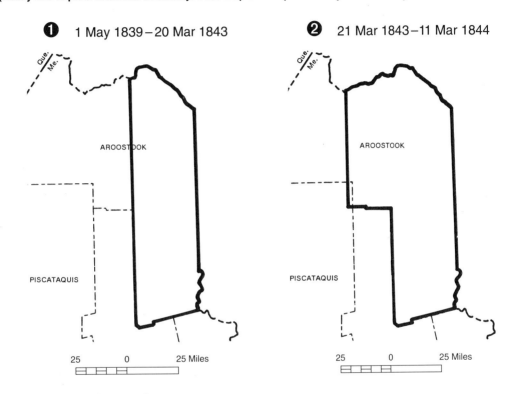

❶ 1 May 1839 – 20 Mar 1843

❷ 21 Mar 1843 – 11 Mar 1844

❸ 12 Mar 1844 – 3 Mar 1885

Chronology of AROOSTOOK

Map	Date	Event	Resulting Area
❹	12 Mar 1844	[Full-scale map of *northwestern* part; for configuration of entire county on this date, see map 3; for further details, see also map 5.]	

(Heavy line depicts historical boundary. Base map shows present-day information.)

❹ Northwestern AROOSTOOK
12 Mar 1844–present

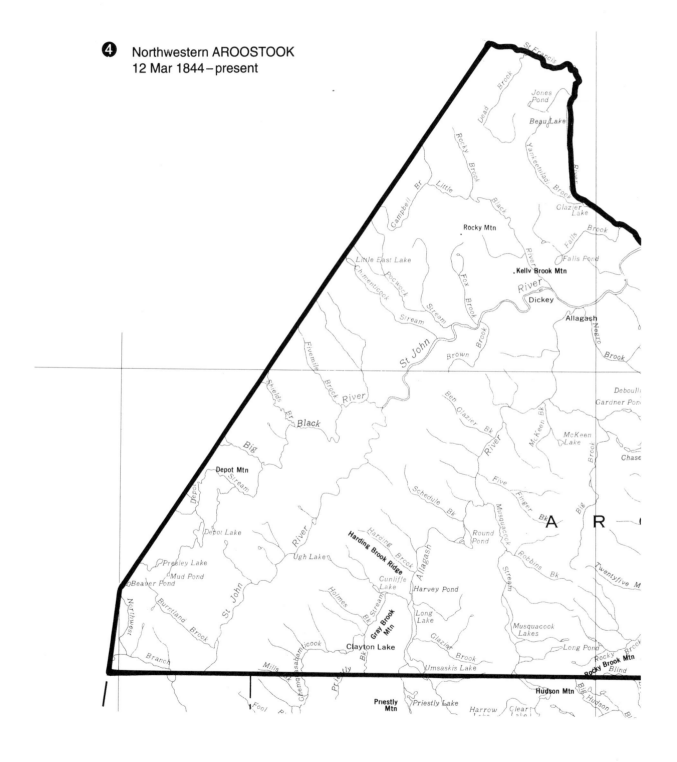

10   0   10   20   30   40 Miles

Chronology of AROOSTOOK

Map	Date	Event	Resulting Area
❺	12 Mar 1844	[Full-scale map of *northeastern* part; for configuration of entire county on this date, see map 3; for further details, see also map 4.]	

(Heavy line depicts historical boundary. Base map shows present-day information.)

❺   Northeastern AROOSTOOK
12 Mar 1844 – present

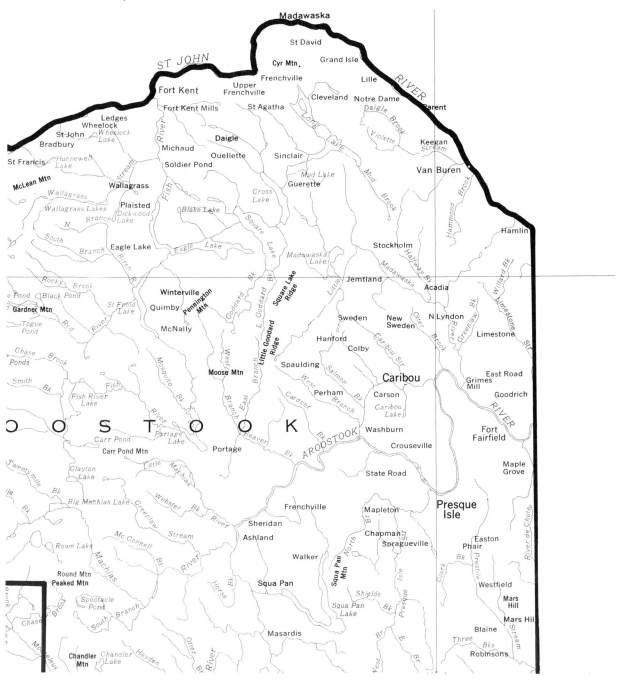

Chronology of AROOSTOOK

Map	Date	Event	Resulting Area
❻	4 Mar 1885	Lost to WASHINGTON when town of Danforth gained from Weston [For configuration of entire county, see maps 4, 5, and 6.]	6,980 sq mi

(Heavy line depicts historical boundary. Base map shows present-day information.)

❻   Southern AROOSTOOK
4 Mar 1885 – 4 Mar 1889
28 Mar 1903 – present

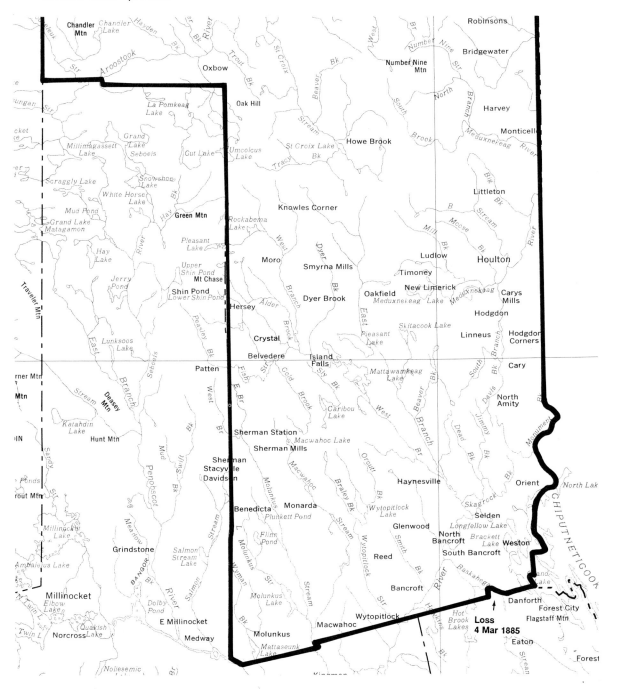

| 10 | 0 | 10 | 20 | 30 | 40 Miles |

Chronology of AROOSTOOK

Map	Date	Event	Resulting Area
7	5 Mar 1889	Gained from PENOBSCOT when Reed Plantation gained from Drew Plantation [For configuration of entire county, see maps 4, 5, and 7.]	6,990 sq mi
6	28 Mar 1903	Lost to PENOBSCOT when Drew Plantation gained from Reed Plantation [For configuration of entire county, see maps 4, 5, and 6.]	6,980 sq mi

(Heavy line depicts historical boundary. Base map shows present-day information.)

7 Southern AROOSTOOK
5 Mar 1889 – 27 Mar 1903

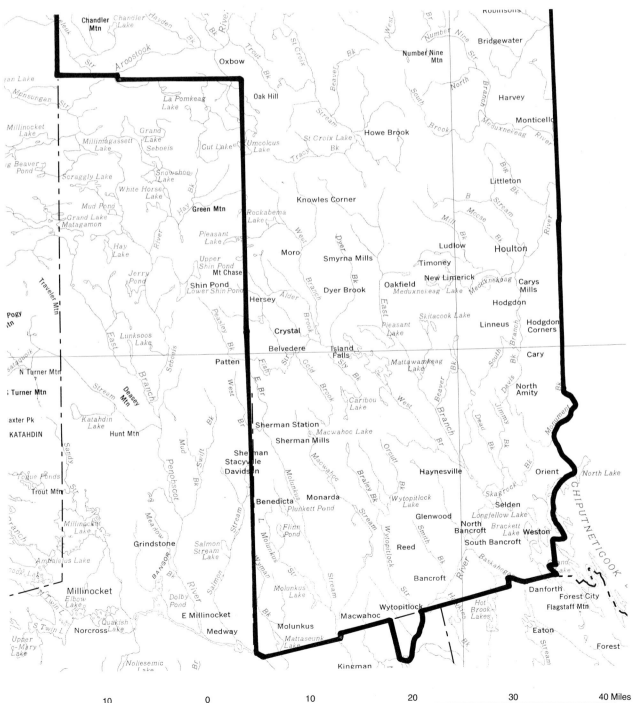

Chronology of CORNWALL (created by New York, extinct)

Map	Date	Event	Resulting Area
❶	5 Sep 1665	Created by New York to cover all of the Duke of York's territory between the Kennebec and St. Croix rivers in present Quebec, Canada, and Maine	25,120 sq mi

(Heavy line depicts historical boundary. Base map shows present-day information.)

❶ 5 Sep 1665 – 6 Oct 1673
   1 Nov 1683 – 19 Dec 1686

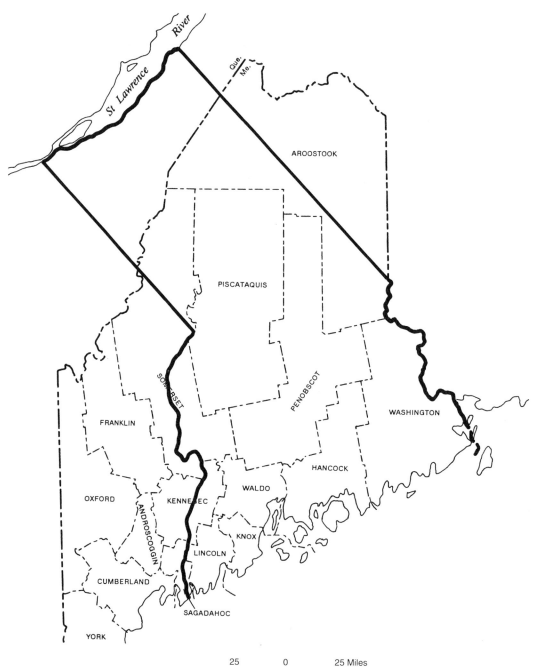

Chronology of CORNWALL (created by New York, extinct)

Map	Date	Event	Resulting Area
❷	by 7 Oct 1673	Implicitly reduced to area north of Massachusetts's claim	24,910 sq mi
	Autumn 1675	Eliminated by Abnaki Indian war	
❶	1 Nov 1683	Re-created by New York	25,120 sq mi
	20 Dec 1686	Eliminated by extension of the Dominion of New England	

(Heavy line depicts historical boundary. Base map shows present-day information.)

❷   by 7 Oct 1673–Autumn 1675

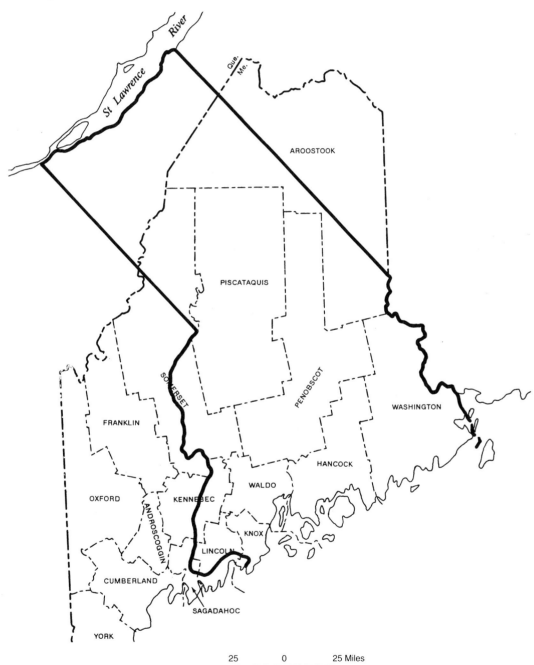

Chronology of CUMBERLAND (created by Mass.)

Map	Date	Event	Resulting Area
❶	1 Nov 1760	Created by Massachusetts from YORK	2,820 sq mi
❷	7 Oct 1763	Extended northward to Atlantic watershed	3,970 sq mi
❸	3 Mar 1786	Gained from YORK	4,160 sq mi

(Heavy line depicts historical boundary. Base map shows present-day information.)

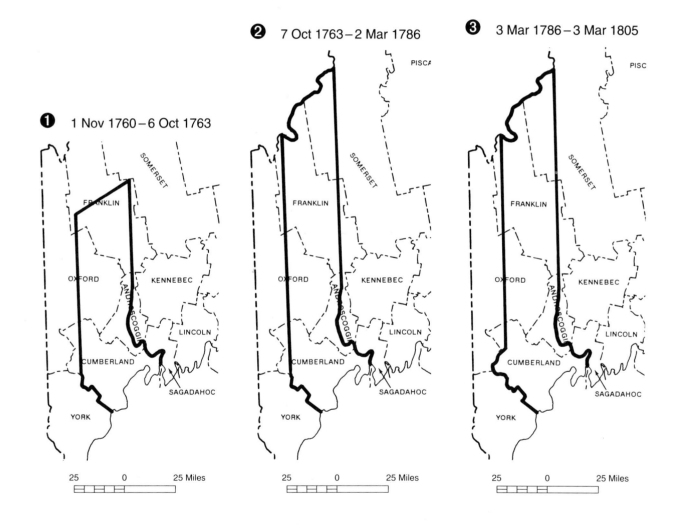

Chronology of CUMBERLAND (created by Mass.)

Map	Date	Event	Resulting Area
❹	4 Mar 1805	Lost to KENNEBEC and to creation of OXFORD	1,190 sq mi
	15 Mar 1820	Separated from Massachusetts when Maine became a state	
	5 Feb 1821	Boundary with OXFORD clarified [no change]	

(Heavy line depicts historical boundary. Base map shows present-day information.)

❹   4 Mar 1805 – 27 Feb 1821

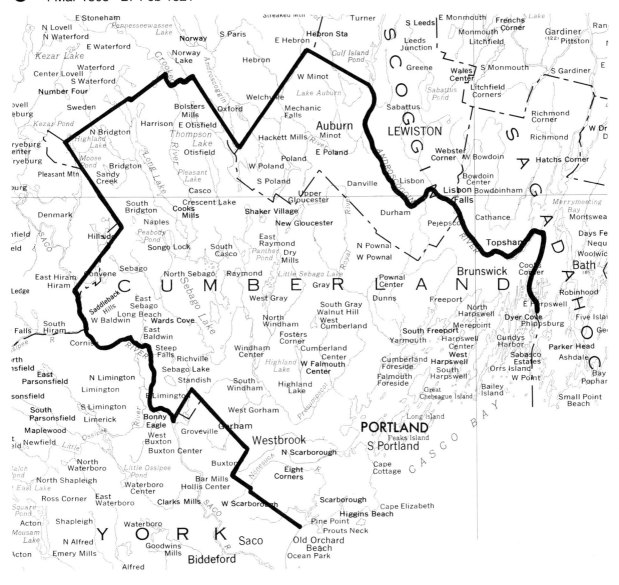

Chronology of CUMBERLAND (created by Mass.)

Map	Date	Event	Resulting Area
❺	28 Feb 1821	Lost to OXFORD	1,190 sq mi

(Heavy line depicts historical boundary. Base map shows present-day information.)

❺ 28 Feb 1821–16 Feb 1824

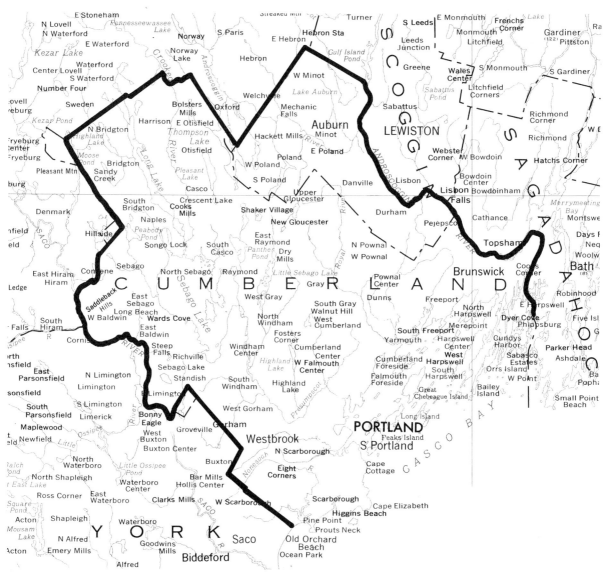

Chronology of CUMBERLAND (created by Mass.)

Map	Date	Event	Resulting Area
❻	17 Feb 1824	Gained from YORK	1,190 sq mi

(Heavy line depicts historical boundary. Base map shows present-day information.)

❻ 17 Feb 1824–11 Mar 1830

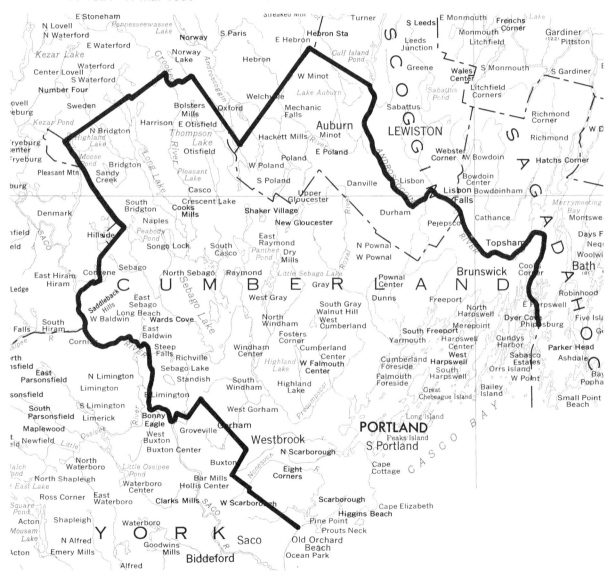

Chronology of CUMBERLAND (created by Mass.)

Map	Date	Event	Resulting Area
❼	12 Mar 1830	Gained from OXFORD when town of Sebago gained from Denmark	1,200 sq mi
❼	17 Mar 1830	Lost to OXFORD when town of Oxford gained from Otisfield	1,200 sq mi
	27 Mar 1841	Lost small area to YORK when town of Saco gained from Scarborough [location unknown, not mapped]	
❼	7 Mar 1842	Gained small area from OXFORD when town of Bridgton gained from Denmark	1,200 sq mi
❼	7 Mar 1844	Lost small area to OXFORD when town of Hiram gained from Baldwin	1,200 sq mi

(Heavy line depicts historical boundary. Base map shows present-day information.)

❼   12 Mar 1830 – 1 Aug 1847

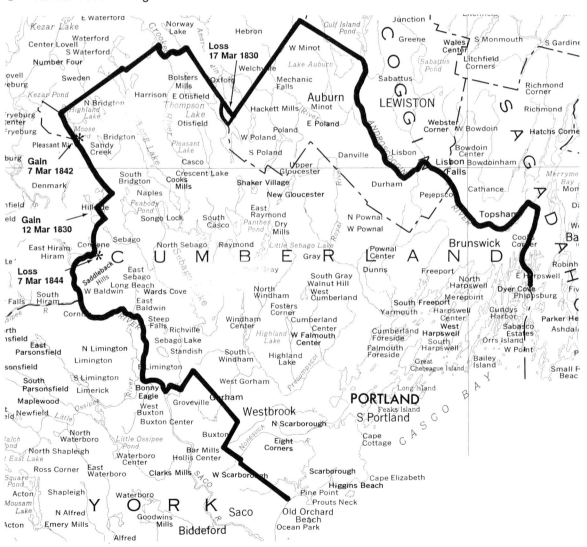

Chronology of CUMBERLAND (created by Mass.)

Map	Date	Event	Resulting Area
❽	2 Aug 1847	Gained from OXFORD when town of Bridgton gained from Fryeburg and Denmark	1,200 sq mi

(Heavy line depicts historical boundary. Base map shows present-day information.)

❽   2 Aug 1847– 30 Mar 1854

Chronology of CUMBERLAND (created by Mass.)

Map	Date	Event	Resulting Area
9	31 Mar 1854	Lost to creation of ANDROSCOGGIN	1,000 sq mi
9	20 Mar 1858	Gained from ANDROSCOGGIN when towns of Casco and Otisfield gained from Poland	1,000 sq mi

(Heavy line depicts historical boundary. Base map shows present-day information.)

9 31 Mar 1854 – 4 Feb 1891

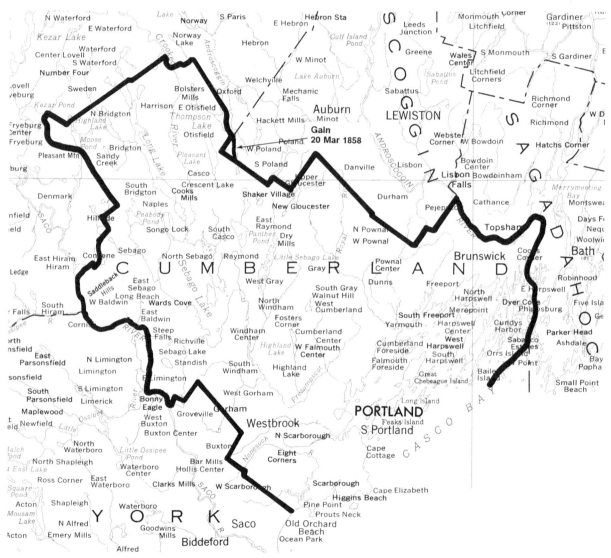

Chronology of CUMBERLAND (created by Mass.)

Map	Date	Event	Resulting Area
⑩	5 Feb 1891	Gained a few islands from SAGADAHOC	1,000 sq mi
	28 Mar 1903	Boundary with SAGADAHOC redefined [no change]	
	15 Mar 1905	Boundary with SAGADAHOC redefined [no change]	
	19 Mar 1917	Boundary with SAGADAHOC redefined [no change]	

(Heavy line depicts historical boundary. Base map shows present-day information.)

⑩ 5 Feb 1891– present

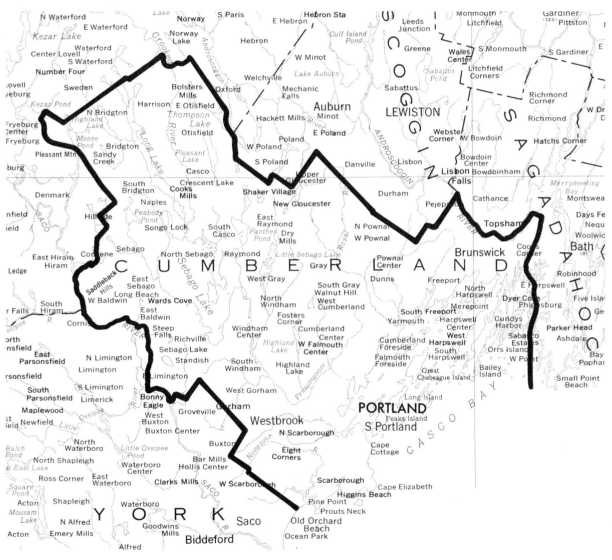

Chronology of DEVONSHIRE (created by Mass., extinct)

Map	Date	Event	Resulting Area
❶	by 7 Oct 1673	Created by Massachusetts without name	Indefinite
	27 May 1674	Named DEVONSHIRE	
	Autumn 1675	Eliminated by Abnaki Indian war	

(Heavy line depicts historical boundary. Base map shows present-day information.)

❶ by 7 Oct 1673–Autumn 1675

| 10 | 0 | 10 | 20 | 30 | 40 Miles |

Chronology of FRANKLIN

Map	Date	Event	Resulting Area
❶/❷	9 May 1838	Created from KENNEBEC, OXFORD, and SOMERSET	1,800 sq mi

(Heavy line depicts historical boundary. Base map shows present-day information.)

❶ Northern FRANKLIN
9 May 1838 – present

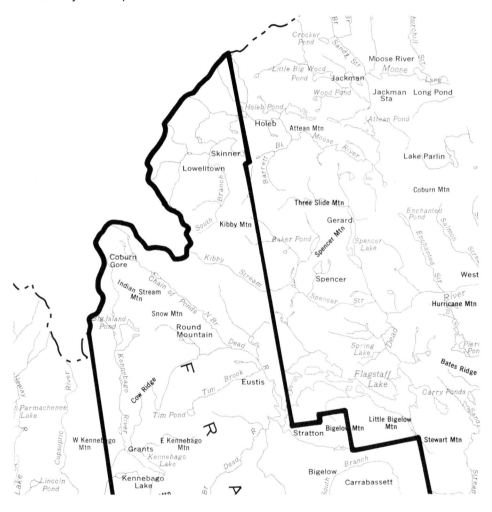

| 10 | 0 | 10 | 20 | 30 | 40 Miles |

Chronology of FRANKLIN

Map	Date	Event	Resulting Area
❷	18 Mar 1840	Lost small area to SOMERSET when town of Anson gained from New Vineyard [For configuration of entire county, see maps 1 and 2.]	1,800 sq mi
❷	6 Apr 1841	Gained from SOMERSET when town of New Sharon gained from Mercer [For configuration of entire county, see maps 1 and 2.]	1,800 sq mi
	9 Aug 1842	Webster–Ashburton Treaty between Great Britain and the United States settled the U.S.–Canadian boundary, fixing northern limits of FRANKLIN [no change]	

(Heavy line depicts historical boundary. Base map shows present-day information.)

❷ Southern FRANKLIN
9 May 1838 – 1 Aug 1847

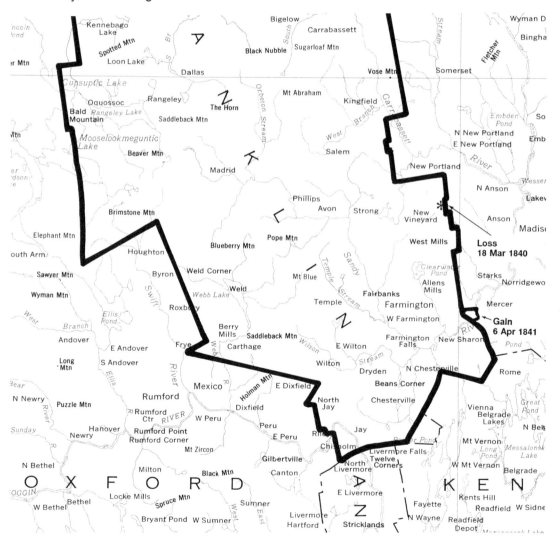

Chronology of FRANKLIN

Map	Date	Event	Resulting Area
❸	2 Aug 1847	Gained from KENNEBEC when town of Chesterville gained from Vienna [For configuration of entire county, see maps 1 and 3.]	1,800 sq mi
	9 Apr 1852	Boundary with KENNEBEC redefined [no change]	

(Heavy line depicts historical boundary. Base map shows present-day information.)

❸ Southern FRANKLIN
2 Aug 1847–present

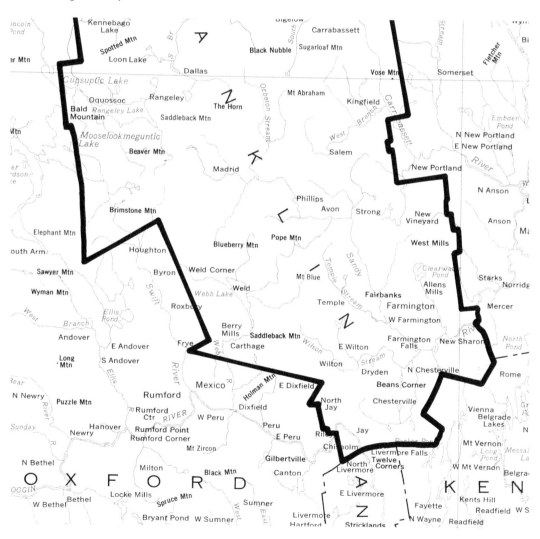

Chronology of HANCOCK (created by Mass.)

Map	Date	Event	Resulting Area
❶	1 May 1790	Created by Massachusetts from LINCOLN	13,610 sq mi
❷	1 May 1791	Lost to LINCOLN	13,420 sq mi
	28 Feb 1799	Boundary with KENNEBEC clarified [no change]	

(Heavy line depicts historical boundary. Base map shows present-day information.)

 ❶ 1 May 1790 – 30 Apr 1791

 ❷ 1 May 1791 – 20 Jun 1811

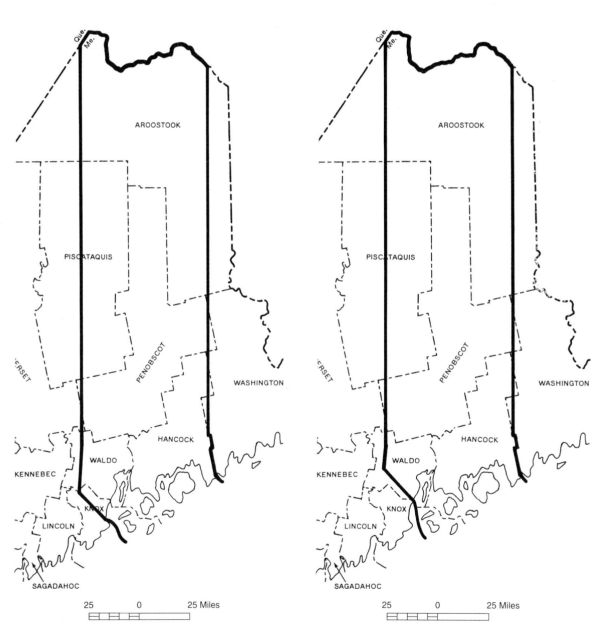

Chronology of HANCOCK (created by Mass.)

Map	Date	Event	Resulting Area
❸	21 Jun 1811	Gained from SOMERSET [For full-scale details of change, see SOMERSET map 2.]	13,440 sq mi
❹	12 Jun 1812	Gained from SOMERSET [For full-scale details of change, see SOMERSET map 3.]	13,460 sq mi

(Heavy line depicts historical boundary. Base map shows present-day information.)

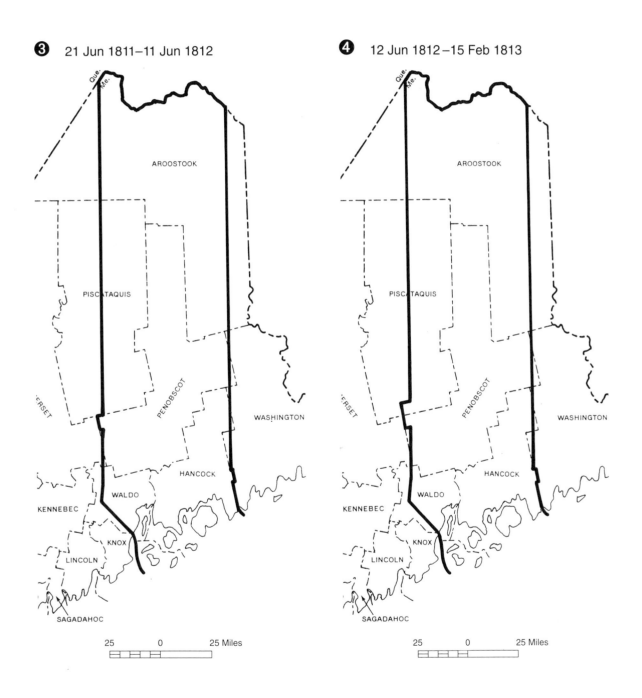

❸ 21 Jun 1811–11 Jun 1812

❹ 12 Jun 1812–15 Feb 1813

Chronology of HANCOCK (created by Mass.)

Map	Date	Event	Resulting Area
❺	16 Feb 1813	Lost to SOMERSET [For full-scale details of change, see SOMERSET map 4.]	13,440 sq mi
❻	15 Feb 1816	Lost to creation of PENOBSCOT	2,360 sq mi

(Heavy line depicts historical boundary. Base map shows present-day information.)

❺   16 Feb 1813–14 Feb 1816

❻   15 Feb 1816–16 Jun 1816

Chronology of HANCOCK (created by Mass.)

Map	Date	Event	Resulting Area
❼	17 Jun 1816	Lost to PENOBSCOT when town of Hampden gained from Frankfurt and Orrington gained from Buckstown [For configuration of entire county, see map 7 and southern part of map 6.]	2,360 sq mi
	15 Mar 1820	Separated from Massachusetts when Maine became a state	

(Heavy line depicts historical boundary. Base map shows present-day information.)

❼ Northern HANCOCK
17 Jun 1816 – 2 Jul 1827

Chronology of HANCOCK (created by Mass.)

Map	Date	Event	Resulting Area
⑧	3 Jul 1827	Lost to creation of WALDO	1,860 sq mi
⑨	17 Mar 1831	Exchanged with WASHINGTON [For configuration of entire county, see map 9 and southern part of map 8.]	1,860 sq mi

(Heavy line depicts historical boundary. Base map shows present-day information.)

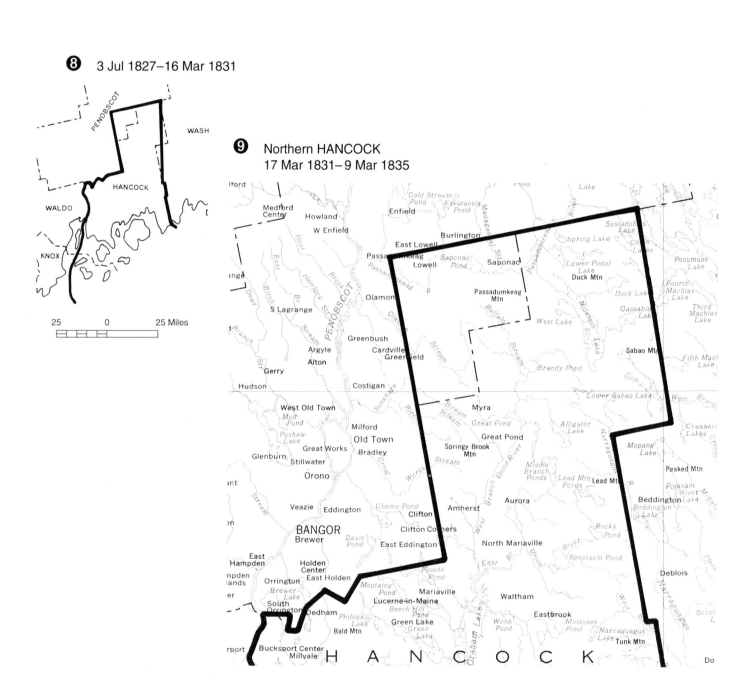

⑧ 3 Jul 1827–16 Mar 1831

⑨ Northern HANCOCK
17 Mar 1831–9 Mar 1835

25   0   25 Miles

10   0   10   20   30   40 Miles

Chronology of HANCOCK (created by Mass.)

Map	Date	Event	Resulting Area
⑩	10 Mar 1835	Lost to PENOBSCOT [For configuration of entire county, see map 10 and southern part of map 8.]	1,850 sq mi

(Heavy line depicts historical boundary. Base map shows present-day information.)

⑩ Northern HANCOCK
10 Mar 1835 – 19 Feb 1841

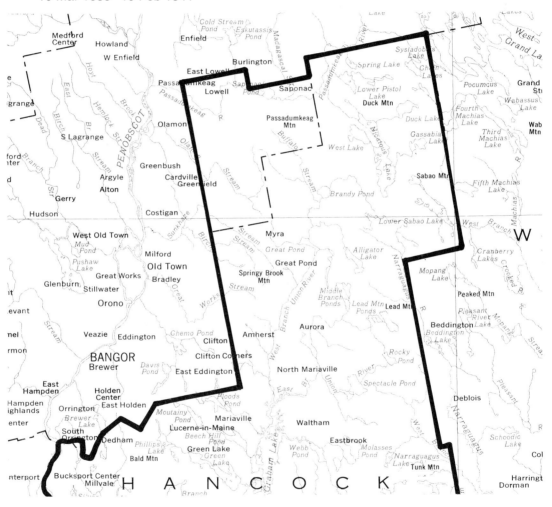

| 10 | 0 | 10 | 20 | 30 | 40 Miles |

Chronology of HANCOCK (created by Mass.)

Map	Date	Event	Resulting Area
⑪	15 Mar 1838	Lost N. Haven I. and Vinalhaven I. to WALDO [For configuration of entire county, see maps 10 and 11.]	1,810 sq mi

(Heavy line depicts historical boundary. Base map shows present-day information.)

⑪   Southern HANCOCK
15 Mar 1838 – 11 Mar 1913

Chronology of HANCOCK (created by Mass.)

Map	Date	Event	Resulting Area
⑫	20 Feb 1841	Lost to PENOBSCOT when town of Lowell gained from Page's Mill Settlement [For configuration of entire county, see maps 11 and 12.]	1,800 sq mi
⑫	10 Apr 1841	Lost small area to PENOBSCOT when town of Brewer gained from Bucksport and Dedham [For configuration of entire county, see maps 11 and 12.]	1,800 sq mi
⑪	24 Mar 1843	Lost Matinicus I. to LINCOLN [For configuration of entire county, see maps 11 and 12.]	1,800 sq mi
	12 Mar 1844	Part of boundary with WASHINGTON clarified [no change]	
⑫	20 Aug 1850	Lost to PENOBSCOT when town of Orrington gained from Bucksport [For configuration of entire county, see maps 11 and 12.]	1,800 sq mi
⑪	9 Apr 1852	Lost islands to LINCOLN [For configuration of entire county, see maps 11 and 12.]	1,800 sq mi

(Heavy line depicts historical boundary. Base map shows present-day information.)

⑫ Northern HANCOCK
20 Feb 1841–14 Mar 1858

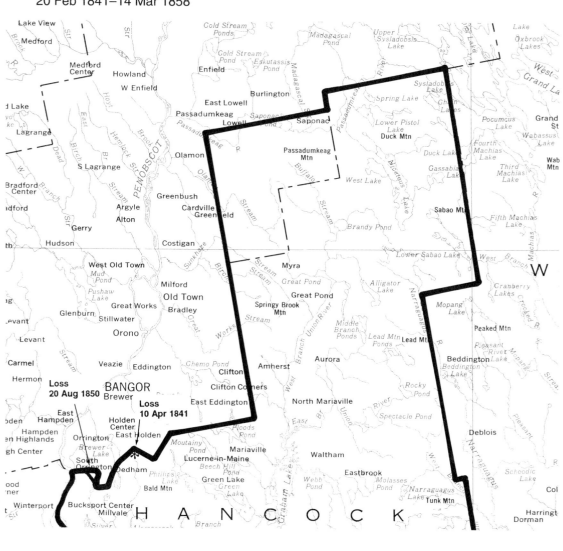

Chronology of HANCOCK (created by Mass.)

Map	Date	Event	Resulting Area
⑬	15 Mar 1858	Lost to PENOBSCOT [For configuration of entire county, see maps 11 and 13.]	1,680 sq mi

(Heavy line depicts historical boundary. Base map shows present-day information.)

⑬ Northern HANCOCK
15 Mar 1858 – present

| 10 | 0 | 10 | 20 | 30 | 40 Miles |

Chronology of HANCOCK (created by Mass.)

Map	Date	Event	Resulting Area
⑭	12 Mar 1913	Lost Isle au Haut to KNOX [For configuration of entire county, see maps 13 and 14.]	1,670 sq mi

(Heavy line depicts historical boundary. Base map shows present-day information.)

⑭ Southern HANCOCK
12 Mar 1913 – present

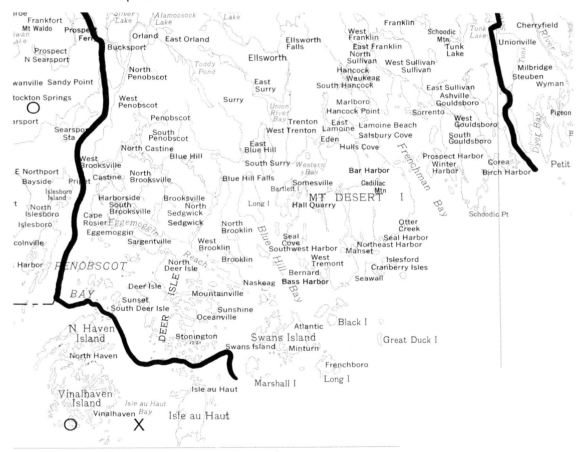

| 10 | | 0 | | 10 | | 20 | | 30 | | 40 Miles |

Chronology of KENNEBEC (created by Mass.)

Map	Date	Event	Resulting Area
❶	20 Feb 1799	Created by Massachusetts from LINCOLN	7,680 sq mi
	28 Feb 1799	Boundary with HANCOCK clarified [no change]	

(Heavy line depicts historical boundary. Base map shows present-day information.)

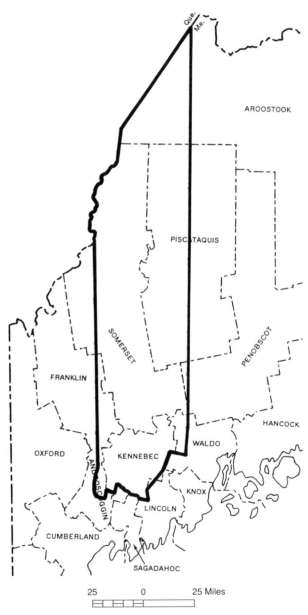

❶   20 Feb 1799 – 3 Mar 1805

25   0   25 Miles

Chronology of KENNEBEC (created by Mass.)

Map	Date	Event	Resulting Area
❷	4 Mar 1805	Gained from CUMBERLAND [For configuration of entire county, see map 2 and northern part of map 1.]	7,910 sq mi

(Heavy line depicts historical boundary. Base map shows present-day information.)

❷ Southern KENNEBEC
4 Mar 1805 – 7 Mar 1808

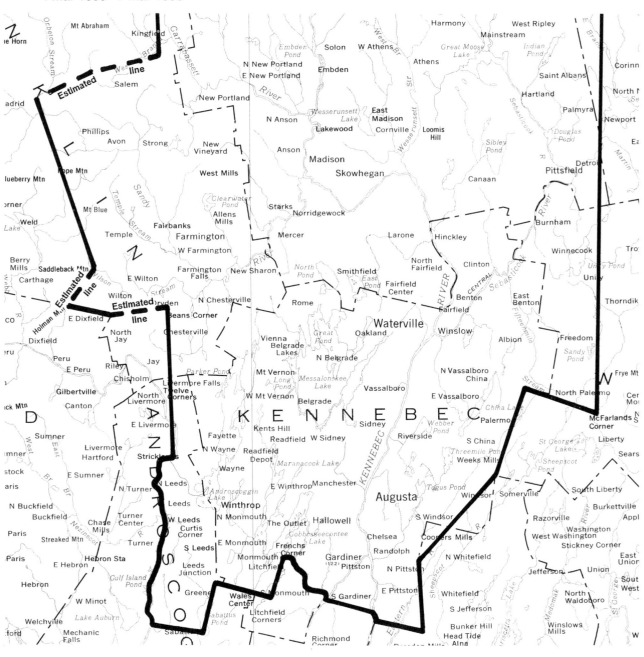

10   0   10   20   30   40 Miles

Chronology of KENNEBEC (created by Mass.)

Map	Date	Event	Resulting Area
❸	8 Mar 1808	Lost to OXFORD [For configuration of entire county, see map 3 and northern part of map 1.]	7,900 sq mi

(Heavy line depicts historical boundary. Base map shows present-day information.)

❸   Southern KENNEBEC
8 Mar 1808 – 31 May 1809

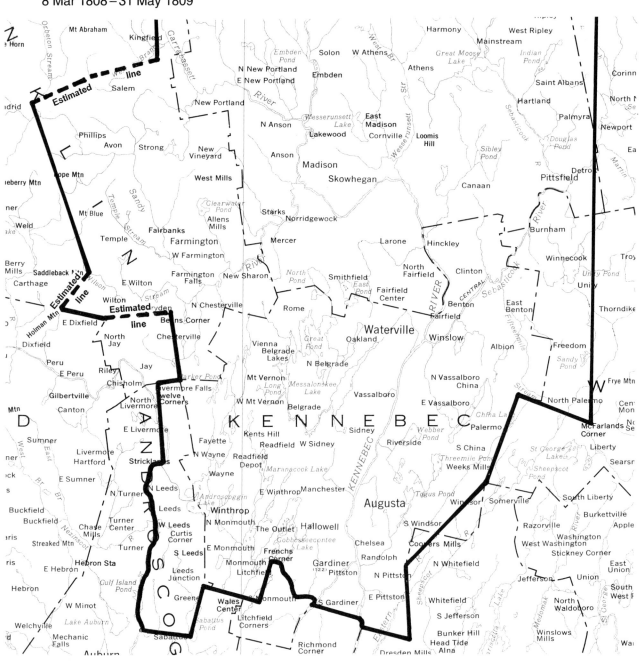

10   0   10   20   30   40 Miles

Chronology of KENNEBEC (created by Mass.)

Map	Date	Event	Resulting Area
❹	1 Jun 1809	Lost to creation of SOMERSET	1,350 sq mi
	6 Mar 1810	Boundary with LINCOLN redefined in part when line between towns of Gardiner and Litchfield redefined [no change]	

(Heavy line depicts historical boundary. Base map shows present-day information.)

❹   1 Jun 1809 – 24 Feb 1811

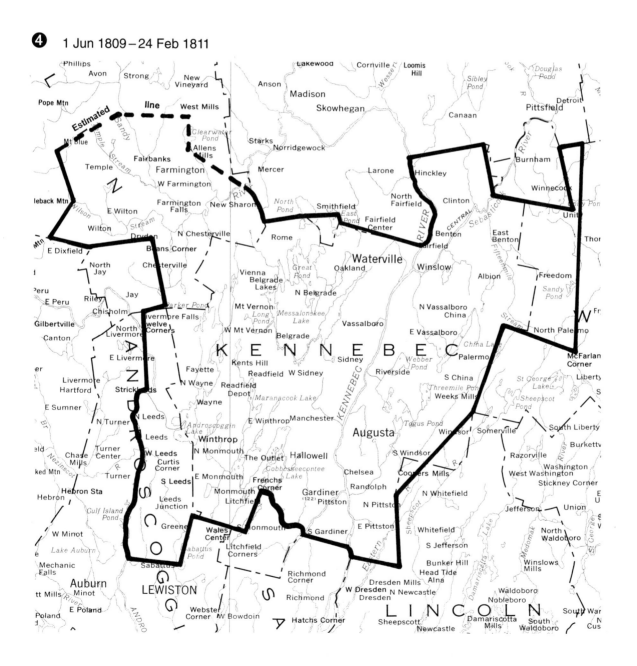

Chronology of KENNEBEC (created by Mass.)

Map	Date	Event	Resulting Area
❺	25 Feb 1811	Lost to LINCOLN	1,350 sq mi

(Heavy line depicts historical boundary. Base map shows present-day information.)

❺   25 Feb 1811–28 Feb 1812

Chronology of KENNEBEC (created by Mass.)

Map	Date	Event	Resulting Area
❻	29 Feb 1812	Exchanged with LINCOLN	1,350 sq mi

(Heavy line depicts historical boundary. Base map shows present-day information.)

❻ 29 Feb 1812 – 25 Feb 1813

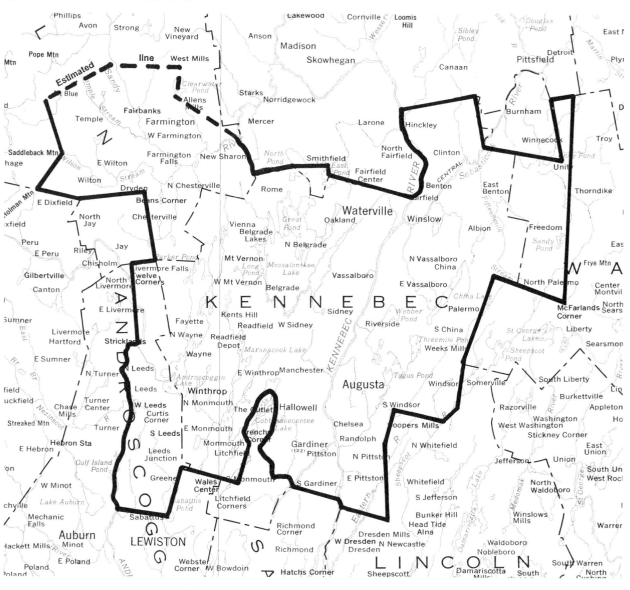

10	0	10	20	30	40 Miles

Chronology of KENNEBEC (created by Mass.)

Map	Date	Event	Resulting Area
❼	26 Feb 1813	Gained from SOMERSET	1,390 sq mi

(Heavy line depicts historical boundary. Base map shows present-day information.)

❼ **26 Feb 1813 – 27 Jan 1814**

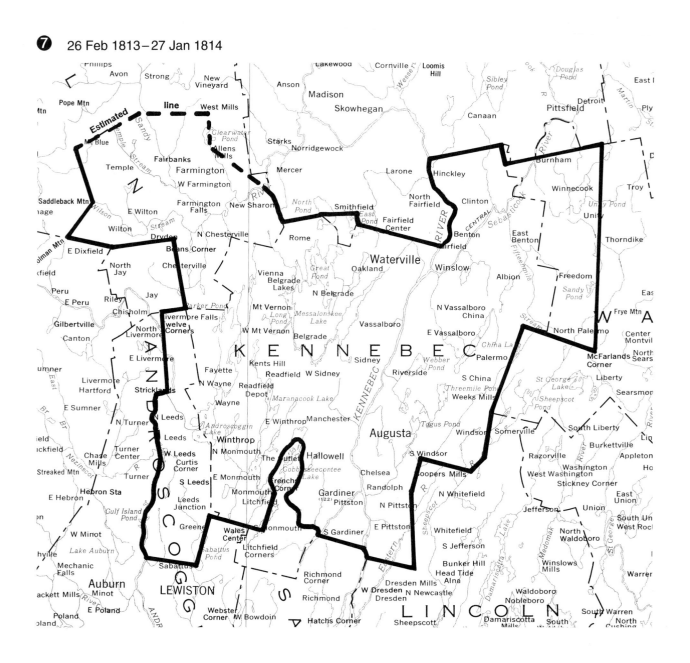

10   0   10   20   30   40 Miles

Chronology of KENNEBEC (created by Mass.)

Map	Date	Event	Resulting Area
⑧	28 Jan 1814	Lost to OXFORD	1,370 sq mi
	15 Mar 1820	Separated from Massachusetts when Maine became a state	
⑧	8 Feb 1821	Gained small area from OXFORD	1,370 sq mi
⑧	8 Mar 1821	Gained from LINCOLN	1,370 sq mi

(Heavy line depicts historical boundary. Base map shows present-day information.)

⑧   28 Jan 1814–16 Mar 1821

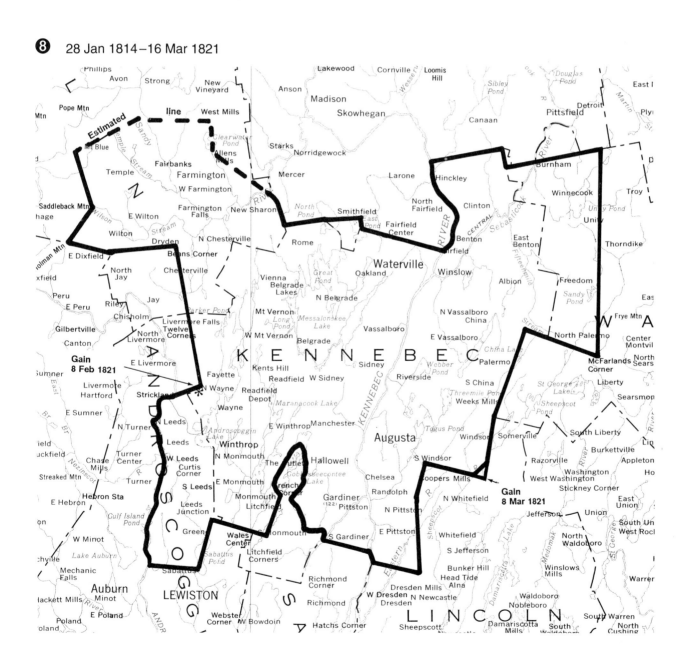

Chronology of KENNEBEC (created by Mass.)

Map	Date	Event	Resulting Area
⑨	17 Mar 1821	Gained from SOMERSET	1,380 sq mi

(Heavy line depicts historical boundary. Base map shows present-day information.)

⑨ 17 Mar 1821–2 Jul 1827

10   0   10   20   30   40 Miles

Chronology of KENNEBEC (created by Mass.)

Map	Date	Event	Resulting Area
⑩	3 Jul 1827	Lost to creation of WALDO	1,270 sq mi
⑩	6 Mar 1830	Gained from SOMERSET	1,270 sq mi

(Heavy line depicts historical boundary. Base map shows present-day information.)

⑩ 3 Jul 1827– 9 Mar 1835

[map of Kennebec County region]

| 10 | 0 | 10 | 20 | 30 | 40 Miles |

Chronology of KENNEBEC (created by Mass.)

Map	Date	Event	Resulting Area
⑪	10 Mar 1835	Gained from LINCOLN	1,320 sq mi

(Heavy line depicts historical boundary. Base map shows present-day information.)

⑪ 10 Mar 1835 – 8 May 1838

Chronology of KENNEBEC (created by Mass.)

Map	Date	Event	Resulting Area
⑫	9 May 1838	Lost to creation of FRANKLIN	1,190 sq mi

(Heavy line depicts historical boundary. Base map shows present-day information.)

⑫   9 May 1838 – 28 Feb 1840

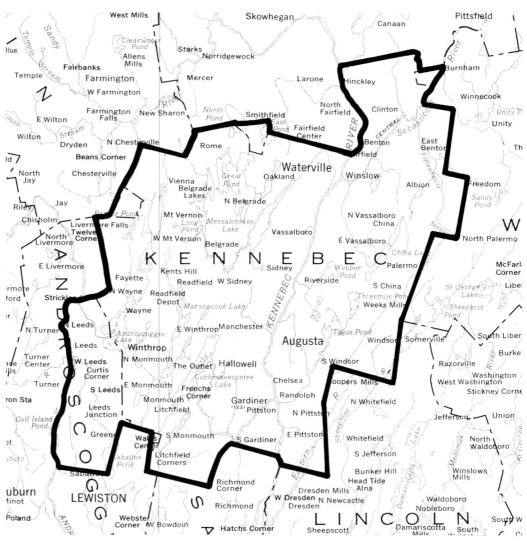

| 10 | 0 | 10 | 20 | 30 | 40 Miles |

Chronology of KENNEBEC (created by Mass.)

Map	Date	Event	Resulting Area
⑬	29 Feb 1840	Lost to SOMERSET	1,180 sq mi

(Heavy line depicts historical boundary. Base map shows present-day information.)

⑬　29 Feb 1840 – 5 Mar 1840

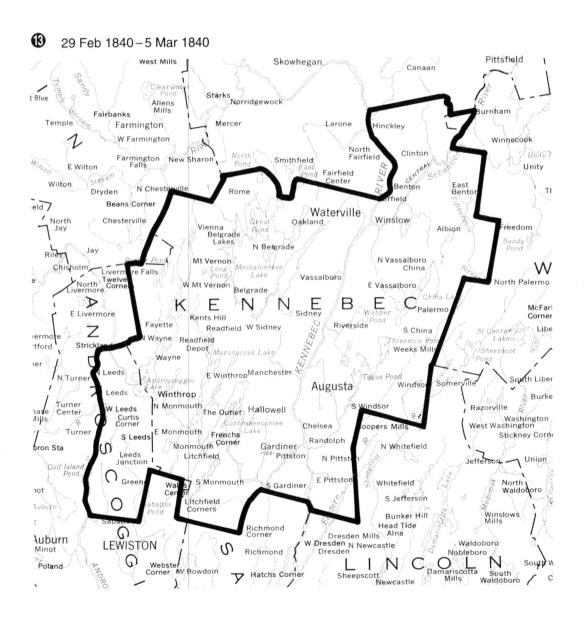

Chronology of KENNEBEC (created by Mass.)

Map	Date	Event	Resulting Area
⑭	6 Mar 1840	Gained from LINCOLN	1,200 sq mi

(Heavy line depicts historical boundary. Base map shows present-day information.)

⑭ 6 Mar 1840 – 29 Feb 1844

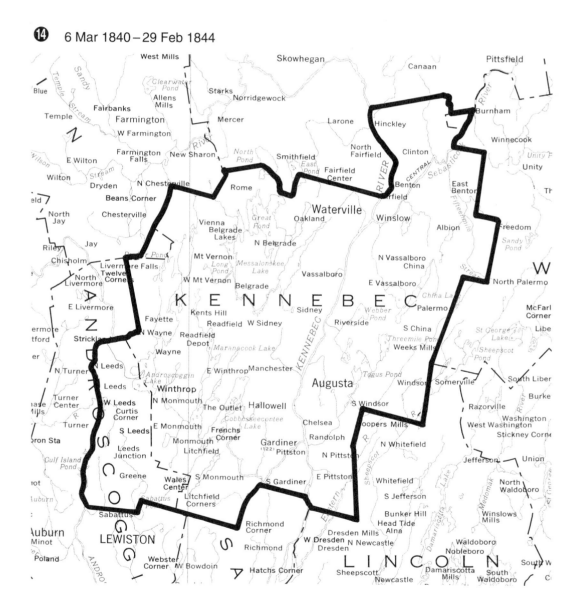

10   0   10   20   30   40 Miles

Chronology of KENNEBEC (created by Mass.)

Map	Date	Event	Resulting Area
⑮	1 Mar 1844	Gained from OXFORD	1,220 sq mi

(Heavy line depicts historical boundary. Base map shows present-day information.)

⑮ **1 Mar 1844 – 1 Aug 1847**

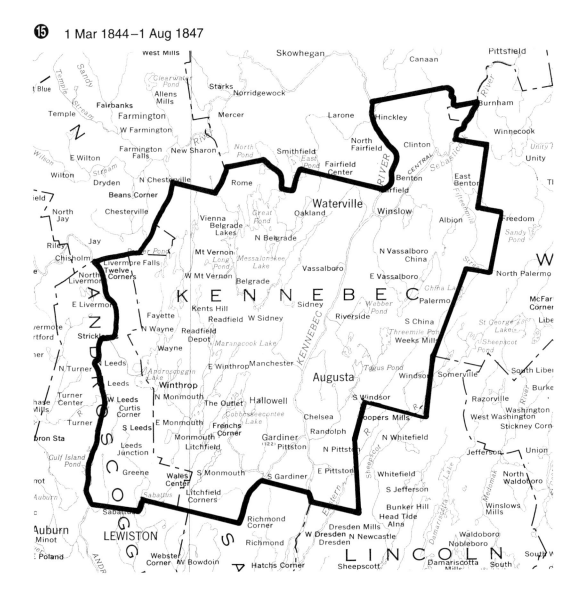

10   0   10   20   30   40 Miles

Chronology of KENNEBEC (created by Mass.)

Map	Date	Event	Resulting Area
⑯	2 Aug 1847	Lost to FRANKLIN when town of Chesterville gained from Vienna	1,210 sq mi
⑯	24 Jul 1849	Lost to SOMERSET when town of Canaan gained from Clinton	1,210 sq mi
⑯	8 Aug 1850	Gained from SOMERSET when town of Clinton gained from Canaan	1,210 sq mi
	9 Apr 1852	Boundary with FRANKLIN redefined [no change]	
	20 Apr 1852	Lost small area to LINCOLN when town of Lewiston gained from Greene to accommodate local property owner [location unknown, not mapped]	

(Heavy line depicts historical boundary. Base map shows present-day information.)

⑯ 2 Aug 1847– 30 Mar 1854

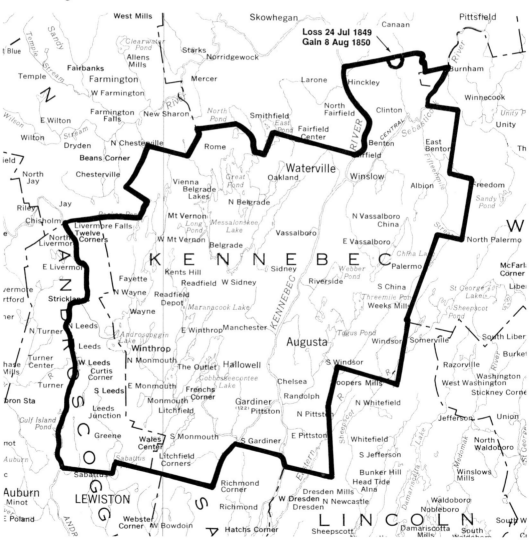

Chronology of KENNEBEC (created by Mass.)

Map	Date	Event	Resulting Area
⑰	31 Mar 1854	Lost to creation of ANDROSCOGGIN	1,090 sq mi
⑰	16 Mar 1855	Lost to ANDROSCOGGIN when town of Wales gained from Monmouth	1,080 sq mi
⑰	12 Mar 1856	Lost to ANDROSCOGGIN when town of Wales gained from Litchfield	1,080 sq mi
⑰	2 Apr 1859	Gained from ANDROSCOGGIN when town of Wayne gained from Leeds	1,080 sq mi
⑰	14 Feb 1867	Lost small area to ANDROSCOGGIN when town of Webster gained from Litchfield	1,080 sq mi

(Heavy line depicts historical boundary. Base map shows present-day information.)

⑰　31 Mar 1854 – 25 Feb 1873

West Mills　Skowhegan　Pittsfield

Mt Blue　Clearwater Pond　Canaan　Burnham

Allens Mills　Starks　Norridgewock

Temple Stream　Sandy Stream

Fairbanks　Mercer　Larone　Hinckley　Winnecook

Temple　Farmington　Unity P.

W Farmington　North Fairfield　Clinton　Unity

E Wilton　Farmington Falls　New Sharon　North Pond　Smithfield　East Pond　Fairfield Center　Benton　East Benton

Wilton　Dryden　N Chesterville　Rome　Fairfield

Beans Corner

N Jay　Chesterville　Vienna　Great Pond　Oakland　Waterville　Winslow　Albion　Freedom

Riley　Jay　Belgrade Lakes　N Belgrade　Sandy Pond

Chisholm　Livermore Falls　Mt Vernon　Long Pond　Messalonskee Lake　N Vassalboro　China　North Palermo

North Livermore　Twelve Corners　W Mt Vernon　Vassalboro　E Vassalboro　China Lake

E Livermore　Belgrade　K E N N E B E C　Palermo　McFarl Corner

Kents Hill　Sidney　Webber Pond　Riverside　Liber

Gain 2 Apr 1859　Fayette　Readfield　W Sidney　S China　St George Lakes

Stricklands　Wayne　Readfield Depot　Maranacook Lake　Threemile Pond　Weeks Mills　Sheepscot Pond

Hartford　Wayne　South Liber

N Turner　N Leeds　E Winthrop　Manchester　Togus Pond　Windsor　Somerville

Chase Mills　Turner Center　Leeds　Winthrop　Augusta　Razorville　Burke

W Leeds　N Monmouth　The Outlet　Hallowell　S Windsor　Washington　West Washington

Curtis Corner　Cobbosseecontee Lake　Chelsea　Coopers Mills　Stickney Corne

Turner　S Leeds　E Monmouth　Frenchs Corner　Randolph　N Whitefield

Hebron Sta　Leeds Junction　Monmouth　Gardiner　Pittston　N Pittst　Jefferson　Union

Loss 16 Mar 1855　Litchfield　N Pittst

Greene　Wayne Cen　S Monmouth　E Pittston　Whitefield　North Waldoboro

Minot　Sabattus Pond　Litchfield Corners　S Jefferson

Loss 12 Mar 1856　Sabattus　Bunker Hill　Head Tide　Winslows Mills

Auburn　Richmond Corner　Alna　Waldoboro

Minot　L E W I S T O N　Dresden Mills　Nobleboro

E Poland　Webster Corner　W Bowdoin　Richmond　W Dresden　N Newcastle　L I N C O L N　South W

Loss 14 Feb 1867　Hatchs Corner　Dresden　Damariscotta Mills　South Waldoboro

Danville　Lisbon　Sheepscott　Newcastle　Damariscotta　Turners Corner

Wiscasset

10　0　10　20　30　40 Miles

Chronology of KENNEBEC (created by Mass.)

Map	Date	Event	Resulting Area
⑱	26 Feb 1873	Lost to WALDO when town of Burnham gained from Clinton Gore Plantation	1,080 sq mi
⑱	27 Feb 1873	Lost small area to SOMERSET when town of Fairfield gained from Benton	1,080 sq mi

(Heavy line depicts historical boundary. Base map shows present-day information.)

⑱ 26 Feb 1873 – 20 Feb 1907

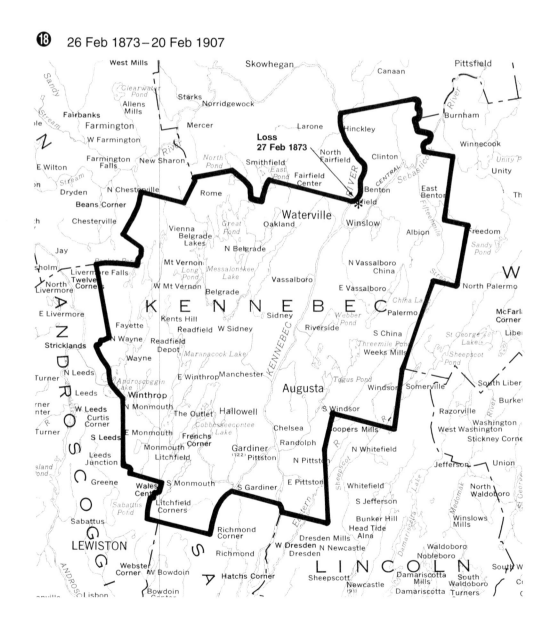

Chronology of KENNEBEC (created by Mass.)

Map	Date	Event	Resulting Area
⑲	21 Feb 1907	Lost to LINCOLN when town of Whitefield gained from Windsor	1,080 sq mi

(Heavy line depicts historical boundary. Base map shows present-day information.)

⑲ 21 Feb 1907–present

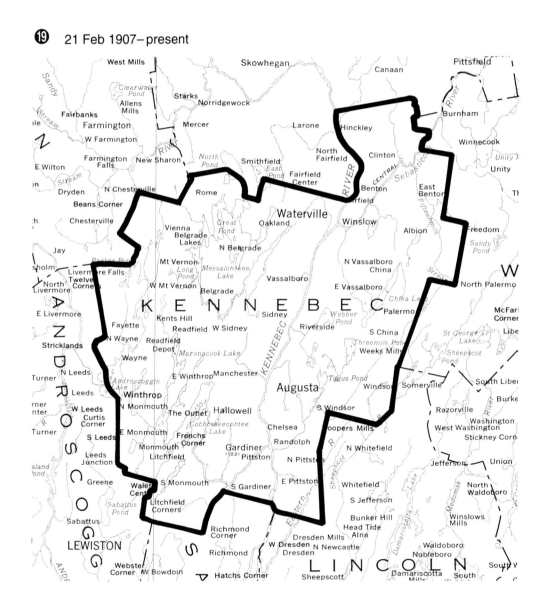

Chronology of KNOX

Map	Date	Event	Resulting Area
❶	1 Apr 1860	Created from LINCOLN and WALDO	350 sq mi

(Heavy line depicts historical boundary. Base map shows present-day information.)

❶   1 Apr 1860 – 11 Mar 1913

10   0   10   20   30   40 Miles

Chronology of KNOX

Map	Date	Event	Resulting Area
❷	12 Mar 1913	Gained Isle au Haut from HANCOCK	360 sq mi

(Heavy line depicts historical boundary. Base map shows present-day information.)

❷ 12 Mar 1913–present

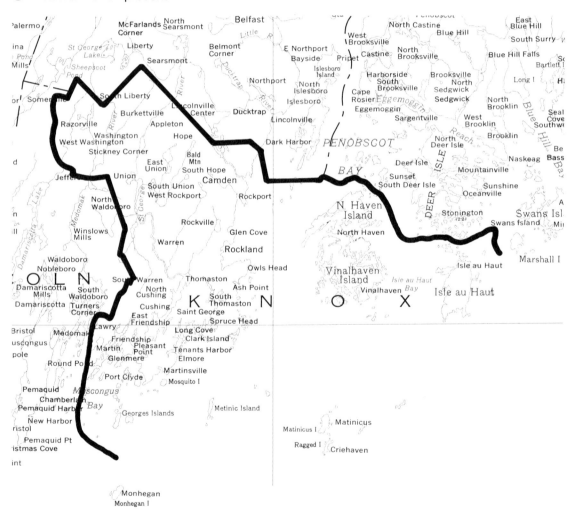

| 10 | 0 | 10 | 20 | 30 | 40 Miles |

Chronology of LINCOLN (created by Mass.)

Map	Date	Event	Resulting Area
❶	1 Nov 1760	Created by Massachusetts from YORK	Indefinite

(Heavy line depicts historical boundary. Base map shows present-day information.)

❶   1 Nov 1760 – 6 Oct 1763

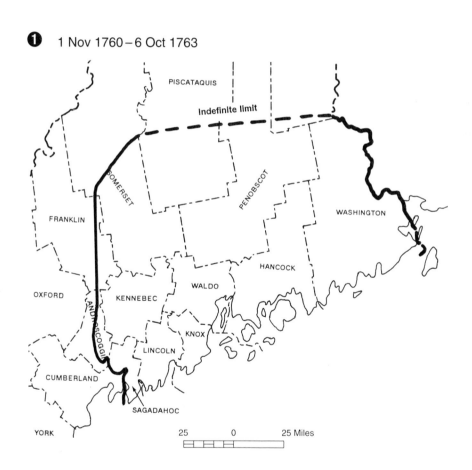

Chronology of LINCOLN (created by Mass.)

Map	Date	Event	Resulting Area
❷	7 Oct 1763	Extended northward to Atlantic watershed	26,090 sq mi

(Heavy line depicts historical boundary. Base map shows present-day information.)

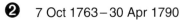

❷   7 Oct 1763 – 30 Apr 1790

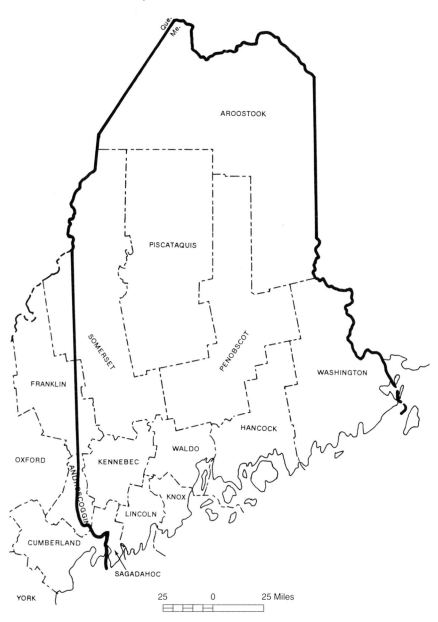

Chronology of LINCOLN (created by Mass.)

Map	Date	Event	Resulting Area
❸	1 May 1790	Lost to creation of HANCOCK and WASHINGTON	9,130 sq mi
❹	1 May 1791	Gained from HANCOCK	9,580 sq mi

(Heavy line depicts historical boundary. Base map shows present-day information.)

❸ 1 May 1790 – 30 Apr 1791   ❹ 1 May 1791 – 19 Feb 1799

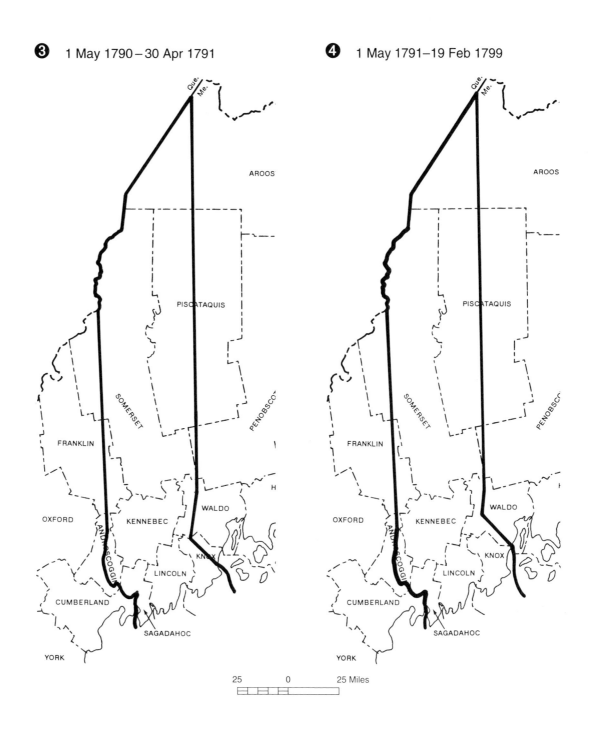

Chronology of LINCOLN (created by Mass.)

Map	Date	Event	Resulting Area
❺	20 Feb 1799	Lost to creation of KENNEBEC	1,450 sq mi
	6 Mar 1810	Boundary with KENNEBEC redefined in part when line between Gardiner and Litchfield redefined [no change]	

(Heavy line depicts historical boundary. Base map shows present-day information.)

❺   20 Feb 1799 – 24 Feb 1811

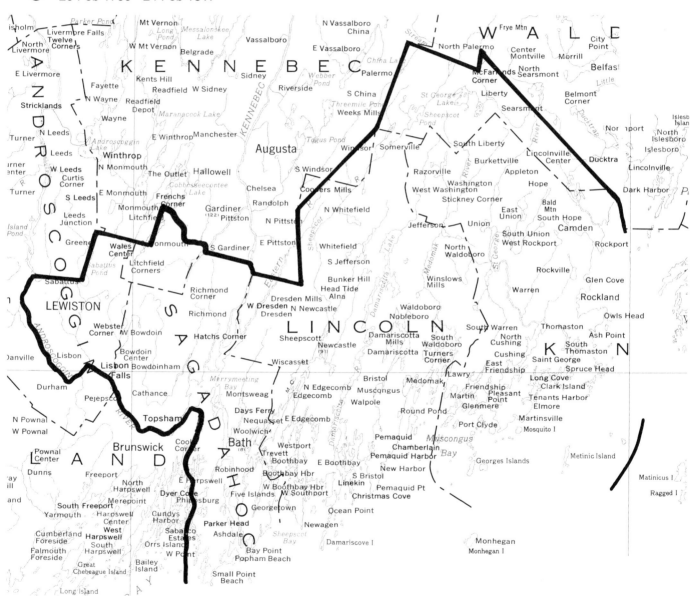

Chronology of LINCOLN (created by Mass.)

Map	Date	Event	Resulting Area
❻	25 Feb 1811	Gained from KENNEBEC	1,460 sq mi

(Heavy line depicts historical boundary. Base map shows present-day information.)

❻ 25 Feb 1811– 28 Feb 1812

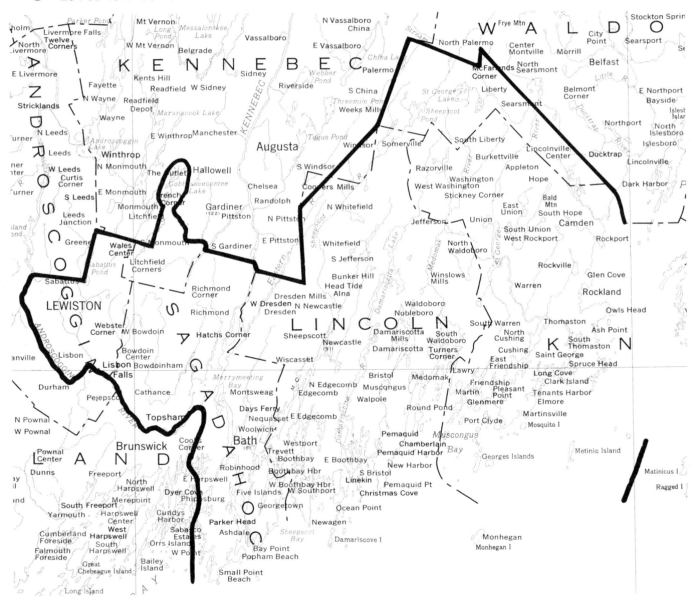

Chronology of LINCOLN (created by Mass.)

Map	Date	Event	Resulting Area
❼	29 Feb 1812	Exchanged with KENNEBEC	1,450 sq mi
	15 Mar 1820	Separated from Massachusetts when Maine became a state	
❼	8 Mar 1821	Lost to KENNEBEC	1,450 sq mi

(Heavy line depicts historical boundary. Base map shows present-day information.)

❼   29 Feb 1812 – 2 Jul 1827

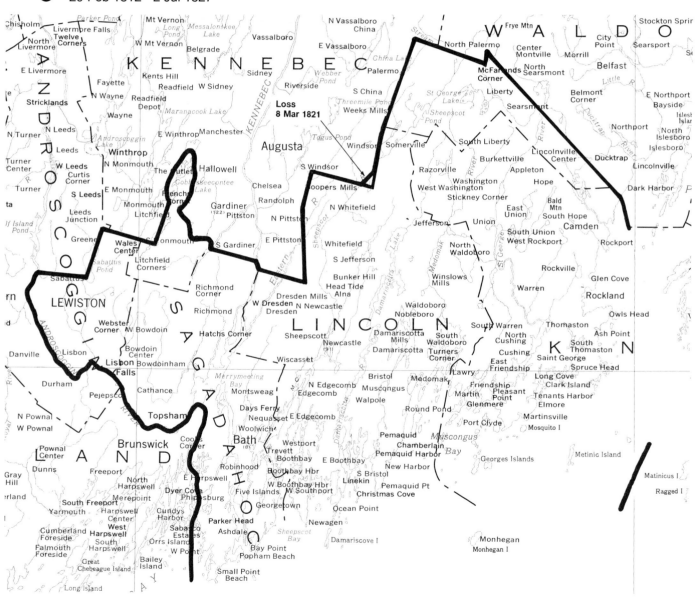

Chronology of LINCOLN (created by Mass.)

Map	Date	Event	Resulting Area
8	3 Jul 1827	Lost to creation of WALDO	1,210 sq mi

(Heavy line depicts historical boundary. Base map shows present-day information.)

8 3 Jul 1827–9 Mar 1835

Chronology of LINCOLN (created by Mass.)

Map	Date	Event	Resulting Area
❾	10 Mar 1835	Lost to KENNEBEC	1,160 sq mi
❾	10 Feb 1836	Lost small area to WALDO when town of Camden gained from Warren	1,160 sq mi

(Heavy line depicts historical boundary. Base map shows present-day information.)

❾ 10 Mar 1835 – 5 Mar 1840

Chronology of LINCOLN (created by Mass.)

Map	Date	Event	Resulting Area
⑩	6 Mar 1840	Lost to KENNEBEC	1,150 sq mi

(Heavy line depicts historical boundary. Base map shows present-day information.)

⑩   6 Mar 1840 – 23 Mar 1843

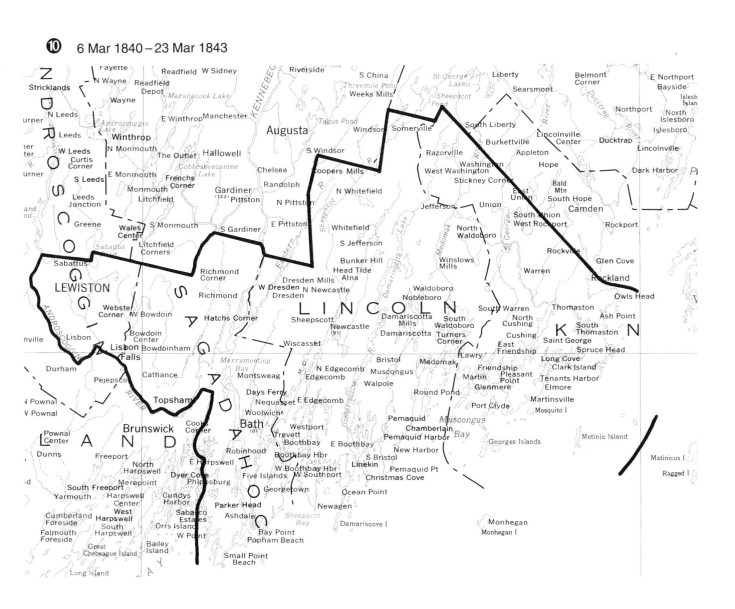

Chronology of LINCOLN (created by Mass.)

Map	Date	Event	Resulting Area
⑪	24 Mar 1843	Gained Matinicus I. from HANCOCK	1,150 sq mi
⑪	9 Apr 1852	Gained islands from HANCOCK	1,150 sq mi
	20 Apr 1852	Gained small area from KENNEBEC when town of Lewiston gained from Greene [location unknown, not mapped]	

(Heavy line depicts historical boundary. Base map shows present-day information.)

⑪ 24 Mar 1843 – 30 Mar 1854

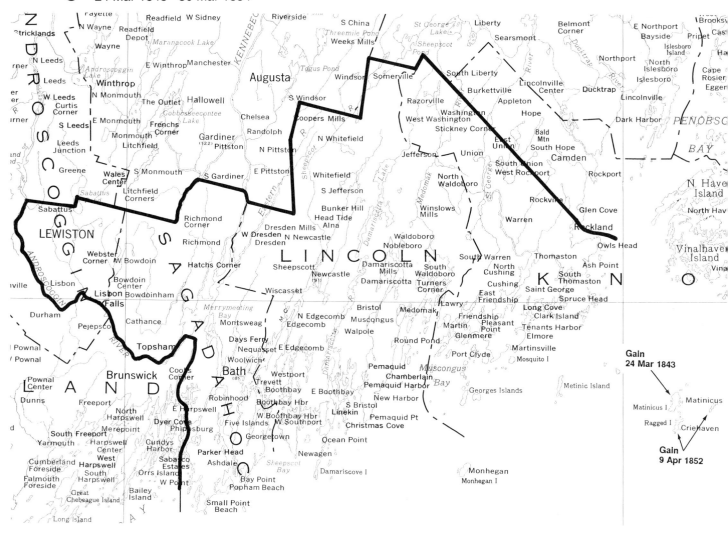

Chronology of LINCOLN (created by Mass.)

Map	Date	Event	Resulting Area
⑫	31 Mar 1854	Lost to creation of ANDROSCOGGIN	1,070 sq mi

(Heavy line depicts historical boundary. Base map shows present-day information.)

⑫   31 Mar 1854 – 3 Apr 1854

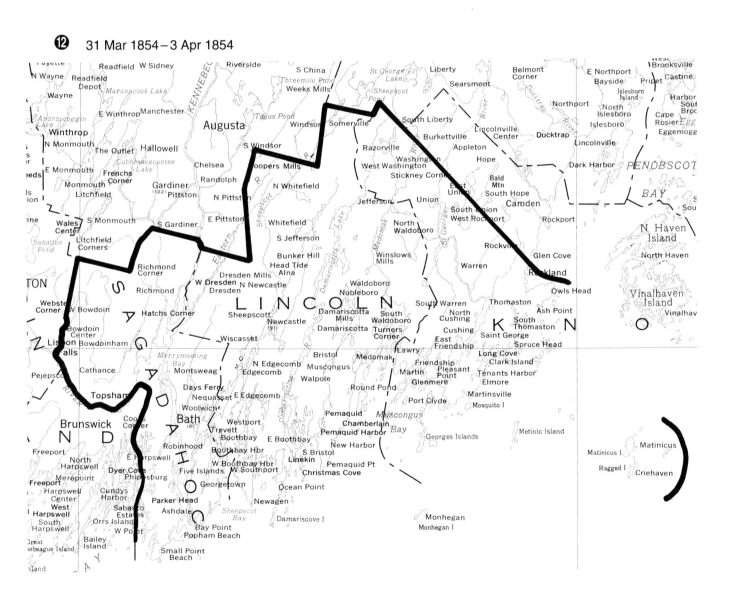

10   0   10   20   30   40 Miles

Chronology of LINCOLN (created by Mass.)

Map	Date	Event	Resulting Area
⑬	4 Apr 1854	Lost to creation of SAGADAHOC	780 sq mi
	11 Apr 1854	Gained small area from WALDO when town of Washington gained from Palermo to accommodate local property owners [location unknown, not mapped]	

(Heavy line depicts historical boundary. Base map shows present-day information.)

⑬   4 Apr 1854 – 31 Mar 1860

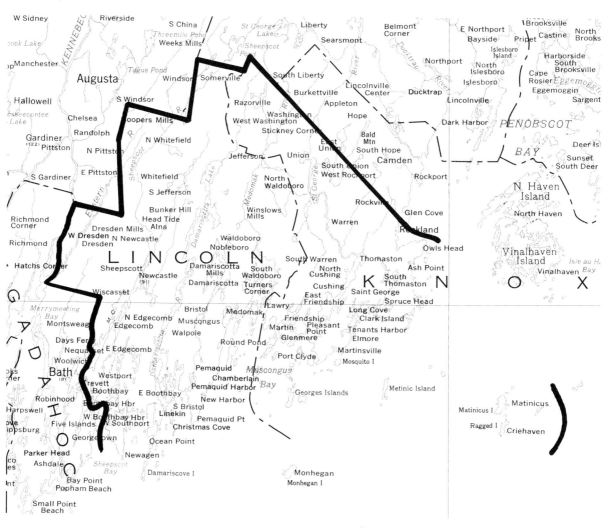

Chronology of LINCOLN (created by Mass.)

Map	Date	Event	Resulting Area
⑭	1 Apr 1860	Lost to creation of KNOX	530 sq mi
⑮	21 Feb 1907	Gained from KENNEBEC when town of Whitefield gained from Windsor	530 sq mi

(Heavy line depicts historical boundary. Base map shows present-day information.)

⑭   1 Apr 1860 – 20 Feb 1907

⑮   21 Feb 1907 – present

10   0   10   20   30   40 Miles

Chronology of OXFORD (created by Mass.)

Map	Date	Event	Resulting Area
❶	4 Mar 1805	Created by Massachusetts from CUMBERLAND and YORK	4,350 sq mi
❷	8 Mar 1808	Gained from KENNEBEC [For configuration of entire county, see map 2 and northern part of map 1.]	4,370 sq mi

(Heavy line depicts historical boundary. Base map shows present-day information.)

❶   4 Mar 1805 – 7 Mar 1808

❷   Southern OXFORD
8 Mar 1808 – 27 Jan 1814

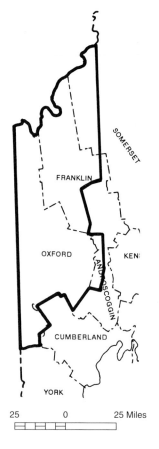

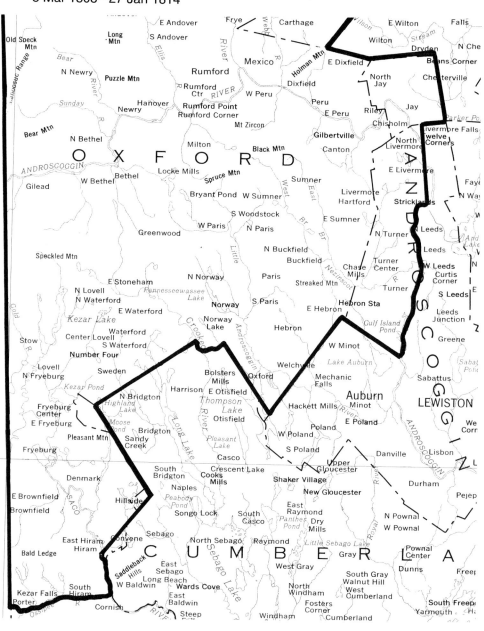

Chronology of OXFORD (created by Mass.)

Map	Date	Event	Resulting Area
❸	28 Jan 1814	Gained from KENNEBEC [For configuration of entire county, see map 3 and northern part of map 1.]	4,390 sq mi

(Heavy line depicts historical boundary. Base map shows present-day information.)

❸   Southern OXFORD
      28 Jan 1814–1 Feb 1819

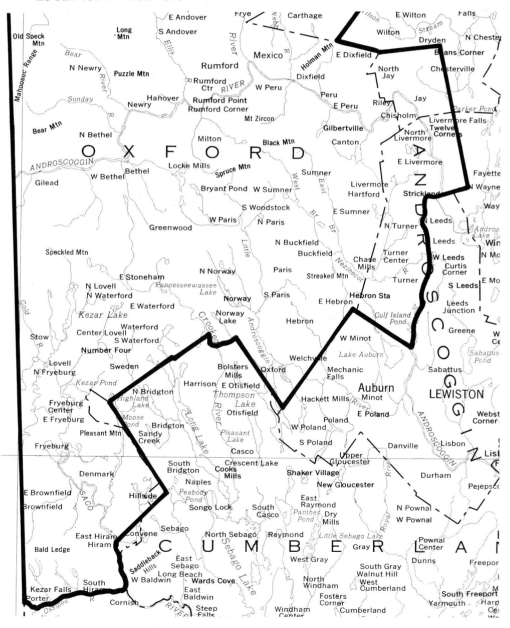

10   0   10   20   30   40 Miles

Chronology of OXFORD (created by Mass.)

Map	Date	Event	Resulting Area
❹	2 Feb 1819	Lost to SOMERSET	3,900 sq mi
	15 Mar 1820	Separated from Massachusetts when Maine became a state	
	5 Feb 1821	Boundary with CUMBERLAND clarified [no change]	
❹	8 Feb 1821	Lost small area to KENNEBEC	3,900 sq mi
❺	28 Feb 1821	Gained from CUMBERLAND [For configuration of entire county, see map 5 and northern part of map 4.]	3,900 sq mi

(Heavy line depicts historical boundary. Base map shows present-day information.)

❹ 2 Feb 1819 – 27 Feb 1821

❺ Southern OXFORD
28 Feb 1821 – 30 Jan 1823

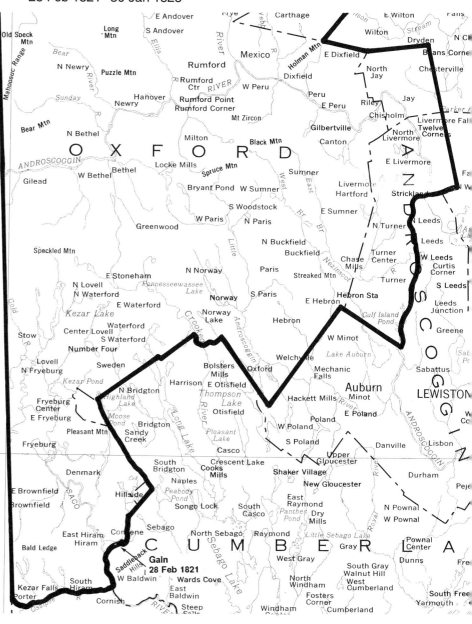

Chronology of OXFORD (created by Mass.)

Map	Date	Event	Resulting Area
❻	31 Jan 1823	Lost to SOMERSET	3,580 sq mi
❼	12 Mar 1830	Lost to CUMBERLAND when town of Sebago gained from Denmark [For configuration of entire county, see map 7 and northern part of map 6.]	3,580 sq mi
❼	17 Mar 1830	Gained from CUMBERLAND when town of Oxford gained from Otisfield	3,580 sq mi

(Heavy line depicts historical boundary. Base map shows present-day information.)

❻ 31 Jan 1823–11 Mar 1830

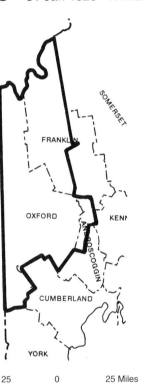

25   0   25 Miles

❼ Southern OXFORD
12 Mar 1830–8 May 1838

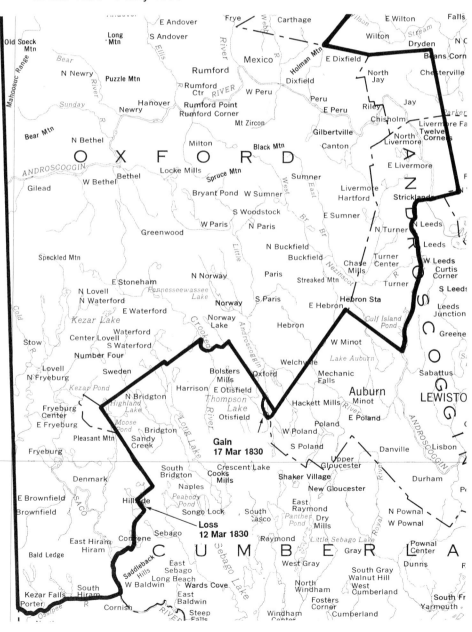

10   0   10   20   30   40 Miles

Chronology of OXFORD (created by Mass.)

Map	Date	Event	Resulting Area
8	9 May 1838	Lost to creation of FRANKLIN [For details of northern part of OXFORD, see map 9.]	2,310 sq mi
9	9 May 1838	[Full-scale map of *northern part*; for configuration of entire county, see map 8.]	
9	7 Mar 1842	Lost small area to CUMBERLAND when town of Bridgton gained from Denmark [For full-scale detail of change, see CUMBERLAND map 7.]	2,310 sq mi
	9 Aug 1842	Webster–Ashburton Treaty between Great Britain and the United States settled the U.S.–Canadian boundary, fixing northern limits of OXFORD [no change]	

(Heavy line depicts historical boundary. Base map shows present-day information.)

8 9 May 1838 – 29 Feb 1844

9 Northern OXFORD
9 May 1838 – present

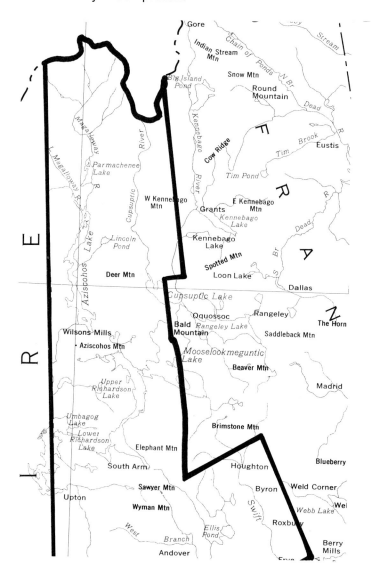

Chronology of OXFORD (created by Mass.)

Map	Date	Event	Resulting Area
⑩	1 Mar 1844	Lost to KENNEBEC [For configuration of entire county, see maps 9 and 10.]	2,290 sq mi
⑩	7 Mar 1844	Gained small area from CUMBERLAND when town of Hiram gained from Baldwin [For configuration of entire county, see maps 9 and 10.]	2,290 sq mi

(Heavy line depicts historical boundary. Base map shows present-day information.)

⑩ Southern OXFORD
1 Mar 1844–1 Aug 1847

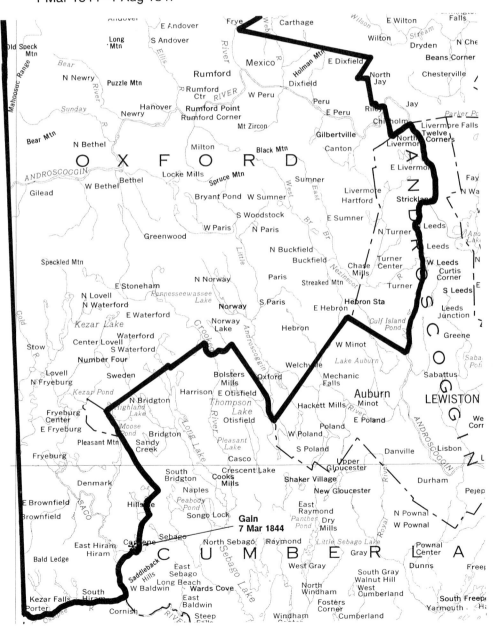

Chronology of OXFORD (created by Mass.)

Map	Date	Event	Resulting Area
⑪	2 Aug 1847	Lost to CUMBERLAND when town of Bridgton gained from Fryeburg and Denmark [For configuration of entire county, see maps 9 and 11.]	2,290 sq mi

(Heavy line depicts historical boundary. Base map shows present-day information.)

⑪   Southern OXFORD
2 Aug 1847 – 30 Mar 1854

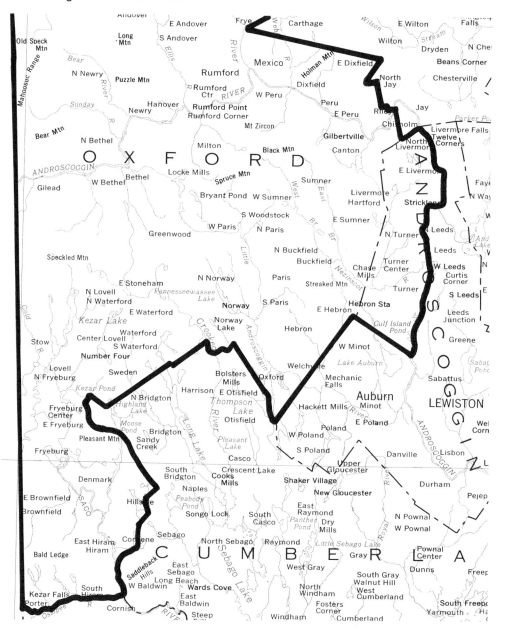

| 10 | 0 | 10 | 20 | 30 | 40 Miles |

Chronology of OXFORD (created by Mass.)

Map	Date	Event	Resulting Area
⑫	31 Mar 1854	Lost to creation of ANDROSCOGGIN [For configuration of entire county, see maps 9 and 12.]	2,180 sq mi

(Heavy line depicts historical boundary. Base map shows present-day information.)

⑫ Southern OXFORD
31 Mar 1854 – present

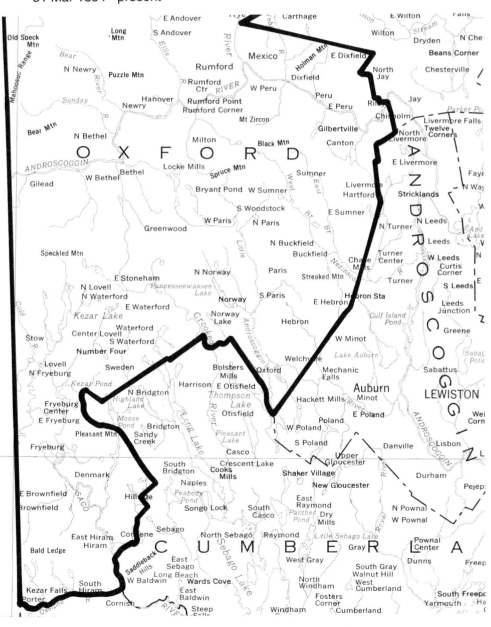

10   0   10   20   30   40 Miles

Chronology of PENOBSCOT (created by Mass.)

Map	Date	Event	Resulting Area
❶	15 Feb 1816	Created by Massachusetts from HANCOCK	10,240 sq mi

(Heavy line depicts historical boundary. Base map shows present-day information.)

❶　15 Feb 1816 – 16 Jun 1816

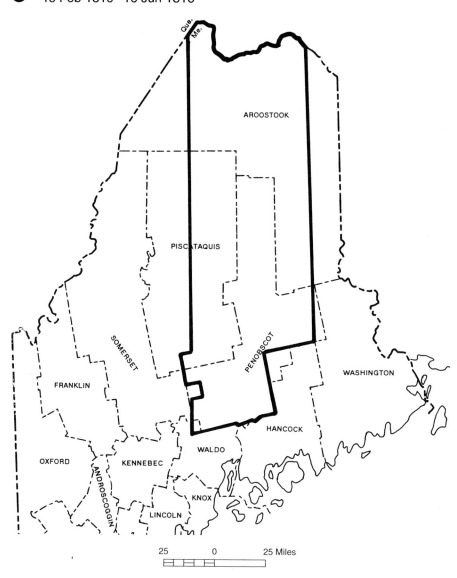

Chronology of PENOBSCOT (created by Mass.)

Map	Date	Event	Resulting Area
❷	17 Jun 1816	Gained from HANCOCK when town of Hampden gained from Frankfurt and Orrington gained from Buckstown [For configuration of entire county, see map 2 and northern part of map 1.]	10,240 sq mi

(Heavy line depicts historical boundary. Base map shows present-day information.)

❷ Southern PENOBSCOT
17 Jun 1816 – 13 Jun 1817

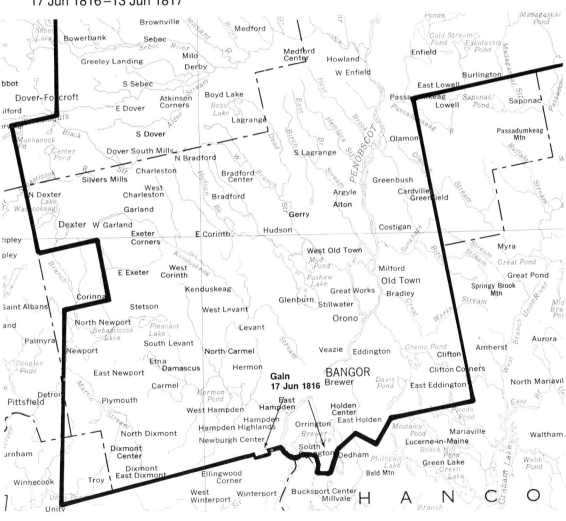

Chronology of PENOBSCOT (created by Mass.)

Map	Date	Event	Resulting Area
❸	14 Jun 1817	Gained from SOMERSET [For configuration of entire county, see map 3 and northern part of map 1.]	10,280 sq mi
	15 Mar 1820	Separated from Massachusetts when Maine became a state	

(Heavy line depicts historical boundary. Base map shows present-day information.)

❸ Southern PENOBSCOT
14 Jun 1817– 2 Jul 1827

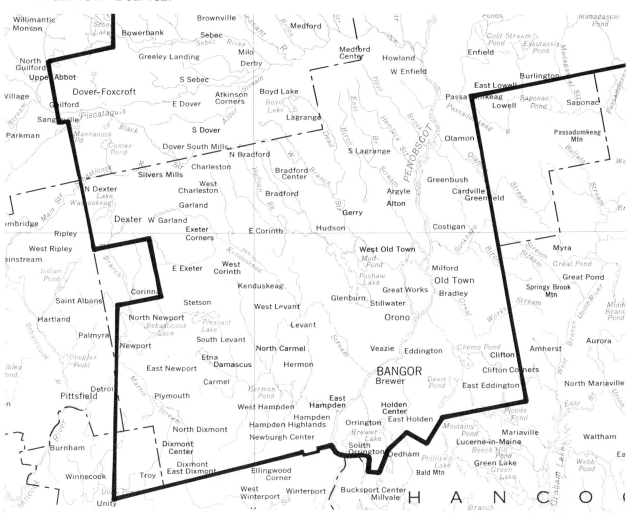

10   0   10   20   30   40 Miles

Chronology of PENOBSCOT (created by Mass.)

Map	Date	Event	Resulting Area
❹	3 Jul 1827	Lost to creation of WALDO [For configuration of entire county, see map 4 and northern part of map 1.]	10,250 sq mi

(Heavy line depicts historical boundary. Base map shows present-day information.)

❹   Southern PENOBSCOT
3 Jul 1827–14 Mar 1831

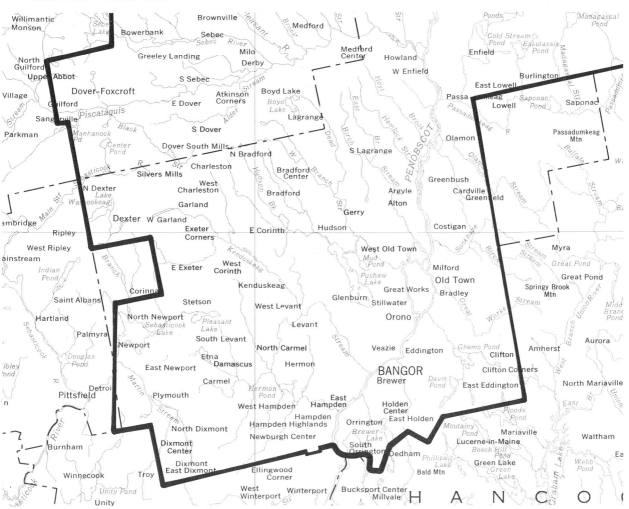

| 10 | | 0 | | 10 | | 20 | | 30 | | 40 Miles |

Chronology of PENOBSCOT (created by Mass.)

Map	Date	Event	Resulting Area
❺	15 Mar 1831	Gained from WASHINGTON	10,560 sq mi

(Heavy line depicts historical boundary. Base map shows present-day information.)

❺   15 Mar 1831– 9 Feb 1833

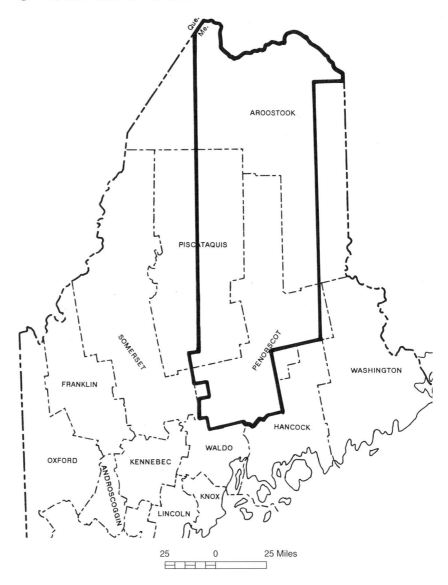

Chronology of PENOBSCOT (created by Mass.)

Map	Date	Event	Resulting Area
❻	10 Feb 1833	Gained from SOMERSET [For configuration of entire county, see map 6 and northern part of map 5.]	10,590 sq mi

(Heavy line depicts historical boundary. Base map shows present-day information.)

❻ Southern PENOBSCOT
10 Feb 1833 – 9 Mar 1835

Chronology of PENOBSCOT (created by Mass.)

Map	Date	Event	Resulting Area
❼	10 Mar 1835	Gained from HANCOCK [For configuration of entire county, see map 7 and northern part of map 5.]	10,600 sq mi

(Heavy line depicts historical boundary. Base map shows present-day information.)

❼ Southern PENOBSCOT
10 Mar 1835 – 29 Apr 1838

| 10 | 0 | 10 | 20 | 30 | 40 Miles |

Chronology of PENOBSCOT (created by Mass.)

Map	Date	Event	Resulting Area
❽	30 Apr 1838	Lost to creation of PISCATAQUIS	6,850 sq mi

(Heavy line depicts historical boundary. Base map shows present-day information.)

❽   30 Apr 1838 – 30 Apr 1839

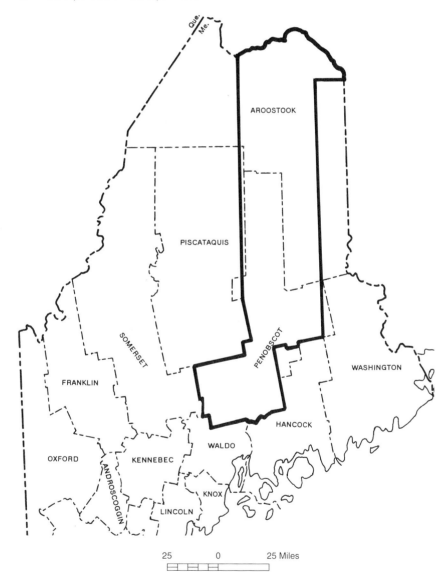

25   0   25 Miles

Chronology of PENOBSCOT (created by Mass.)

Map	Date	Event	Resulting Area
❾	1 May 1839	Lost to creation of AROOSTOOK	4,670 sq mi

(Heavy line depicts historical boundary. Base map shows present-day information.)

❾ 1 May 1839–19 Feb 1841

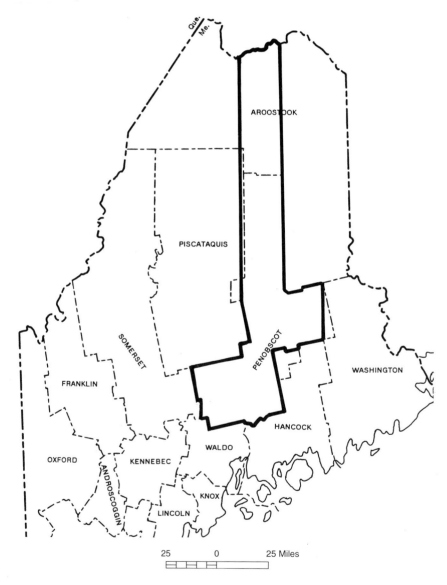

25   0   25 Miles

Chronology of PENOBSCOT (created by Mass.)

Map	Date	Event	Resulting Area
⑩	20 Feb 1841	Gained from HANCOCK when town of Lowell gained from Page's Mill Settlement [For configuration of entire county, see map 10 and northern part of map 9.]	4,680 sq mi
⑩	10 Apr 1841	Gained small area from HANCOCK when town of Brewer gained from Bucksport and Dedham [For configuration of entire county, see map 10 and northern part of map 9.]	4,680 sq mi
	9 Aug 1842	Webster–Ashburton Treaty between Great Britain and the United States settled the U.S.–Canadian boundary, fixing northern limits of PENOBSCOT [no change]	

(Heavy line depicts historical boundary. Base map shows present-day information.)

⑩ Southern PENOBSCOT
20 Feb 1841– 20 Mar 1843

Chronology of PENOBSCOT (created by Mass.)

Map	Date	Event	Resulting Area
⑪	21 Mar 1843	Lost to AROOSTOOK	3,460 sq mi

(Heavy line depicts historical boundary. Base map shows present-day information.)

⑪   21 Mar 1843 – 28 Feb 1844

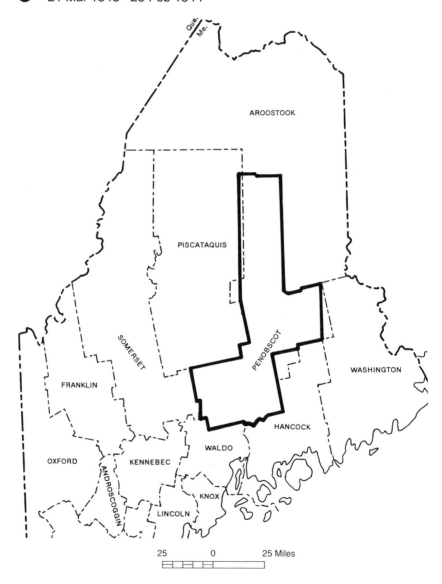

Chronology of PENOBSCOT (created by Mass.)

Map	Date	Event	Resulting Area
⑫ by 29 Feb 1844		Exchanged with SOMERSET, putting line along town boundaries [For configuration of entire county, see map 12 and northern part of map 11.]	3,460 sq mi

(Heavy line depicts historical boundary. Base map shows present-day information.)

⑫   Southern PENOBSCOT
by 29 Feb 1844 – 14 Mar 1858

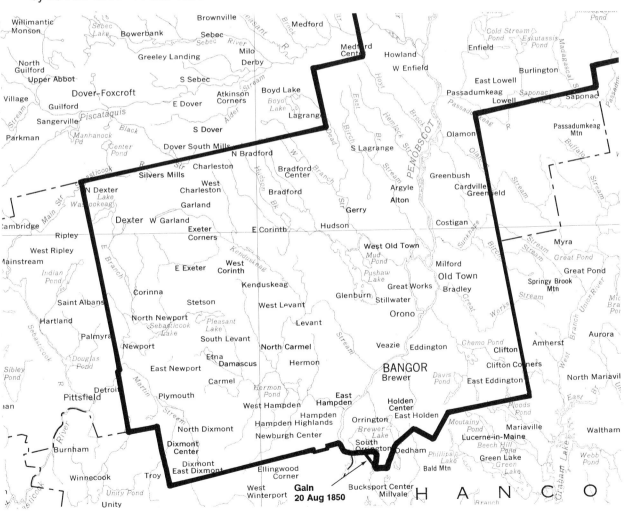

Chronology of PENOBSCOT (created by Mass.)

Map	Date	Event	Resulting Area
⑬	12 Mar 1844	Gained from WASHINGTON and exchanged with PISCATAQUIS [For full-scale details of northern and central parts, see maps 14 and 15.]	3,390 sq mi
⑭	12 Mar 1844	[Full-scale map of *northern part*; for configuration of entire county, see map 13; for further details, see also map 15.]	

(Heavy line depicts historical boundary. Base map shows present-day information.)

⑬ 12 Mar 1844 – 19 Aug 1850

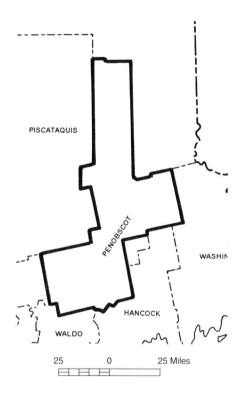

⑭ Northern PENOBSCOT
12 Mar 1844 – present

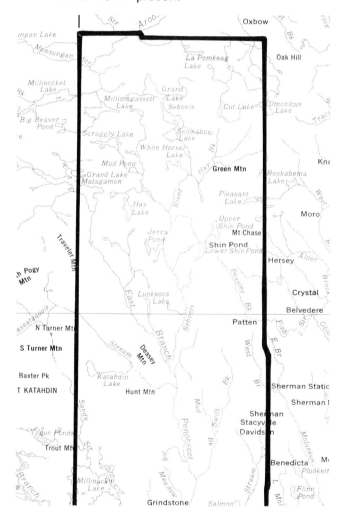

Chronology of PENOBSCOT (created by Mass.)

Map	Date	Event	Resulting Area
⑮	12 Mar 1844	[Full-scale map of *central part;* for configuration of entire county, see map 13; for further details, see also map 14.]	
⑫	20 Aug 1850	Gained from HANCOCK when town of Orrington gained from Bucksport [For configuration of entire county, see maps 12, 14, and 15.]	3,390 sq mi

(Heavy line depicts historical boundary. Base map shows present-day information.)

⑮   Central PENOBSCOT
12 Mar 1844 – 4 Mar 1889
28 Mar 1903 – present

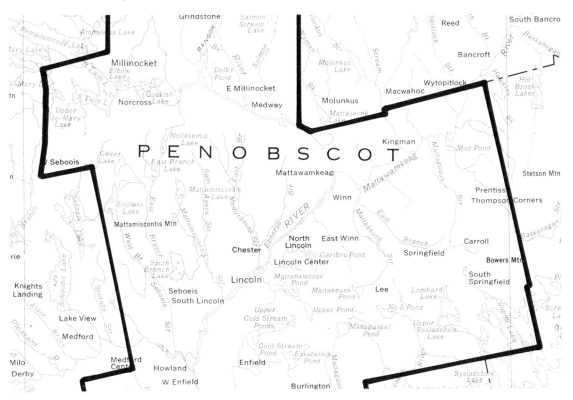

Chronology of PENOBSCOT (created by Mass.)

Map	Date	Event	Resulting Area
⑯	15 Mar 1858	Gained from HANCOCK [For configuration of entire county, see maps 14, 15, and 16.]	3,400 sq mi

(Heavy line depicts historical boundary. Base map shows present-day information.)

⑯ Southern PENOBSCOT
15 Mar 1858 – present

Chronology of PENOBSCOT (created by Mass.)

Map	Date	Event	Resulting Area
⑰	5 Mar 1889	Lost to AROOSTOOK when Reed Plantation gained from Drew Plantation [For configuration of entire county, see maps 14, 16, and 17.]	3,390 sq mi
⑮	28 Mar 1903	Gained from AROOSTOOK when Drew Plantation gained from Reed Plantation [For configuration of entire county, see maps 14, 15, and 16.]	3,400 sq mi

(Heavy line depicts historical boundary. Base map shows present-day information.)

⑰ Central PENOBSCOT
5 Mar 1889 – 27 Mar 1903

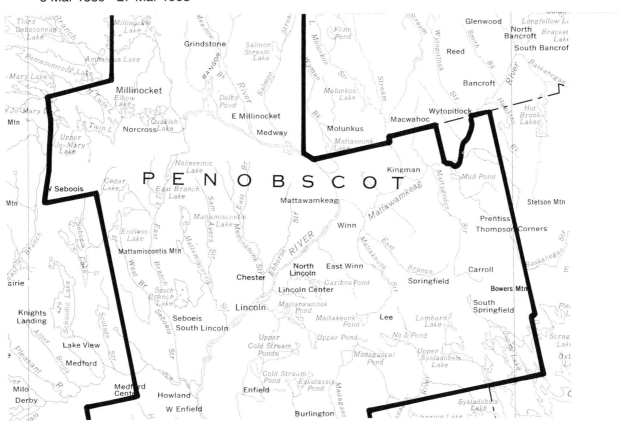

| 10 | 0 | 10 | 20 | 30 | 40 Miles |

Chronology of PISCATAQUIS

Map	Date	Event	Resulting Area
❶	30 Apr 1838	Created from SOMERSET and PENOBSCOT	6,340 sq mi
	9 Aug 1842	Webster–Ashburton Treaty between Great Britain and the United States settled the U.S.–Canadian boundary, fixing northern limits of PISCATAQUIS [no change]	
❷	12 Mar 1844	Exchanged with AROOSTOOK and PENOBSCOT, lost to SOMERSET [For full-scale details, see maps 3 and 4.]	4,500 sq mi

(Heavy line depicts historical boundary. Base map shows present-day information.)

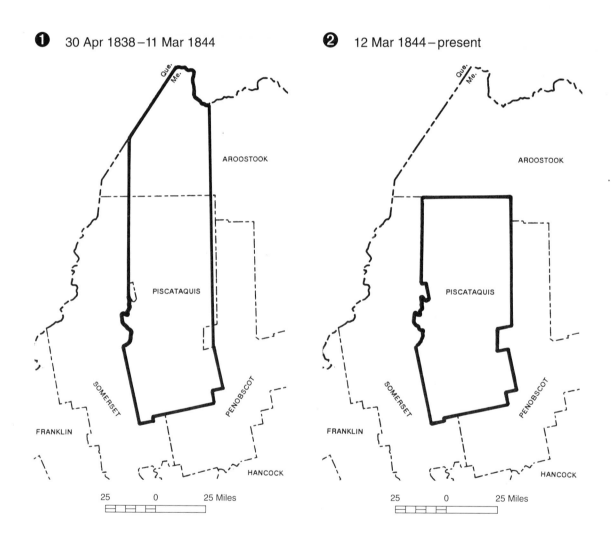

❶ 30 Apr 1838 – 11 Mar 1844

❷ 12 Mar 1844 – present

Chronology of PISCATAQUIS

Map	Date	Event	Resulting Area
❸	12 Mar 1844	[Full-scale map of *northern part*; for configuration of entire county, see map 2; for further details, see also map 4.]	

(Heavy line depicts historical boundary. Base map shows present-day information.)

❸ Northern PISCATAQUIS
12 Mar 1844 – present

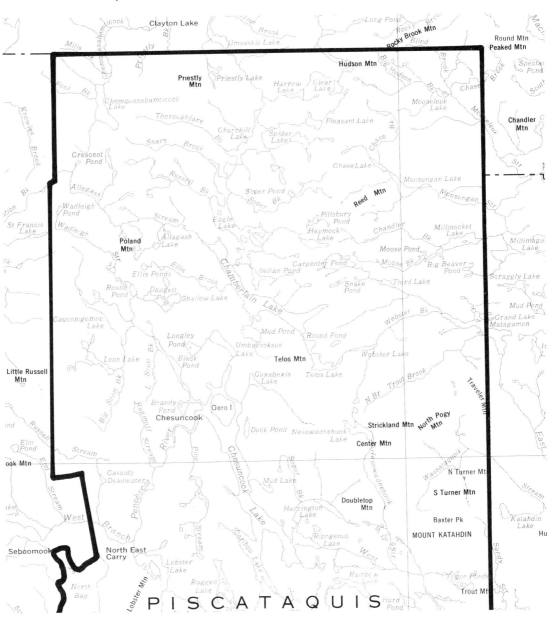

Chronology of PISCATAQUIS

Map	Date	Event	Resulting Area
❹	12 Mar 1844	[Full-scale map of *southern part*; for configuration of entire county, see map 2; for further details, see also map 3.]	
	13 Mar 1883	Boundary with SOMERSET redefined [no change]	
❹	27 Feb 1885	Lost small area to SOMERSET when town of Cambridge gained from Wellington [For configuration of entire county, see maps 3 and 4.]	4,500 sq mi

(Heavy line depicts historical boundary. Base map shows present-day information.)

❹ Southern PISCATAQUIS
12 Mar 1844–present

Chronology of SAGADAHOC

Map	Date	Event	Resulting Area
❶	4 Apr 1854	Created from LINCOLN	300 sq mi
❷	5 Feb 1891	Lost a few islands to CUMBERLAND	300 sq mi
	28 Mar 1903	Boundary with CUMBERLAND redefined [no change]	
	15 Mar 1905	Boundary with CUMBERLAND redefined [no change]	
	19 Mar 1917	Boundary with CUMBERLAND redefined [no change]	

(Heavy line depicts historical boundary. Base map shows present-day information.)

❶ 4 Apr 1854 – 4 Feb 1891

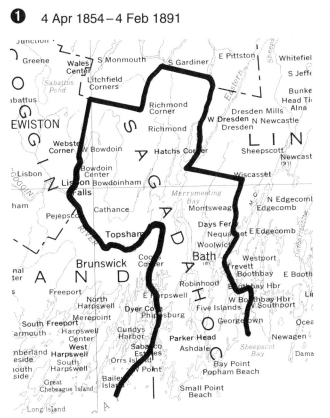

❷ 5 Feb 1891 – present

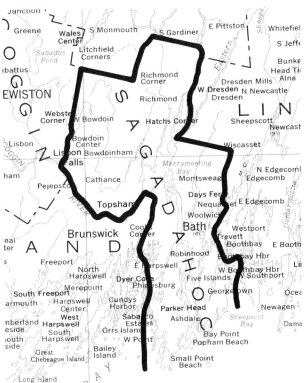

Chronology of SOMERSET (created by Mass.)

Map	Date	Event	Resulting Area
❶	1 Jun 1809	Created by Massachusetts from KENNEBEC	6,720 sq mi

(Heavy line depicts historical boundary. Base map shows present-day information.)

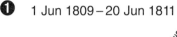

❶   1 Jun 1809 – 20 Jun 1811

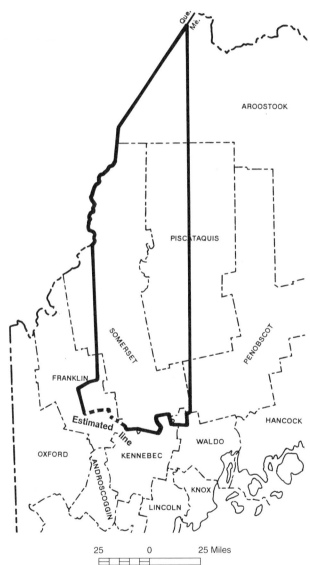

25   0   25 Miles

Chronology of SOMERSET (created by Mass.)

Map	Date	Event	Resulting Area
❷	21 Jun 1811	Lost to HANCOCK [For configuration of entire county, see map 2 and northern part of map 1.]	6,700 sq mi

(Heavy line depicts historical boundary. Base map shows present-day information.)

❷   Southern SOMERSET
21 Jun 1811–11 Jun 1812

[map of southern Somerset County, Maine showing towns, mountains, lakes, rivers, and historical boundary lines]

Scale: 10   0   10   20   30   40 Miles

Chronology of SOMERSET (created by Mass.)

Map	Date	Event	Resulting Area
❸	12 Jun 1812	Lost to HANCOCK [For configuration of entire county, see map 3 and northern part of map 1.]	6,680 sq mi

(Heavy line depicts historical boundary. Base map shows present-day information.)

❸ Southern SOMERSET
12 Jun 1812 – 15 Feb 1813

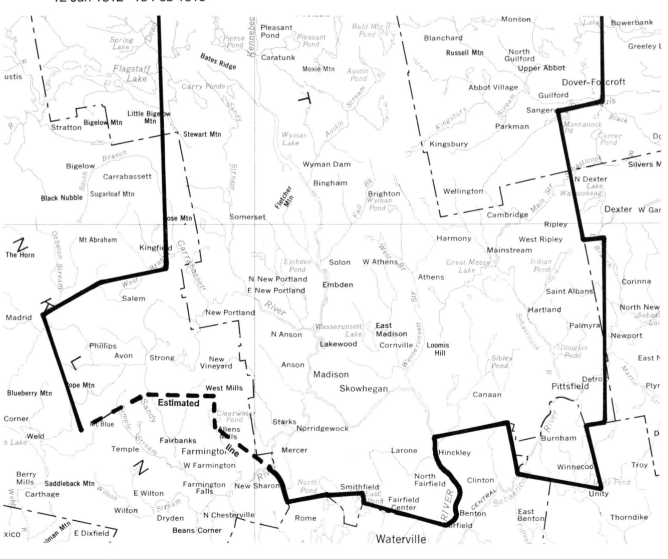

Chronology of SOMERSET (created by Mass.)

Map	Date	Event	Resulting Area
❹	16 Feb 1813	Gained from HANCOCK [For configuration of entire county, see map 4 and northern part of map 1.]	6,700 sq mi

(Heavy line depicts historical boundary. Base map shows present-day information.)

❹ Southern SOMERSET
16 Feb 1813–25 Feb 1813

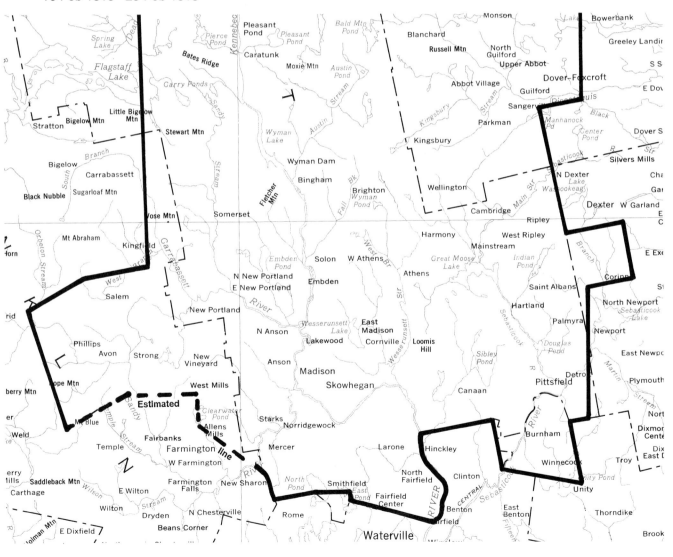

Chronology of SOMERSET (created by Mass.)

Map	Date	Event	Resulting Area
❺	26 Feb 1813	Lost to KENNEBEC [For configuration of entire county, see map 5 and northern part of map 1.]	6,670 sq mi

(Heavy line depicts historical boundary. Base map shows present-day information.)

❺   Southern SOMERSET
26 Feb 1813–13 Jun 1817

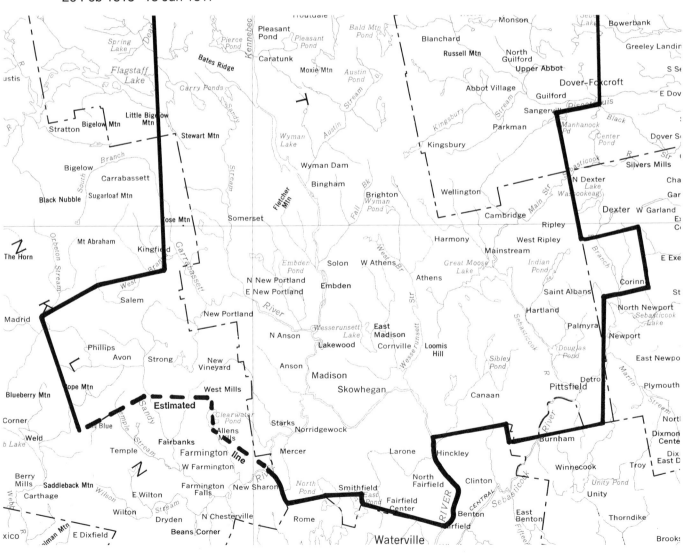

| 10 | 0 | 10 | 20 | 30 | 40 Miles |

Chronology of SOMERSET (created by Mass.)

Map	Date	Event	Resulting Area
❻	14 Jun 1817	Lost to PENOBSCOT [For configuration of entire county, see map 6 and northern part of map 1.]	6,640 sq mi

(Heavy line depicts historical boundary. Base map shows present-day information.)

❻ Southern SOMERSET
14 Jun 1817–1 Feb 1819

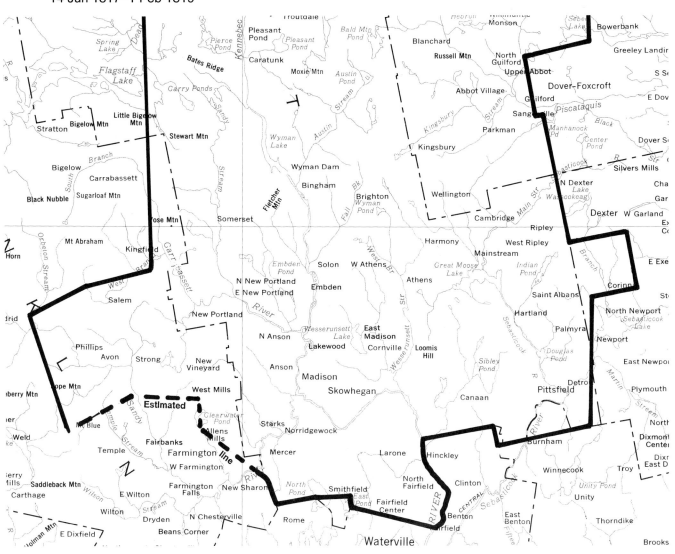

Chronology of SOMERSET (created by Mass.)

Map	Date	Event	Resulting Area
❼	2 Feb 1819	Gained from OXFORD	7,230 sq mi
	15 Mar 1820	Separated from Massachusetts when Maine became a state	

(Heavy line depicts historical boundary. Base map shows present-day information.)

❼   2 Feb 1819–16 Mar 1821

AROOSTOOK

PISCATAQUIS

SOMERSET

FRANKLIN

PENOBSCOT

HANCOCK

Estimated line

WALDO

OXFORD

KENNEBEC

ANDROSCOGGIN

KNOX

LINCOLN

25   0   25 Miles

Chronology of SOMERSET (created by Mass.)

Map	Date	Event	Resulting Area
❽	17 Mar 1821	Lost to KENNEBEC [For configuration of entire county, see map 8 and northern part of map 7.]	7,220 sq mi

(Heavy line depicts historical boundary. Base map shows present-day information.)

❽   Southern SOMERSET
17 Mar 1821 – 30 Jan 1823
6 Mar 1830 – 9 Feb 1833

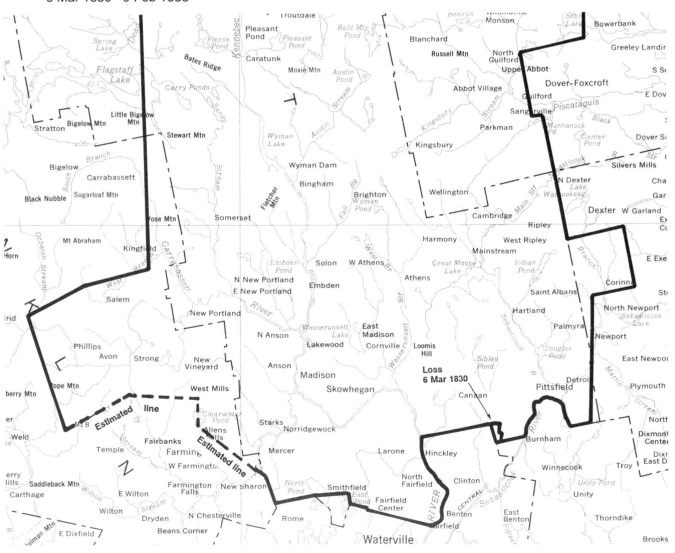

Chronology of SOMERSET (created by Mass.)

Map	Date	Event	Resulting Area
9	31 Jan 1823	Gained from OXFORD	7,680 sq mi
8	6 Mar 1830	Lost to KENNEBEC [For configuration of entire county, see map 8 and northern part of map 9.]	7,220 sq mi

(Heavy line depicts historical boundary. Base map shows present-day information.)

9 31 Jan 1823 – 5 Mar 1830

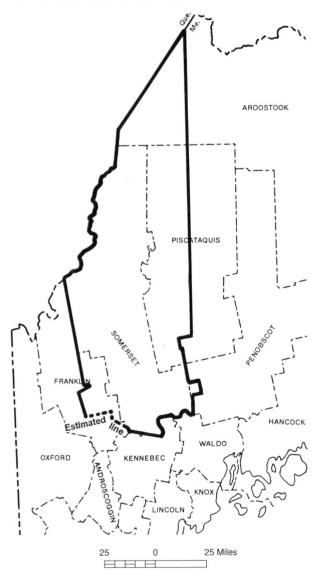

Chronology of SOMERSET (created by Mass.)

Map	Date	Event	Resulting Area
⑩	10 Feb 1833	Lost to PENOBSCOT [For configuration of entire county, see map 10 and northern part of map 9.]	7,760 sq mi

(Heavy line depicts historical boundary. Base map shows present-day information.)

⑩   Southern SOMERSET
10 Feb 1833 – 29 Apr 1838

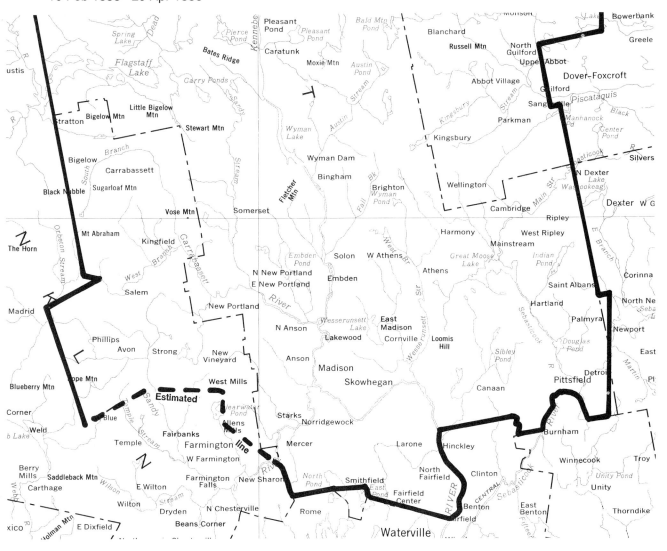

Chronology of SOMERSET (created by Mass.)

Map	Date	Event	Resulting Area
⑪	30 Apr 1838	Lost to creation of PISCATAQUIS	4,740 sq mi
⑫	9 May 1838	Lost to creation of FRANKLIN [For full-scale detail of central part of county, see map 13.]	4,420 sq mi

(Heavy line depicts historical boundary. Base map shows present-day information.)

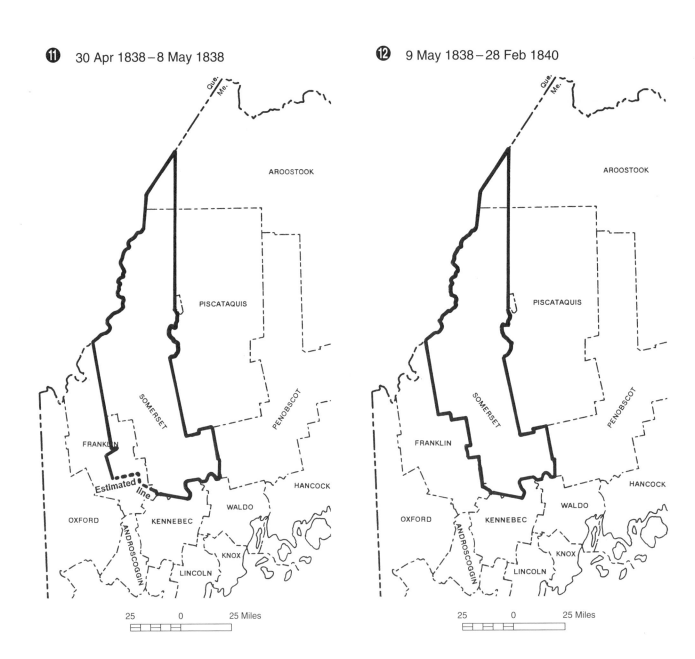

⑪ 30 Apr 1838 – 8 May 1838

⑫ 9 May 1838 – 28 Feb 1840

Chronology of SOMERSET (created by Mass.)

Map	Date	Event	Resulting Area
⓭	9 May 1838	[Full-scale map of *central part*; for configuration of entire county, see map 12.]	

(Heavy line depicts historical boundary. Base map shows present-day information.)

⓭ Central SOMERSET
9 May 1838 – present

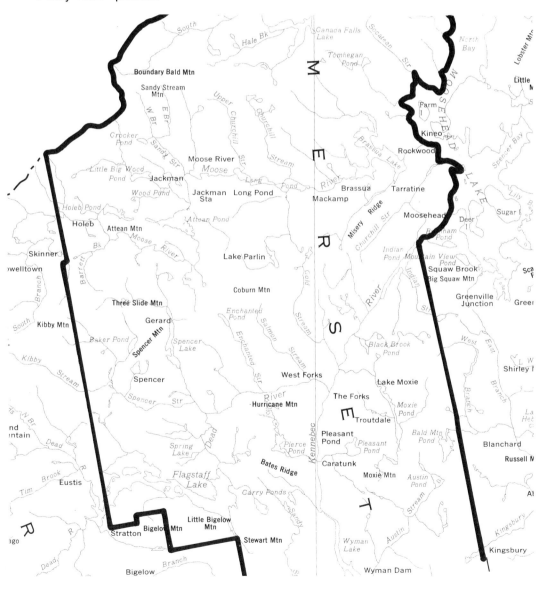

| 10 | 0 | 10 | 20 | 30 | 40 Miles |

Chronology of SOMERSET (created by Mass.)

Map	Date	Event	Resulting Area
⑭	29 Feb 1840	Gained from KENNEBEC [For configuration of entire county, see maps 13 and 14 and northern part of map 12.]	4,420 sq mi
⑭	18 Mar 1840	Gained small area from FRANKLIN when town of Anson gained from New Vineyard [For configuration of entire county, see maps 13 and 14 and northern part of map 12.]	4,420 sq mi
⑭	6 Apr 1841	Lost to FRANKLIN when town of New Sharon gained from Mercer [For configuration of entire county, see maps 13 and 14 and northern part of map 12.]	4,410 sq mi
	9 Aug 1842	Webster–Ashburton Treaty between Great Britain and the United States settled the U.S.– Canadian boundary, fixing northern limits of SOMERSET [no change]	

(Heavy line depicts historical boundary. Base map shows present-day information.)

⑭ Southern SOMERSET
29 Feb 1840 – 28 Feb 1844

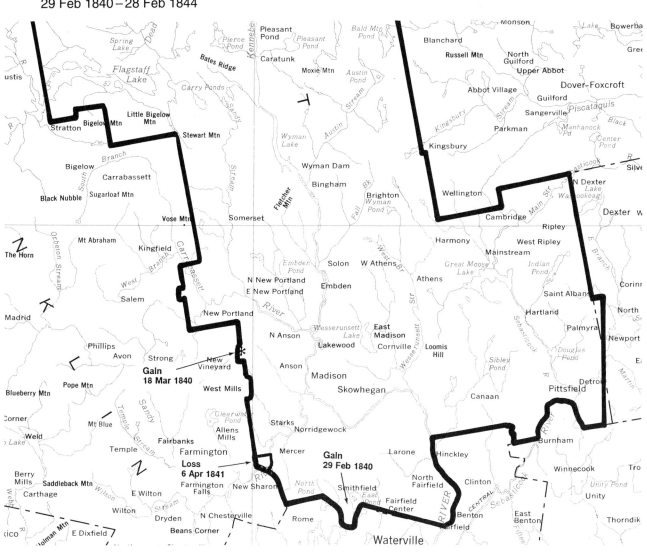

Chronology of SOMERSET (created by Mass.)

Map	Date	Event	Resulting Area
⑮	by 29 Feb 1844	Exchanged with PENOBSCOT, putting southeastern segment of line along town boundaries [For configuration of entire county, see maps 13 and 15 and northern part of map 12.]	4,410 sq mi

(Heavy line depicts historical boundary. Base map shows present-day information.)

⑮ Southern SOMERSET
by 29 Feb 1844 – present

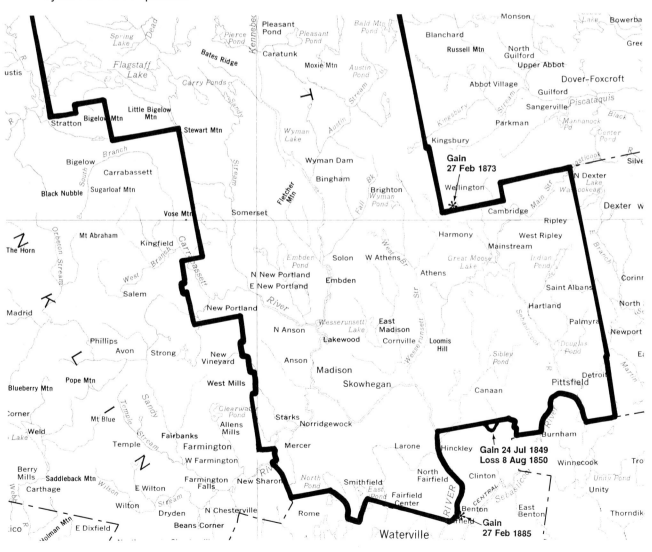

Chronology of SOMERSET (created by Mass.)

Map	Date	Event	Resulting Area
⑯	12 Mar 1844	Gained from PISCATAQUIS, lost to AROOSTOOK [For configuration of entire county, see maps 13, 15, and 16.]	4,200 sq mi
⑮	24 Jul 1849	Gained from KENNEBEC when town of Canaan gained from Clinton [For configuration of entire county, see maps 13, 15, and 16.]	4,200 sq mi
⑮	8 Aug 1850	Lost to KENNEBEC when town of Clinton gained from Canaan [For configuration of entire county, see maps 13, 15, and 16.]	4,200 sq mi
⑮	27 Feb 1873	Gained small area from KENNEBEC when town of Fairfield gained from Benton [For configuration of entire county, see maps 13, 15, and 16.]	4,200 sq mi
	13 Mar 1883	Boundary with PISCATAQUIS redefined [no change]	
⑮	27 Feb 1885	Gained small area from PISCATAQUIS when town of Cambridge gained from Wellington [For configuration of entire county, see maps 13, 15, and 16.]	4,200 sq mi

(Heavy line depicts historical boundary. Base map shows present-day information.)

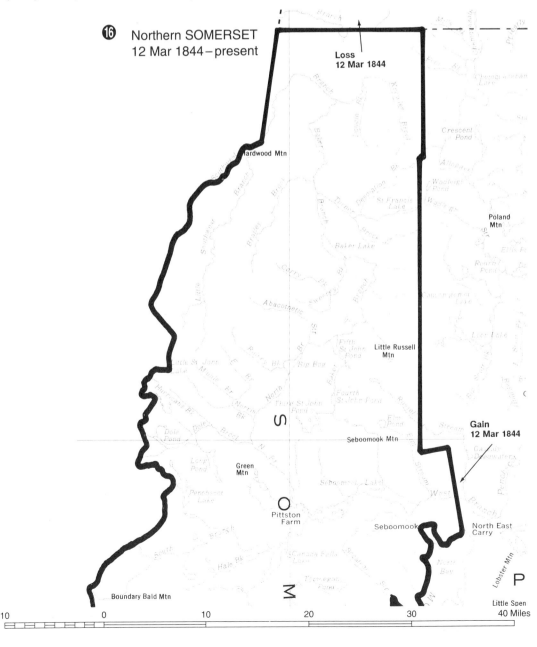

⑯ Northern SOMERSET
12 Mar 1844 – present

Chronology of WALDO

Map	Date	Event	Resulting Area
❶	3 Jul 1827	Created from HANCOCK, KENNEBEC, and LINCOLN	880 sq mi
❶	10 Feb 1836	Gained small area from LINCOLN when town of Camden gained from Warren	880 sq mi

(Heavy line depicts historical boundary. Base map shows present-day information.)

❶   3 Jul 1827–14 Mar 1838

Pittsfield
Detroit
Canaan
Plymouth
Carmel
Brewe
East
Hampden
West Hampden
Hold
Cent
Eas
Hampden
Hampden Highlands
Orrington
North Dixmont
Newburgh Center
Burnham
Dixmont
Center
Dixmont
East Dixmont
Ellingwood
Corner
South
Orrington
De
Winnecook
Troy
Clinton
West
Winterport
Winterport
Bucksport Cent
Millvale
enton
East
Benton
Unity
Jackson
Monroe
Frankfort
Mt Waldo
Prospe
Ferr
Orla
Buocksport
Thorndike
Swan
Lake
Prospect
Albion
Freedom
Brooks
Prospect
N Searsport
North
Penot
East Knox
Waldo
Swanville   Sandy Point
salboro
China
W
Frye Mtn
A
L
D
O
Stockton Springs
West
Penobsc
North Palermo
City
Point
Searsport
Searspo
Sta
boro
Center
Montville
Morrill
Belfast
North C
C
Palermo
McFarlands
Corner
North
Searsmont
West
Brooksville
North
Brool
S China
Liberty
Belmont
Corner
E Northport
Bayside
Castine
eeks Mills
Searsmont
Prip t
Islesboro
Island
Harborside
South
Brooksville
Windsor
Somerville
South Liberty
Northport
North
Islesboro
Cape
Rosier
Eggemoggin
Burkettville
Lincolnville
Center
Ducktrap
Islesboro
Eggemoggin
Sarge
Razorville
Appleton
Lincolnville
Washington
West Washington
Hope
Dark Harbor
PENOBSCOT
Ils
Stickney Corne
Bald
Mtn
South Hope
itefield
East
Union
BAY
Deer
Jefferson
Union
Sout
West Ro
Camden
Rockport
Sunset
South Dee
ield
North
Waldoboro
N Haven
Island
fferson
Rockvil
ker Hill
Tide
Winslows
Mills
Rockland
Glen Cove
North Haven
Warren
GaIn
10 Feb 1836
Owls Head
Vinalhaven
Island
Isle au
Waldoboro
Nobleboro
C   O   L   N
Damariscotta
Mills
South
Waldoboro
South Warren
North
Cushing
Thomaston
Ash Point
Vinalhaven
Ba
stle
Damariscotta
Turners
Corner
Cushing
East
Friendship
Saint George
South
Thomaston
K
Spruce Head
N
O
X

| 10 | 0 | 10 | 20 | 30 | 40 Miles |

Chronology of WALDO

Map	Date	Event	Resulting Area
❷	15 Mar 1838	Gained N. Haven I. and Vinalhaven I. from HANCOCK	920 sq mi
	11 Apr 1854	Lost small area to LINCOLN when town of Washington gained from Palermo to accommodate local property owners [location unknown, not mapped]	

(Heavy line depicts historical boundary. Base map shows present-day information.)

❷   15 Mar 1838 – 31 Mar 1860

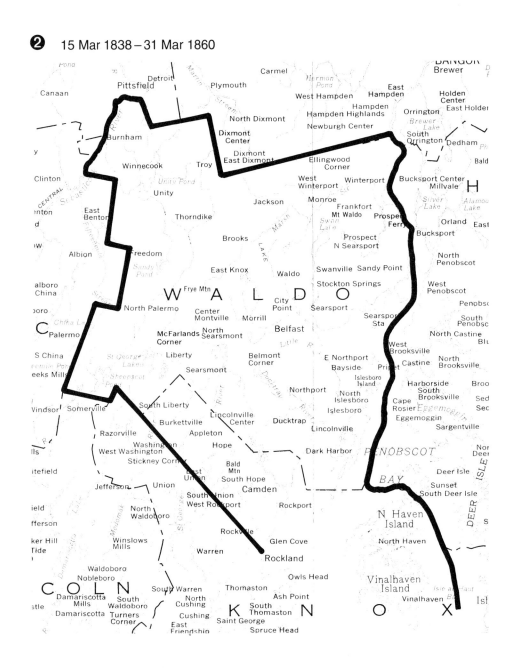

Chronology of WALDO

Map	Date	Event	Resulting Area
❸	1 Apr 1860	Lost to creation to KNOX	780 sq mi

(Heavy line depicts historical boundary. Base map shows present-day information.)

❸ 1 Apr 1860 – 25 Feb 1873

Chronology of WALDO

Map	Date	Event	Resulting Area
❹	26 Feb 1873	Gained from KENNEBEC when town of Burnham gained from Clinton Gore Plantation	780 sq mi

(Heavy line depicts historical boundary. Base map shows present-day information.)

❹   26 Feb 1873–present

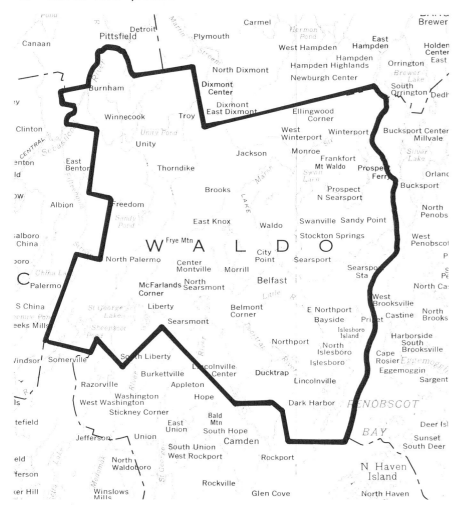

Chronology of WASHINGTON (created by Mass.)

Map	Date	Event	Resulting Area
❶	.1 May 1790	Created by Massachusetts from LINCOLN	3,840 sq mi
	24 Nov 1817	Gained islands in Pasamaquoddy Bay: Mouse, Dudley (now Trent), and Frederick (now Dudley) [no mappable change]	
	15 Mar 1820	Separated from Massachusetts when Maine became a state	
❷	15 Mar 1831	Lost to PENOBSCOT	3,780 sq mi

(Heavy line depicts historical boundary. Base map shows present-day information.)

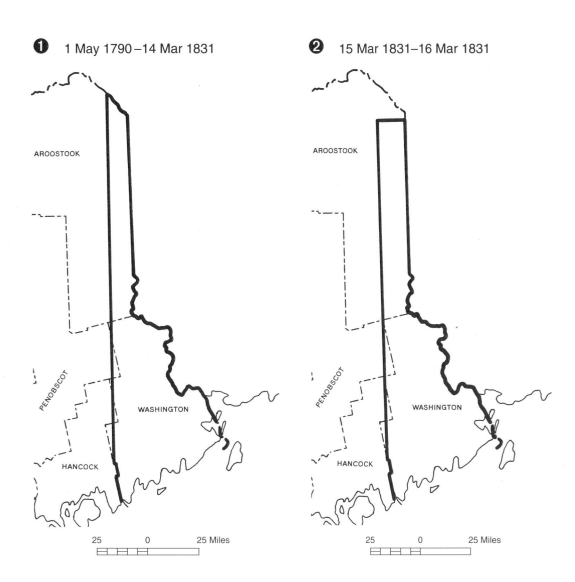

❶ 1 May 1790–14 Mar 1831

❷ 15 Mar 1831–16 Mar 1831

Chronology of WASHINGTON (created by Mass.)

Map	Date	Event	Resulting Area
❸	17 Mar 1831	Exchanged with HANCOCK [For configuration of entire county, see map 3 and northern part of map 2.]	3,780 sq mi

(Heavy line depicts historical boundary. Base map shows present-day information.)

❸ Southern WASHINGTON
17 Mar 1831–present

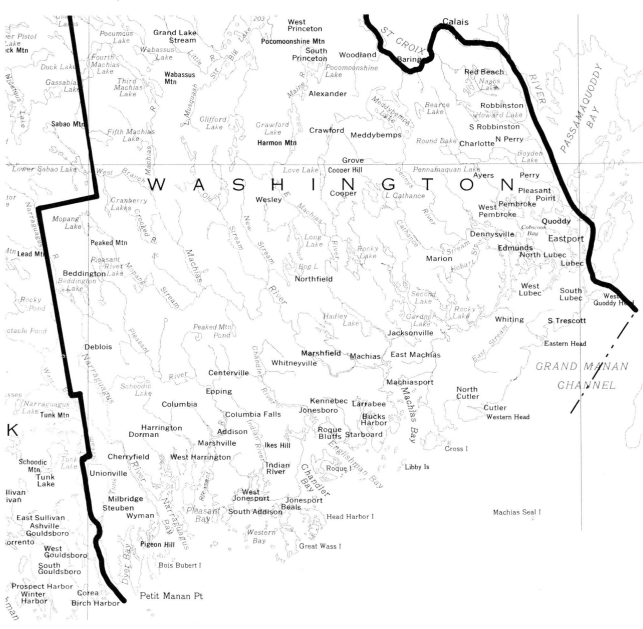

| 10 | | 0 | | 10 | | 20 | | 30 | | 40 Miles |

Chronology of WASHINGTON (created by Mass.)

Map	Date	Event	Resulting Area
❹	1 May 1839	Lost to creation of AROOSTOOK	2,880 sq mi
❺	12 Mar 1844	Part of boundary with HANCOCK clarified [no change]; lost to PENOBSCOT	2,800 sq mi

(Heavy line depicts historical boundary. Base map shows present-day information.)

❹ 1 May 1839 – 11 Mar 1844

25   0   25 Miles

❺ 12 Mar 1844 – 3 Mar 1885

25   0   25 Miles

Chronology of WASHINGTON (created by Mass.)

Map	Date	Event	Resulting Area
❻	4 Mar 1885	Gained from AROOSTOOK when town of Danforth gained from Weston [For configuration of entire county, see maps 3 and 6.]	2,800 sq mi

(Heavy line depicts historical boundary. Base map shows present-day information.)

❻ Northern WASHINGTON
4 Mar 1885–present

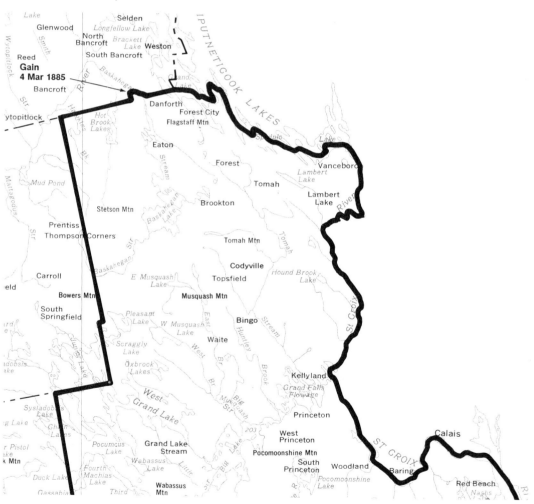

| 10 | 0 | 10 | 20 | 30 | 40 Miles |

Chronology of YORK (created by Mass.)

Map	Date	Event	Resulting Area
❶	20 Nov 1652	Created by Massachusetts as YORKSHIRE	Indefinite
	Nov 1664	YORKSHIRE went into abeyance	
❶	27 May 1668	YORK (formerly called YORKSHIRE) reinstated by Massachusetts	
	17 Mar 1679/1680	Eliminated when Massachusetts organized a new government for Maine	
❶	7 Oct 1691	Reinstated under new Massachusetts charter	

(Heavy line depicts historical boundary. Base map shows present-day information.)

❶ 20 Nov 1652 – Nov 1664
27 May 1668 – 16 Mar 1679/1680
7 Oct 1691 – 25 Jun 1716

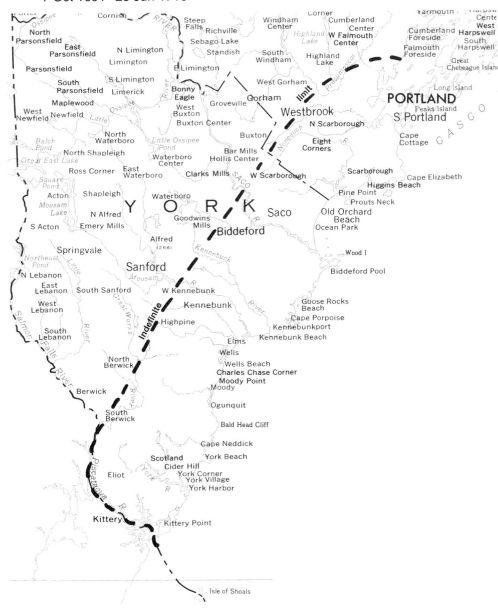

Chronology of YORK (created by Mass.)

Map	Date	Event	Resulting Area
❷	26 Jun 1716	Gained all Massachusetts territory between Kennebec and St. Croix rivers	Indefinite
	12 Apr 1753	Jurisdiction clarified [no change]	
❸	1 Nov 1760	Lost to creation of CUMBERLAND and LINCOLN	2,400 sq mi

(Heavy line depicts historical boundary. Base map shows present-day information.)

❷   26 Jun 1716 – 31 Oct 1760

❸   1 Nov 1760 – 6 Oct 1763

Chronology of YORK (created by Mass.)

Map	Date	Event	Resulting Area
❹	7 Oct 1763	Extended northward to Atlantic watershed	2,940 sq mi
❺	3 Mar 1786	Lost to CUMBERLAND	2,910 sq mi

(Heavy line depicts historical boundary. Base map shows present-day information.)

❹ 7 Oct 1763 – 2 Mar 1786

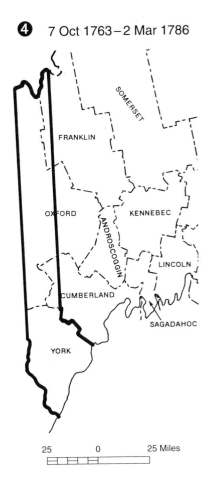

❺ 3 Mar 1786 – 3 Mar 1805

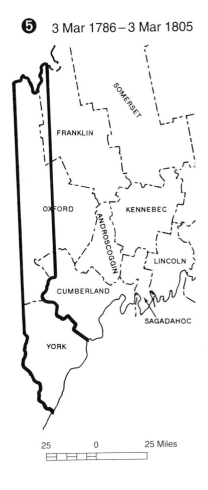

Chronology of YORK (created by Mass.)

Map	Date	Event	Resulting Area
❻	4 Mar 1805	Lost to creation of OXFORD	1,050 sq mi
	15 Mar 1820	Separated from Massachusetts when Maine became a state	

(Heavy line depicts historical boundary. Base map shows present-day information.)

❻   4 Mar 1805 – 16 Feb 1824

10   0   10   20   30   40 Miles

Chronology of YORK (created by Mass.)

Map	Date	Event	Resulting Area
❼	17 Feb 1824	Lost to CUMBERLAND	1,040 sq mi
	27 Mar 1841	Gained small area from CUMBERLAND when town of Saco gained from Scarborough [location unknown, not mapped]	

(Heavy line depicts historical boundary. Base map shows present-day information.)

❼   17 Feb 1824 – present

| 10 | 0 | 10 | 20 | 30 | 40 Miles |

Colonial, State, and Federal Censuses in Maine

Date	Census
1764–1765	Colonial census. Statistics for CUMBERLAND, LINCOLN, and YORK (Benton; Greene and Harrington, 21–30); no names.
20 Aug 1771	Tax list. No statistics; some names (Pruitt).
20 Mar 1776	Colonial census. Statistics (Felt, 157–165; Greene and Harrington, 31–40); some names at Massachusetts State Archives, Boston.
1784	Poll list. Statistics (Felt, 166–170; Greene and Harrington, 40–46); no names.
2 Aug 1790	Federal census. Statistics and names.
1798	Direct tax of 1798. No statistics; names at New England Historic Genealogical Society, Boston.
4 Aug 1800	Federal census. Statistics and names.
6 Aug 1810	Federal census. Statistics and names.
7 Aug 1820	Federal census. Statistics and names.
1 Jun 1830	Federal census. Statistics and names.
1 Mar 1837	State census [not mapped]. No statistics; some names at Maine State Archives, Augusta.
1 Jun 1840	Federal census. Statistics and names.
1 Jun 1850	Federal census. Statistics and names.
1 Jun 1860	Federal census. Statistics and names.
1 Jun 1870	Federal census. Statistics and names.
1 Jun 1880	Federal census. Statistics and names.
2 Jun 1890	Federal census. Statistics; names from special census of Union Veterans only.
1 Jun 1900	Federal census. Statistics and names.
15 Apr 1910	Federal census. Statistics and names.
1 Jan 1920	Federal census. Statistics and names.
1 Apr 1930	Federal census. Statistics; names not available until 2002.
1 Apr 1940	Federal census. Statistics; names not available until 2012.

Date	Census
1 Apr 1950	Federal census. Statistics; names not available until 2022.
1 Apr 1960	Federal census. Statistics; names not available until 2032.
1 Apr 1970	Federal census. Statistics; names not available until 2042.
1 Apr 1980	Federal census. Statistics; names not available until 2052.
1 Apr 1990	Federal census. Statistics; names not available until 2062.

Sources

Benton, J. H., Jr. *Early Census Making in Massachusetts, 1643–1765, with a Reproduction of the Lost Census of 1765 (Recently Found) and Documents Relating Thereto, Now First Collected and Published*. Boston: Charles E. Goodspeed, 1905.

Felt, Joseph B. "Population of Massachusetts." *Collections of the American Statistical Association* 1, pt. 2 (1845): 121–216. No other volumes published.

Greene, Evarts Boutell, and Virginia D. Harrington. *American Population before the Federal Census of 1790*. New York: Columbia University Press, 1932.

Lainhart, Ann S. *State Census Records*. [Baltimore]: Genealogical Publishing Co., 1992.

Pruitt, Bettye Hobbs, ed. *Massachusetts Tax Valuation List of 1771*. Boston: G. K. Hall, 1978.

Wells, Robert V. *Population of the British Colonies in America before 1776: A Survey of Census Data*. Princeton, N.J.: Princeton University Press, 1975.

Census Outline
Maps for Maine

Federal Census 1820

PENOBSCOT

SOMERSET

WASHINGTON

HANCOCK

OXFORD

KENNEBEC

LINCOLN

CUMBERLAND

YORK

25   0   25 Miles

Federal Census 1830

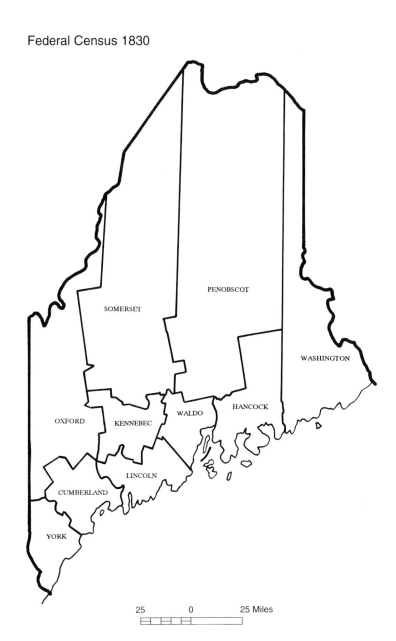

PENOBSCOT

SOMERSET

WASHINGTON

OXFORD

KENNEBEC

WALDO

HANCOCK

LINCOLN

CUMBERLAND

YORK

25   0   25 Miles

Federal Census 1840

AROOSTOOK

PISCATAQUIS

SOMERSET

PENOBSCOT

FRANKLIN

WASHINGTON

OXFORD

KENNEBEC

WALDO

HANCOCK

LINCOLN

CUMBERLAND

YORK

25   0   25 Miles

Federal Census 1850

Federal Censuses 1860–1910

25   0   25 Miles

Federal Censuses 1920–1990

25   0   25 Miles

MASSACHUSETTS

Massachusetts County Creations

County	Source	Dates	
		Authorization	Creation Effective
BARNSTABLE	Ply. Laws, ch. 6/p. 19	2 Jun 1685	same
BERKSHIRE	Mass. Col. Acts, vol. 4, ch. 33/p. 432	21 Apr 1761	30 Jun 1761
BRISTOL	Ply. Laws, ch. 6/p. 19	2 Jun 1685	same
CORNWALL (created by N.Y. in present Me., extinct)	*See* Maine County Creations.		
CUMBERLAND (now in Me.)	*See* Maine County Creations.		
DEVONSHIRE (extinct)	*See* Maine County Creations.		
DUKES (created by N.Y., extinct)	N.Y. Col. Laws, vol. 1, ch. 4/p. 122	1 Nov 1683	same
DUKES	Mass. Col. Acts, vol. 1, ch. 7/p. 216	22 Jun 1695	same
ESSEX	Mass. Recs., 2:38	10 May 1643	same
FRANKLIN	Mass. Acts 1811, ch. 61/p. 467	24 Jun 1811	2 Dec 1811
HAMPDEN	Mass. Acts 1812, ch. 137/p. 291	25 Feb 1812	1 Aug 1812
HAMPSHIRE	Mass. Recs., vol. 4, pt. 2:52	7 May 1662	same
HANCOCK (now in Me.)	*See* Maine County Creations.		
KENNEBEC (now in Me.)	*See* Maine County Creations.		
LINCOLN (now in Me.)	*See* Maine County Creations.		
MIDDLESEX	Mass. Recs., 2:38	10 May 1643	same
NANTUCKET	Mass. Col. Acts, vol. 1, ch. 7/p. 216	22 Jun 1695	same
NORFOLK (original, extinct)	Mass. Recs., 2:38	10 May 1643	same
NORFOLK	Mass. Acts 1793, ch. 43/p. 272	26 Mar 1793	20 Jun 1793
OXFORD (now in Me.)	*See* Maine County Creations.		
PENOBSCOT (now in Me.)	*See* Maine County Creations.		
PLYMOUTH	Ply. Laws, ch. 6/p. 19	2 Jun 1685	same
SOMERSET (now in Me.)	*See* Maine County Creations.		

County	Source	Dates	
		Authorization	Creation Effective
SUFFOLK	Mass. Recs., 2:38	10 May 1643	same
WASHINGTON (now in Me.)	*See* Maine County Creations.		
WORCESTER	Mass. Col. Acts, vol. 2, ch. 8/p. 584	2 Apr 1731	10 Jul 1731
YORK (now in Me.)	*See* Maine County Creations.		

Counties established by Massachusetts beyond its present limits

In Maine (1652–1820)   CUMBERLAND (1760)

DEVONSHIRE (1673)

HANCOCK (1789)

KENNEBEC (1799)

LINCOLN (1760)

OXFORD (1805)

PENOBSCOT (1816)

SOMERSET (1809)

WASHINGTON (1790)

YORK (1652)

Counties established within present Massachusetts by other authorities

By New York (1665–1687)   DUKES (1683)

Consolidated Chronology of Massachusetts State and County Boundaries

10 April 1606

King James I chartered two Virginia companies, head-quartered in different cities, to establish colonies along the coast of North America: the Virginia Company of London, assigned coast between 34 degrees and 41 degrees north latitude; and the Virginia Company of Plymouth, assigned coast between 38 degrees and 45 degrees north latitude, including present Maine and Massachusetts. Colonies of the two companies were to be at least 100 miles apart, even in area of overlapping grants. (Paullin, pl. 42; Swindler, 10:17–23; Van Zandt, 92)

3 November 1620

King James I replaced the charter to the Virginia Company of Plymouth with a charter for a Council for New England to establish colonies in a region between 40 degrees and 48 degrees north latitude and extending from the Atlantic to the Pacific Ocean, including present Maine and Massachusetts. (Swindler, 5:16–26)

25 December 1620

The Pilgrims and other colonists aboard the Mayflower decided to settle at the place that became Plymouth, Massachusetts. Because their land grant was from the Virginia Company of London and they had landed in a region outside the authority of that company, their plantation had no specified or recognized limits and no governmental authority. The Pilgrims acquired a new land patent for their settlement on 1 June 1621. (Andrews, 1:259, 272, 279)

20 August 1622

The Council for New England granted to Ferdinando Gorges and John Mason all land along the Atlantic coast between the Merrimack and Sagadahoc (now Kennebec) rivers, to be called the province of Maine. Covered present eastern New Hampshire and southwestern Maine. (Andrews, 1:334; Swindler, 4:264)

4 March 1628/1629

King Charles I chartered the Massachusetts Bay Company to establish a colony in the territory stretching from three miles north of the Merrimack R. ("to the Northward of any and every Parte thereof") to three miles south of the Charles R. and extending westward from the Atlantic coast to the Pacific Ocean, thereby taking a three-mile wide strip of Maine (area south of the Kennebec R.) north of the Merrimack R. (Andrews, 1:359; Swindler, 5:32–42)

7 November 1629

After Ferdinando Gorges and John Mason divided their 1622 land grant, the Council for New England granted to Mason the territory lying between the Merrimack and Piscataqua rivers and extending up to 60 miles inland from the coast, to be called New Hampshire. Maine, the remainder of the 1622 grant that lay between the Piscataqua and Kennebec rivers, was left to Gorges. (Swindler, 6:304)

13 January 1629/1630

The Council for New England issued a new land patent (the "Old Charter") that granted land title and trading rights, but no powers of government, to New Plymouth colony for the area bounded on the west by Narragansett Bay and on the north by a line from near the Pawtucket (now Blackstone) R. to the mouth of the Cohassett R. (Andrews, 1:295; Paullin, 28, pl. 43A; Swindler, 5:28)

26 June 1630

The Council for New England patented the Province of Lygonia, consisting of a square territory south and west of the Sagadahoc (now Kennebec) R. measuring 40 miles long and 40 miles wide. Overlapped part of Maine (area between the Kennebec and Piscataqua rivers). Patent included "power to make Laws &c". (Farnham, 7:134)

1633

Residents of the town of Exeter and nearby settlements in southern New Hampshire, under the mistaken belief that they were located outside New Hampshire, placed themselves under the jurisdiction of Massachusetts. (Morison and Morison, 12)

7 June 1635

The Council for New England, faced with competition from Massachusetts and less success than expected in managing its own colonies, tried to protect the interests of its principal members, including Ferdinando Gorges (for Me.) and John Mason (for N.H.), by first distributing all its land among them and then, on this date, surrendering its charter to the crown. Members hoped the king would a) confirm the land grants they had made to themselves, b) abrogate the Massachusetts charter, and c) create a new royal colony for all of New England with Gorges as its governor. Technically, this threw all of former New England, outside Massachusetts, under the direct jurisdiction of the crown, but some earlier grants remained effective. (Preston, 305)

3 April 1639

King Charles I granted Maine to Ferdinando Gorges as a proprietary colony. Territory included the area in present western Maine between the Piscataqua and Kennebec rivers inland (up river) 120 miles from the Atlantic coast, plus two islands south of Cape Cod in present Massachusetts, Martha's Vineyard and Nantucket. Thomas Gorges, a distant relative of Ferdinando Gorges, established a government in 1640, and created several "counties" (without specified names or boundaries), and conducted the colony's affairs until annexation by Massachusetts in 1652. (Preston, 321–322, 334, 344; Swindler, 4:269)

9 June 1640

Massachusetts and New Plymouth agreed on the course of their mutual boundary from the mouth of Bound Brook at the Cohasset marshes through Accord Pond to a point three miles south of the Charles R., a refinement of their charter boundary descriptions. (Bradford, 426)

14 June 1641

Massachusetts gained all of New Hampshire when the colonists there voluntarily accepted Massachusetts's jurisdiction; there had been no effective government or judicial system there since the dissolution of the Council for New England and the death of John Mason, New Hampshire's principal land holder. (Swindler, 6:319)

1642

Nathaniel Woodward and Solomon Saffrey officially demarcated the southern limit of Massachusetts, supposedly three miles south of the Charles R., as prescribed in its charter of 1628/1629. (Hooker, 16–17; Van Zandt, 66–67)

Massachusetts, responding to a request from disgruntled Rhode Islanders, extended jurisdiction over the settlement of Pawtuxet; these colonists reaffiliated with Rhode Island in 1658. (Arnold, 1:111)

10 May 1643

Massachusetts created four original counties: ESSEX, MIDDLESEX, NORFOLK (original), and SUFFOLK. Original NORFOLK covered territory north of the Merrimack R., including settlements in present New Hampshire. (Mass. Recs., 2:38)

1644

Based upon its participation with Connecticut and New Plymouth in the Pequot War (1636–1637), Massachusetts claimed much of the territory formerly controlled by the Pequots, roughly between the Thames and Pawcatuck rivers at the eastern end of present Connecticut, plus Block I. in present Rhode Island. Massachusetts established a settlement (now Pawcatuck, Conn.) near mouth of the Pawcatuck R. (Bowen, *Disputes*, 31)

27 August 1645

Massachusetts claimed to have secured a patent for the whole area of Rhode Island on 10 December 1643, and subsequently tried to enforce its authority in the western and southwestern parts of Rhode Island. This patent was later deemed invalid and possibly fraudulent. (Arnold, 1:118–119)

March 1645/1646

Lygonia gained from Maine when the English government settled the jurisdictional dispute between the two provinces in favor of Lygonia, effectively reducing Maine to a few settlements between the Piscataqua and Kennebec rivers. (Williamson, 1:302)

26 May 1652

Massachusetts declared an interpretation of its 1628/1629 charter that would make its northern boundary an east-west line through a point three miles north of the most northerly part of the Merrimack R., which it decided later (1 Aug. 1652) was the parallel of 43 degrees, 40 minutes, 12 seconds north latitude, cutting the Atlantic Coast near present Casco Bay, Maine. Massachusetts used this interpretation to claim part of Maine and, until 1740, to create a few towns in present southern Vermont and southwestern New Hampshire. (Van Zandt, 64; Williamson, 1:337)

20 November 1652

Massachusetts, after towns in southern Maine (area between the Kennebec and Piscataqua rivers) acknowledged its jurisdiction, created YORKSHIRE in Maine to cover all territory within the new bounds declared on 26 May 1652. Towns located farther north near Casco Bay gave their allegiance later, the last in 1658, practically eliminating Lygonia. (Farnham, 7:274, 288; Mass. Recs., vol. 4, pt. 1:124; Reid, *Maine*, 21)

26 May 1658

The Pawtuxet settlers, who gave their allegiance to Massachusetts in 1642, returned to Rhode Island jurisdiction. (Arnold, 1:267)

ESSEX gained small area (15 acres) from MIDDLESEX when Andover gained from Billerica [location unknown, not mapped]. (Mass. Recs., vol. 4, pt. 1:333)

18 September 1658

Commissioners of the United Colonies of New England, a confederation of Connecticut, Massachusetts, New Haven, and New Plymouth (1643–c. 1686), tried to settle the dispute between Connecticut and Massachusetts over the Pequot Country (area in present eastern Connecticut) when it decided the Mystic R. was their boundary, leaving Massachusetts with the territory between the Mystic and Pawcatuck rivers in present eastern Connecticut. Massachusetts asserted that the Pequot Country extended well east of the Pawcatuck into present western Rhode Island, a claim Rhode Island resisted, but Massachusetts imposed its authority on both sides of the Pawcatuck for the next several years. (Arnold, 1:277–278; Bowen, *Disputes*, 32)

23 April 1662

King Charles II granted Connecticut a charter as a self-governing corporate colony, consolidating Hartford and other settlements on the Connecticut R. with New Haven and other coastal settlements into a single colony. Bounds included the southern Massachusetts line on the north and Narragansett Bay on the east. Massachusetts did not concede its claim to territory between the Mystic and Pawcatuck rivers in present eastern Connecticut, but Connecticut quickly took control of the area. (Bowen, *Disputes*, 32; Swindler, 2:135–136)

7 May 1662

HAMPSHIRE created from non-county area (towns of Springfield, Northampton, Hadley, and all territory within 30 miles), effectively covering entire western part of the province. (Mass. Recs., vol. 4, pt. 2:52)

8 July 1663

King Charles II granted Rhode Island a charter as a self-governing corporate colony. It was bounded on the north by the southern line of Massachusetts; on the east by a straight north-south line between Massachusetts and Pawtucket Falls (a gain for Rhode Island from SUFFOLK), thence down the Seekonk R. to Narragansett Bay and along a line three miles inland from the Bay (a gain for Rhode Island from the colony at New Plymouth); on the south by the ocean, including Block I. (claimed by Massachusetts after the Pequot War); and on the west by the Pawcatuck R. and a line due north to Massachusetts. (Bowen, *Disputes*, 33; Swindler, 8:368)

12 March 1663/1664

King Charles II granted to the Duke of York the following: all territory between the Connecticut and Delaware rivers; the islands of Long Island, Martha's Vineyard, and Nantucket; and the area between the Kennebec and St. Croix rivers extending inland from the Atlantic coast to the St. Lawrence R. Covered most of present Maine and both the major coastal islands and the western third of the mainland in present Massachusetts. (Swindler, 4:278–280)

May 1664

SUFFOLK lost to the New Plymouth colony when a joint commission from Massachusetts and Plymouth demarcated their mutual boundary. Starting at a tree that they determined to be three miles south of the Charles R., they went both northeast to Accord Pond, as agreed in 1640, and west to the Pawtucket (now Blackstone) R., across the northeastern corner of present Rhode Island (an additional gain for Plymouth). This boundary, known as the "Old Colony Line," remained in effect until the two colonies were united in 1691. (Bradford, 427 n.)

8 June 1664

New Plymouth colony protested that Rhode Island's new charter infringed upon Plymouth's territory under its 1629/1630 patent. (Arnold, 1:308)

19 October 1664

Massachusetts, faced with new charters for Connecticut and Rhode Island, gave up its claim to the Pequot Country east of Connecticut's Mystic R. and including Block I. in present western Rhode Island. (Arnold, 1:308)

November 1664

Representatives of the Gorges family rejected Massachusetts's 1652 claim and resumed government of Maine (area between the Kennebec and Piscataqua rivers). YORKSHIRE (Me.) went into abeyance. (York County, 2:5)

Autumn 1664

Royal commissioners tried to settle the implicit conflict between the recent grant (12 Mar. 1663/1664) of New York to the Duke of York and the western limit of Massachusetts, as specified in its 1629 charter, by proposing a boundary line running 20 miles east of the Hudson R. Never formalized, this proposal was widely accepted in principle but did not prevent a long, serious dispute between the two colonies. (Schwarz, 20; Van Zandt, 70)

27 February 1664/1665

SUFFOLK gained from Rhode Island when royal commissioners, charged with solving inter-colonial disputes in New England, established the eastern boundary of Rhode Island with Massachusetts and New Plymouth along the east side of Narragansett Bay (intended as a temporary arrangement until the king should settle the matter definitively). Contemporary understanding of what constituted the Narragansett R. and Bay apparently included the Seekonk and Pawtucket (now Blackstone) rivers, which left the present northeastern corner of Rhode Island to Massachusetts and Plymouth. (Arnold, 1:315)

20 March 1664/1665

Royal commissioners decided the dispute over the Narragansett Country (present southwestern Rhode Island) by dismissing Massachusetts's claim and placing the area directly under royal jurisdiction. They named it King's Province and on 8 April 1665 gave Rhode Island temporary administrative authority over this new province until a royal decision should settle the competing claims of Connecticut and Rhode Island; this did not occur until 1686. (Arnold, 1:315; James, 86–87; Potter, 178, 181)

23 June 1665

Royal commissioners replaced Gorges's jurisdiction over Maine (between the Kennebec and Piscataqua rivers) with a new government under direct authority of the crown. (Farnham, 7:308)

5 September 1665

New York created the county of CORNWALL to cover all of the Duke of York's territory between the Kennebec and St. Croix rivers in present Maine. (Williamson, 1:421)

21 July 1667

The Peace of Breda, between England and France and the Netherlands, confirmed the English conquest of New York from the Dutch in 1664 and removed Acadia (now Nova Scotia) from English to French control, including a fort on the Penobscot R. in present Maine. Actual transfer of Acadia did not occur until 1670. (Farnham, 7:311, 314; Parry, 10:231)

27 May 1668

Massachusetts reasserted authority over all of Maine west of the Kennebec R., an area that had been put under royal government in June 1665. YORK (Me.) (formerly called YORKSHIRE) reinstated. (Farnham, 7:317)

19 May 1669

Massachusetts created town of Westfield from Springfield in HAMPSHIRE west of the Connecticut R. Part of Westfield (now Southwick) extended into present Connecticut, the result of uncertain geographic knowledge and disagreement over the line between Connecticut and Massachusetts. (Bowen, *Disputes*, 53–58; Mass. Recs., vol. 4, pt. 2:432)

1670

England surrendered to France the forts of Acadia (now Nova Scotia), including one on the Penobscot R. in present Maine. France claimed remainder of territory east of the Kennebec R. in present Maine. (Farnham, 7:312; Hart, 1:511)

by 7 October 1673

Massachusetts, relying on a new survey of its northern limit and responding to the Dutch capture of New York (Aug. 1673), claimed some of the Duke of York's territory east of the Kennebec R. in present Maine, including the Pemaquid settlement, and established a new county there. On 27 May 1674 this county was named DEVON-SHIRE. New York's CORNWALL implicitly reduced to area north of the Massachusetts claim. (Mass. Recs., 5:16; Reid, *Maine,* 138; Williamson, 1:443)

3 June 1674

Town of Suffield created as part of HAMPSHIRE. This town lay entirely within present Connecticut, the result of uncertain geographic knowledge and disagreement over the line between Connecticut and Massachusetts. (Bowen, *Disputes,* 53–58; Mass. Recs., 5:13)

29 June 1674

Following the Treaty of Westminster (9 Feb. 1673/1674) that restored New York to the English (following rule by the Dutch since Aug. 1673), King Charles II regranted to the Duke of York the territory he had granted on 12 March 1663/1664, including all territory between the Connecticut and Delaware rivers, the islands of Martha's Vineyard and Nantucket, and the area between the Kennebec and St. Croix rivers extending inland from the Atlantic coast to the St. Lawrence R. Covered most of present Maine and both the major coastal islands and the western third of the mainland in present Massachusetts. DEVONSHIRE continued to operate for settlements in present Maine situated east of the Kennebec R., although they were within the formally defined jurisdiction of New York's CORNWALL. (Parry, 13:136; Swindler, 4:282; Williamson, 1:446)

Autumn 1675

Outbreak of war between the Abnaki Indians and the English in present Maine apparently eliminated New York's CORNWALL and its rival Massachusetts county DEVONSHIRE. (Williamson, 1:446)

20 July 1677

England's Committee for Trade and Plantations ruled that the 1639 proprietary grant of Maine (area between the Kennebec and Piscataqua rivers) to Ferdinando Gorges was valid and that Massachusetts had exceeded the intent of its charter by extending its jurisdiction more than three miles north of where the Merrimack R. meets the Atlantic coast. YORK continued as a de facto county in southeastern Maine. (Farnham, 7:339)

15 March 1677/1678

Massachusetts purchased the proprietary rights granted in 1635 to Ferdinando Gorges, an attempt to legitimate the extension of its jurisdiction northeastward to the Kennebec R. in present New Hampshire and Maine. (Farnham, 7:350)

18 September 1679

King Charles II made New Hampshire a royal colony separate from Massachusetts. Jurisdiction of New Hampshire was defined as the area from three miles north of the Merrimack R. to Maine (i.e., the Piscataqua R.), but no western boundary was specified. Massachusetts's original NORFOLK eliminated and, as a result, ESSEX gained Amesbury, Haverhill, and Salisbury; changes implemented in 1680. (Swindler, 6:322; Van Zandt, 61)

17 March 1679/1680

Massachusetts organized a new government for Maine (area between the Piscataqua and Kennebec rivers) in accordance with terms of Ferdinando Gorges's 1635 grant. YORK (Me.) eliminated. (Farnham, 7:356; Williamson, 1:556, 563)

16 May 1683

Massachusetts created Enfield east of the Connecticut R. as part of HAMPSHIRE. This town lay almost entirely within present Connecticut, the result of uncertain geographic knowledge and disagreement over the line between Connecticut and Massachusetts. (Bowen, *Disputes,* 53–58; Mass. Recs., 5:410–411)

1 November 1683

New York re-created CORNWALL to cover all of the Duke of York's grant in area of present Maine and Quebec between the Kennebec and St. Croix rivers and extending from the Atlantic coast to the St. Lawrence R., including the Pemaquid settlement governed since 1674 by Massachusetts. New York created its DUKES in present Massachusetts to cover the Elizabeth Is., Martha's Vineyard, and Nantucket. (N.Y. Col. Laws, ch. 4/1:122)

18 June 1684

England's Court of Chancery annulled the Massachusetts charter, technically putting Massachusetts and Maine (area between New Hampshire and the Kennebec R.) directly under the authority of the crown. Actual transfer of authority occurred when royal governor arrived 17 May 1686. (Farnham, 7:359; Van Zandt, 66)

2 June 1685

New Plymouth colony created three original counties: BARNSTABLE, BRISTOL, and PLYMOUTH. (Ply. Laws, ch. 6/p. 19)

17 May 1686

Arrival of its first royal governor inaugurated the Dominion of New England, the new single province that King James II created (8 Oct. 1685) by uniting King's Province (present southwestern Rhode Island, formerly termed Narragansett Country), Massachusetts, New Hampshire, and Maine (area between New Hampshire and the Kennebec R.). No change in counties. (Farnham, 7:367; Hart, 1:573; N.H. Early Laws, 1:99; Williamson, 1:576)

20 December 1686

New royal governor of the Dominion of New England added New Plymouth and territory east of the Kennebec R. ("Country of Pemaquid") to the Dominion, according to his commission (3 Jun. 1686) and royal order (12 Sep. 1686). New York's CORNWALL eliminated from present Maine and Quebec in spring of 1687. (Barnes, 69; N.H. Early Laws, 1:144)

18 April 1689

Upon learning of the Glorious Revolution (replacement of King James II by King William III and Queen Mary II) in England, Bostonians imprisoned the royal governor and others, thereby ending the Dominion of New England. Massachusetts resumed self-government. Massachusetts also attempted to re-establish its authority in southern Maine, but a new war between England and France left the area east of New Hampshire either in turmoil or under French control until the Treaty of Ryswick in 1697. (Craven, 224; Morris and Kelly, pl. 11)

22 April 1689

New Plymouth reinstated its former government after the fall of the Dominion of New England. (Craven, 225)

15 March 1689/1690

Massachusetts created Woodstock as part of SUFFOLK. This town lay almost entirely on the Connecticut side of the provincial boundary, the result of uncertain geographic knowledge and disagreement over the line between Connecticut and Massachusetts. (Bowen, *Disputes*, 53–58; Bowen, *Woodstock*, 1:31)

19 March 1689/1690

Massachusetts formally extended its jurisdiction over New Hampshire, which had petitioned (20 Feb. 1689 / 1690) for the annexation as a means to fill the governmental void left by the fall of the Dominion of New England. No change in counties. (N.H. Early Laws, 1:261, 371)

7 October 1691

King William III and Queen Mary II issued a new charter for the province of Massachusetts Bay, limiting its western extent to match Connecticut's (c. 20 miles east of the Hudson R.) and extending its boundaries to encompass the New Plymouth colony, the islands of Nantucket and Martha's Vineyard, the former colonies of Maine (area between the Kennebec and Piscataqua rivers) and Acadia (now Nova Scotia), and all remaining territory of present Maine between Acadia and the Kennebec R. Massachusetts formally continued its counties, namely ESSEX, HAMPSHIRE, MIDDLESEX, and SUFFOLK, reinstated YORK (Me.) in present southwestern Maine, and took over BARNSTABLE, BRISTOL, and PLYMOUTH from New Plymouth. New York's DUKES eliminated. (Mass. Col. Acts, vol. 1, ch. 27 [1692–1693], sec. 1/p. 63; Swindler, 5:80)

1 March 1691/1692

King William III and Queen Mary II commissioned a royal governor for New Hampshire, effectively separating it from Massachusetts. Jurisdiction extended from three miles north of the Merrimack R. to the Piscataqua R., but, as in 1679, no western limit was specified. Both Massachusetts and New Hampshire granted land and established towns in present New Hampshire west of the Merrimack R., often in conflict with each other. (N.H. State Papers, 2:57)

22 June 1695

DUKES created from Martha's Vineyard and the Elizabeth Is. NANTUCKET created from Nantucket I. (Mass. Col. Acts, vol. 1, ch. 7 [1695–1696]/p. 216)

20 September 1697

Acadia (now Nova Scotia) effectively separated from Massachusetts and confirmed to France by the Treaty of Ryswick that ended King William's War between England and France and restored the pre-war empires. No boundaries were specified and France threw jurisdiction of present Maine into doubt by claiming all territory east of the Kennebec R. (Farnham, 8:29; Hart, 2:76–77)

1705

The northern boundary of Rhode Island with Massachusetts came into question when the towns of Providence (R.I.) and Mendon (Mass.) complained of the line's uncertain location. Commissioners redefined the boundary in 1711 but it was never surveyed. The effective division between the colonies continued along the present line west of the Pawtucket (now Blackstone) R. and down that river south to the Seekonk R. (Arnold, 2:18, 26–27)

19 November 1707

PLYMOUTH gained town of Rochester from BARNSTABLE. (Mass. Col. Acts, vol. 21, ch. 60 [1707]/p. 755)

29 October 1708

PLYMOUTH gained non-county area between BRISTOL and PLYMOUTH. (Mass. Col. Acts, vol. 21, ch. 76 [1708]/p. 767)

18 March 1711/1712

The "Old Colony Line" that divided Massachusetts and New Plymouth when they were separate colonies was declared the boundary separating SUFFOLK from BRISTOL and PLYMOUTH [no change]. (Mass. Col. Acts, vol. 21, ch. 152 [1711]/p. 799)

15 April 1713

Following the Treaty of Utrecht (31 Mar. 1713), by which Acadia (now Nova Scotia) was formally transferred from France to Great Britain, Massachusetts lost nominal jurisdiction over Nova Scotia when that area was made a separate province. Limits specified in the treaty ("ancient boundaries") were vague, but from this date Massachusetts held actual control of territory west of the St. Croix R. that is present Maine. (Farnham, 8:33; Gipson, 3:29 n.74, 5:334)

13 July 1713

Agents of Connecticut and Massachusetts accepted a 1702 survey as the definitive rendition of their mutual chartered limits east of the Connecticut R. (substantially the same as the present line and up to eight miles north of the Woodward-Saffrey line of 1642). They also agreed that Massachusetts would retain its jurisdiction over the border towns of Enfield and Woodstock that it had formed when the 1642 line was believed accurate, even though those towns extended south of the new line into Connecticut's territory. This agreement was accepted by both colonies (13 Feb. 1713/1714) but never confirmed by London. Demarcation of the new line was completed in 1717. [No change.] (Bowen, *Disputes*, 58; Hooker, 20)

26 June 1716

YORK (Me.) gained all territory between the Kennebec and St. Croix rivers in present Maine. (Mass. Col. Acts, vol. 9, ch. 75 [1716–1717]/p. 485)

1717

Commissioners from Connecticut and Massachusetts settled their boundary from the Connecticut R. westward to New York. Massachusetts retained its jurisdiction over the border towns of Suffield and Westfield, which it had created earlier and which extended south of the line into Connecticut. (Bowen, *Disputes*, 59)

1729

Renewal of the boundary dispute between Massachusetts and Rhode Island was sparked by a petition for annexation to Rhode Island by some citizens of Attleborough (Mass.) who believed they resided west of the due-north line from Pawtucket Falls to the southern limit of Massachusetts (the eastern boundary line prescribed in Rhode Island's 1663 charter but indefinitely set aside by royal commissioners in 1664). Several attempts to settle the issue failed, and in 1733 Rhode Island appealed to the king. [No change.] (Arnold, 2:99, 101, 113)

10 July 1731

WORCESTER created from HAMPSHIRE, MIDDLESEX, and SUFFOLK. This completed definite limits for HAMPSHIRE, MIDDLESEX, and SUFFOLK. (Mass. Col. Acts, vol. 2, ch. 8 [1730–1731], sec. 1/p. 584)

29 June 1732

MIDDLESEX exchanged with WORCESTER when town of Harvard created from Groton, Lancaster, and Stow. (Mass. Col. Acts, vol. 2, ch. 4 [1732–1733], sec. 1/p. 644)

14 June 1735

WORCESTER gained from MIDDLESEX when town of Upton created from Hopkinton. (Mass. Col. Acts, vol. 2, ch. 11 [1735–1736], sec. 1/p. 764)

5 August 1740

King George II settled the lines between Massachusetts and New Hampshire substantially as they are today. Eastern boundary of New Hampshire went up the Piscataqua and Salmon Falls rivers and thence on a straight line north to a point 120 miles inland or, if closer, the limit of the colony; the southern boundary of New Hampshire was to run three miles north of the Merrimack R. from the coast westward to a point north of Pautucket Falls (now Lowell, Mass.) and thence in a straight line west to New York. Demarcation of the southern boundary of New Hampshire in 1741 actually ran a little north of west, an error that later occasioned some controversy but has remained unchanged to the present. (Farnham, 8:47; Van Zandt, 59)

16 January 1741/1742

WORCESTER gained from HAMPSHIRE when town of Western (now Warren) created from Brookfield, Brimfield, and Kingsfield. (Mass. Col. Acts, vol. 2, ch. 17 [1741–1742], sec. 2/p. 1088)

28 May 1746

King George II settled the dispute between Massachusetts and Rhode Island in favor of Rhode Island by confirming the judgment of a royal commission that had decided (30 Jun. 1741) on a line substantially the same as that prescribed in Rhode Island's 1663 charter. As a result, Rhode Island gained its present northeast corner (the "Attleborough Gore") and a three-mile wide strip east of Narragansett Bay. Decision implemented in 1747. (Arnold, 2:132–134)

17 February 1746/1747

BRISTOL (R.I.) created from BRISTOL, PROVIDENCE (R.I.) gained from BRISTOL and SUFFOLK, and NEWPORT (R.I.) gained from BRISTOL when Rhode Island implemented the 1746 royal settlement of the boundary with Massachusetts. (Arnold, 2:157; R.I. Recs., 5:207–209)

May 1749

Connecticut gained the towns of Enfield, Somers (created from Enfield in 1734), and Suffield from HAMPSHIRE and Woodstock from WORCESTER when it responded to the towns' requests for annexation by extending its jurisdiction over all portions of them south of the 1713 provincial line. These towns lay mostly on Connecticut's side of the boundary with Massachusetts, but had been founded by Massachusetts and continued under its government as a result of the 1713 and 1717 agreements.

This left jogs in the intercolonial line along the northern limit of Enfield and where Westfield (now Southwick) extended into Connecticut west of Suffield. (Bowen, *Disputes*, 62; Hooker, 22, 26)

October 1750

Rhode Island surveyors, acting without cooperation of Massachusetts to demarcate the lines confirmed by the king in 1746, discovered that the 1642 Woodward-Saffrey line, recognized for a century as the southern line of Massachusetts, ran far south of where it should have been according to the original Massachusetts charter. Rhode Island did not push the issue to a resolution during the colonial period; in 1846 a U.S. Supreme Court ruling left the line unchanged because it had functioned so long as the effective boundary. [No change.] (Arnold, 2:183, 299 n.; Van Zandt, 67)

12 April 1753

HAMPSHIRE redefined to cover all territory west of the Connecticut R. WORCESTER redefined to cover all adjacent territory not already specifically part of another county. YORK (Me.) redefined to cover all territory east of New Hampshire not specifically part of another county. [No change.] (Mass. Col. Acts, vol. 3, ch. 27 [1752–1753]/p. 656)

9 June 1756

Boundary between HAMPSHIRE and WORCESTER adjusted when dispute between towns of Greenwich and Hardwick settled [no discernible change]. (Mass. Col. Acts, vol. 15, ch. 51 [1756–1757]/p. 550)

1 November 1760

CUMBERLAND (Me.) and LINCOLN (Me.) created from YORK (Me.). All three counties were to extend northward to limit of the province. (Mass. Col. Acts, vol. 4, ch. 7 [1760–1761], secs. 1, 2, 6/pp. 372–374)

30 June 1761

BERKSHIRE created from HAMPSHIRE. (Mass. Col. Acts, vol. 4, ch. 33 [1760–1761], sec. 1/p. 432)

7 October 1763

King George III, by his Proclamation of 1763, created the new royal province of Quebec in Canada, bounded on the south in part by the watershed between rivers flowing into the St. Lawrence R. and those flowing into the

Atlantic Ocean, implicitly setting the northern limit for Maine (then part of Mass.) and its counties of CUMBERLAND (Me.), LINCOLN (Me.), and YORK (Me.) along the watershed. (Cappon, Petchenik, and Long, 1, 77; Shortt and Doughty, 119–120)

5 January 1764

WORCESTER gained from HAMPSHIRE when town of Western (now Warren) gained from Palmer. (Mass. Col. Acts, vol. 17, ch. 14 [1764–1765]/p. 516)

5 February 1765

HAMPSHIRE gained from WORCESTER when town of Greenwich gained from Hardwick. (Mass. Col. Acts, vol. 17, ch. 218 [1764–1765]/p. 603)

6 March 1767

MIDDLESEX gained small area from WORCESTER when town of Ashby created from Fitchburg and Ashburnham. (Mass. Col. Acts, vol. 4, ch. 15 [1766–1767]/p. 908)

30 June 1768

HAMPSHIRE gained from BERKSHIRE when town of Worthington created from Plantation #3. (Mass. Col. Acts, vol. 4, ch. 16 [1768], sec. 1/p. 1028)

20 November 1770

PLYMOUTH gained small area from SUFFOLK when town of Bridgewater gained from Stoughton to accommodate local property owners [location unknown, not mapped]. (Mass. Col. Acts, vol. 5, ch. 15 [1770–1771], sec. 1/p. 116)

18 May 1773

Massachusetts and New York agreed on the course of their boundary (a straight line roughly parallel to and 20 miles east of the Hudson R., in accord with the informal agreement of 1664), thereby ending over a century of uncertainty and dispute. The line was demarcated in 1787. [No change.] (Cappon, Petchenik, and Long, 89; Schwarz, 220; Van Zandt, 70)

1774

HARTFORD (Conn.) gained from HAMPSHIRE when Connecticut unilaterally took over the small part of town of Southwick (Mass.), formerly part of Westfield (Mass.), that extended south of the 1713 boundary. (Bowen, *Disputes*, 65; Hooker, 25)

4 July 1776

Massachusetts became an independent state. (*Declaration of Independence*)

23 June 1779

HAMPSHIRE gained from BERKSHIRE when town of Cummington created from Plantation #5. (Mass. Col. Acts, vol. 5, ch. 6 [1779–1780], sec. 1/pp. 1072–1073)

25 February 1783

MIDDLESEX gained from WORCESTER when town of Boxborough gained from Harvard. (Mass. Acts 1783, ch. 8, sec. 1/p. 214)

12 March 1783

HAMPSHIRE gained from BERKSHIRE when town of Middlefield created from Worthington, Chester, Partridgefield (now Peru), Becket, Washington, and Prescott's Grant (now Middlefield). (Mass. Acts 1783, ch. 19, sec. 1/p. 228)

3 September 1783

Commissioners from Great Britain and the United States signed the Treaty of Paris (ratifications exchanged 12 May 1784) ending the War of the American Revolution, recognizing American independence, and defining northern U.S. boundary around Maine (then part of Mass.) as the St. Croix R. to the Atlantic watershed and thence westward to the parallel of 45 degrees north latitude. Later treaties and surveys settled details of this boundary (and some disputes over them), but there were no later changes in its essential definition. (Parry, 48:481–486; Van Zandt, 12)

15 October 1783

HAMPSHIRE gained from WORCESTER when town of Orange created from Athol and Royalston. (Mass. Acts 1783, ch. 2, sec. 1/p. 38)

16 March 1784

WORCESTER gained from MIDDLESEX when town of Berlin created from Marlborough, Northborough, and Bolton. (Mass. Acts 1784, ch. 23, sec. 1/p. 98)

9 February 1785

HAMPSHIRE gained from BERKSHIRE when town of Rowe created from the Myrifield Grant and non-town territory. (Mass. Acts 1785, ch. 2, sec. 1/p. 230)

3 March 1786

CUMBERLAND (Me.) gained from YORK (Me.). (Mass. Acts 1786, ch. 18, sec. 1/p. 407)

7 March 1786

WORCESTER gained small area from MIDDLESEX when town of Southborough gained from Framingham. (Mass. Acts 1786, ch. 21, sec. 1/p. 410)

1 May 1790

HANCOCK (Me.) and WASHINGTON (Me.) created from LINCOLN (Me.). (Mass. Acts 1789, ch. 25, sec. 1/p. 25)

1 May 1791

LINCOLN (Me.) gained from HANCOCK (Me.). (Mass. Acts 1790, ch. 10, sec. 1/p. 81)

3 March 1792

Boundary between MIDDLESEX and SUFFOLK redefined in part when boundary between towns of Medway and Sherburne redefined [no change]. (Mass. Acts 1792, ch. 23, sec. 1/p. 155)

16 November 1792

MIDDLESEX gained from WORCESTER when town of Ashby gained from Ashburnham. (Mass. Acts 1792, ch. 2, sec. 1/p. 224)

9 March 1793

HAMPSHIRE gained from BERKSHIRE when town of Hawley gained from non-town area called Plantation #7. (Mass. Acts 1793, ch. 18, sec. 1/p. 242)

20 June 1793

NORFOLK created from SUFFOLK. (Mass. Acts 1793, ch. 43, sec. 1/p. 272 and ch. 9, sec. 1/p. 314)

15 July 1794

WORCESTER gained small area from HAMPSHIRE when town of Western (now Warren) gained from Palmer to accommodate local property owners [location unknown, not mapped]. (Temple, 10)

22 June 1797

MIDDLESEX exchanged with NORFOLK when town of Natick exchanged with Needham. (Mass. Acts 1797, ch. 22, sec. 1/p. 142)

8 February 1798

PLYMOUTH gained small strip from NORFOLK when town of Bridgewater gained from Stoughton [not mapped]. (Mass. Acts 1798, ch. 10, sec. 1/p. 164)

25 October 1798

Commissioners from Great Britain and the United States agreed on the true course of the St. Croix R., fixing part of the U.S.–Canadian boundary in accordance with the Treaty of Paris of 1783 and settling a dispute between Massachusetts and Nova Scotia that dated back to 1764 [no change]. (Van Zandt, 12)

20 February 1799

KENNEBEC (Me.) created from LINCOLN (Me.). (Mass. Acts 1799, ch. 23, sec. 1/p. 257)

28 February 1799

Boundary between KENNEBEC (Me.) and HANCOCK (Me.) clarified [no change]. (Mass. Acts 1799, ch. 39, sec. 1/p. 275)

18 February 1801

WORCESTER gained from HAMPSHIRE when town of Dana created from Greenwich, Hardwick, and Petersham. (Mass. Acts 1801, ch. 14, sec. 1/p. 453)

18 June 1803

PLYMOUTH gained towns of Hingham and Hull from SUFFOLK. (Mass. Acts 1803, ch. 14, sec. 1/p. 246)

6 March 1804

SUFFOLK gained from NORFOLK when Boston gained from Dorchester. (Mass. Acts 1804, ch. 45, sec. 1/p. 412)

1804

HAMPSHIRE gained from HARTFORD (Conn.) when Massachusetts gained part of the town of Southwick (the "Southwick Jog") that lay south of the Connecticut boundary and that had been annexed from Massachusetts in 1774. (Hooker, 25–26; Van Zandt, 69)

4 March 1805

OXFORD (Me.) created from CUMBERLAND (Me.) and YORK (Me.). KENNEBEC (Me.) gained from CUMBERLAND (Me.). (Mass. Acts 1805, ch. 24, secs. 1–2/pp. 573–574)

20 June 1807

WORCESTER gained from MIDDLESEX when town of Northborough gained from Marlborough. (Mass. Acts 1807, p. 52)

8 March 1808

OXFORD (Me.) gained from KENNEBEC (Me.). (Mass. Acts 1808, ch. 97/p. 323)

WORCESTER gained small area from MIDDLESEX when town of Upton gained from Hopkinton to accommodate local property owner [location unknown, not mapped]. (Mass. Acts 1808, ch. 106, sec. 1/p. 336)

1 June 1809

SOMERSET (Me.) created from KENNEBEC (Me.). (Mass. Acts 1809, ch. 62, sec. 1/p. 459)

6 March 1810

Boundary between KENNEBEC (Me.) and LINCOLN (Me.) redefined in part when line between towns of Gardiner and Litchfield redefined [no change]. (Mass. Acts 1810, ch. 108/p. 194)

25 February 1811

LINCOLN (Me.) gained from KENNEBEC (Me.). (Mass. Acts 1811, ch. 61/p. 290)

21 June 1811

HANCOCK (Me.) gained from SOMERSET (Me.). (Mass. Acts 1811, ch. 36/p. 430)

2 December 1811

FRANKLIN created from HAMPSHIRE. (Mass. Acts 1811, ch. 61/p. 467)

29 February 1812

KENNEBEC (Me.) exchanged with LINCOLN (Me.). (Mass. Acts 1812, ch. 160/p. 309)

12 June 1812

HANCOCK (Me.) gained from SOMERSET (Me.). (Mass. Acts 1812, ch. 4/p. 7)

1 August 1812

HAMPDEN created from HAMPSHIRE. (Mass. Acts 1812, ch. 137/p. 291)

16 February 1813

SOMERSET (Me.) gained from HANCOCK (Me.). (Mass. Acts 1813, ch. 85/p. 157)

26 February 1813

KENNEBEC (Me.) gained from SOMERSET (Me.). (Mass. Acts 1813, ch. 108/p. 179)

28 January 1814

OXFORD (Me.) gained from KENNEBEC (Me.). (Mass. Acts 1814, ch. 79/pp. 316–317)

7 February 1816

WORCESTER gained from FRANKLIN when town of Athol gained from Orange. (Mass. Acts 1816, ch. 62/p. 71)

15 February 1816

PENOBSCOT (Me.) created from HANCOCK (Me.). (Mass. Acts 1816, ch. 121, sec. 1/p. 156)

17 June 1816

PENOBSCOT (Me.) gained from HANCOCK (Me.) when town of Hampden gained from Frankfurt and town of Orrington gained from Buckstown. (Mass. Acts 1816, ch. 13, sec. 1/p. 195 and ch. 14/p. 196)

14 June 1817

PENOBSCOT (Me.) gained from SOMERSET (Me.). (Mass. Acts 1817, ch. 15/p. 398)

24 November 1817

Under authority of the Treaty of Ghent (24 Dec. 1814) commissioners from Great Britain and the United States agreed on the division of the islands in Passamaquoddy Bay, part of the Bay of Fundy: Mouse, Dudley (now

Trent), and Frederick (now Dudley) islands assigned to the United States, as part of WASHINGTON (Me.) [no change]. (Paullin, 59)

2 February 1819

SOMERSET (Me.) gained from OXFORD (Me.). (Mass. Acts 1819, ch. 41, sec. 1/p. 71)

15 March 1820

State of Maine admitted to the Union, separate from Massachusetts; boundaries same as present day. CUMBERLAND (Me.), HANCOCK (Me.), KENNEBEC (Me.), LINCOLN (Me.), OXFORD (Me.), PENOBSCOT (Me.), SOMERSET (Me.), WASHINGTON (Me.), and YORK (Me.) eliminated from Massachusetts. (U.S. Stat., vol. 3, ch. 19 [1820]/p. 544)

28 January 1822

HAMPSHIRE gained from FRANKLIN when town of Prescott created from Pelham and New Salem. (Mass. Acts 1822, ch. 34, sec. 1/p. 614)

21 February 1822

FRANKLIN gained from BERKSHIRE when town of Monroe created from Rowe and non-town area called the Gore. (Mass. Acts 1822, ch. 93, sec. 1/p. 707)

8 February 1823

HAMPSHIRE gained from WORCESTER when town of Ware gained from Western (now Warren). (Mass. Acts 1823, ch. 76/p. 114)

14 June 1823

NORFOLK gained small area from PLYMOUTH when town of Cohasset gained from Scituate to accommodate local property owners [location unknown, not mapped]. (Mass. Acts 1823, ch. 28/p. 237)

22 February 1825

Boundary between SUFFOLK and NORFOLK adjusted when line between Boston and Brookline adjusted. (Mass. Acts 1825, ch. 90/p. 73)

3 November 1826

HAMPDEN and WORCESTER exchanged narrow strips with TOLLAND (Conn.) and WINDHAM (Conn.)

when an irregularity in the state boundary was straightened [not mapped]. (Bowen, *Disputes*, 66; Hooker, 28)

11 February 1829

WORCESTER gained small area (one acre) from MIDDLESEX when town of Bolton gained from Marlborough to accommodate local property owner [location unknown, not mapped]. (Mass. Acts 1829, ch. 47/p. 72)

3 March 1829

MIDDLESEX gained small area from WORCESTER when town of Ashby gained from Fitchburg to accommodate local property owner [location unknown, not mapped] and exchanged with NORFOLK when town of Holliston gained from Medway. (Mass. Acts 1829, ch. 125/p. 200 and ch. 133/p. 209)

5 February 1830

WORCESTER gained from FRANKLIN when town of Athol gained from New Salem. (Mass. Acts 1830, ch. 33/p. 300)

18 February 1830

Boundary between BRISTOL and NORFOLK clarified when line between town of Attleborough and Wrentham clarified [no change]. (Mass. Acts 1830, ch. 48/p. 319)

7 February 1831

HAMPDEN gained from WORCESTER when town of Palmer gained from Western (now Warren). (Mass. Acts 1831, ch. 37/p. 545)

25 March 1834

SUFFOLK gained from NORFOLK when Boston gained Thompson I. from Dorchester. (Mass. Acts 1834, ch. 102/p. 129)

27 March 1835

MIDDLESEX exchanged with WORCESTER when towns of Holliston, Hopkinton, and Milford exchanged. (Mass. Acts 1835, ch. 72/p. 382)

16 March 1836

Boundary between SUFFOLK and NORFOLK redefined when line between Boston and Roxbury redefined [not mapped]. (Mass. Acts 1836, ch. 37/p. 681)

9 April 1836

Boundary between PLYMOUTH and BRISTOL redefined in part when line between towns of Rochester and Fairhaven redefined [no change]. (Mass. Acts 1836, ch. 193, sec. 1/p. 876)

16 March 1837

WORCESTER gained from FRANKLIN when town of Athol gained from New Salem. (Mass. Acts 1837, ch. 80, sec. 1/p. 70)

19 April 1837

Boundary between NORFOLK and SUFFOLK adjusted slightly when line through water between Roxbury and Boston adjusted [not mapped]. (Mass. Acts 1837, ch. 202, sec. 1/p. 222)

16 March 1838

Boundary between MIDDLESEX and WORCESTER redefined in part when line between towns of Marlborough and Bolton redefined [no change]. (Mass. Acts 1838, ch. 36/p. 330)

2 April 1838

FRANKLIN gained from BERKSHIRE when towns of Charlemont and Rowe gained from Zoar. (Mass. Acts 1838, ch. 56, sec. 1/p. 344 and ch. 57, sec. 1/p. 345)

23 April 1838

NORFOLK gained from MIDDLESEX when town of Roxbury gained from Newton. (Mass. Acts 1838, ch. 167, sec. 1/p. 481)

20 March 1840

PLYMOUTH gained small area from NORFOLK when town of Scituate gained from Cohasset to accommodate local property owner [location unknown, not mapped]. (Mass. Acts 1840, ch. 58, sec. 1/p. 206)

22 February 1841

ESSEX gained from SUFFOLK when town of Saugus gained from Chelsea. (Mass. Acts 1841, ch. 30, sec. 1/p. 350)

24 March 1843

MIDDLESEX gained small area from WORCESTER when town of Marlborough gained from Southborough to accommodate local property owners [location unknown, not mapped]. (Mass. Acts 1843, ch. 89, sec. 1/ p. 53)

3 March 1846

Boundary between MIDDLESEX and WORCESTER redefined in part when line between towns of Shirley and Lunenburg redefined [no change]. (Mass. Acts 1846, ch. 74/p. 35)

31 March 1847

Boundary between NORFOLK and PLYMOUTH clarified in part when line between towns of Weymouth and Abington clarified [no change]. (Mass. Acts 1847, ch. 138/p. 391)

25 April 1848

Boundary between MIDDLESEX and WORCESTER redefined in part when line between towns of Shirley and Lunenburg redefined [no change]. (Mass. Acts 1848, ch. 194, sec. 1/p. 708)

2 February 1849

Boundary between HAMPSHIRE and FRANKLIN clarified when line between towns of Williamsburg and Whately clarified [no change]. (Mass. Acts 1849, ch. 3/ p. 198)

3 May 1850

Boundary between SUFFOLK and NORFOLK adjusted when line through water between Boston and Roxbury adjusted [not mapped]. (Mass. Acts 1850, ch. 281, sec. 1/ p. 460)

4 May 1853

Boundary between BERKSHIRE and HAMPDEN clarified when line between towns of Sandisfield and Tolland clarified [no change]. (Mass. Acts 1853, ch. 293/p. 535)

25 May 1853

HAMPSHIRE gained from HAMPDEN when town of Norwich (now Huntington) gained from Chester and Blandford. (Mass. Acts 1853, ch. 421, sec. 1/p. 639)

10 April 1854

MIDDLESEX gained from ESSEX when town of Reading gained from Lynnfield. (Mass. Acts 1854, ch. 246, sec. 1/ p. 163)

11 January 1855

COLUMBIA (N.Y.) gained from BERKSHIRE when New York acquired the southwestern corner of Massachusetts, known as Boston Corner. (Pratt, 2:223; Van Zandt, 70, 76)

15 May 1855

Boundary between BERKSHIRE and HAMPDEN redefined when line between towns of Sandisfield and Tolland redefined [no change]. (Mass. Acts 1855, ch. 358, sec. 1/p. 755)

21 May 1855

SUFFOLK gained small area from NORFOLK when Boston gained from Dorchester. (Mass. Acts 1855, ch. 468, sec. 1/p. 907)

7 January 1858

MIDDLESEX gained from ESSEX when town of North Reading gained from Lynnfield. (Mass. Acts 1857, ch. 238, sec. 1/p. 572; Mass. Sec. Comm., 41)

1 April 1859

WORCESTER gained from MIDDLESEX when town of Milford gained from Holliston. (Mass. Acts 1859, ch. 149/p. 312)

3 April 1860

Boundary between SUFFOLK and NORFOLK adjusted slightly when line along streets between Boston and Roxbury shifted to sides of streets from centerlines [not mapped]. (Mass. Acts 1860, ch. 172, sec. 1/p. 138)

21 March 1861

Boundary between NORFOLK and PLYMOUTH clarified in part when boundary between towns of Abington and Randolph clarified [no change]. (Mass. Acts 1861, ch. 86/p. 390)

1 March 1862

BRISTOL gained from NEWPORT (R.I.) and lost to PROVIDENCE (R.I.) when Massachusetts and Rhode Island implemented the U.S. Supreme Court settlement (31 Dec. 1861) of their boundary to the Atlantic Ocean. (Bayles, *Providence*, 1:29; R.I. Acts 1861, ch. 379/ pp. 4–6; Ullman, 83–84; Van Zandt, 68)

1 June 1867

Boundary between BRISTOL and PLYMOUTH clarified in part when boundary between towns of Lakeville and Taunton clarified [no change]. (Mass. Acts 1867, ch. 352, sec. 1/p. 745)

6 January 1868

SUFFOLK gained from NORFOLK when Boston gained all of Roxbury. (Mass. Acts 1867, ch. 359, sec. 1/p. 754)

20 March 1868

MIDDLESEX gained from WORCESTER when town of Hudson gained from Bolton. (Mass. Acts 1868, ch. 79, sec. 1/p. 62)

3 January 1870

SUFFOLK gained from NORFOLK when Boston gained all of Dorchester. (Mass. Acts 1869, ch. 349, sec. 1/p. 646)

2 April 1870

Boundary between NORFOLK and SUFFOLK adjusted slightly when line along streets between Boston and West Roxbury shifted from one side to the other [not mapped]. (Mass. Acts 1870, ch. 146, sec. 1/pp. 21, 95)

18 June 1870

SUFFOLK gained small area from NORFOLK when Boston gained from Brookline. (Mass. Acts 1870, ch. 374, sec. 1/p. 290)

7 March 1872

NORFOLK exchanged with WORCESTER when town of Bellingham exchanged with Mendon. (Mass. Acts 1872, ch. 69, sec. 1/p. 57)

12 April 1872

SUFFOLK gained small area from NORFOLK when Boston gained Mt. Hope Cemetery from town of West Roxbury. (Mass. Acts 1872, ch. 197, sec. 1/p. 143)

27 April 1872

SUFFOLK and NORFOLK exchanged small areas when Boston and Brookline exchanged. (Mass. Acts 1872, ch. 267, sec. 1/p. 210)

5 January 1874

SUFFOLK gained from MIDDLESEX and NORFOLK when Boston gained all of Brighton, Charlestown, and West Roxbury. (Mass. Acts 1873, ch. 286, sec. 1/p. 716, ch. 303, sec. 1/p. 747, and ch. 314, sec. 1/p. 810)

8 May 1874

SUFFOLK gained from NORFOLK when Boston gained from Brookline. (Mass. Acts 1874, ch. 220, sec. 1/p. 143)

29 May 1874

Boundary between SUFFOLK and MIDDLESEX adjusted when line between Boston and Newton adjusted. (Mass. Acts 1874, ch. 277, sec. 1/p. 189)

1 July 1875

MIDDLESEX gained small area from SUFFOLK when Newton gained from Boston. (Mass. Acts 1875, ch. 184, sec. 1/p. 773)

27 May 1890

Boundary between SUFFOLK and NORFOLK adjusted when line between Boston and Brookline adjusted. (Mass. Acts 1890, ch. 339, sec. 1/p. 299)

4 May 1891

Boundary between SUFFOLK and MIDDLESEX adjusted when line between Boston and Somerville adjusted. (Mass. Acts 1891, ch. 294, sec. 1/p. 856)

13 April 1894

Boundary between NORFOLK and SUFFOLK adjusted slightly when line between northern Brookline and Boston adjusted [not mapped]. (Mass. Acts 1894, ch. 242, sec. 1/p. 219)

14 April 1897

Boundary between PLYMOUTH and BARNSTABLE clarified in part when line between towns of Wareham and Bourne clarified [no change]. (Mass. Acts 1897, ch. 281, sec. 1/p. 258)

30 April 1897

Boundary between NORFOLK and PLYMOUTH adjusted when line between towns of Cohasset and Hingham adjusted [no discernible change]. (Mass. Acts 1897, ch. 330, sec. 1/p. 318)

29 March 1898

Boundary between SUFFOLK and MIDDLESEX adjusted when line through the Charles R. between Boston and Cambridge adjusted [not mapped] and line between Boston and Newton adjusted. (Mass. Acts 1898, ch. 242, sec. 1/p. 178 and ch. 243/p. 179)

1 April 1898

Boundary between SUFFOLK and NORFOLK adjusted when line between Boston and Hyde Park adjusted. (Mass. Acts 1898, ch. 251, sec. 1/p. 185)

13 May 1898

Boundary between SUFFOLK and MIDDLESEX adjusted when line between Boston and Newton adjusted. (Mass. Acts 1898, ch. 431, sec. 1/p. 376)

3 June 1899

Many small adjustments prescribed for eastern boundary of Rhode Island with Massachusetts, substituting a series of straight lines for indefinite lines such as high-water boundaries [not mapped]. (Ullman, 84; Van Zandt, 68)

16 May 1901

Boundary between MIDDLESEX and WORCESTER redefined when line between towns of Marlborough and Southborough redefined [no discernible change]. (Mass. Acts 1901, ch. 393, sec. 1/p. 306)

21 May 1903

Boundary between MIDDLESEX and ESSEX redefined in part when line between towns of Tewkesbury and Andover redefined [no change]. (Mass. Acts 1903, ch. 373, sec. 1/p. 343)

12 March 1904

Boundary between ESSEX and MIDDLESEX redefined in part when line between towns of North Andover and North Reading redefined [no change]. (Mass. Acts 1904, ch. 149, sec. 1/p. 98)

22 April 1904

Boundary between ESSEX and MIDDLESEX redefined in part when line between towns of North Reading and Andover redefined [no change]. (Mass. Acts 1904, ch. 250, sec. 1/p. 213)

1 May 1905

Boundary between MIDDLESEX and WORCESTER redefined in part when line between towns of Berlin and Hudson redefined [no change] and adjusted when line between towns of Marlborough and Berlin adjusted. (Mass. Acts 1905, ch. 357, sec. 1/p. 283 and ch. 358, sec. 1/p. 284)

2 May 1905

Boundary between ESSEX and MIDDLESEX redefined in part when line between towns of Lynnfield and Reading redefined [no change]. (Mass. Acts 1905, ch. 361, sec. 1/p. 286)

14 June 1906

MIDDLESEX gained small area from WORCESTER when towns of Boxborough and Littleton gained from Harvard. (Mass. Acts 1906, ch. 483, sec. 1/p. 654 and ch. 484, sec. 1/p. 655)

28 March 1907

Boundary between MIDDLESEX and NORFOLK redefined in part when line between towns of Newton and Brookline redefined [no change]. (Mass. Acts 1907, ch. 249, sec. 1/p. 194)

16 May 1907

Boundary between MIDDLESEX and WORCESTER redefined in part when town of Hopkinton's boundary with Milford and Upton redefined [no change]. (Mass. Acts 1907, ch. 423, sec. 1 and ch. 424, sec. 1/pp. 362–363)

9 June 1909

HAMPDEN gained from HAMPSHIRE when town of Holyoke gained from Northampton. (Mass. Acts 1909, ch. 480, sec. 1/p. 498)

29 March 1910

Boundary between SUFFOLK and MIDDLESEX adjusted when line in the Charles R. between Boston and Cambridge adjusted [not mapped]. (Mass. Acts 1910, ch. 312, sec. 1/p. 239)

Boundary between HAMPSHIRE and HAMPDEN redefined in part when line between towns of Ware and Palmer redefined [no change]. (Mass. Acts 1910, ch. 471, sec. 1/p. 422)

27 April 1911

Boundary between FRANKLIN and WORCESTER redefined in part when line between towns of New Salem and Prescott redefined [no change]. (Mass. Acts 1911, ch. 340, sec. 1/p. 310)

1 January 1912

SUFFOLK gained from NORFOLK when Boston gained all of Hyde Park. (Mass. Acts 1911, ch. 469, sec. 1/p. 450 and ch. 583, sec. 1/p. 600)

23 March 1928

Boundary between PLYMOUTH and NORFOLK adjusted when line between towns of Hingham and Cohasset adjusted [no discernible change]. (Mass. Acts 1928, ch. 160, sec. 1/p. 184)

18 September 1933

MIDDLESEX gained small area from ESSEX when town of Wakefield gained from Saugus. (Mass. Acts 1933, ch. 298, sec. 1/p. 453; Mass. Sec. Comm., 59)

28 April 1938

FRANKLIN gained from HAMPSHIRE when town of New Salem gained from Enfield, Greenwich, and Prescott; WORCESTER gained from HAMPSHIRE when Petersham gained from Dana, Greenwich, and Prescott and Hardwick gained from Greenwich. (Mass. Acts 1927, ch. 321, sec. 1/p. 384; Mass. Acts 1938, ch. 240, sec. 1/p. 188; Mass. Sec. Comm., 48)

10 April 1947

ESSEX exchanged with MIDDLESEX when town of Lynnfield exchanged with Reading. (Mass. Acts 1947, ch. 243, sec. 1/p. 222)

Individual County
Chronologies, Maps,
and Areas for Massachusetts

Chronology of BARNSTABLE

Map	Date	Event	Resulting Area
❶	2 Jun 1685	Created as one of three original counties in New Plymouth Colony	500 sq mi

(Heavy line depicts historical boundary. Base map shows present-day information.)

❶ 2 Jun 1685 – 18 Nov 1707

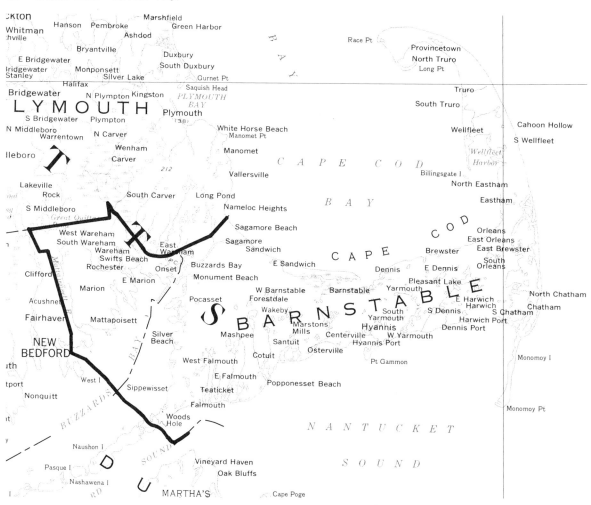

Chronology of BARNSTABLE

Map	Date	Event	Resulting Area
	7 Oct 1691	Became a Massachusetts county when Massachusetts absorbed New Plymouth [no change]	
❷	19 Nov 1707	Lost town of Rochester to PLYMOUTH	410 sq mi
	14 Apr 1897	Boundary with PLYMOUTH clarified in part when line between towns of Wareham and Bourne clarified [no change]	

(Heavy line depicts historical boundary. Base map shows present-day information.)

❷ 19 Nov 1707–present

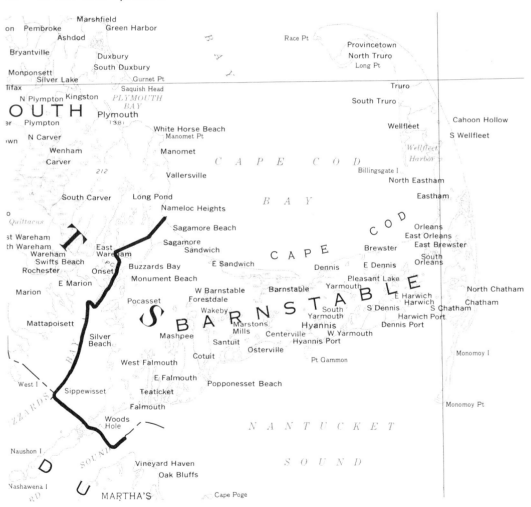

Chronology of BERKSHIRE

Map	Date	Event	Resulting Area
❶	30 Jun 1761	Created from HAMPSHIRE	1,040 sq mi

(Heavy line depicts historical boundary. Base map shows present-day information.)

❶ 30 Jun 1761– 29 Jun 1768

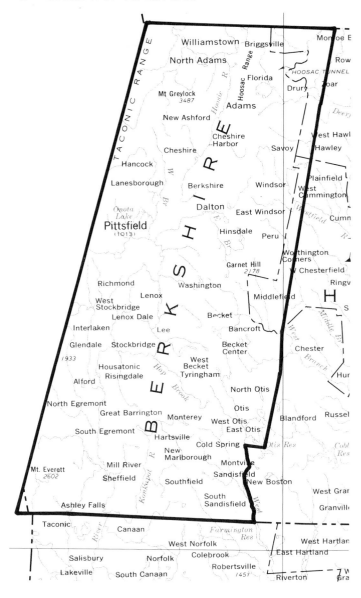

| 10 | 0 | 10 | 20 | 30 | 40 Miles |

Chronology of BERKSHIRE

Map	Date	Event	Resulting Area
❷	30 Jun 1768	Lost to HAMPSHIRE when town of Worthington created from Plantation #3	1,020 sq mi

(Heavy line depicts historical boundary. Base map shows present-day information.)

❷   30 Jun 1768 – 22 Jun 1779

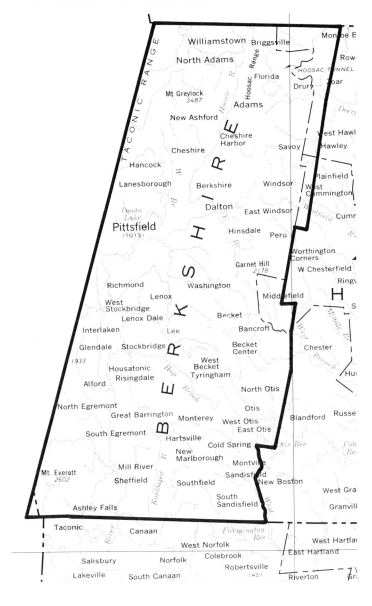

Chronology of BERKSHIRE

Map	Date	Event	Resulting Area
❸	23 Jun 1779	Lost to HAMPSHIRE when town of Cummington created from Plantation #5	1,010 sq mi

(Heavy line depicts historical boundary. Base map shows present-day information.)

❸   23 Jun 1779 – 11 Mar 1783

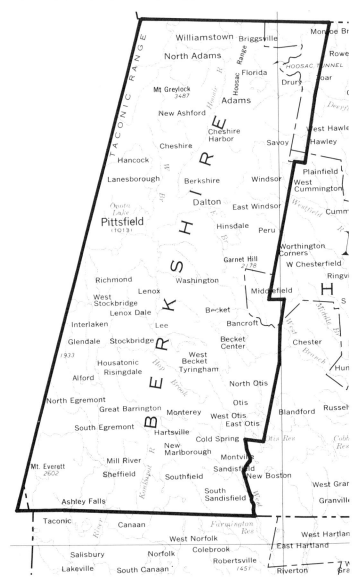

10   0   10   20   30   40 Miles

Chronology of BERKSHIRE

Map	Date	Event	Resulting Area
❹	12 Mar 1783	Lost to HAMPSHIRE when town of Middlefield created from Worthington, Chester, Partridgefield (now Peru), Becket, Washington, and Prescott's Grant (now Middlefield)	1,000 sq mi

(Heavy line depicts historical boundary. Base map shows present-day information.)

❹   12 Mar 1783 – 8 Feb 1785

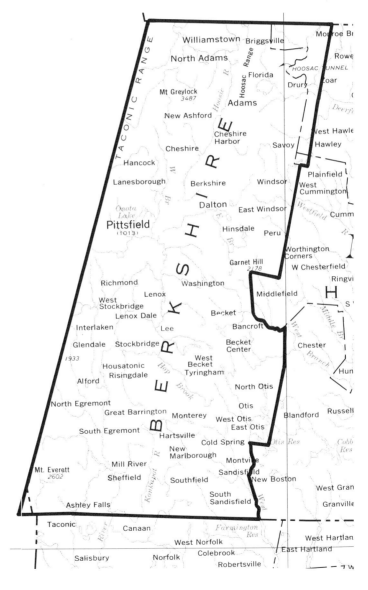

Chronology of BERKSHIRE

Map	Date	Event	Resulting Area
❺	9 Feb 1785	Lost to HAMPSHIRE when town of Rowe created from the Myrifield Grant and non-town territory	1,000 sq mi

(Heavy line depicts historical boundary. Base map shows present-day information.)

❺   9 Feb 1785 – 8 Mar 1793

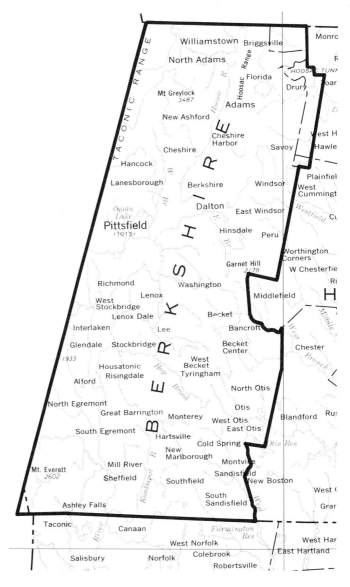

10	0	10	20	30	40 Miles

Chronology of BERKSHIRE

Map	Date	Event	Resulting Area
❻	9 Mar 1793	Lost to HAMPSHIRE when town of Hawley gained from Plantation #7	990 sq mi

(Heavy line depicts historical boundary. Base map shows present-day information.)

❻ 9 Mar 1793–20 Feb 1822

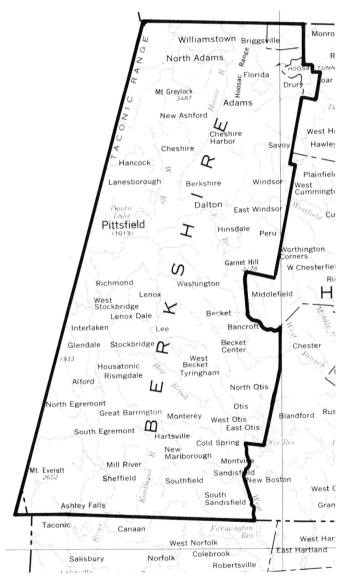

10   0   10   20   30   40 Miles

Chronology of BERKSHIRE

Map	Date	Event	Resulting Area
❼	21 Feb 1822	Lost to FRANKLIN when town of Monroe created from Rowe and non-town area called Gore	980 sq mi

(Heavy line depicts historical boundary. Base map shows present-day information.)

❼   21 Feb 1822 – 1 Apr 1838

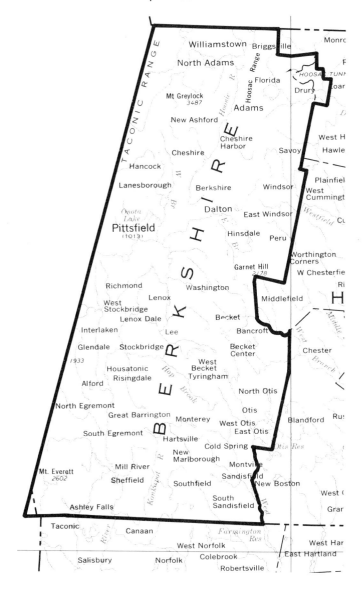

| 10 | 0 | 10 | 20 | 30 | 40 Miles |

Chronology of BERKSHIRE

Map	Date	Event	Resulting Area
❽	2 Apr 1838	Lost to FRANKLIN when towns of Charlemont and Rowe gained from Zoar	970 sq mi
	4 May 1853	Boundary with HAMPDEN clarified when line between towns of Sandisfield and Tolland clarified [no change]	

(Heavy line depicts historical boundary. Base map shows present-day information.)

❽   2 Apr 1838 – 10 Jan 1855

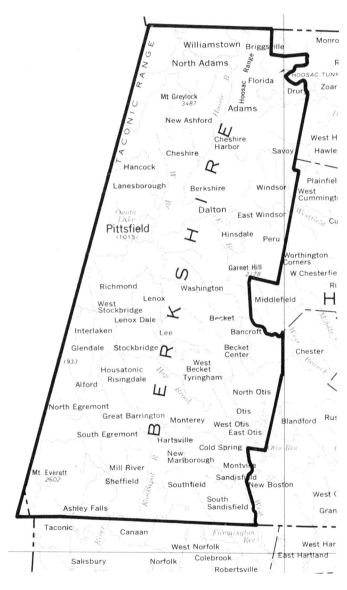

| 10 | 0 | 10 | 20 | 30 | 40 Miles |

Chronology of BERKSHIRE

Map	Date	Event	Resulting Area
❾	11 Jan 1855	Lost to COLUMBIA (N.Y.) when New York acquired the southwestern corner of Massachusetts, known as Boston Corner	960 sq mi
	15 May 1855	Boundary with HAMPDEN redefined when line between towns of Sandisfield and Tolland redefined [no change]	

(Heavy line depicts historical boundary. Base map shows present-day information.)

❾ 11 Jan 1855 – present

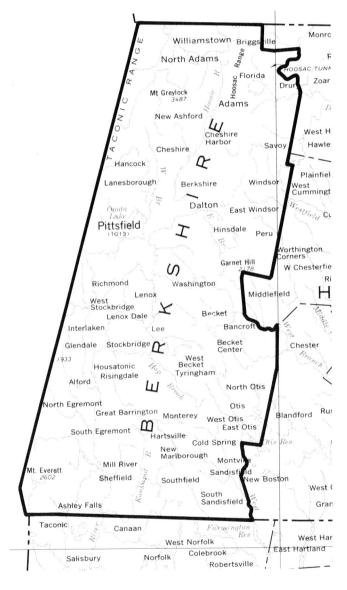

10	0	10	20	30	40 Miles

Chronology of BRISTOL

Map	Date	Event	Resulting Area
❶	2 Jun 1685	Created as one of three original counties in New Plymouth Colony	730 sq mi
	7 Oct 1691	Became a Massachusetts county when Massachusetts absorbed New Plymouth [no change]	
	18 Mar 1711	Boundary with SUFFOLK redefined as the "Old Colony Line" [no change]	

(Heavy line depicts historical boundary. Base map shows present-day information.)

❶   2 Jun 1685 – 16 Feb 1746/1747

10	0	10	20	30	40 Miles

Chronology of BRISTOL

Map	Date	Event	Resulting Area
❷	17 Feb 1746/1747	Lost to creation of BRISTOL (R.I.) and to PROVIDENCE (R.I.) when provincial boundary with Rhode Island adjusted	600 sq mi
	18 Feb 1830	Boundary with NORFOLK clarified when line between towns of Attleborough and Wrentham clarified [no change]	
	9 Apr 1836	Boundary with PLYMOUTH redefined in part when line between towns of Rochester and Fairhaven redefined [no change]	

(Heavy line depicts historical boundary. Base map shows present-day information.)

❷ 17 Feb 1746/1747– 28 Feb 1862

(Map showing the historical boundary of Bristol County with present-day place names including Norfolk, Sharon, Stoughton, Brockton, Franklin, Wrentham, Foxboro, Mansfield, North Attleboro, Attleboro, Taunton, East Providence, BRISTOL, Fall River, New Bedford, Newport, Middletown, and surrounding areas.)

Chronology of BRISTOL

Map	Date	Event	Resulting Area
❸	1 Mar 1862	Gained from NEWPORT (R.I.) and lost to PROVIDENCE (R.I.) when Massachusetts and Rhode Island implemented the U.S. Supreme Court settlement of their boundary	590 sq mi
	1 Jun 1867	Boundary with PLYMOUTH clarified in part when boundary between towns of Lakeville and Taunton clarified [no change]	

(Heavy line depicts historical boundary. Base map shows present-day information.)

❸   1 Mar 1862 – present

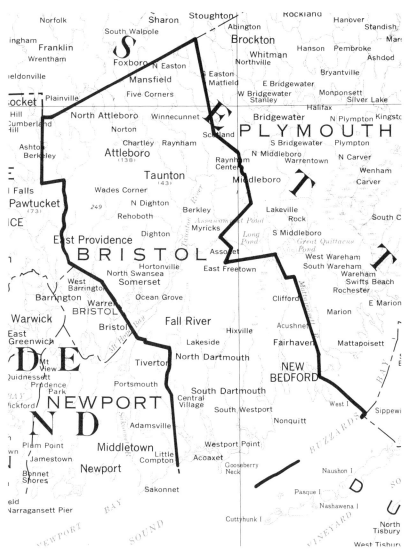

Chronology of DUKES (created by N.Y., extinct)

Map	Date	Event	Resulting Area
❶	1 Nov 1683	Created by New York from Nantucket, Martha's Vineyard, and the Elizabeth Is.	150 sq mi
	7 Oct 1691	Eliminated when Massachusetts gained the islands	

(Heavy line depicts historical boundary. Base map shows present-day information.)

❶ 1 Nov 1683 – 6 Oct 1691

NEW BEDFORD
Beach
Santuit
Hyannis-Port
Monomoy I
Dartmouth
West Falmouth
Cotuit
Osterville
Pt Gammon
outh Westport
West I
E Falmouth
Monomoy Pt
Nonquitt
Sippewisset
Teaticket
Popponesset Beach
tport Point
Falmouth
Gooseberry Neck
Woods Hole
N A N T U C K E T
Naushon I
BUZZARDS BAY
S O U N D
Pasque I
SOUND
Vineyard Haven
Nashawena I
Oak Bluffs
Cuttyhunk I
VINEYARD
D U K E S
Cape Poge
Great Point
North Tisbury
MARTHA'S
Edgartown
West Tisbury
VINEYARD
Chappaquiddick I
Menemsha
Katama
Gay Head
Chilmark
MUSKEGET CHANNEL
Muskeget I
Wauwinet
Nashaquitsa
Tuckernuck I
N A N T U C K E T
Quidnet
Polpis
Nantucket
Sankaty Head
Madaket
Siasconset
NANTUCKET I
Surfside

10   0   10   20   30   40 Miles

Chronology of DUKES

Map	Date	Event	Resulting Area
❶	22 Jun 1695	Created from Martha's Vineyard and the Elizabeth Is.	100 sq mi

(Heavy line depicts historical boundary. Base map shows present-day information.)

❶ 22 Jun 1695 – present

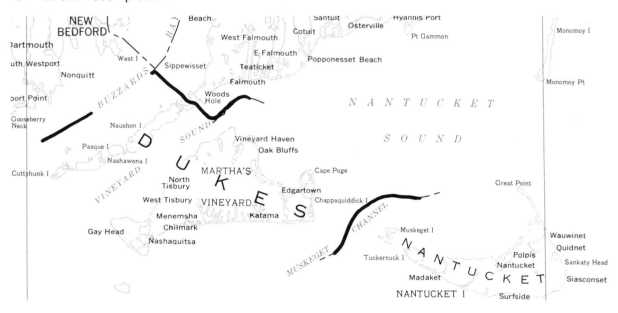

10   0   10   20   30   40 Miles

Chronology of ESSEX

Map	Date	Event	Resulting Area
❶	10 May 1643	Created as one of four original counties in Massachusetts	440 sq mi
	26 May 1658	Gained small area (15 acres) from MIDDLESEX when town of Andover gained from Billerica [location unknown, not mapped]	

(Heavy line depicts historical boundary. Base map shows present-day information.)

❶   10 May 1643–17 Sep 1679

10   0   10   20   30   40 Miles

Chronology of ESSEX

Map	Date	Event	Resulting Area
❷	18 Sep 1679	Gained towns of Amesbury, Haverhill, and Salisbury when original NORFOLK eliminated	550 sq mi
	7 Oct 1691	Continued under new provincial charter [no change]	
❸	22 Feb 1841	Gained from SUFFOLK when town of Saugus gained from Chelsea	550 sq mi

(Heavy line depicts historical boundary. Base map shows present-day information.)

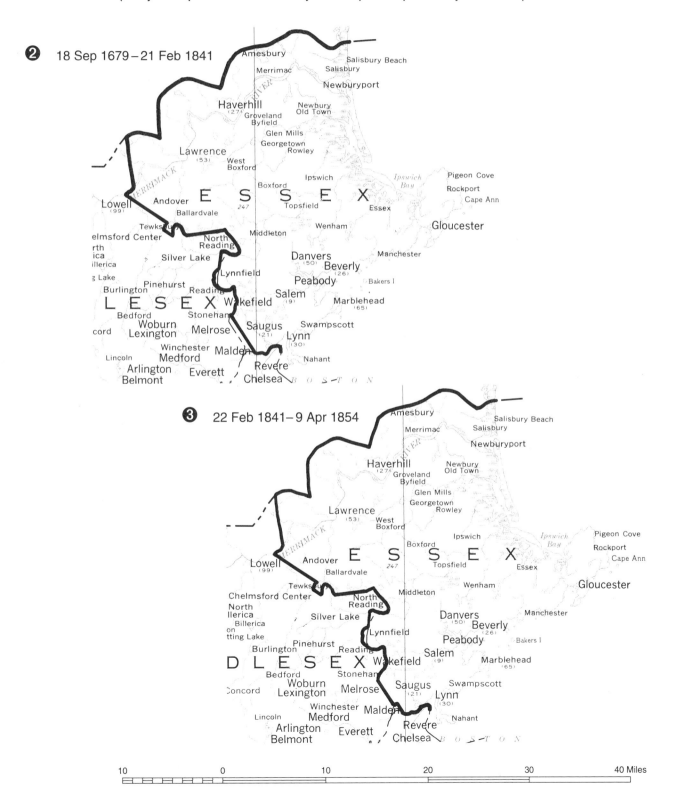

❷ 18 Sep 1679 – 21 Feb 1841

❸ 22 Feb 1841 – 9 Apr 1854

10   0   10   20   30   40 Miles

Chronology of ESSEX

Map	Date	Event	Resulting Area
❹	10 Apr 1854	Lost to MIDDLESEX when town of Reading gained from Lynnfield	550 sq mi
❹	7 Jan 1858	Lost to MIDDLESEX when town of North Reading gained from Lynnfield	540 sq mi
	21 May 1903	Boundary with MIDDLESEX redefined in part when line between towns of Tewkesbury and Andover redefined [no change]	
	12 Mar 1904	Boundary with MIDDLESEX redefined in part when line between towns of North Andover and North Reading redefined [no change]	
	22 Apr 1904	Boundary with MIDDLESEX redefined in part when line between towns of North Reading and Andover redefined [no change]	
	2 May 1905	Boundary with MIDDLESEX redefined in part when line between towns of Lynnfield and Reading redefined [no change]	
❹	18 Sep 1933	Lost small area to MIDDLESEX when town of Wakefield gained from Saugus	540 sq mi

(Heavy line depicts historical boundary. Base map shows present-day information.)

❹   10 Apr 1854 – 9 Apr 1947

Chronology of ESSEX

Map	Date	Event	Resulting Area
❺	10 Apr 1947	Exchanged with MIDDLESEX when town of Lynnfield exchanged with Reading	540 sq mi

(Heavy line depicts historical boundary. Base map shows present-day information.)

❺   10 Apr 1947– present

Chronology of FRANKLIN

Map	Date	Event	Resulting Area
❶	2 Dec 1811	Created from HAMPSHIRE	700 sq mi
❷	7 Feb 1816	Lost to WORCESTER when town of Athol gained from Orange	690 sq mi

(Heavy line depicts historical boundary. Base map shows present-day information.)

❶ 2 Dec 1811–6 Feb 1816

❷ 7 Feb 1816–27 Jan 1822

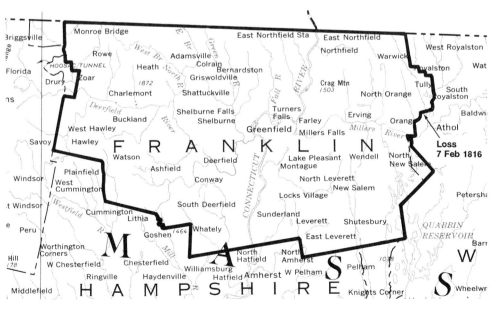

10   0   10   20   30   40 Miles

Chronology of FRANKLIN

Map	Date	Event	Resulting Area
❸	28 Jan 1822	Lost to HAMPSHIRE when town of Prescott created from Pelham and New Salem	680 sq mi
❹	21 Feb 1822	Gained from BERKSHIRE when town of Monroe created from Rowe and non-town area called the Gore	700 sq mi

(Heavy line depicts historical boundary. Base map shows present-day information.)

❸ 28 Jan 1822 – 20 Feb 1822

❹ 21 Feb 1822 – 4 Feb 1830

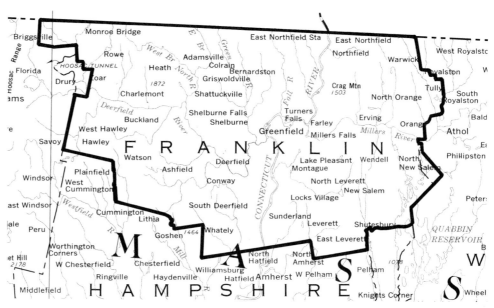

Chronology of FRANKLIN

Map	Date	Event	Resulting Area
⑤	5 Feb 1830	Lost to WORCESTER when town of Athol gained from New Salem	700 sq mi
⑥	16 Mar 1837	Lost to WORCESTER when town of Athol gained from New Salem	700 sq mi

(Heavy line depicts historical boundary. Base map shows present-day information.)

⑤ 5 Feb 1830–15 Mar 1837

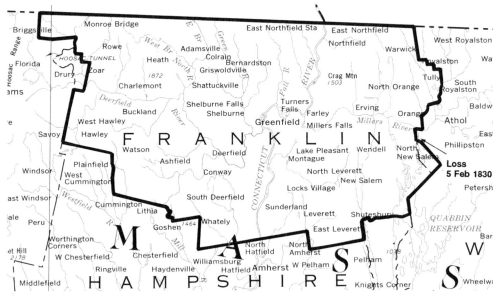

⑥ 16 Mar 1837–1 Apr 1838

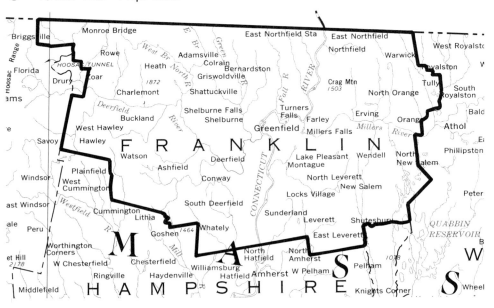

Chronology of FRANKLIN

Map	Date	Event	Resulting Area
❼	2 Apr 1838	Gained from BERKSHIRE when towns of Charlemont and Rowe gained from Zoar	710 sq mi
	2 Feb 1849	Boundary with HAMPSHIRE clarified when line between towns of Williamsburg and Whately clarified [no change]	
	27 Apr 1911	Boundary with WORCESTER redefined in part when line between towns of New Salem and Prescott redefined [no change]	
❽	28 Apr 1938	Gained from HAMPSHIRE when town of New Salem gained from Enfield, Greenwich, and Prescott	740 sq mi

(Heavy line depicts historical boundary. Base map shows present-day information.)

❼ 2 Apr 1838 – 27 Apr 1938

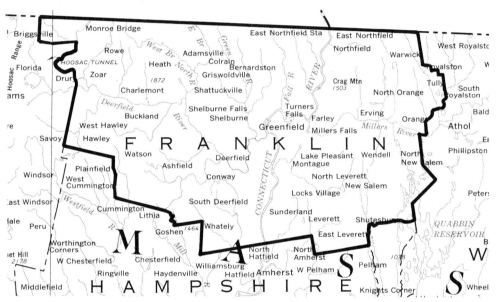

❽ 28 Apr 1938 – present

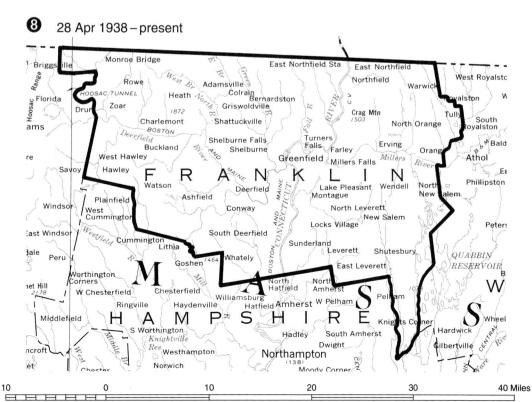

10   0   10   20   30   40 Miles

Chronology of HAMPDEN

Map	Date	Event	Resulting Area
❶	1 Aug 1812	Created from HAMPSHIRE	640 sq mi
	3 Nov 1826	Exchanged small strips with TOLLAND (Conn.) when an irregularity in the state boundary was straightened [not mapped]	
❷	7 Feb 1831	Gained from WORCESTER when town of Palmer gained from Western (now Warren)	650 sq mi
	4 May 1853	Boundary with BERKSHIRE clarified when line between towns of Sandisfield and Tolland clarified [no change]	

(Heavy line depicts historical boundary. Base map shows present-day information.)

❶ 1 Aug 1812 – 6 Feb 1831

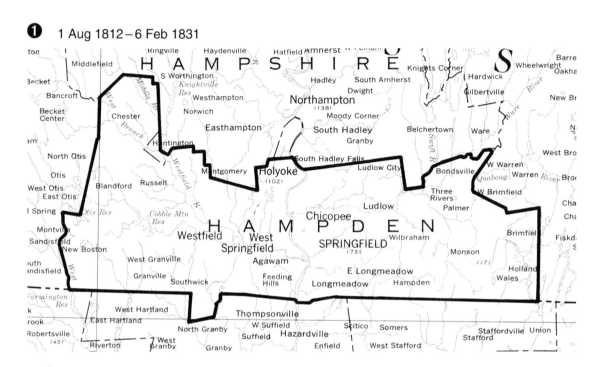

❷ 7 Feb 1831 – 24 May 1853

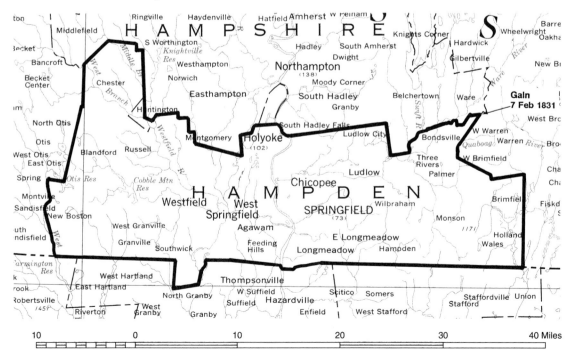

10   0   10   20   30   40 Miles

Chronology of HAMPDEN

Map	Date	Event	Resulting Area
❸	25 May 1853	Lost to HAMPSHIRE when town of Norwich (now Huntington) gained from Chester and Blandford	650 sq mi
	15 May 1855	Boundary with BERKSHIRE redefined when line between towns of Sandisfield and Tolland redefined [no change]	
❹	9 Jun 1909	Gained from HAMPSHIRE when town of Holyoke gained from Northampton	650 sq mi
	29 Apr 1910	Boundary with HAMPSHIRE redefined in part when line between towns of Ware and Palmer redefined [no change]	

(Heavy line depicts historical boundary. Base map shows present-day information.)

❸ 25 May 1853 – 8 Jun 1909

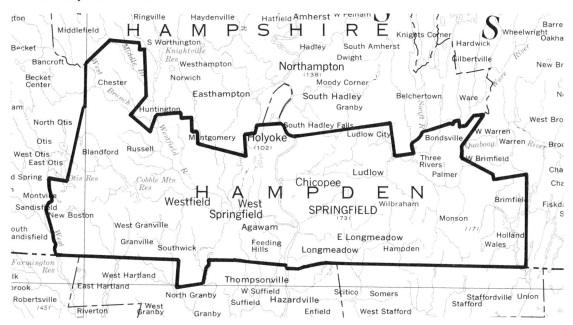

❹ 9 Jun 1909 – present

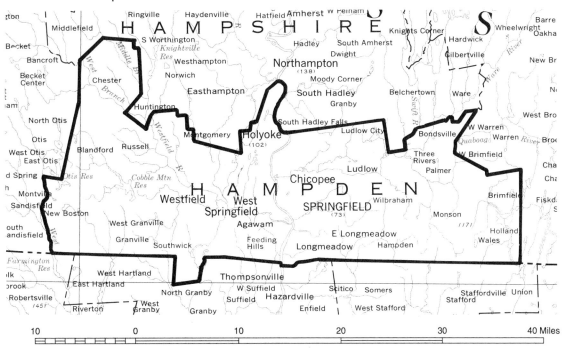

10   0   10   20   30   40 Miles

Chronology of HAMPSHIRE

Map	Date	Event	Resulting Area
❶	7 May 1662	Created from non-county area (towns of Springfield, Northampton, Hadley, and all territory within 30 miles), effectively covering entire western part of the province	Indefinite
❷	19 May 1669	Gained from Connecticut when town of Westfield (now Southwick) created in present Connecticut	Indefinite
❸	3 Jun 1674	Gained from Connecticut when town of Suffield created within present Connecticut	Indefinite

(Heavy line depicts historical boundary. Base map shows present-day information.)

❶   7 May 1662 – 18 May 1669

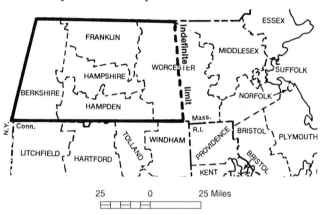

❷   19 May 1669 – 2 Jun 1674

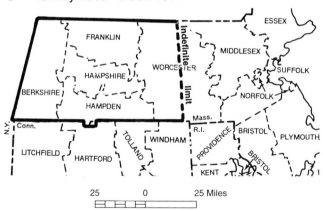

❸   3 Jun 1674 – 15 May 1683

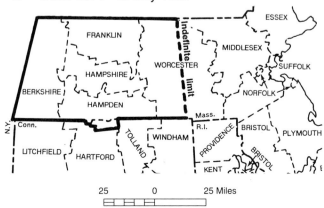

Chronology of HAMPSHIRE

Map	Date	Event	Resulting Area
❹	16 May 1683	Gained from Connecticut when town of Enfield created within present Connecticut	Indefinite
	7 Oct 1691	Continued under new provincial charter [no change]	
❺	10 Jul 1731	Lost to creation of WORCESTER	3,090 sq mi
❻	16 Jan 1741/1742	Lost to WORCESTER when town of Western (now Warren) created from Brookfield, Brimfield, and Kingsfield	3,080 sq mi
❼	May 1749	Lost towns of Enfield, Somers (formerly part of Enfield), and Suffield to Connecticut	3,020 sq mi
	12 Apr 1753	Redefined to cover all territory west of Connecticut R. [no change]	
	9 Jun 1756	Boundary with WORCESTER adjusted when dispute between towns of Greenwich and Hardwick settled [no discernible change]	

(Heavy line depicts historical boundary. Base map shows present-day information.)

❹ 16 May 1683 – 9 Jul 1731

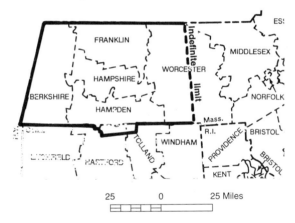

25   0   25 Miles

❺ 10 Jul 1731 – 15 Jan 1741/1742

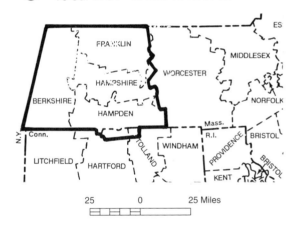

25   0   25 Miles

❻ 16 Jan 1741/1742 – May 1749

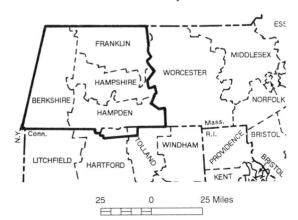

25   0   25 Miles

❼ May 1749 – 29 Jun 1761

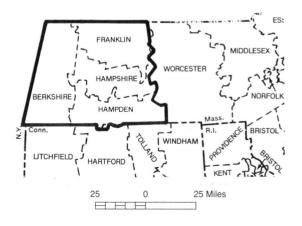

25   0   25 Miles

Chronology of HAMPSHIRE

Map	Date	Event	Resulting Area
8	30 Jun 1761	Lost to creation of BERKSHIRE	1,880 sq mi
8	5 Jan 1764	Lost to WORCESTER when town of Western (now Warren) gained from Palmer	1,880 sq mi
8	5 Feb 1765	Gained from WORCESTER when town of Greenwich gained from Hardwick	1,880 sq mi

(Heavy line depicts historical boundary. Base map shows present-day information.)

8 30 Jun 1761–29 Jun 1768

Chronology of HAMPSHIRE

Map	Date	Event	Resulting Area
⑨	30 Jun 1768	Gained from BERKSHIRE when town of Worthington created from Plantation #3	1,890 sq mi

(Heavy line depicts historical boundary. Base map shows present-day information.)

⑨   30 Jun 1768–1774

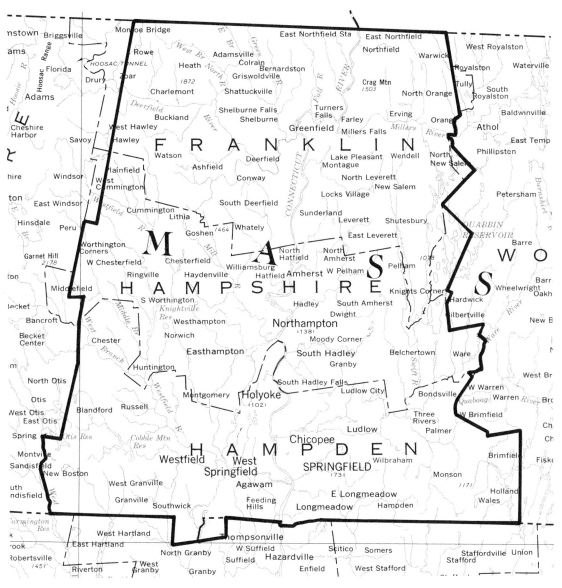

Chronology of HAMPSHIRE

Map	Date	Event	Resulting Area
⑩	1774	Lost to HARTFORD (Conn.) when Connecticut took over that part of town of Southwick that extended south of the provincial boundary	1,880 sq mi

(Heavy line depicts historical boundary. Base map shows present-day information.)

⑩   1774 – 22 Jun 1779

10	0	10	20	30	40 Miles

Chronology of HAMPSHIRE

Map	Date	Event	Resulting Area
⑪	23 Jun 1779	Gained from BERKSHIRE when town of Cummington created from Plantation #5	1,890 sq mi

(Heavy line depicts historical boundary. Base map shows present-day information.)

⑪   23 Jun 1779 – 11 Mar 1783

10	0	10	20	30	40 Miles

Chronology of HAMPSHIRE

Map	Date	Event	Resulting Area
⑫	12 Mar 1783	Gained from BERKSHIRE when town of Middlefield created from Worthington, Chester, Partridgefield (now Peru), Becket, Washington, and Prescott's Grant (now Middlefield)	1,900 sq mi

(Heavy line depicts historical boundary. Base map shows present-day information.)

⑫   12 Mar 1783–14 Oct 1783

Chronology of HAMPSHIRE

Map	Date	Event	Resulting Area
⑬	15 Oct 1783	Gained from WORCESTER when town of Orange created from Athol and Royalston	1,910 sq mi

(Heavy line depicts historical boundary. Base map shows present-day information.)

⑬ 15 Oct 1783 – 8 Feb 1785

Chronology of HAMPSHIRE

Map	Date	Event	Resulting Area
⑭	9 Feb 1785	Gained from BERKSHIRE when town of Rowe created from the Myrifield Grant and non-town territory	1,920 sq mi

(Heavy line depicts historical boundary. Base map shows present-day information.)

⑭   9 Feb 1785 – 8 Mar 1793

[Map showing county boundaries with towns including Briggsville, Monroe Bridge, East Northfield, West Royalston, Waterville, Rowe, Adamsville, Colrain, Northfield, Warwick, Florida, Heath, Bernardston, Griswoldville, Crag Mtn, North Orange, South Royalston, Drury, Zoar, Charlemont, Shattuckville, Shelburne Falls, Turners Falls, Farley, Erving, Orange, Athol, Baldwinville, East Templ, Buckland, Shelburne, Greenfield, Millers Falls, Phillipston, West Hawley, Savoy, Hawley, Watson, Deerfield, Lake Pleasant, Montague, Wendell, North New Salem, Petersham, Plainfield, West Cummington, Ashfield, Conway, North Leverett, New Salem, Locks Village, Cummington, Lithia, South Deerfield, Sunderland, Leverett, Shutesbury, Quabbin Reservoir, Barre, Goshen, Whately, East Leverett, Worthington Corners, W Chesterfield, Chesterfield, Williamsburg, North Hatfield, North Amherst, Pelham, Wheelwright, Oakh, Garnet Hill, Ringville, Haydenville, Hatfield, Amherst, W Pelham, Middlefield, S Worthington, Knightville Res, Hadley, South Amherst, Knights Corner, Hardwick, Gilbertville, Bancroft, Westhampton, Dwight, Belchertown, Ware, New B, Becket Center, Chester, Norwich, Northampton, Moody Corner, Easthampton, South Hadley, Belchertown, West Br, North Otis, Huntington, Montgomery, Holyoke, Granby, South Hadley Falls, Ludlow City, Bondsville, W Warren, Warren, Otis, Russell, Ludlow, Three Rivers, Palmer, W Brimfield, West Otis, Blandford, Chicopee, East Otis, Springfield, Montville, Westfield, West Springfield, Wilbraham, Monson, Brimfield, Sandisfield, New Boston, Agawam, E Longmeadow, Holland, West Granville, Feeding Hills, Longmeadow, Hampden, Wales, Granville, Southwick, West Hartland, East Hartland, Thompsonville, W Suffield, Scitico, Somers, Staffordville, Union, Robertsville, North Granby, Suffield, Hazardville, Stafford, Riverton, West Granby, Granby, Enfield, West Stafford]

10   0   10   20   30   40 Miles

Chronology of HAMPSHIRE

Map	Date	Event	Resulting Area
⑮	9 Mar 1793	Gained from BERKSHIRE when town of Hawley gained from Plantation #7	1,930 sq mi
	15 Jul 1794	Lost small area to WORCESTER when town of Western (now Warren) gained from Palmer to accommodate local property owners [location unknown, not mapped]	

(Heavy line depicts historical boundary. Base map shows present-day information.)

⑮ 9 Mar 1793–17 Feb 1801

Chronology of HAMPSHIRE

Map	Date	Event	Resulting Area
⑯	18 Feb 1801	Lost to WORCESTER when town of Dana created from Greenwich, Hardwick, and Petersham	1,920 sq mi

(Heavy line depicts historical boundary. Base map shows present-day information.)

⑯   18 Feb 1801–1804

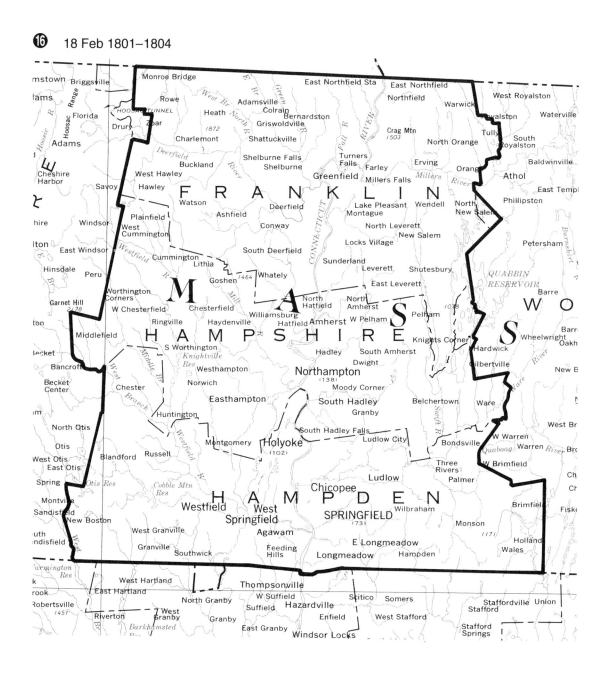

| 10 | 0 | 10 | 20 | 30 | 40 Miles |

Chronology of HAMPSHIRE

Map	Date	Event	Resulting Area
⑰	1804	Gained from HARTFORD (Conn.) when state boundary adjusted (the "Southwick Jog")	1,930 sq mi

(Heavy line depicts historical boundary. Base map shows present-day information.)

⑰ 1804–1 Dec 1811

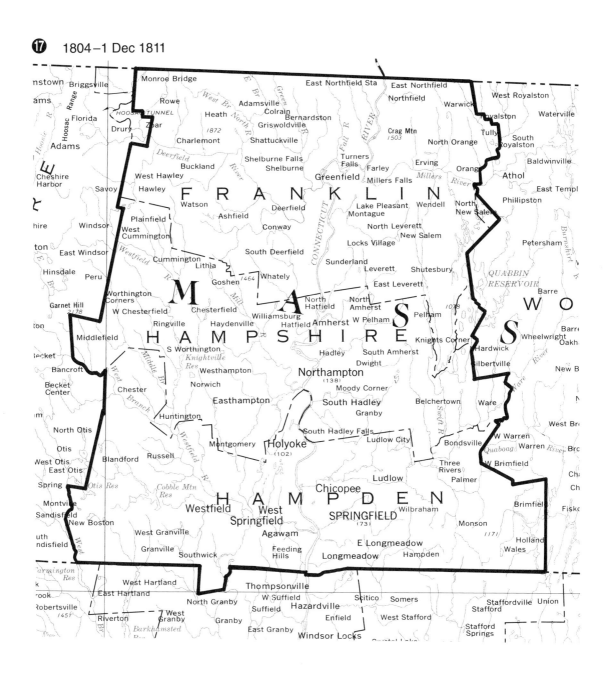

10   0   10   20   30   40 Miles

Chronology of HAMPSHIRE

Map	Date	Event	Resulting Area
⑱	2 Dec 1811	Lost to creation of FRANKLIN	1,230 sq mi

(Heavy line depicts historical boundary. Base map shows present-day information.)

⑱   2 Dec 1811–31 Jul 1812

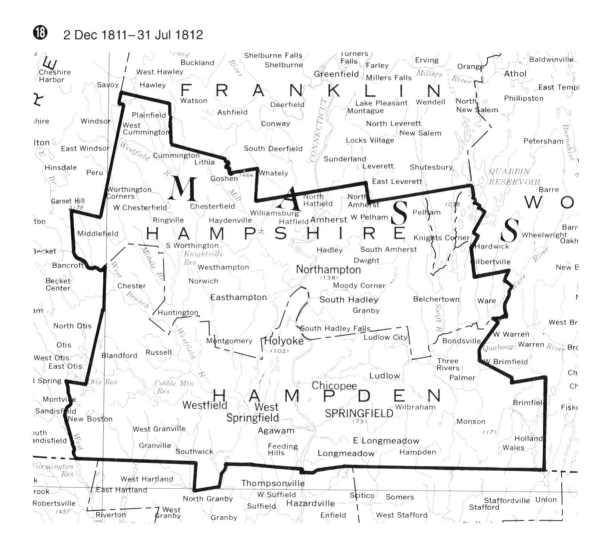

10   0   10   20   30   40 Miles

Chronology of HAMPSHIRE

Map	Date	Event	Resulting Area
⑲	1 Aug 1812	Lost to creation of HAMPDEN	590 sq mi
⑳	28 Jan 1822	Gained from FRANKLIN when town of Prescott created from Pelham and New Salem	600 sq mi
⑳	8 Feb 1823	Gained small area from WORCESTER when town of Ware gained from Western (now Warren)	600 sq mi
	2 Feb 1849	Boundary with FRANKLIN clarified when line between towns of Williamsburg and Whately clarified [no change]	

(Heavy line depicts historical boundary. Base map shows present-day information.)

⑲   1 Aug 1812 – 27 Jan 1822

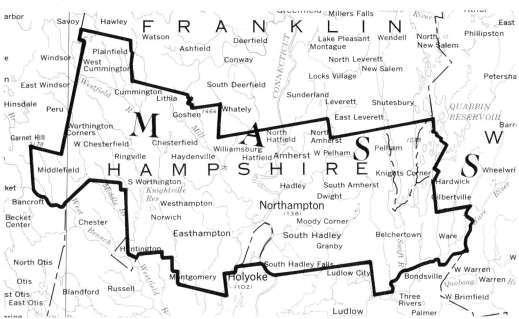

⑳   28 Jan 1822 – 24 May 1853

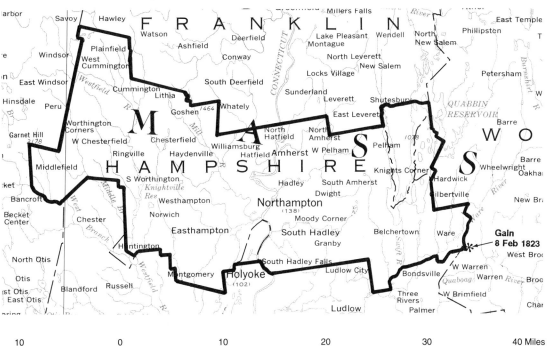

10	0	10	20	30	40 Miles

Chronology of HAMPSHIRE

Map	Date	Event	Resulting Area
㉑	25 May 1853	Gained from HAMPDEN when town of Norwich (now Huntington) gained from Chester and Blandford	610 sq mi
㉒	9 Jun 1909	Lost to HAMPDEN when town of Holyoke gained from Northampton	600 sq mi
	29 Apr 1910	Boundary with HAMPDEN redefined in part when line between towns of Ware and Palmer redefined [no change]	

(Heavy line depicts historical boundary. Base map shows present-day information.)

㉑   25 May 1853–8 Jun 1909

㉒   9 Jun 1909–27 Apr 1938

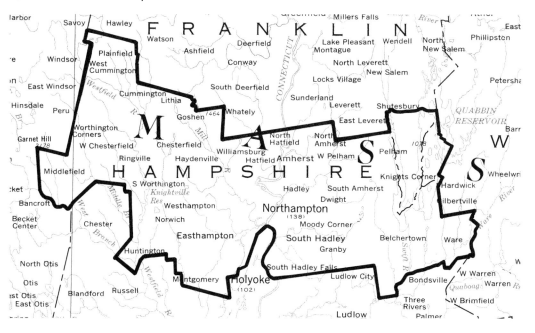

10	0	10	20	30	40 Miles

Chronology of HAMPSHIRE

Map	Date	Event	Resulting Area
㉓	28 Apr 1938	Lost to FRANKLIN when town of New Salem gained from Enfield, Greenwich, and Prescott; lost to WORCESTER when town of Petersham gained from Dana, Greenwich, and Prescott and when town of Hardwick gained from Greenwich	580 sq mi

(Heavy line depicts historical boundary. Base map shows present-day information.)

㉓   28 Apr 1938 – present

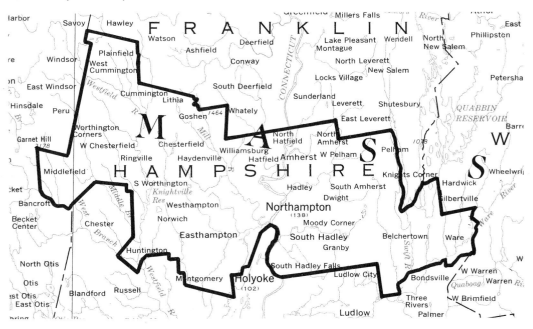

Chronology of MIDDLESEX

Map	Date	Event	Resulting Area
❶	10 May 1643	Created as one of four original counties in Massachusetts	Indefinite
	26 May 1658	Lost small area (15 acres) to ESSEX when town of Andover gained from Billerica [location unknown, not mapped]	

(Heavy line depicts historical boundary. Base map shows present-day information.)

❶   10 May 1643 – 9 Jul 1731

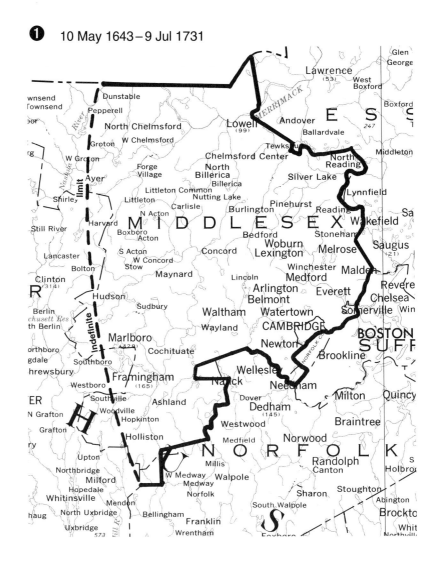

| 10 | 0 | 10 | 20 | 30 | 40 Miles |

Chronology of MIDDLESEX

Map	Date	Event	Resulting Area
	7 Oct 1691	Continued under new provincial charter [no change]	
❷	10 Jul 1731	Lost to creation of WORCESTER	880 sq mi

(Heavy line depicts historical boundary. Base map shows present-day information.)

❷   10 Jul 1731– 28 Jun 1732

| 10 | | 0 | | 10 | | 20 | | 30 | | 40 Miles |

Chronology of MIDDLESEX

Map	Date	Event	Resulting Area
❸	29 Jun 1732	Exchanged with WORCESTER when town of Harvard created from Groton, Lancaster, and Stow	870 sq mi

(Heavy line depicts historical boundary. Base map shows present-day information.)

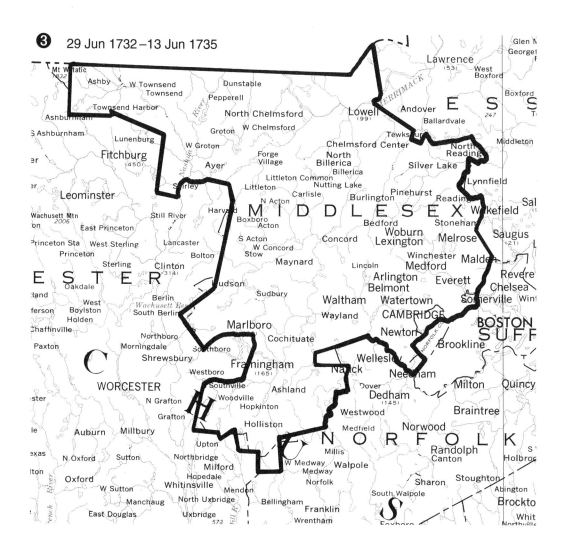

❸ 29 Jun 1732 – 13 Jun 1735

Chronology of MIDDLESEX

Map	Date	Event	Resulting Area
❹	14 Jun 1735	Lost to WORCESTER when town of Upton created from Hopkinton	870 sq mi
❹	6 Mar 1767	Gained small area from WORCESTER when town of Ashby created from Fitchburg and Ashburnham	870 sq mi

(Heavy line depicts historical boundary. Base map shows present-day information.)

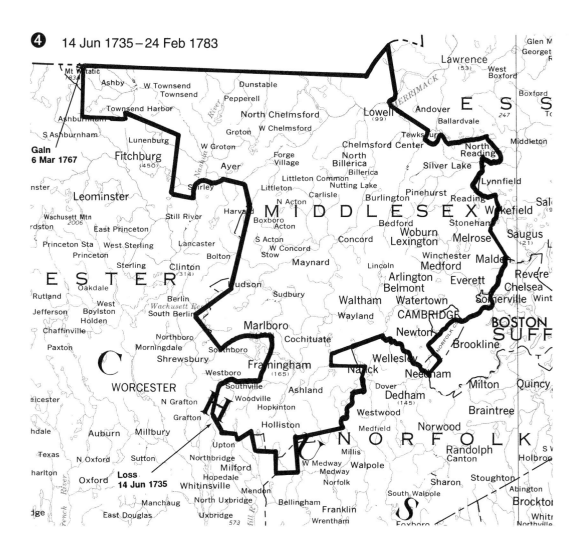

❹ 14 Jun 1735 – 24 Feb 1783

| 10 | 0 | 10 | 20 | 30 | 40 Miles |

Chronology of MIDDLESEX

Map	Date	Event	Resulting Area
❺	25 Feb 1783	Gained from WORCESTER when town of Boxborough gained from Harvard	870 sq mi

(Heavy line depicts historical boundary. Base map shows present-day information.)

❺　25 Feb 1783 – 15 Mar 1784

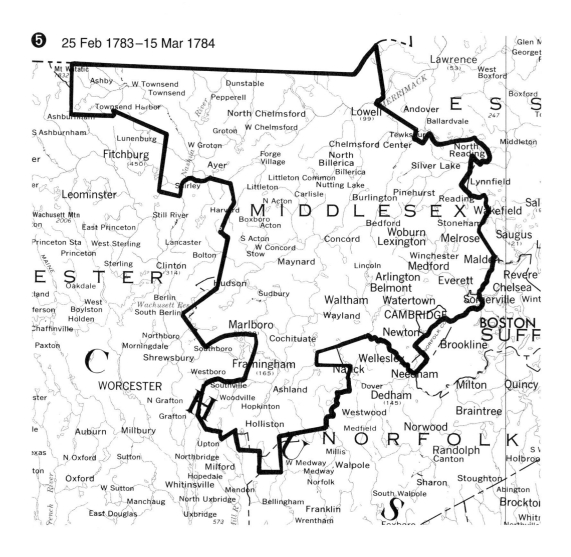

Chronology of MIDDLESEX

Map	Date	Event	Resulting Area
❻	16 Mar 1784	Lost to WORCESTER when town of Berlin created from Marlborough, Northborough, and Bolton	870 sq mi
❻	7 Mar 1786	Lost small area to WORCESTER when town of Southborough gained from Framingham	870 sq mi
	3 Mar 1792	Boundary with SUFFOLK redefined in part when boundary between towns of Medway and Sherburne redefined [no change]	

(Heavy line depicts historical boundary. Base map shows present-day information.)

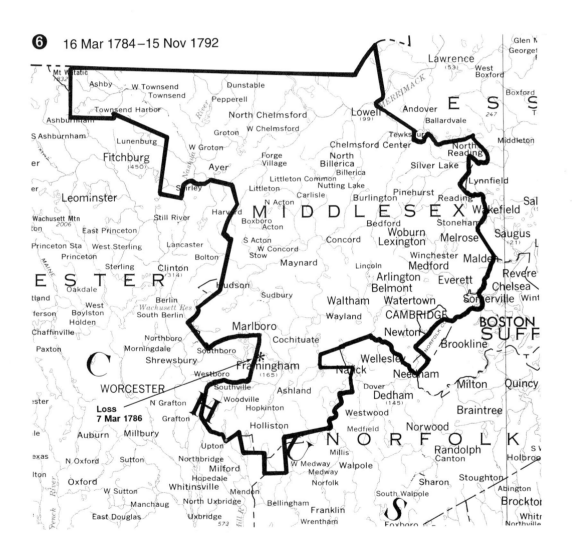

❻   16 Mar 1784–15 Nov 1792

10   0   10   20   30   40 Miles

Chronology of MIDDLESEX

Map	Date	Event	Resulting Area
❼	16 Nov 1792	Gained from WORCESTER when town of Ashby gained from Ashburnham	870 sq mi

(Heavy line depicts historical boundary. Base map shows present-day information.)

❼ 16 Nov 1792 – 21 Jun 1797

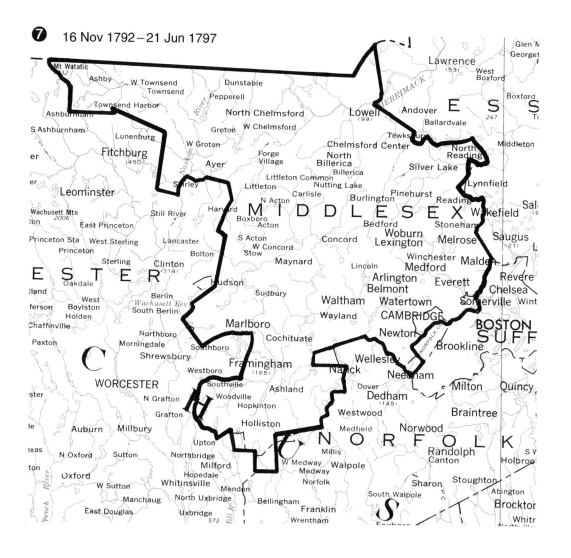

Chronology of MIDDLESEX

Map	Date	Event	Resulting Area
⑧	22 Jun 1797	Exchanged with NORFOLK when town of Natick exchanged with Needham	870 sq mi
⑧	20 Jun 1807	Lost to WORCESTER when town of Northborough gained from Marlborough	870 sq mi
	8 Mar 1808	Lost small area to WORCESTER when town of Upton gained from Hopkinton to accommodate local property owner [location unknown, not mapped]	
	11 Feb 1829	Lost small area (one acre) to WORCESTER when town of Bolton gained from Marlborough to accommodate local property owner [location unknown, not mapped]	

(Heavy line depicts historical boundary. Base map shows present-day information.)

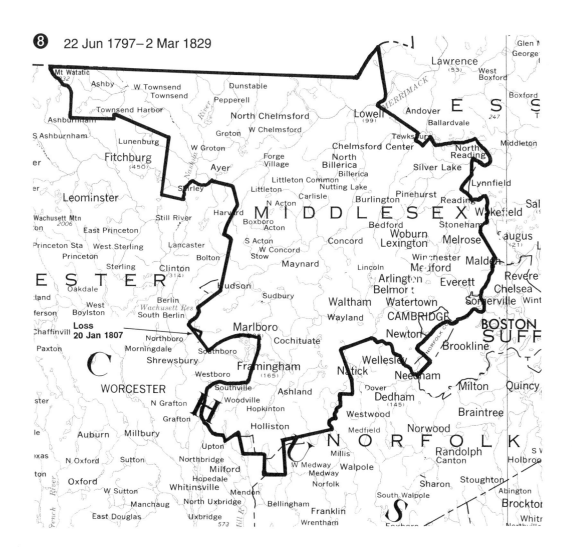

Chronology of MIDDLESEX

Map	Date	Event	Resulting Area
⑨	3 Mar 1829	Gained small area from WORCESTER when town of Ashby gained from Fitchburg to accommodate local property owner [location unknown, not mapped]; exchanged with NORFOLK when Holliston gained from Medway	870 sq mi

(Heavy line depicts historical boundary. Base map shows present-day information.)

⑨   3 Mar 1829 – 26 Mar 1835

Chronology of MIDDLESEX

Map	Date	Event	Resulting Area
⑩	27 Mar 1835	Exchanged with WORCESTER when towns of Holliston, Hopkinton, and Milford exchanged	870 sq mi
	16 Mar 1838	Boundary with WORCESTER redefined in part when line between towns of Marlborough and Bolton redefined [no change]	

(Heavy line depicts historical boundary. Base map shows present-day information.)

⑩   27 Mar 1835 – 22 Apr 1838

Chronology of MIDDLESEX

Map	Date	Event	Resulting Area
⑪	23 Apr 1838	Lost to NORFOLK when town of Roxbury gained from Newton	870 sq mi
	24 Mar 1843	Gained small area from WORCESTER when town of Marlborough gained from Southborough to accommodate local property owners [location unknown, not mapped]	
	3 Mar 1846	Boundary with WORCESTER redefined in part when line between towns of Shirley and Lunenburg redefined [no change]	
	25 Apr 1848	Boundary with WORCESTER redefined in part when line between towns of Shirley and Lunenburg redefined [no change]	

(Heavy line depicts historical boundary. Base map shows present-day information.)

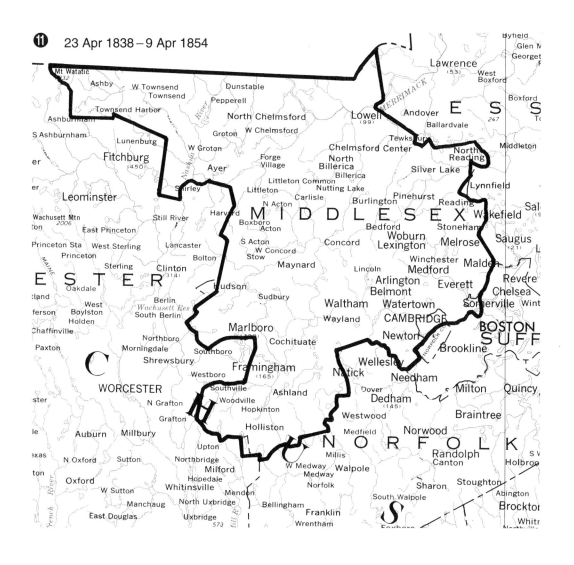

⑪   23 Apr 1838 – 9 Apr 1854

| 10 | 0 | 10 | 20 | 30 | 40 Miles |

Chronology of MIDDLESEX

Map	Date	Event	Resulting Area
⑫	10 Apr 1854	Gained from ESSEX when town of Reading gained from Lynnfield	870 sq mi
⑫	7 Jan 1858	Gained from ESSEX when town of North Reading gained from Lynnfield	870 sq mi

(Heavy line depicts historical boundary. Base map shows present-day information.)

⑫   10 Apr 1854 – 31 Mar 1859

Chronology of MIDDLESEX

Map	Date	Event	Resulting Area
⑬	1 Apr 1859	Lost to WORCESTER when town of Milford gained from Holliston	870 sq mi

(Heavy line depicts historical boundary. Base map shows present-day information.)

⑬   1 Apr 1859 – 19 Mar 1868

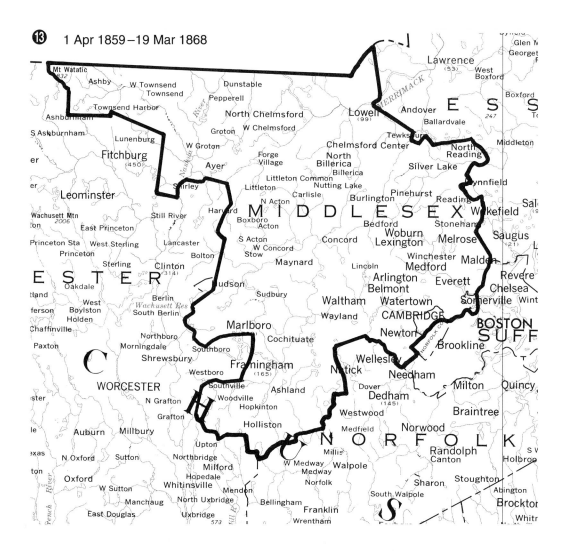

10   0   10   20   30   40 Miles

Chronology of MIDDLESEX

Map	Date	Event	Resulting Area
⑭	20 Mar 1868	Gained from WORCESTER when town of Hudson gained from Bolton	870 sq mi

(Heavy line depicts historical boundary. Base map shows present-day information.)

⑭   20 Mar 1868 – 4 Jan 1874

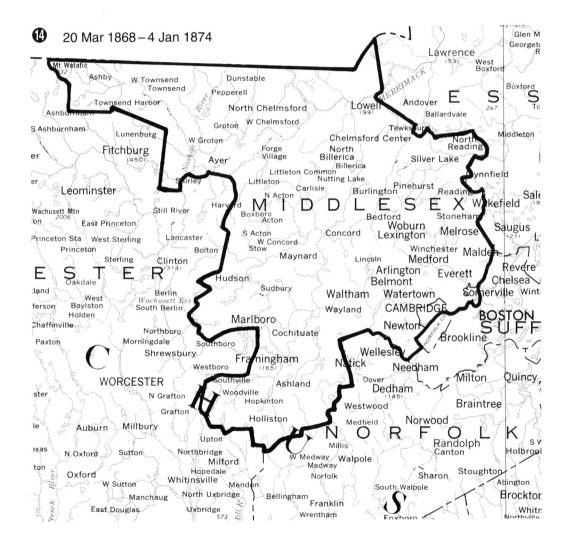

10   0   10   20   30   40 Miles

Chronology of MIDDLESEX

Map	Date	Event	Resulting Area
⑮	5 Jan 1874	Lost to SUFFOLK when Boston gained all of Brighton and Charlestown	870 sq mi
⑮	29 May 1874	Boundary with SUFFOLK adjusted when line between Boston and Newton adjusted	870 sq mi
⑮	1 Jul 1875	Gained small area from SUFFOLK when town of Newton gained from Boston	870 sq mi
⑮	4 May 1891	Boundary with SUFFOLK adjusted when line between Boston and Somerville adjusted	870 sq mi
⑮	29 Mar 1898	Boundary with SUFFOLK adjusted when line through the Charles R. between Boston and Cambridge adjusted [not mapped] and line between Boston and Newton adjusted	870 sq mi
⑮	13 May 1898	Boundary with SUFFOLK adjusted when line between Boston and Newton adjusted	870 sq mi
	16 May 1901	Boundary with WORCESTER redefined when line between towns of Marlborough and Southborough redefined [no discernible change]	
	21 May 1903	Boundary with ESSEX redefined in part when line between towns of Tewkesbury and Andover redefined [no change]	
	12 Mar 1904	Boundary with ESSEX redefined in part when line between towns of North Andover and North Reading redefined [no change]	
	22 Apr 1904	Boundary with ESSEX redefined in part when line between towns of North Reading and Andover redefined [no change]	

(Heavy line depicts historical boundary. Base map shows present-day information.)

⑮   5 Jan 1874 – 9 Apr 1947

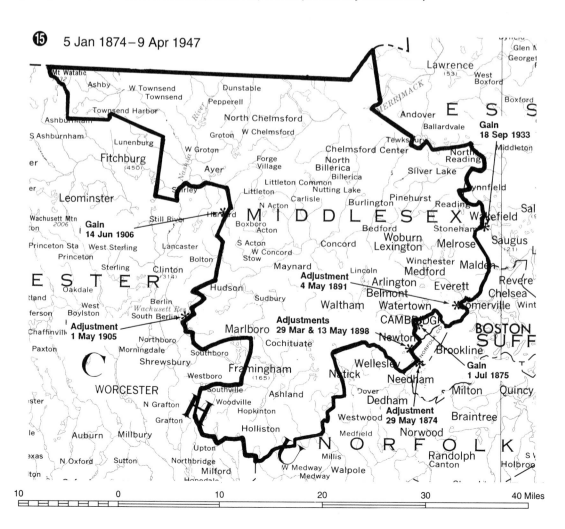

Chronology of MIDDLESEX

Map	Date	Event	Resulting Area
⑮	1 May 1905	Boundary with WORCESTER adjusted when line between towns of Berlin and Hudson redefined [no change] and line between Berlin and Marlborough adjusted	870 sq mi
	2 May 1905	Boundary with ESSEX redefined in part when line between towns of Lynnfield and Reading redefined [no change]	
⑮	14 Jun 1906	Gained small area from WORCESTER when towns of Boxborough and Littleton gained from Harvard	870 sq mi
	28 Mar 1907	Boundary with NORFOLK redefined in part when line between towns of Newton and Brookline redefined [no change]	
	16 May 1907	Boundary with WORCESTER redefined when town of Hopkinton's boundary with Milford and Upton redefined [no change]	
	29 Mar 1910	Boundary with SUFFOLK adjusted when line between Boston and Cambridge in the Charles R. adjusted [not mapped]	
⑮	18 Sep 1933	Gained small area from ESSEX when town of Wakefield gained from Saugus	870 sq mi
⑯	10 Apr 1947	Exchanged with ESSEX when town of Lynnfield exchanged with Reading	870 sq mi

(Heavy line depicts historical boundary. Base map shows present-day information.)

⑯   10 Apr 1947–present

10   0   10   20   30   40 Miles

Chronology of NANTUCKET

Map	Date	Event	Resulting Area
❶	22 Jun 1695	Created from Nantucket I.	50 sq mi

(Heavy line depicts historical boundary. Base map shows present-day information.)

❶ 22 Jun 1695 – present

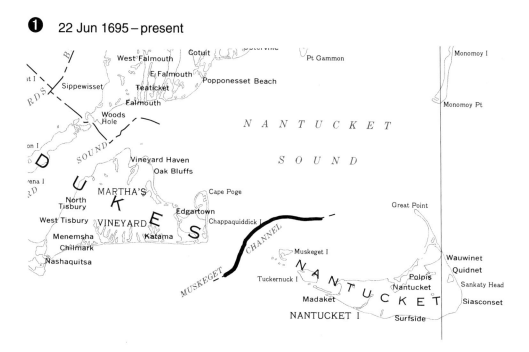

Chronology of NORFOLK (original, extinct)

Map	Date	Event	Resulting Area
❶	10 May 1643	Created as one of four original counties in Massachusetts, covered part of present New Hampshire	Indefinite
	18 Sep 1679	Eliminated when New Hampshire made a separate colony	

(Heavy line depicts historical boundary. Base map shows present-day information.)

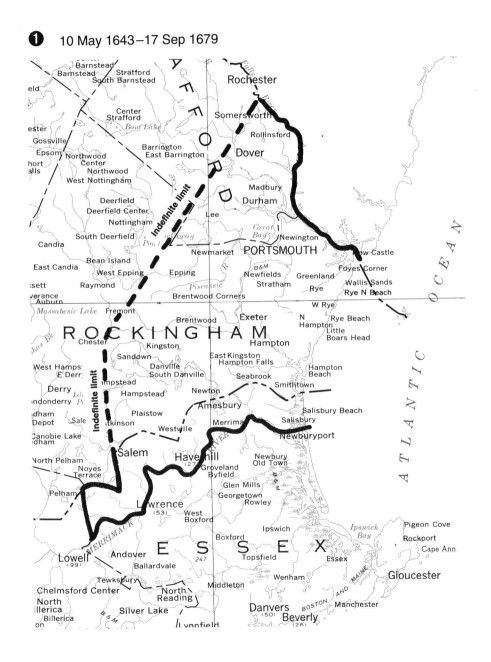

❶ 10 May 1643–17 Sep 1679

Chronology of NORFOLK

Map	Date	Event	Resulting Area
❶	20 Jun 1793	Created from SUFFOLK	440 sq mi
❷	22 Jun 1797	Exchanged with MIDDLESEX when town of Natick exchanged with Needham	440 sq mi
	8 Feb 1798	Lost small strip to PLYMOUTH when town of Bridgewater gained from Stoughton [not mapped]	

(Heavy line depicts historical boundary. Base map shows present-day information.)

❶   20 Jun 1793 – 21 Jun 1797

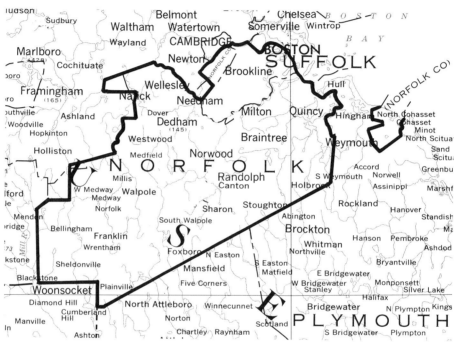

❷   22 Jun 1797 – 5 Mar 1804

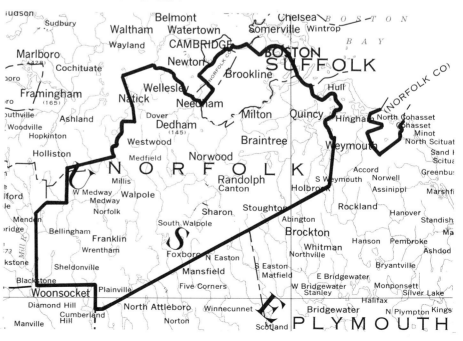

10   0   10   20   30   40 Miles

Chronology of NORFOLK

Map	Date	Event	Resulting Area
❸	6 Mar 1804	Lost to SUFFOLK when Boston gained from Dorchester	430 sq mi
	14 Jun 1823	Gained small area from PLYMOUTH when town of Cohasset gained from Scituate to accommodate local property owners [location unknown, not mapped]	
❸	22 Feb 1825	Boundary with SUFFOLK adjusted when line between Boston and Brookline adjusted	430 sq mi
❹	3 Mar 1829	Exchanged with MIDDLESEX when town of Holliston gained from Medway	440 sq mi
	18 Feb 1830	Boundary with BRISTOL clarified when line between towns of Attleborough and Wrentham clarified [no change]	

(Heavy line depicts historical boundary. Base map shows present-day information.)

❸ 6 Mar 1804 – 2 Mar 1829

❹ 3 Mar 1829 – 24 Mar 1834

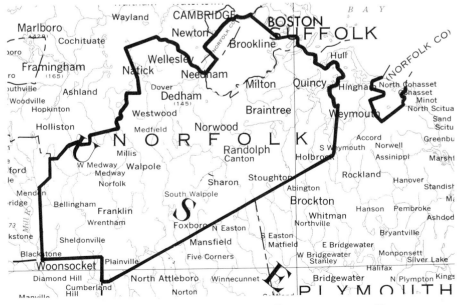

Chronology of NORFOLK

Map	Date	Event	Resulting Area
❺	25 Mar 1834	Lost to SUFFOLK when Boston gained Thompson I. from Dorchester	440 sq mi
	16 Mar 1836	Boundary with SUFFOLK redefined when line between Boston and Roxbury redefined [not mapped]	
	19 Apr 1837	Boundary with SUFFOLK adjusted slightly when line through water between Boston and Roxbury adjusted [not mapped]	

(Heavy line depicts historical boundary. Base map shows present-day information.)

❺   25 Mar 1834 – 22 Apr 1838

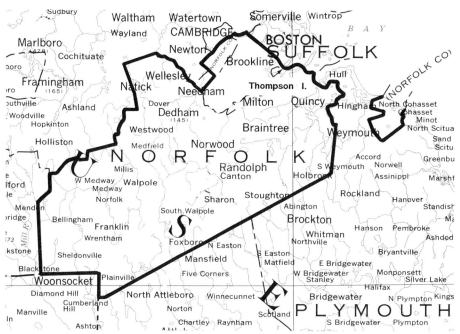

10   0   10   20   30   40 Miles

Chronology of NORFOLK

Map	Date	Event	Resulting Area
6	23 Apr 1838	Gained from MIDDLESEX when town of Roxbury gained from Newton	440 sq mi
	20 Mar 1840	Lost small area to PLYMOUTH when town of Scituate gained from Cohasset to accommodate local property owners [location unknown, not mapped]	
	31 Mar 1847	Boundary with PLYMOUTH clarified in part when line between towns of Weymouth and Abington clarified [no change]	
	3 May 1850	Boundary with SUFFOLK adjusted when line through water between Boston and Roxbury adjusted [not mapped]	
6	21 May 1855	Lost small area to SUFFOLK when Boston gained from Dorchester	440 sq mi
	3 Apr 1860	Boundary with SUFFOLK adjusted slightly when line along streets between Boston and Roxbury shifted to sides of streets from centerlines [not mapped]	
	21 Mar 1861	Boundary with PLYMOUTH clarified in part when boundary between towns of Abington and Randolph clarified [no change]	

(Heavy line depicts historical boundary. Base map shows present-day information.)

6   23 Apr 1838 – 5 Jan 1868

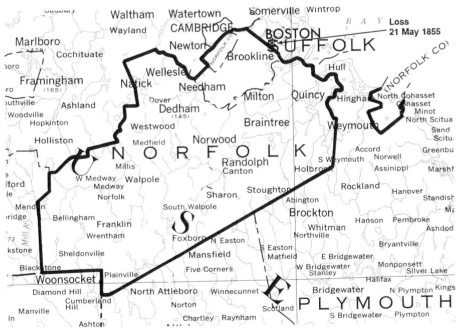

Chronology of NORFOLK

Map	Date	Event	Resulting Area
❼	6 Jan 1868	Lost to SUFFOLK when Boston gained all of Roxbury	430 sq mi

(Heavy line depicts historical boundary. Base map shows present-day information.)

❼ 6 Jan 1868 – 2 Jan 1870

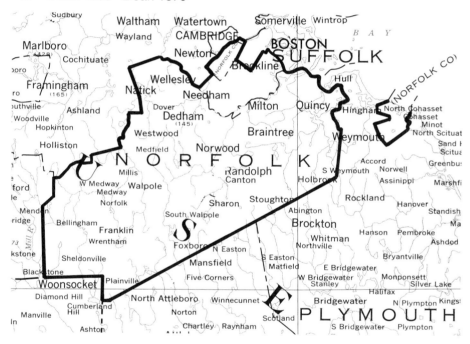

Chronology of NORFOLK

Map	Date	Event	Resulting Area
⑧	3 Jan 1870	Lost to SUFFOLK when Boston gained all of Dorchester	420 sq mi
	2 Apr 1870	Boundary with SUFFOLK adjusted slightly when line along streets between Boston and West Roxbury shifted from one side to the other [not mapped]	
⑧	18 Jun 1870	Lost small area to SUFFOLK when Boston gained from Brookline	420 sq mi
⑧	7 Mar 1872	Exchanged with WORCESTER when town of Bellingham exchanged with Mendon	420 sq mi
⑧	12 Apr 1872	Lost small area to SUFFOLK when Boston gained Mt. Hope Cemetery from West Roxbury	420 sq mi
⑧	27 Apr 1872	Exchanged small areas with SUFFOLK when Boston and Brookline exchanged	420 sq mi

(Heavy line depicts historical boundary. Base map shows present-day information.)

⑧   3 Jan 1870 – 4 Jan 1874

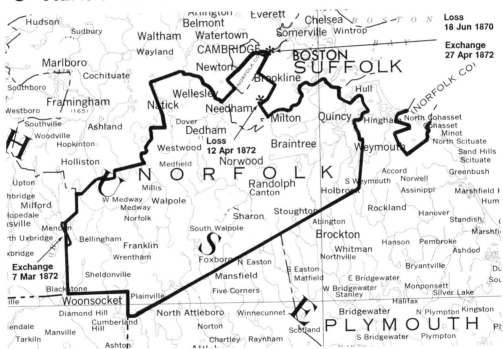

Chronology of NORFOLK

Map	Date	Event	Resulting Area
9	5 Jan 1874	Lost to SUFFOLK when Boston gained West Roxbury	410 sq mi
10	8 May 1874	Lost to SUFFOLK when Boston gained from Brookline	410 sq mi
10	27 May 1890	Boundary with SUFFOLK adjusted when line between Boston and Brookline adjusted	410 sq mi
	13 Apr 1894	Boundary with SUFFOLK adjusted slightly when line between Boston and northern Brookline adjusted [not mapped]	
	30 Apr 1897	Boundary with PLYMOUTH adjusted when line between towns of Cohasset and Hingham adjusted [no discernible change]	
10	1 Apr 1898	Boundary with SUFFOLK adjusted when line between Boston and Hyde Park adjusted	410 sq mi
	28 Mar 1907	Boundary with MIDDLESEX redefined in part when line between towns of Newton and Brookline redefined [no change]	

(Heavy line depicts historical boundary. Base map shows present-day information.)

9   5 Jan 1874 – 7 May 1874

10   8 May 1874 – 31 Dec 1911

Chronology of NORFOLK

Map	Date	Event	Resulting Area
⑪	1 Jan 1912	Lost to SUFFOLK when Boston gained all of Hyde Park	400 sq mi
	23 Mar 1928	Boundary with PLYMOUTH adjusted when line between towns of Cohasset and Hingham adjusted [no discernible change]	

(Heavy line depicts historical boundary. Base map shows present-day information.)

⑪   1 Jan 1912 – present

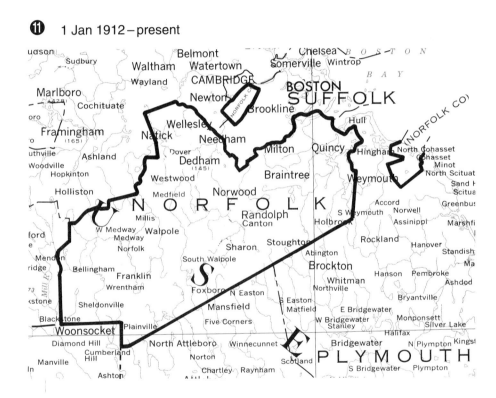

Chronology of PLYMOUTH

Map	Date	Event	Resulting Area
❶	2 Jun 1685	Created as one of three original counties in New Plymouth Colony	590 sq mi
	7 Oct 1691	Became a Massachusetts county when Massachusetts absorbed New Plymouth [no change]	

(Heavy line depicts historical boundary. Base map shows present-day information.)

❶   2 Jun 1685 – 18 Nov 1707

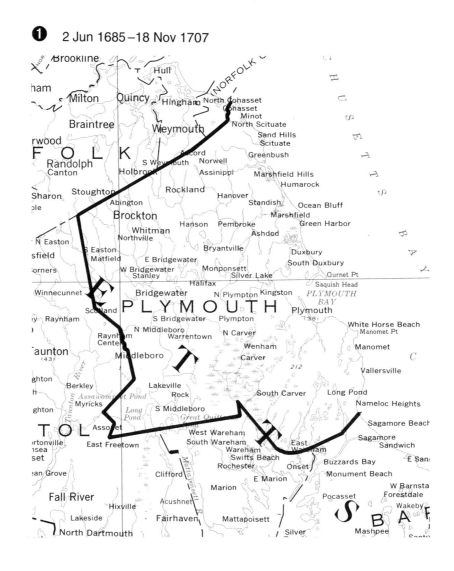

Chronology of PLYMOUTH

Map	Date	Event	Resulting Area
❷	19 Nov 1707	Gained town of Rochester from BARNSTABLE	680 sq mi
❷	29 Oct 1708	Gained small non-county area between BRISTOL and PLYMOUTH	680 sq mi
	18 Mar 1711	Boundary with SUFFOLK redefined as the "Old Colony Line" [no change]	
	20 Nov 1770	Gained small area from SUFFOLK when town of Bridgewater gained from Stoughton to accommodate local property owners [location unknown, not mapped]	
	8 Feb 1798	Gained small strip from NORFOLK when town of Bridgewater gained from Stoughton [not mapped]	
❸	18 Jun 1803	Gained towns of Hingham and Hull from SUFFOLK [see following page]	710 sq mi
	14 Jun 1823	Lost small area to NORFOLK when town of Cohasset gained from Scituate to accommodate local property owners [location unknown, not mapped]	

(Heavy line depicts historical boundary. Base map shows present-day information.)

❷ 19 Nov 1707–17 Jun 1803

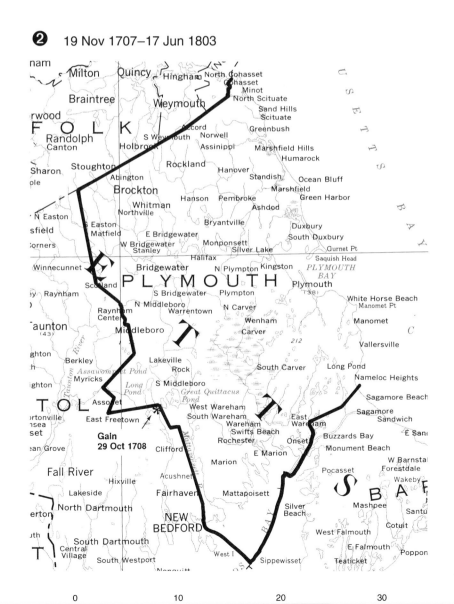

Chronology of PLYMOUTH

Map	Date	Event	Resulting Area
	9 Apr 1836	Boundary with BRISTOL redefined in part when line between towns of Rochester and Fairhaven redefined [no change]	
	20 Mar 1840	Gained small area from NORFOLK when town of Scituate gained from Cohasset to accommodate local property owners [location unknown, not mapped]	
	31 Mar 1847	Boundary with NORFOLK clarified in part when line between towns of Weymouth and Abington clarified [no change]	
	21 Mar 1861	Boundary with NORFOLK clarified in part when boundary between towns of Abington and Randolph clarified [no change]	
	1 Jun 1867	Boundary with BRISTOL clarified in part when boundary between towns of Lakeville and Taunton clarified [no change]	
	14 Apr 1897	Boundary with BARNSTABLE clarified in part when line between towns of Wareham and Bourne clarified [no change]	
	30 Apr 1897	Boundary with NORFOLK adjusted when line between towns of Cohasset and Hingham adjusted [no discernible change]	
	23 Mar 1928	Boundary with NORFOLK adjusted when line between towns of Cohasset and Hingham adjusted [no discernible change]	

(Heavy line depicts historical boundary. Base map shows present-day information.)

❸ 18 Jun 1803 – present

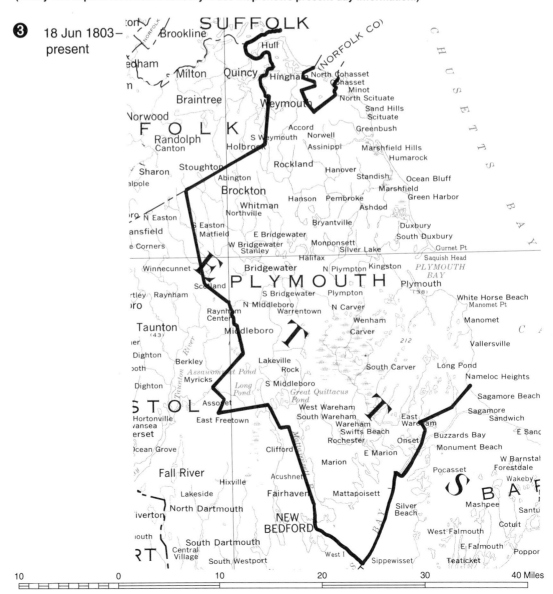

Chronology of SUFFOLK

Map	Date	Event	Resulting Area
❶	10 May 1643	Created as one of four original counties in Massachusetts	Indefinite

(Heavy line depicts historical boundary. Base map shows present-day information.)

❶ 10 May 1643 – 7 Jul 1663

Chronology of SUFFOLK

Map	Date	Event	Resulting Area
❷	8 Jul 1663	Lost to Rhode Island when provincial boundary adjusted	Indefinite

(Heavy line depicts historical boundary. Base map shows present-day information.)

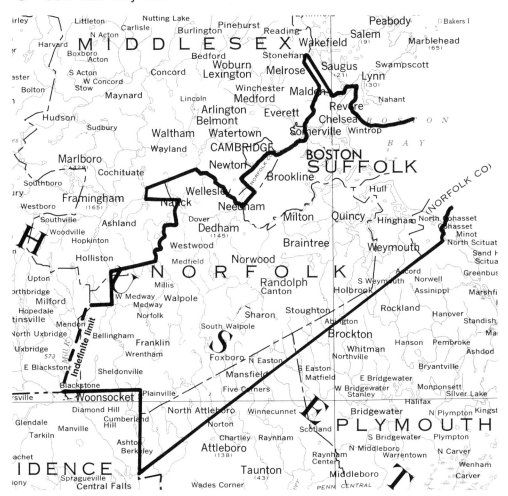

❷ 8 Jul 1663–May 1664

10   0   10   20   30   40 Miles

Chronology of SUFFOLK

Map	Date	Event	Resulting Area
❸	May 1664	Lost to New Plymouth Colony when provincial boundary demarcated	Indefinite

(Heavy line depicts historical boundary. Base map shows present-day information.)

❸ May 1664 – 26 Feb 1664/1665

10		0		10		20		30		40 Miles

Chronology of SUFFOLK

Map	Date	Event	Resulting Area
❹	27 Feb 1664/1665	Gained from Rhode Island when provincial boundary adjusted	Indefinite
❺	15 Mar 1690	Gained from Connecticut when town of Woodstock created within present Connecticut	Indefinite
	7 Oct 1691	Continued under new provincial charter [no change]	
	18 Mar 1711	Boundary with PLYMOUTH redefined as the "Old Colony Line" [no change]	

(Heavy line depicts historical boundary. Base map shows present-day information.)

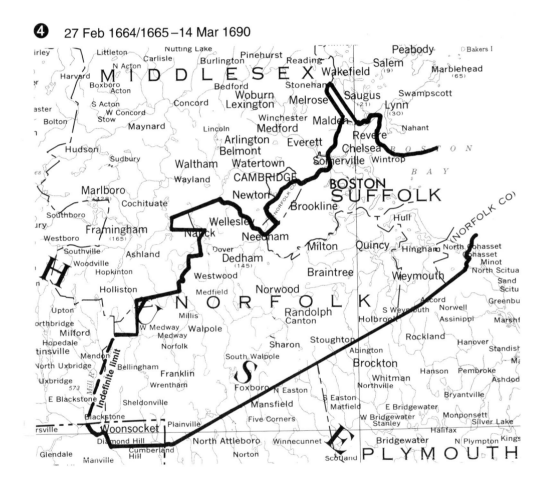

❹ 27 Feb 1664/1665 – 14 Mar 1690

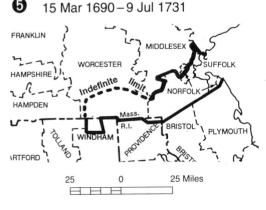

❺ 15 Mar 1690 – 9 Jul 1731

25 0 25 Miles

10 0 10 20 30 40 Miles

Chronology of SUFFOLK

Map	Date	Event	Resulting Area
❻	10 Jul 1731	Lost to creation of WORCESTER	500 sq mi

(Heavy line depicts historical boundary. Base map shows present-day information.)

❻   10 Jul 1731–16 Feb 1746/1747

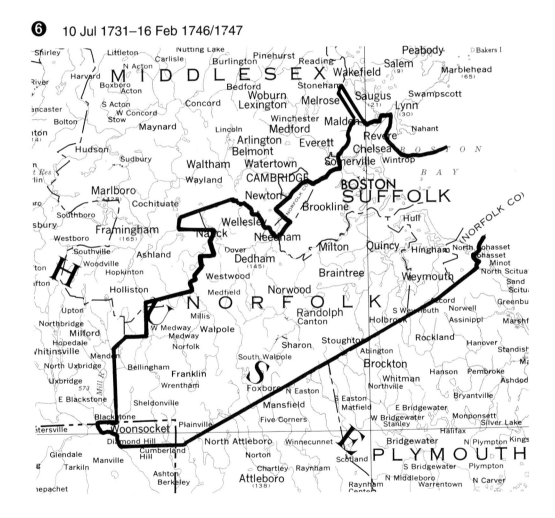

Chronology of SUFFOLK

Map	Date	Event	Resulting Area
❼	17 Feb 1746/1747	Lost to PROVIDENCE (R.I.) when Rhode Island implemented the 1745 royal settlement of the provincial boundary	490 sq mi
	20 Nov 1770	Lost small area to PLYMOUTH when town of Bridgewater gained from Stoughton to accommodate local property owners [location unknown, not mapped]	
	3 Mar 1792	Boundary with MIDDLESEX redefined in part when boundary between towns of Medway and Sherburne redefined [no change]	

(Heavy line depicts historical boundary. Base map shows present-day information.)

❼   17 Feb 1746/1747–19 Jun 1793

Chronology of SUFFOLK

Map	Date	Event	Resulting Area
❽	20 Jun 1793	Lost to creation of NORFOLK	50 sq mi
❾	18 Jun 1803	Lost towns of Hingham and Hull to PLYMOUTH	30 sq mi

(Heavy line depicts historical boundary. Base map shows present-day information.)

❽   20 Jun 1793–17 Jun 1803

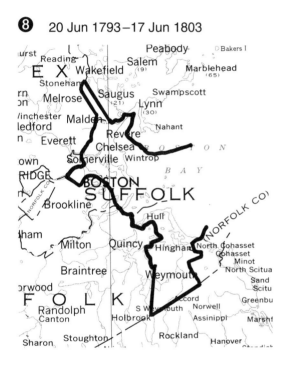

❾   18 Jun 1803–5 Mar 1804

| 10 | 0 | 10 | 20 | 30 | 40 Miles |

Chronology of SUFFOLK

Map	Date	Event	Resulting Area
⑩	6 Mar 1804	Gained from NORFOLK when Boston gained from Dorchester	30 sq mi
⑩	22 Feb 1825	Boundary with NORFOLK adjusted when line between Boston and Brookline adjusted	30 sq mi
⑪	25 Mar 1834	Gained from NORFOLK when Boston gained Thompson I. from Dorchester	30 sq mi
	16 Mar 1836	Boundary with NORFOLK redefined when line between Boston and Roxbury redefined [not mapped]	
	19 Apr 1837	Boundary with NORFOLK adjusted slightly when line through water between Boston and Roxbury adjusted [not mapped]	

(Heavy line depicts historical boundary. Base map shows present-day information.)

⑩ 6 Mar 1804 – 24 Mar 1834

⑪ 25 Mar 1834 – 21 Feb 1841

| 10 | 0 | 10 | 20 | 30 | 40 Miles |

Chronology of SUFFOLK

Map	Date	Event	Resulting Area
⑫	22 Feb 1841	Lost to ESSEX when town of Saugus gained from Chelsea	30 sq mi
	3 May 1850	Boundary with NORFOLK adjusted when line through water between Boston and Roxbury adjusted [not mapped]	
⑫	21 May 1855	Gained small area from NORFOLK when Boston gained from Dorchester	30 sq mi
	3 Apr 1860	Boundary with NORFOLK adjusted slightly when line along streets between Boston and Roxbury shifted to sides of streets from centerlines [not mapped]	
⑬	6 Jan 1868	Gained from NORFOLK when Boston gained all of Roxbury	30 sq mi

(Heavy line depicts historical boundary. Base map shows present-day information.)

⑫ 22 Feb 1841– 5 Jan 1868

⑬ 6 Jan 1868– 2 Jan 1870

10	0	10	20	30	40 Miles

Chronology of SUFFOLK

Map	Date	Event	Resulting Area
⑭	3 Jan 1870	Gained from NORFOLK when Boston gained all of Dorchester	40 sq mi
	2 Apr 1870	Boundary with NORFOLK adjusted slightly when line along streets between Boston and West Roxbury shifted from one side to the other [not mapped]	
⑭	18 Jun 1870	Gained small area from NORFOLK when Boston gained from Brookline	40 sq mi
⑭	12 Apr 1872	Gained small area from NORFOLK when Boston gained Mt. Hope Cemetery from West Roxbury	40 sq mi
⑭	27 Apr 1872	Exchanged small areas with NORFOLK when Boston and Brookline exchanged	40 sq mi
⑮	5 Jan 1874	Gained from MIDDLESEX and NORFOLK when Boston gained Brighton, Charlestown, and West Roxbury	50 sq mi

(Heavy line depicts historical boundary. Base map shows present-day information.)

⑭   3 Jan 1870 – 4 Jan 1874

⑮   5 Jan 1874 – 7 May 1874

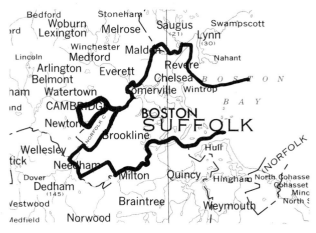

10   0   10   20   30   40 Miles

Chronology of SUFFOLK

Map	Date	Event	Resulting Area
⓰	8 May 1874	Gained from NORFOLK when Boston gained from Brookline	50 sq mi
⓰	29 May 1874	Boundary with MIDDLESEX adjusted when line between Boston and Newton adjusted	50 sq mi
⓰	1 Jul 1875	Lost small area to MIDDLESEX when town of Newton gained from Boston	50 sq mi
⓰	27 May 1890	Boundary with NORFOLK adjusted when line between Boston and Brookline adjusted	50 sq mi
⓰	4 May 1891	Boundary with MIDDLESEX adjusted when line between Boston and Somerville adjusted	50 sq mi
	13 Apr 1894	Boundary with NORFOLK adjusted slightly when line between northern Brookline and Boston adjusted [not mapped]	
⓰	29 Mar 1898	Boundary with MIDDLESEX adjusted when line through the Charles R. between Boston and Cambridge adjusted [not mapped] and line between Boston and Newton adjusted	50 sq mi
⓰	1 Apr 1898	Boundary with NORFOLK adjusted when line between Boston and Hyde Park adjusted	50 sq mi
⓰	13 May 1898	Boundary with MIDDLESEX adjusted when line between Boston and Newton adjusted	50 sq mi
	29 Mar 1910	Boundary with MIDDLESEX adjusted when line in the Charles R. between Boston and Cambridge adjusted [not mapped]	
⓱	1 Jan 1912	Gained from NORFOLK when Boston gained all of Hyde Park	60 sq mi

(Heavy line depicts historical boundary. Base map shows present-day information.)

⓰ 8 May 1874–31 Dec 1911

⓱ 1 Jan 1912–present

Chronology of WORCESTER

Map	Date	Event	Resulting Area
❶	10 Jul 1731	Created from HAMPSHIRE, MIDDLESEX, and SUFFOLK	1,630 sq mi

(Heavy line depicts historical boundary. Base map shows present-day information.)

❶   10 Jul 1731– 28 Jun 1732

thfield

Warwick

West Royalston

Royalston

Waterville

Winchendon

Mt Watatic
1832

Ashby

W Townsend
Townsend

Dunstable

Pepperell

Tully

North Orange

South
Royalston

Townsend Harbor

North Chelms

Orang

Baldwinville

Otter River

Ashburnham

S Ashburnham

Lunenburg

Groton

W Chelmsf

W Groton

Forge
Village

Athol

East Templeton

Gardner

Fitchburg
(450)

Ayer

Shirley

Little
Littleton

Phillipston

Templeton

Westminster
1285

Leominster

N Acto

endell

North
New Salem

Wachusett Mtn
2006

Still River

Harvard

Boxboro
Acton

lem

Petersham

Hubbardston

East Princeton

Lancaster

S Acton
W Conco
Stow

tesbury

Williamsville

Princeton Sta

West Sterling

Princeton

Bolton

QUABBIN
RESERVOIR

Barre

Sterling

Clinton
314

M

am
1018

W O R C E S T E R

Oakdale

Berlin

Hudson

Sudbur

ghts Corner

S

Wheelwright

Barre Plains

Oakham

Rutland

West
Boylston

Jefferson

Holden

Wachusett Res
South Berlin

Marlboro

Coc

Hardwick

Gilbertville

New Braintree

Chaffinville

Paxton

A

Northboro

Morningdale

Shrewsbury

Southboro

Framingha
(165)

Westboro

C

chertown

Ware

North Brookfield

Spencer

West Brookfield

Leicester

WORCESTER

N Grafton

Southville

Woodville

Hopkinton

Asl

W Warren

E Brookfield

Brookfield

Rochdale

Grafton

Holliston

Bondsville

Warren River

Three
Rivers

W Brimfield

1022

Charlton Depot

Texas

Auburn

Millbury

Upton

Palmer

Charlton City

N Oxford

Sutton

Northbridge

Milford

Brimfiel

Fiskdale

Charlton

Oxford

Hopedale

Mend

am

Monson
1171

Sturbridge

W Sutton

Whitinsville

Manchaug

North Uxbridge

Bellin

Holland
Wales

Southbridge

East Douglas

Uxbridge
573

ien

Dudley

Webster

Douglas

E Blackstone

Shel

Quinebau

E Thompson

Wallum Lake

Slatersville

Blackstone

Woonso

Staffordville

Stafford

Union

E Woodstock

N Grosvenor Dale

Grosvenor Dale

Harrisville

Glendale

Diamond H

Cu
Hil

Manville

Stafford
Springs

Thompson

Pascoag

Tarkiln

845

Woodstock
Valley

Woodstock

S Woodstock

Quaddick

W Glocester

Chepachet

Westford

Eastford

(290)

P R O V I D E N C E

Chronology of WORCESTER

Map	Date	Event	Resulting Area
❷	29 Jun 1732	Exchanged with MIDDLESEX when town of Harvard created from Groton, Lancaster, and Stow	1,640 sq mi

(Heavy line depicts historical boundary. Base map shows present-day information.)

❷ 29 Jun 1732–13 Jun 1735

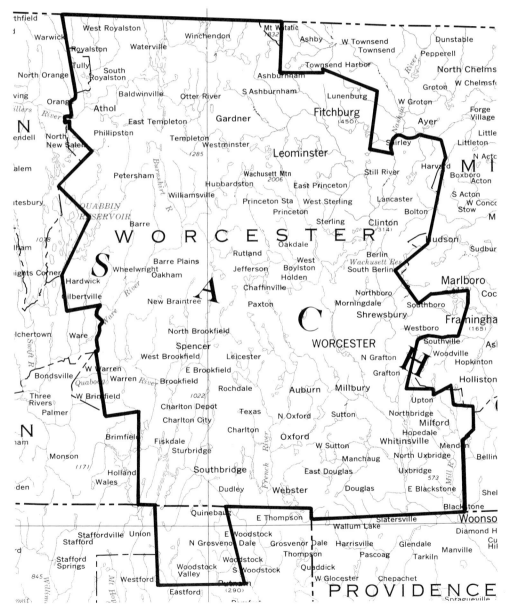

Chronology of WORCESTER

Map	Date	Event	Resulting Area
❸	14 Jun 1735	Gained from MIDDLESEX when town of Upton created from Hopkinton	1,640 sq mi

(Heavy line depicts historical boundary. Base map shows present-day information.)

❸ 14 Jun 1735–15 Jan 1741/1742

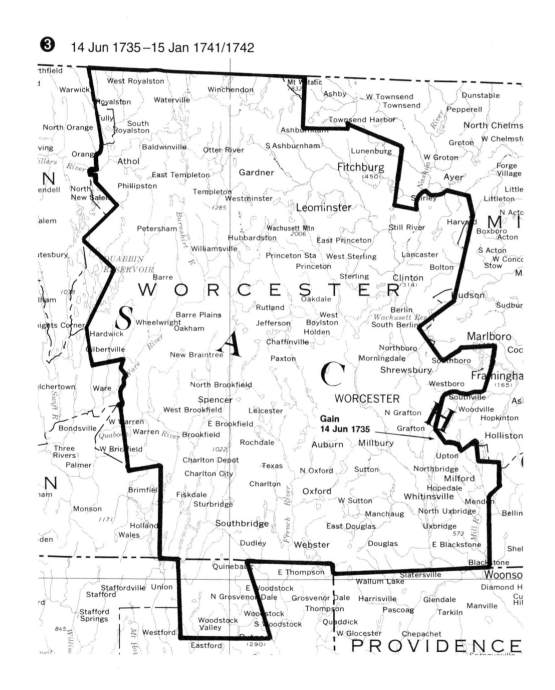

| 10 | 0 | 10 | 20 | 30 | 40 Miles |

Chronology of WORCESTER

Map	Date	Event	Resulting Area
❹	16 Jan 1741/1742	Gained from HAMPSHIRE when town of Western (now Warren) created from Brookfield, Brimfield, and Kingsfield	1,650 sq mi

(Heavy line depicts historical boundary. Base map shows present-day information.)

❹   16 Jan 1741/1742 – May 1749

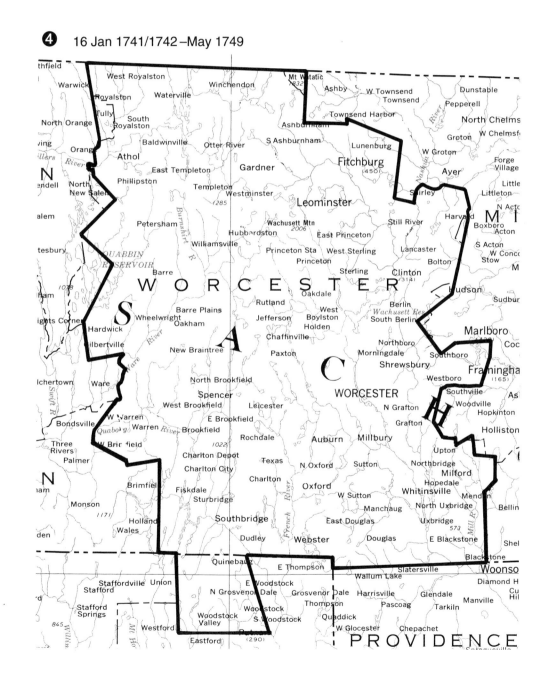

Chronology of WORCESTER

Map	Date	Event	Resulting Area
❺	May 1749	Lost town of Woodstock to Connecticut	1,580 sq mi
	12 Apr 1753	Boundaries redefined [no change]	
	9 Jun 1756	Boundary with HAMPSHIRE adjusted when dispute between towns of Greenwich and Hardwick settled [no discernible change]	

(Heavy line depicts historical boundary. Base map shows present-day information.)

❺ May 1749 – 4 Jan 1764

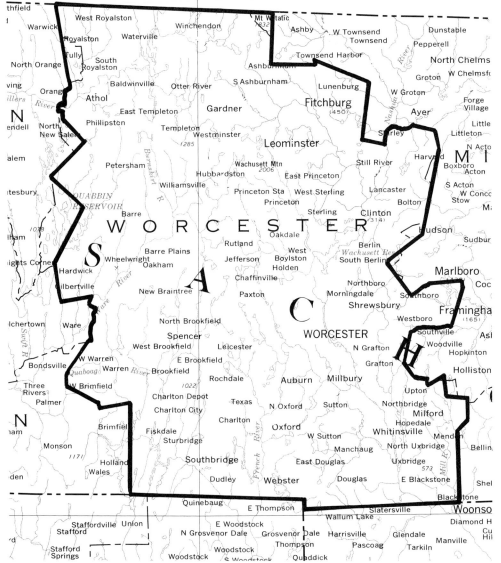

Chronology of WORCESTER

Map	Date	Event	Resulting Area
❻	5 Jan 1764	Gained from HAMPSHIRE when town of Western (now Warren) gained from Palmer	1,580 sq mi

(Heavy line depicts historical boundary. Base map shows present-day information.)

❻ 5 Jan 1764 – 4 Feb 1765

thfield
Warwick
West Royalston
Winchendon
Mt Watatic 1832
Ashby
W Townsend
Townsend
Dunstable
Pepperell
Royalston
Waterville
Townsend Harbor
North Chelms
North Orange
South Royalston
Ashburnham
Groton
W Chelmsf
ving
Tully
S Ashburnham
Lunenburg
W Groton
Orange
Atnol
Baldwinville
Otter River
Fitchburg (450)
Ayer
Forge Village
East Templeton
Gardner
North New Salem
Phillipston
Templeton
Westminster 1285
Leominster
Shirley
Harvard
Little Littleton
N Acto
N
endell
salem
Petersham
Wachusett Mtn 2006
Hubbardston
East Princeton
Still River
Boxboro
Acton
MI
Williamsville
Princeton Sta
West Sterling
Lancaster
S Acton
W Conc
Stow
itesbury
QUABBIN RESERVOIR
Barre
Princeton
Sterling
Bolton
M
lham
1078
WORCESTER
Oakdale
Clinton (314)
udson
Sudbur
Rutland
West Boylston
Berlin
nights Corner
Hardwick
Wheelwright
Oakham
Barre Plains
Jefferson
Holden
South Berlin
Wachusett Res
Marlboro
Gilbertville
S
New Braintree
Chaffinville
Paxton
Northboro
Morningdale
Shrewsbury
Southboro
Coc
Framingha (165)
A
C
Westboro
Gain 5 Jan 1764
Ware
North Brookfield
Spencer
West Brookfield
Leicester
WORCESTER
N Grafton
Southville
Woodville
Hopkinton
Bondsville
W Warren
Quaboag
Warren River
Brookfield
E Brookfield
Grafton
Holliston
Three Rivers
W Brimfield
Rochdale
1022
Auburn
Millbury
Upton
Palmer
Charlton Depot
Texas
N Oxford
Sutton
Northbridge
Milford
N
Brimfiel
Charlton City
Charlton
Oxford
W Sutton
Whitinsville
Hopedale
Mend
ham
Fiskdale
Sturbridge
Manchaug
North Uxbridge
Bellin
Monson
1171
Southbridge
East Douglas
Uxbridge 573
Holland
Wales
Dudley
Webster
Douglas
E Blackstone
Shel
oden
Quinebaug
E Thompson
Slatersville
Blackstone
Woonso
Wallum Lake
Staffordville Union
Stafford
E Woodstock
N Grosvenor Dale
Grosvenor Dale
Harrisville
Glendale
Diamond H
Cu Hil
rd
Stafford Springs
Woodstock
Thompson
Pascoag
Tarkiln
Manville
S Woodstock
Quaddick

10   0   10   20   30   40 Miles

Chronology of WORCESTER

Map	Date	Event	Resulting Area
❼	5 Feb 1765	Lost to HAMPSHIRE when town of Greenwich gained from Hardwick	1,580 sq mi
❼	6 Mar 1767	Lost small area to MIDDLESEX when town of Ashby created from Fitchburg and Ashburnham	1,580 sq mi

(Heavy line depicts historical boundary. Base map shows present-day information.)

❼   5 Feb 1765 – 24 Feb 1783

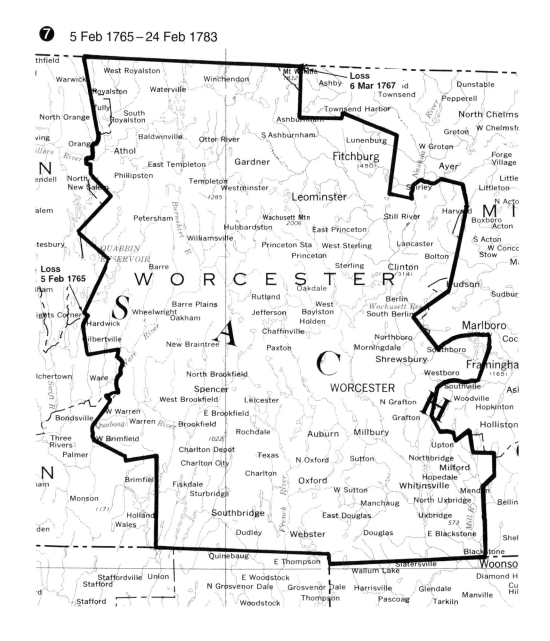

Chronology of WORCESTER

Map	Date	Event	Resulting Area
❽	25 Feb 1783	Lost to MIDDLESEX when town of Boxborough gained from Harvard	1,580 sq mi

(Heavy line depicts historical boundary. Base map shows present-day information.)

❽   25 Feb 1783 – 14 Oct 1783

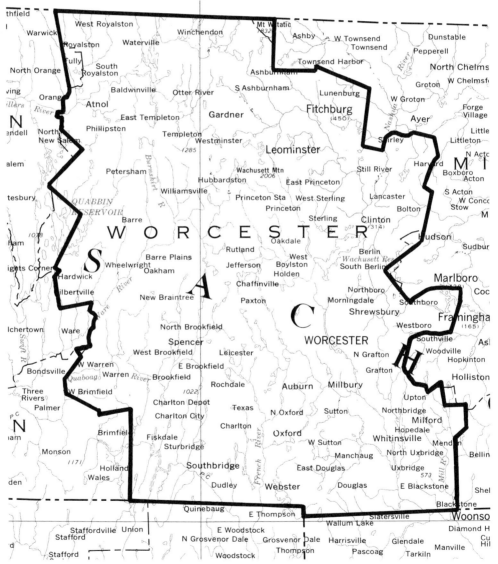

| 10 | 0 | 10 | 20 | 30 | 40 Miles |

Chronology of WORCESTER

Map	Date	Event	Resulting Area
➒	15 Oct 1783	Lost to HAMPSHIRE when town of Orange created from Athol and Royalston	1,570 sq mi

(Heavy line depicts historical boundary. Base map shows present-day information.)

➒   15 Oct 1783–15 Mar 1784

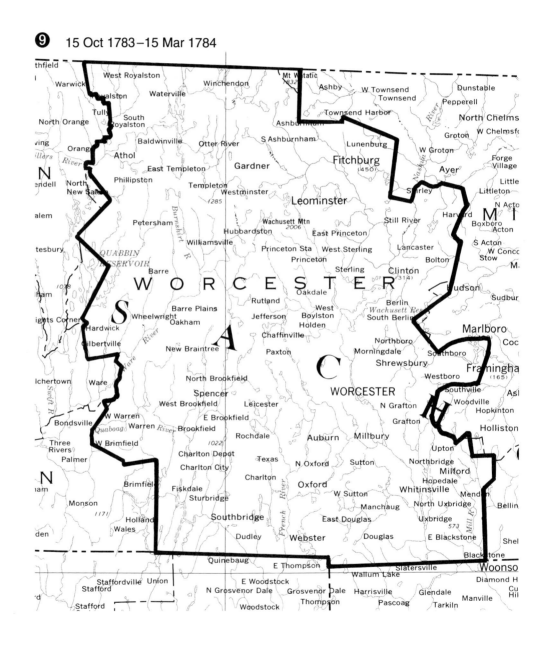

| 10 | | 0 | 10 | 20 | 30 | 40 Miles |

Chronology of WORCESTER

Map	Date	Event	Resulting Area
⑩	16 Mar 1784	Gained from MIDDLESEX when town of Berlin created from Marlborough, Northborough, and Bolton	1,580 sq mi
⑩	7 Mar 1786	Gained small area from MIDDLESEX when town of Southborough gained from Framingham	1,580 sq mi

(Heavy line depicts historical boundary. Base map shows present-day information.)

⑩   16 Mar 1784–15 Nov 1792

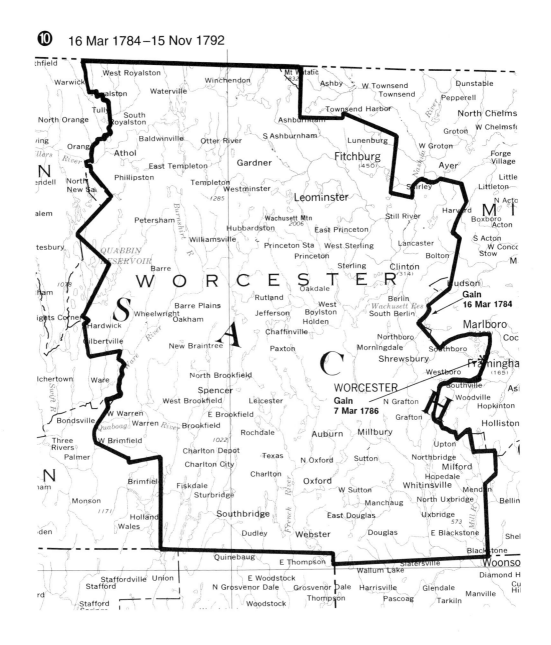

| 10 | 0 | 10 | 20 | 30 | 40 Miles |

Chronology of WORCESTER

Map	Date	Event	Resulting Area
⑪	16 Nov 1792	Lost to MIDDLESEX when town of Ashby gained from Ashburnham	1,570 sq mi
	15 Jul 1794	Gained small area from HAMPSHIRE when town of Western (now Warren) gained from Palmer to accommodate local property owners [location unknown, not mapped]	

(Heavy line depicts historical boundary. Base map shows present-day information.)

⑪ 16 Nov 1792 – 17 Feb 1801

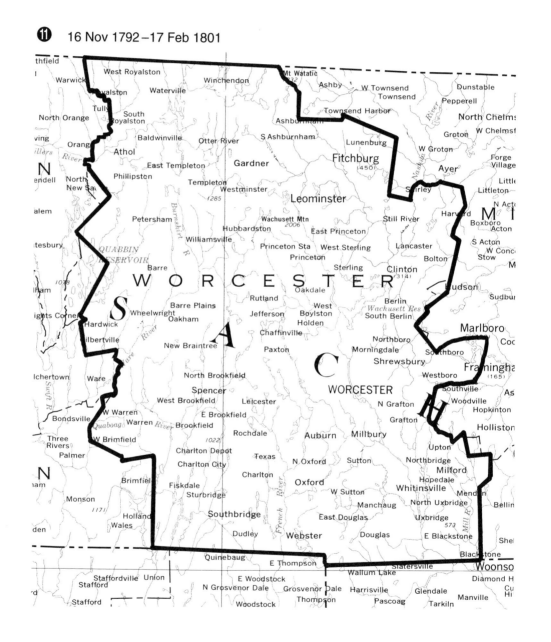

10   0   10   20   30   40 Miles

Chronology of WORCESTER

Map	Date	Event	Resulting Area
⑫	18 Feb 1801	Gained from HAMPSHIRE when town of Dana created from Greenwich, Hardwick, and Petersham	1,580 sq mi

(Heavy line depicts historical boundary. Base map shows present-day information.)

⑫ 18 Feb 1801–19 Jun 1807

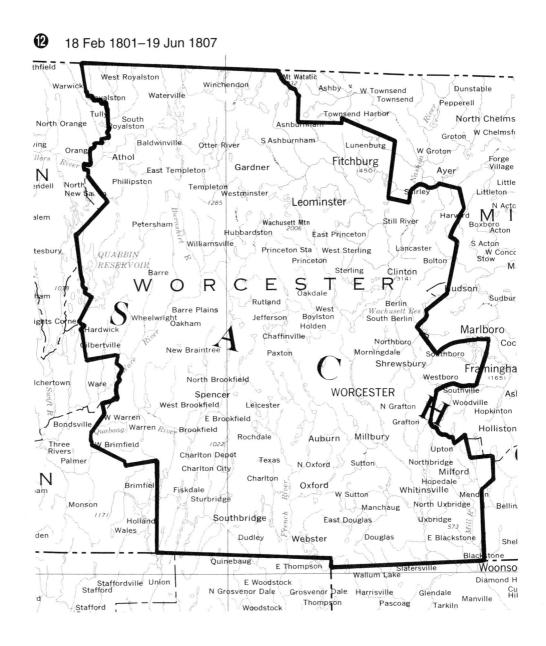

Chronology of WORCESTER

Map	Date	Event	Resulting Area
⑬	20 Jun 1807	Gained from MIDDLESEX when town of Northborough gained from Marlborough	1,580 sq mi
	8 Mar 1808	Gained small area from MIDDLESEX when town of Upton gained from Hopkinton to accommodate local property owner [location unknown, not mapped]	
⑬	7 Feb 1816	Gained from FRANKLIN when town of Athol gained from Orange	1,580 sq mi
⑬	8 Feb 1823	Lost small area to HAMPSHIRE when town of Ware gained from Western (now Warren)	1,580 sq mi
	3 Nov 1826	Exchanged narrow strips with WINDHAM (Conn.) when an irregularity in the state boundary was straightened [not mapped]	

(Heavy line depicts historical boundary. Base map shows present-day information.)

⑬   20 Jun 1807– 26 Mar 1835

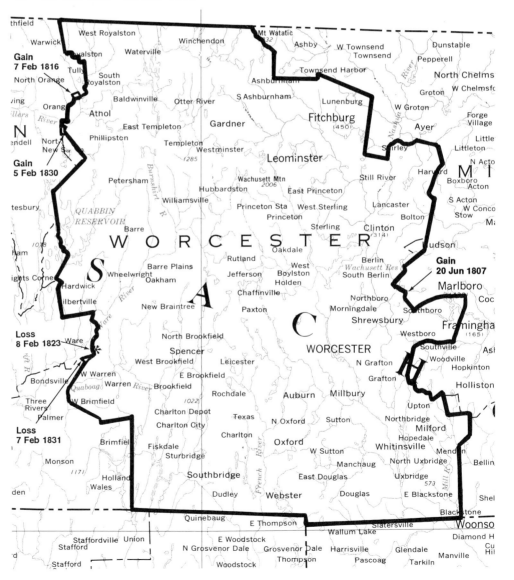

10   0   10   20   30   40 Miles

Chronology of WORCESTER

Map	Date	Event	Resulting Area
	11 Feb 1829	Gained small area (one acre) from MIDDLESEX when town of Bolton gained from Marlborough to accommodate local property owner [location unknown, not mapped]	
	3 Mar 1829	Lost small area to MIDDLESEX when town of Ashby gained from Fitchburg to accommodate local property owner [location unknown, not mapped]	
⑬	5 Feb 1830	Gained from FRANKLIN when town of Athol gained from New Salem	1,580 sq mi
⑬	7 Feb 1831	Lost to HAMPDEN when town of Palmer gained from Western (now Warren)	1,580 sq mi
⑭	27 Mar 1835	Exchanged with MIDDLESEX when towns of Holliston, Hopkinton, and Milford exchanged	1,580 sq mi

(Heavy line depicts historical boundary. Base map shows present-day information.)

⑭ 27 Mar 1835–15 Mar 1837

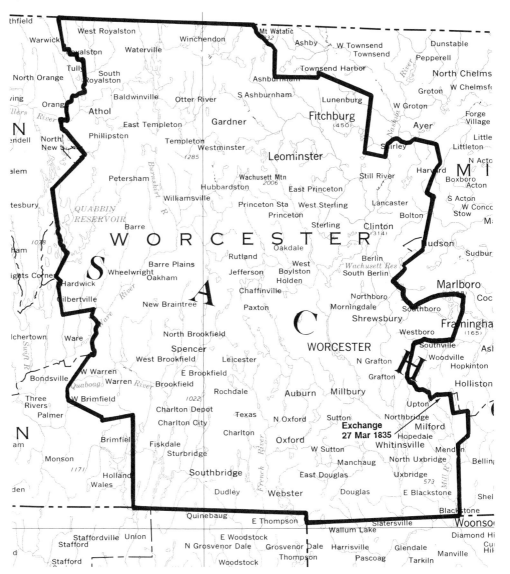

10   0   10   20   30   40 Miles

Chronology of WORCESTER

Map	Date	Event	Resulting Area
⓯	16 Mar 1837	Gained from FRANKLIN when town of Athol gained from New Salem	1,590 sq mi
	16 Mar 1838	Boundary with MIDDLESEX redefined in part when line between towns of Marlborough and Bolton redefined [no change]	
	24 Mar 1843	Lost small area to MIDDLESEX when town of Marlborough gained from Southborough to accommodate local property owners [location unknown, not mapped]	
	3 Mar 1846	Boundary with MIDDLESEX redefined in part when line between towns of Shirley and Lunenburg redefined [no change]	
	25 Apr 1848	Boundary with MIDDLESEX redefined in part when line between towns of Shirley and Lunenburg redefined [no change]	

(Heavy line depicts historical boundary. Base map shows present-day information.)

⓯ 16 Mar 1837– 31 Mar 1859

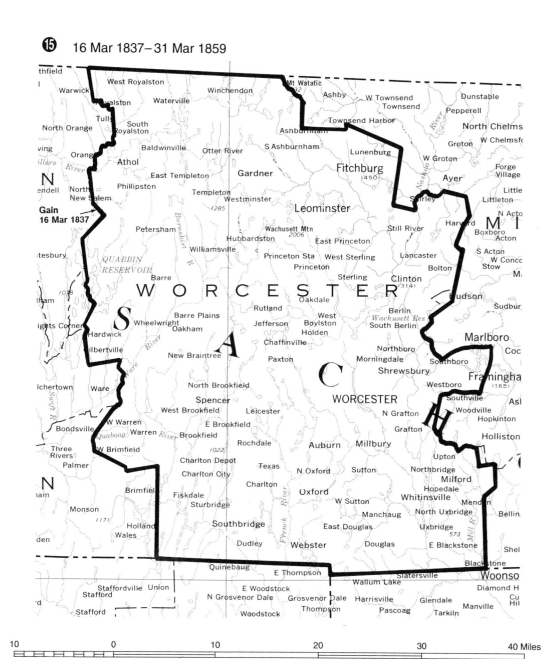

10   0   10   20   30   40 Miles

Chronology of WORCESTER

Map	Date	Event	Resulting Area
⑯	1 Apr 1859	Gained from MIDDLESEX when town of Milford gained from Holliston	1,590 sq mi

(Heavy line depicts historical boundary. Base map shows present-day information.)

⑯ 1 Apr 1859 – 19 Mar 1868

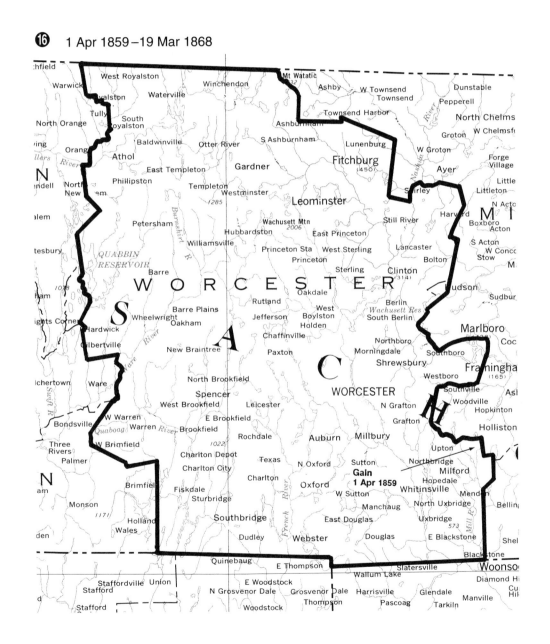

10   0   10   20   30   40 Miles

Chronology of WORCESTER

Map	Date	Event	Resulting Area
	20 Mar 1868	Lost to MIDDLESEX when town of Hudson gained from Bolton	1,590 sq mi
	7 Mar 1872	Exchanged with NORFOLK when town of Bellingham exchanged with Mendon	1,590 sq mi
	16 May 1901	Boundary with MIDDLESEX redefined when line between towns of Marlborough and Southborough redefined [no discernible change]	
	1 May 1905	Boundary with MIDDLESEX adjusted when line between towns of Berlin and Hudson redefined [no change] and line between Berlin and Marlborough adjusted	1,590 sq mi
	14 Jun 1906	Lost small area to MIDDLESEX when towns of Boxborough and Littleton gained from Harvard	1,590 sq mi
	16 May 1907	Boundary with MIDDLESEX redefined when town of Hopkinton's boundary with Milford and Upton redefined [no change]	
	27 Apr 1911	Boundary with FRANKLIN redefined in part when line between towns of New Salem and Prescott redefined [no change]	

(Heavy line depicts historical boundary. Base map shows present-day information.)

17 20 Mar 1868 – 27 Apr 1938

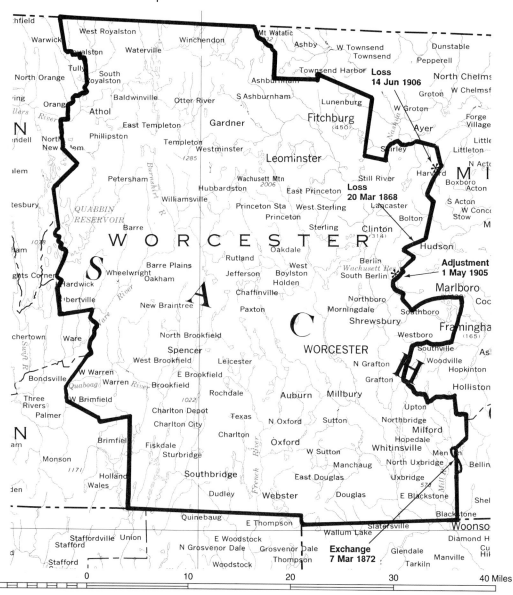

Chronology of WORCESTER

Map	Date	Event	Resulting Area
⑱	28 Apr 1938	Gained from HAMPSHIRE when town of Petersham gained from Dana, Greenwich, and Prescott and when town of Hardwick gained from Greenwich	1,600 sq mi

(Heavy line depicts historical boundary. Base map shows present-day information.)

⑱   28 Apr 1938 – present

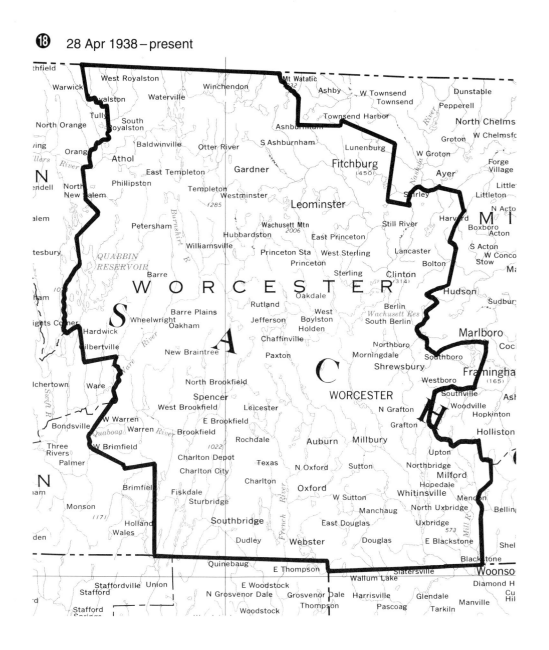

| 10 | | 0 | | 10 | | 20 | | 30 | | 40 Miles |

Colonial, State, and
Federal Censuses in Massachusetts

Date	Census
1764–1765	Colonial census. Statistics (Benton; Greene and Harrington, 21–30); no names.
20 Aug 1771	Tax list. No statistics; names for approximately half the towns (Pruitt).
20 Mar 1776	Colonial census. Statistics (Felt, 157–165; Greene and Harrington, 31–40); some names at Massachusetts State Archives, Boston.
1784	Poll list. Statistics (Felt, 166–170; Greene and Harrington, 40–46); no names.
2 Aug 1790	Federal census. Statistics and names.
1798	Direct tax of 1798. No statistics; names at New England Historic Genealogical Society, Boston.
4 Aug 1800	Federal census. Statistics and names.
6 Aug 1810	Federal census. Statistics and names.
7 Aug 1820	Federal census. Statistics and names.
1 Jun 1830	Federal census. Statistics and names.
1 May 1837	State census. Statistics (Dubester, 24); no names.
1 May 1840	State census. Statistics (Dubester, 24–25); no names.
1 Jun 1840	Federal census. Statistics and names.
1 May 1850	State census. Statistics (Dubester, 24–25); no names.
1 Jun 1850	Federal census. Statistics and names.
1 Jun 1855	State census. Statistics (Dubester, 25); names at Massachusetts State Archives, Boston.
1 Jun 1860	Federal census. Statistics and names.
1 May 1865	State census. Statistics (Dubester, 25); names at Massachusetts State Archives, Boston.
1 Jun 1870	Federal census. Statistics and names.
1 May 1875	State census. Statistics (Dubester, 26); no names.
1 Jun 1880	Federal census. Statistics and names.
1 May 1885	State census. Statistics (Dubester, 26–27); no names.
2 Jun 1890	Federal census. Statistics; names from special census of Union Veterans only.
1 May 1895	State census. Statistics (Dubester, 27); no names.
1 Jun 1900	Federal census. Statistics and names.
1 May 1905	State census. Statistics (Dubester, 27–28); no names.
15 Apr 1910	Federal census. Statistics and names.
1 Apr 1915	State census. Statistics (Dubester, 28); no names.
1 Jan 1920	Federal census. Statistics and names.

Date	Census
31 Mar 1925	State census. Statistics (Dubester, 28); no names.
1 Apr 1930	Federal census. Statistics; names not available until 2002.
1 Jan 1935	State census. Statistics (Dubester, 29); no names.
1 Apr 1940	Federal census. Statistics; names not available until 2012.
1 Jan 1945	State census. Statistics (Dubester, 29); no names.
1 Apr 1950	Federal census. Statistics; names not available until 2022.
1 Apr 1960	Federal census. Statistics; names not available until 2032.
1 Apr 1970	Federal census. Statistics; names not available until 2042.
1 Apr 1980	Federal census. Statistics; names not available until 2052.
1 Apr 1990	Federal census. Statistics; names not available until 2062.

Sources

Benton, J. H., Jr. *Early Census Making in Massachusetts, 1643–1765, with a Reproduction of the Lost Census of 1765 (Recently Found) and Documents Relating Thereto, Now First Collected and Published.* Boston: Charles E. Goodspeed, 1905.

Dubester, Henry J. *State Censuses: An Annotated Bibliography of Censuses of Population Taken after the Year 1790 by States and Territories of the United States.* 1948. Reprint. New York: Burt Franklin, 1969.

Felt, Joseph B. "Population of Massachusetts." *Collections of the American Statistical Association* 1, pt. 2 (1845): 121–216. No other volumes published.

Greene, Evarts Boutell, and Virginia D. Harrington. *American Population before the Federal Census of 1790.* New York: Columbia University Press, 1932.

Lainhart, Ann S. *State Census Records.* [Baltimore]: Genealogical Publishing Co., 1992.

Massachusetts. Bureau of Statistics. *Decennial Census, 1915.* Boston, 1918. See appendices.

Pruitt, Bettye Hobbs, ed. *Massachusetts Tax Valuation List of 1771.* Boston: G. K. Hall, 1978.

Wells, Robert V. *Population of the British Colonies in America before 1776: A Survey of Census Data.* Princeton, N.J.: Princeton University Press, 1975.

Census Outline
Maps for Massachusetts

Colonial Censuses 1764/1765, 1771

LINCOLN

CUMBERLAND

YORK

ESSEX

MIDDLESEX

BERKSHIRE

HAMPSHIRE

WORCESTER

SUFFOLK

PLYMOUTH

BRISTOL

BARNSTABLE

DUKES

NANTUCKET

25   0   25 Miles

Colonial Census 1776

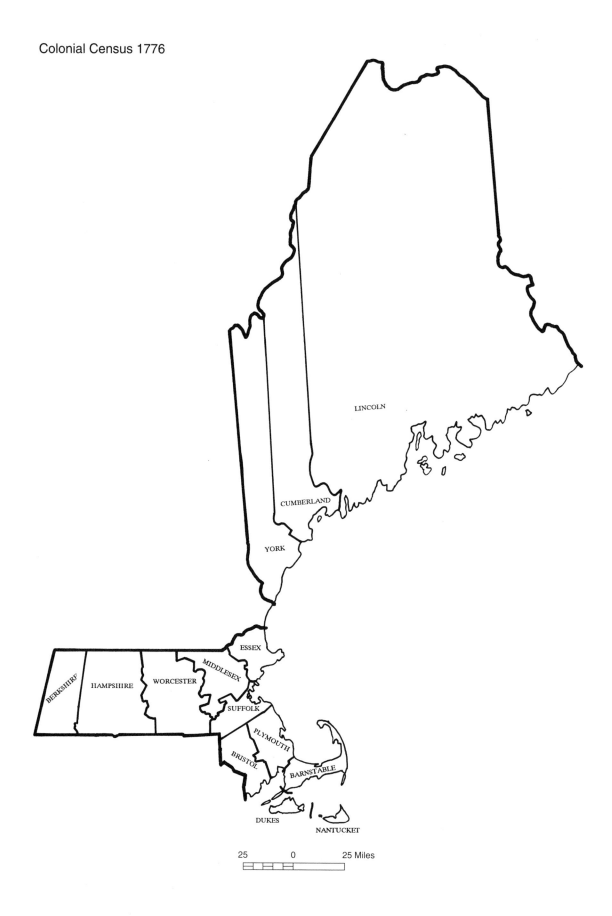

LINCOLN

CUMBERLAND

YORK

ESSEX

MIDDLESEX

BERKSHIRE

HAMPSHIRE

WORCESTER

SUFFOLK

PLYMOUTH

BRISTOL

BARNSTABLE

DUKES

NANTUCKET

25   0   25 Miles

State Poll List 1784

LINCOLN

CUMBERLAND

YORK

ESSEX

BERKSHIRE   HAMPSHIRE   WORCESTER   MIDDLESEX

SUFFOLK

PLYMOUTH

BRISTOL   BARNSTABLE

DUKES

NANTUCKET

25   0   25 Miles

Federal Census 1790

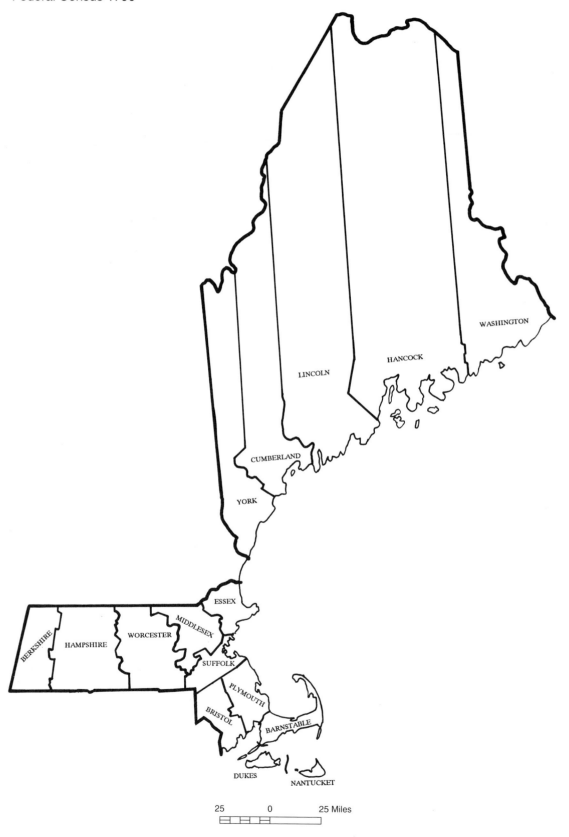

25   0   25 Miles

State Tax List 1798

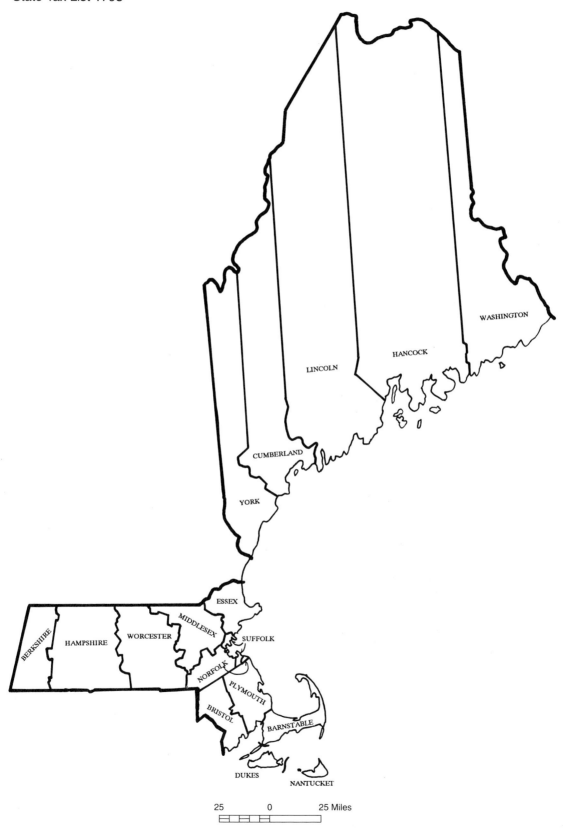

WASHINGTON

HANCOCK

LINCOLN

CUMBERLAND

YORK

ESSEX

MIDDLESEX

BERKSHIRE

HAMPSHIRE

WORCESTER

SUFFOLK

NORFOLK

PLYMOUTH

BRISTOL

BARNSTABLE

DUKES

NANTUCKET

25   0   25 Miles

Federal Census 1800

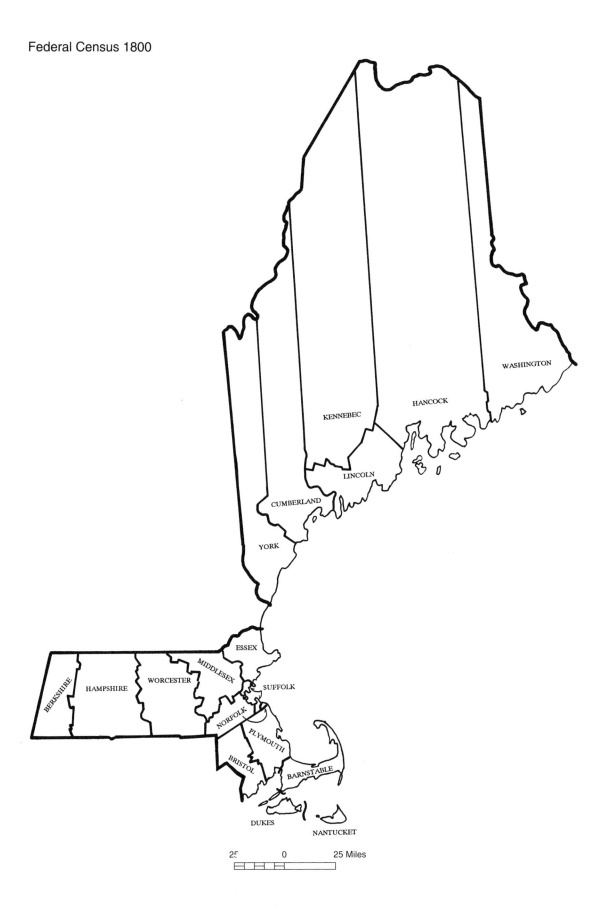

WASHINGTON

HANCOCK

KENNEBEC

LINCOLN

CUMBERLAND

YORK

ESSEX

MIDDLESEX

SUFFOLK

BERKSHIRE

HAMPSHIRE

WORCESTER

NORFOLK

PLYMOUTH

BRISTOL

BARNSTABLE

DUKES

NANTUCKET

25   0   25 Miles

Federal Census 1810

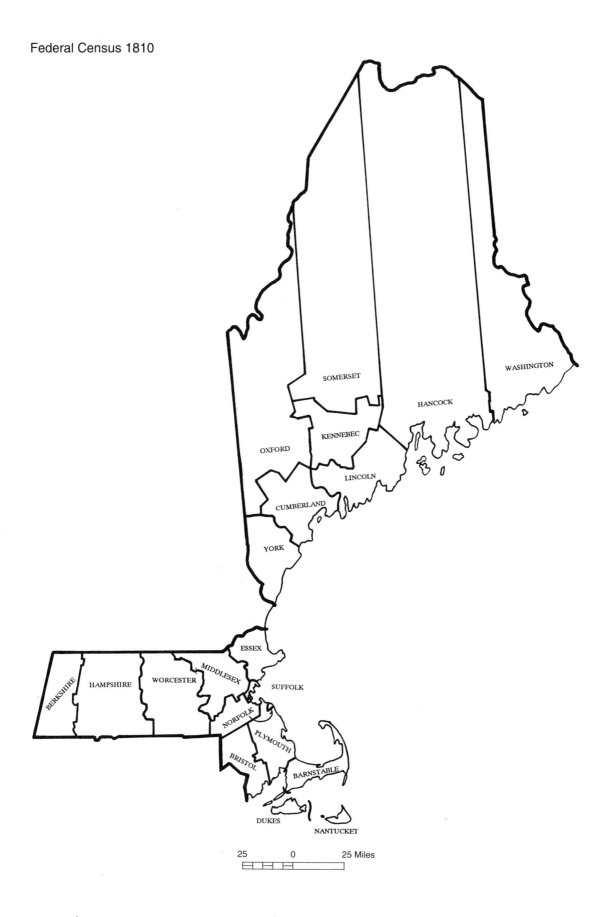

25   0   25 Miles

Federal Census 1820

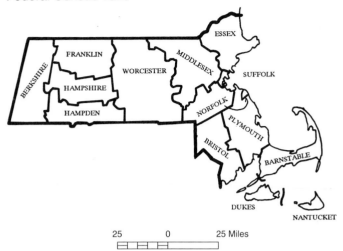

State and Federal Censuses 1830, 1837

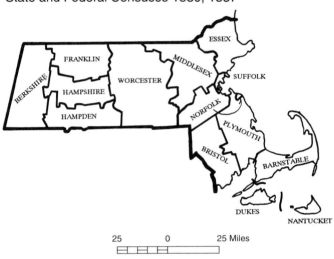

State and Federal Censuses 1840, 1850

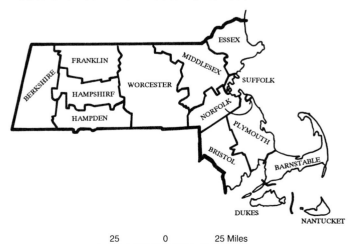

State and Federal Censuses 1855, 1860

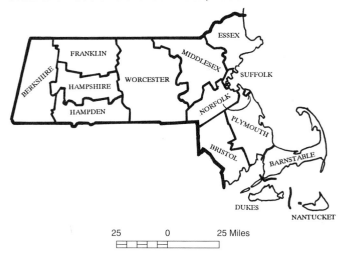

State Census 1865

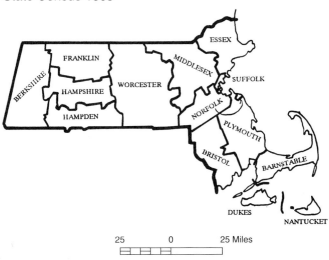

Federal Census 1870

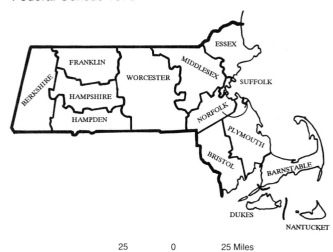

State and Federal Censuses 1875–1905

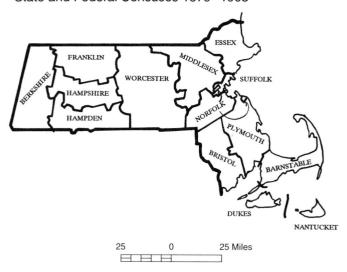

25   0   25 Miles

Federal Census 1910

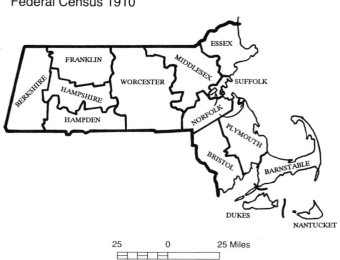

25   0   25 Miles

State and Federal Censuses 1915–1935

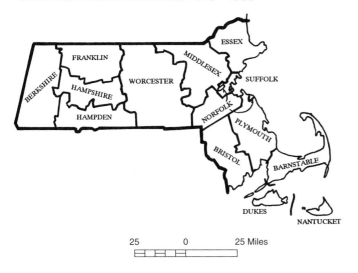

25   0   25 Miles

State and Federal Censuses 1940–1990

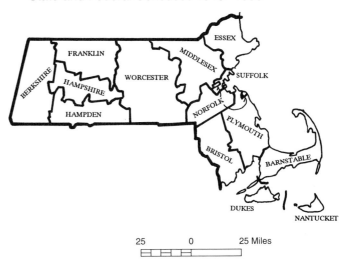

25   0   25 Miles

RHODE ISLAND

Rhode Island County Creations

County	Source	Dates	
		Authorization	**Creation Effective**
BRISTOL	R.I. Recs., 5:207–209	17 Feb 1746/1747	same
KENT	R.I. Recs., 5:301	11 Jun 1750	same
KINGS (see WASHINGTON)			
NEWPORT (created as RHODE ISLAND)	R.I. Recs., 3:477–478	22 Jun 1703	same
PROVIDENCE (created as PROVIDENCE PLANTATIONS)	R.I. Recs., 3:477–478	22 Jun 1703	same
PROVIDENCE PLANTA-TIONS (see PROVIDENCE)			
RHODE ISLAND (see NEWPORT)			
WASHINGTON (created as KINGS)	R.I. Recs., 4:427	16 Jun 1729	same

Consolidated Chronology of Rhode Island State and County Boundaries

1636

Roger Williams secured permission from the Narragansett Indians to establish a community at the head of Narragansett Bay. This community, Providence, was the first European settlement in the area of present Rhode Island. Over the years other, independent settlements were established in the region as a new, unauthorized colony grew spontaneously around Narragansett Bay. (James, 13–32)

1642

Nathaniel Woodward and Solomon Saffrey officially demarcated the southern limit of neighboring Massachusetts, supposedly three miles south of the Charles R., as specified in its charter, implicitly setting the northern limit of Rhode Island. (Hooker, 16–17; Van Zandt, 66–67)

Massachusetts, responding to a request from disgruntled Rhode Islanders, extended its jurisdiction over the settlement of Pawtuxet; these colonists reaffiliated with Rhode Island in 1658. (Arnold, 1:111)

14 March 1643/1644

Roger Williams secured a Parliamentary patent for Rhode Island (then called "Providence Plantations") that granted authority for self-government. Boundaries were defined as Massachusetts on the north, Plymouth on the east, and Pequot Indian country on the west, which implied a western limit at the Pawcatuck R. That put the Narragansett Country (roughly all of present WASHINGTON and southern half of KENT) inside the patent. (James, 57; Swindler, 8:360)

1644

Based upon its participation with Connecticut and New Plymouth in the Pequot War (1636–1637), Massachusetts claimed much of the territory formerly controlled by the Pequots, roughly between the Thames and Pawcatuck rivers at the eastern end of present Connecticut, plus Block I. in present Rhode Island. (Bowen, *Disputes*, 31)

26 May 1658

The Pawtuxet settlers, who gave their allegiance to Massachusetts in 1642, returned to Rhode Island jurisdiction. (Arnold, 1:267)

18 September 1658

Massachusetts asserted that the Pequot Country (territory it had claimed in present eastern Connecticut) extended well east of the Pawcatuck R. into present western Rhode Island and, despite Rhode Island's protests, imposed its authority on both sides of the Pawcatuck for the next several years. (Arnold, 1:277–278)

23 April 1662

King Charles II granted Connecticut a charter as a self-governing corporate colony, consolidating Hartford and other settlements on the Connecticut R. with New Haven and other coastal settlements into a single colony. Boundary set at Narragansett Bay on the east. Rhode Island did not concede its claim to territory between the Pawcatuck R. and Narragansett Bay (present southwestern Rhode Island, then known as Narragansett Country), but Connecticut quickly took control of the area. (Bowen, *Disputes*, 32; Swindler, 2:135–136)

8 July 1663

King Charles II granted Rhode Island a charter as a self-governing corporate colony. It was bounded on the north by Massachusetts's south line; on the east by a straight north-south line between Massachusetts and Pawtucket Falls (a gain for Rhode Island from Massachusetts), thence down the Seekonk R. to Narragansett Bay and along a line three miles inland from the Bay (a gain for Rhode Island from the colony of New Plymouth); on the south by the ocean, including Block I. (claimed by Massachusetts after the Pequot War); and on the west by the Pawcatuck R. and a line due north to Massachusetts. This charter also supposedly implemented a 1662 agreement between agents of Connecticut and Rhode Island to establish their boundary along the Pawcatuck, but

Connecticut rejected that agreement and pressed for control of the Narragansett Country, including present Rhode Island southwest of Narragansett Bay. (Bowen, *Disputes*, 33; Swindler, 8:368)

May 1664

Rhode Island lost the northeast corner of the present state to New Plymouth when a joint commission from Massachusetts and Plymouth demarcated their mutual boundary ("Old Colony Line"), including its westward extension to the Pawtucket (now Blackstone) R. This boundary remained in effect until Massachusetts and Plymouth were united in 1691. (Bradford, 427 n.)

8 June 1664

Plymouth protested that Rhode Island's new charter infringed upon its territory under its 1629/1630 patent. (Arnold, 1:308)

19 October 1664

Massachusetts, faced with new charters for Connecticut and Rhode Island, gave up its claim to the Pequot Country east of Connecticut's Mystic R., including Block I. in present Rhode Island. (Arnold, 1:308)

27 February 1664/1665

Rhode Island lost to Massachusetts when royal commissioners, charged with solving inter-colonial disputes in New England, established the eastern boundary of Rhode Island with Massachusetts and New Plymouth along the east side of Narragansett Bay (intended as a temporary arrangement until the king should settle the matter definitively). Contemporary understanding of what constituted the Narragansett R. and Bay apparently included the Seekonk and Pawtucket (now Blackstone) rivers, which left the present northeastern corner of Rhode Island to Massachusetts and Plymouth. (Arnold, 1:315)

20 March 1664/1665

Royal commissioners decided the dispute over the Narragansett Country (present southwestern Rhode Island) by dismissing Massachusetts's claim and placing the area directly under royal jurisdiction. They named it King's Province and on 8 April 1665 gave Rhode Island temporary administrative authority over this new province until a royal decision should settle the competing claims of Connecticut and Rhode Island; this did not occur until 1686. (Arnold, 1:315; James, 86–87; Potter, 178, 181)

17 May 1686

Arrival of its first royal governor inaugurated the Dominion of New England, the new single province that King James II created (8 Oct. 1685) by uniting King's Province (present southwestern Rhode Island, formerly termed Narragansett Country), Massachusetts, Maine (area between New Hampshire and the Kennebec R.), and New Hampshire. (Farnham, 7:367; Hart, 1:573; N.H. Early Laws, 1:99; Williamson, 1:576)

28 May 1686

The governor of the Dominion of New England proclaimed a provisional government for the King's Province in present southwestern Rhode Island and prohibited both Connecticut and Rhode Island from further attempts to exercise authority in the area. (R.I. Recs., 3:197)

30 December 1686

The governor of the Dominion of New England incorporated Rhode Island into the new province, following instructions (13 Sep. 1686) from King James II. (N.H. Early Laws, 1:168; R.I. Recs., 3:210, 220)

18 April 1689

Upon learning of the Glorious Revolution (replacement of King James II by King William III and Queen Mary II) in England, Bostonians imprisoned the royal governor and others, thereby ending the Dominion of New England. Over the next months Rhode Island and the other colonies that had been united to form the Dominion had to resume self-government. (Craven, 224; Morris and Kelly, pl. 11)

1 May 1689

Rhode Island reinstated its former government after the fall of the Dominion of New England, including the former King's Province (present southwestern Rhode Island), but shortly thereafter, Connecticut challenged Rhode Island's authority in that area. (Craven, 225; R.I. Recs., 3:257)

12 May 1703

Connecticut and Rhode Island settled their dispute over present southwestern Rhode Island substantially along the line agreed by colonial agents in 1662, described in Rhode Island's 1663 charter, and claimed since then by Rhode Island. Boundary was to run up the Pawcatuck R. to the junction with the Ashaway R., thence a straight line to the southwestern corner of the Warwick Purchase, and thence due north to the southern line of Massachusetts. Although not confirmed in London until February 1726/1727, this line appears to have become effective almost immediately, and, except for small refinements through surveying, it has remained unchanged to the present. (Potter, 206–211; R.I. Recs., 3:474; Van Zandt, 71)

22 June 1703

Two original counties created in Rhode Island: PROVIDENCE PLANTATIONS for the mainland and RHODE ISLAND for Block I. and the islands in Narragansett Bay. (R.I. Recs., 3:477–478)

1705

The northern boundary of Rhode Island with Massachusetts came into question when the towns of Providence (R.I.) and Mendon (Mass.) complained of the line's uncertain location. Commissioners redefined the boundary in 1711 but it was never surveyed. The effective division between the colonies continued along the present line west of the Pawtucket (now Blackstone) R. and down that river south to the Seekonk R. (Arnold, 2:18, 26–27)

16 June 1729

KINGS created from PROVIDENCE PLANTATIONS. PROVIDENCE PLANTATIONS renamed PROVIDENCE. RHODE ISLAND renamed NEWPORT. (R.I. Recs., 4:427)

1729

Renewal of the boundary dispute between Rhode Island and Massachusetts was sparked by a petition for annexation to Rhode Island by some citizens of the town of Attleborough (Mass.), who believed they resided west of the due-north line from Pawtucket Falls to the southern limit of Massachusetts (the eastern boundary line prescribed in Rhode Island's 1663 charter but indefinitely set aside by royal commissioners in 1664). Several attempts to settle the issue failed, and in 1733 Rhode Island appealed to the king. [No change.] (Arnold, 2:99, 101, 113)

28 May 1746

King George II settled the dispute between Massachusetts and Rhode Island in favor of Rhode Island by confirming the judgment of a royal commission that had decided (30 Jun. 1741) on a line substantially the same as that prescribed in Rhode Island's 1663 charter. As a result, Rhode Island gained its present northeast corner (the "Attleborough Gore") and a three-mile wide strip east of Narragansett Bay. Decision implemented in 1747. (Arnold, 2:132–134)

17 February 1746/1747

BRISTOL created from BRISTOL (Mass.), PROVIDENCE gained from BRISTOL (Mass.) and SUFFOLK (Mass.), and NEWPORT gained from BRISTOL (Mass.) when Rhode Island implemented the 1746 royal settlement of the boundary with Massachusetts. (Arnold, 2:157; R.I. Recs., 5:207–209)

11 June 1750

KENT created from PROVIDENCE. (R.I. Recs., 5:301)

October 1750

Rhode Island surveyors, acting without cooperation of Massachusetts to demarcate the lines confirmed by the king in 1746, discovered that the 1642 Woodward-Saffrey line, recognized for a century as the southern line of Massachusetts, ran far south of where it should have been according to the original Massachusetts charter. Except for occasional protestations, Rhode Island did not push the issue to a resolution during the colonial period; in 1846 a U.S. Supreme Court ruling left the line unchanged because it had functioned so long as the effective boundary. [No change.] (Arnold, 2:183, 299 n.; Van Zandt, 67)

4 July 1776

Rhode Island became an independent state. (*Declaration of Independence*)

29 October 1781

KINGS renamed WASHINGTON. (R.I. Recs., 9:484)

1 March 1862

NEWPORT lost to BRISTOL (Mass.) and PROVIDENCE gained from BRISTOL (Mass.) when Massachusetts and Rhode Island implemented the U. S. Supreme Court settlement (31 Dec. 1861) of their boundary to the Atlantic Ocean. (Bayles, *Providence*, 1:29; R.I. Acts and Resolves, 1861, ch. 379, sec. 2/p. 4; Ullman, 83–84; Van Zandt, 68)

6 May 1963

WASHINGTON gained Block I. from NEWPORT. (R.I. Acts and Resolves, 1963, ch. 84, sec. 1/p. 300)

Individual County Chronologies, Maps, and Areas for Rhode Island

Chronology of BRISTOL

Map	Date	Event	Resulting Area
❶	17 Feb 1746/1747	Created from BRISTOL (Mass.)	30 sq mi

(Heavy line depicts historical boundary. Base map shows present-day information.)

❶   17 Feb 1746/1747– present

Chronology of KENT

Map	Date	Event	Resulting Area
❶	11 Jun 1750	Created from PROVIDENCE	180 sq mi

(Heavy line depicts historical boundary. Base map shows present-day information.)

❶   11 Jun 1750 – present

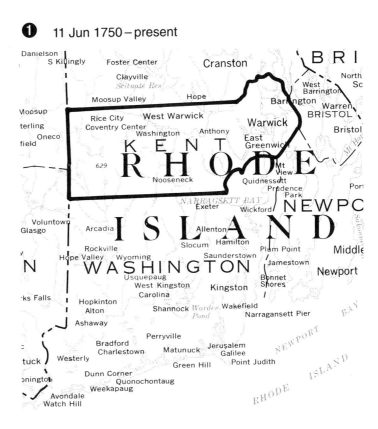

Chronology of NEWPORT (created as RHODE ISLAND)

Map	Date	Event	Resulting Area
❶	22 Jun 1703	Created as RHODE ISLAND	70 sq mi
	16 Jun 1729	Renamed NEWPORT	
❷	17 Feb 1746/1747	Gained from BRISTOL (Mass.)	140 sq mi

(Heavy line depicts historical boundary. Base map shows present-day information.)

❶ 22 Jun 1703–16 Feb 1746/1747

❷ 17 Feb 1746/1747–28 Feb 1862

10	0	10	20	30	40 Miles

Chronology of NEWPORT (created as RHODE ISLAND)

Map	Date	Event	Resulting Area
❸	1 Mar 1862	Lost to BRISTOL (Mass.)	130 sq mi
❹	6 May 1963	Lost to WASHINGTON	120 sq mi

(Heavy line depicts historical boundary. Base map shows present-day information.)

❸ 1 Mar 1862 – 5 May 1963

❹ 6 May 1963 – present

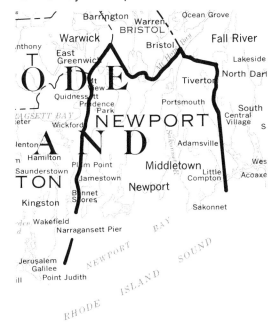

10	0	10	20	30	40 Miles

Chronology of PROVIDENCE (created as PROVIDENCE PLANTATIONS)

Map	Date	Event	Resulting Area
❶	22 Jun 1703	Created as PROVIDENCE PLANTATIONS	920 sq mi

(Heavy line depicts historical boundary. Base map shows present-day information.)

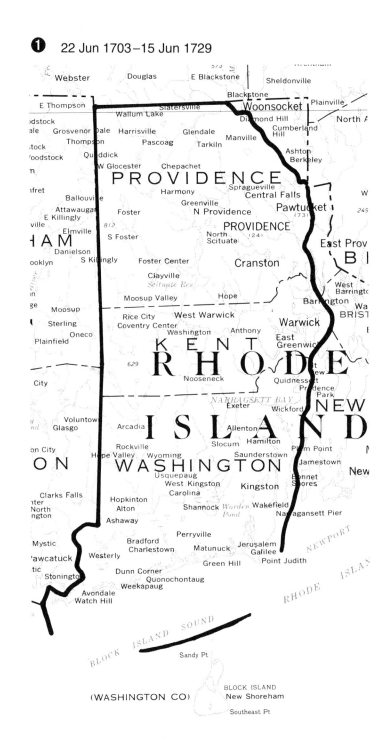

❶ 22 Jun 1703–15 Jun 1729

(WASHINGTON CO)

| 10 | 0 | 10 | 20 | 30 | 40 Miles |

Chronology of PROVIDENCE (created as PROVIDENCE PLANTATIONS)

Map	Date	Event	Resulting Area
❷	16 Jun 1729	Lost to creation of KINGS (now WASHINGTON); renamed PROVIDENCE	560 sq mi
❸	17 Feb 1746/1747	Gained from BRISTOL (Mass.) and SUFFOLK (Mass.)	600 sq mi

(Heavy line depicts historical boundary. Base map shows present-day information.)

❷ 16 Jun 1729 – 16 Feb 1746/1747

❸ 17 Feb 1746/1747 – 10 Jun 1750

| 10 | 0 | 10 | 20 | 30 | 40 Miles |

Chronology of PROVIDENCE (created as PROVIDENCE PLANTATIONS)

Map	Date	Event	Resulting Area
❹	11 Jun 1750	Lost to creation of KENT	420 sq mi
❺	1 Mar 1862	Gained from BRISTOL (Mass.)	440 sq mi

(Heavy line depicts historical boundary. Base map shows present-day information.)

❹ 11 Jun 1750 – 28 Feb 1862

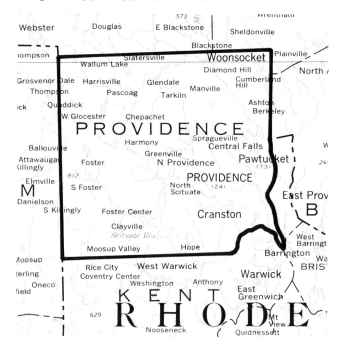

❺ 1 Mar 1862 – present

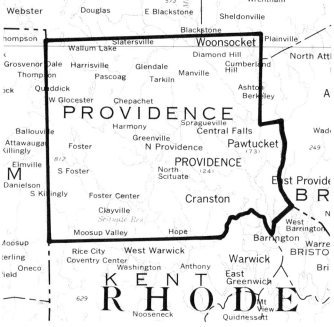

10   0   10   20   30   40 Miles

Chronology of WASHINGTON (created as KINGS)

Map	Date	Event	Resulting Area
❶	16 Jun 1729	Created as KINGS from PROVIDENCE PLANTATIONS (now PROVIDENCE)	360 sq mi
	29 Oct 1781	Renamed WASHINGTON	
❷	6 May 1963	Gained from NEWPORT	370 sq mi

(Heavy line depicts historical boundary. Base map shows present-day information.)

❶ 16 Jun 1729 – 5 May 1963

❷ 6 May 1963 – present

| 10 | 0 | 10 | 20 | 30 | 40 Miles |

Colonial, State, and Federal Censuses in Rhode Island

Date	Census
1708	Colonial census. Statistics (R.I. Recs., 4:59); no names.
1730	Colonial census. Statistics (Greene and Harrington, 66); no names.
1748–1749	Colonial census. Statistics (R.I. Recs., 5:270); no names.
1755	Colonial census. Statistics (Greene and Harrington, 67); no names.
1 Jun 1774	Colonial census. Statistics (R.I. Recs., 7:299); names (Bartlett).
1776	Colonial census. Statistics (R.I. Recs., 7:616–617); some names at Rhode Island State Archives, Providence.
1777	Military census. No statistics; names for all but 6 towns (Chamberlain).
1782	State census. Statistics (Greene and Harrington, 69; Holbrook); names (Holbrook).
2 Aug 1790	Federal census. Statistics and names.
1798	Direct tax of 1798. No statistics; names for 14 towns at Rhode Island State Archives, Providence.
4 Aug 1800	Federal census. Statistics and names.
6 Aug 1810	Federal census. Statistics and names.
7 Aug 1820	Federal census. Statistics and names.
1 Jun 1830	Federal census. Statistics and names.
1 Jun 1840	Federal census. Statistics and names.
1 Jun 1850	Federal census. Statistics and names.
1 Jun 1860	Federal census. Statistics and names.
1 Jun 1865	State census. Statistics (Dubester, 54); names at Rhode Island Historical Society, Providence.
1 Jun 1870	Federal census. Statistics and names.
1 Jun 1875	State census. Statistics (Dubester, 54–55); names at Rhode Island State Archives, Providence.
1 Jun 1880	Federal census. Statistics and names.
1 Jun 1885	State census. Statistics (Dubester, 55); names at Rhode Island State Archives, Providence.
2 Jun 1890	Federal census. Statistics; names from special census of Union Veterans only.
1 Jun 1895	State census. Statistics (Dubester, 55); no names.
1 Jun 1900	Federal census. Statistics and names.
1 Jun 1905	State census. Statistics and names at Rhode Island State Records Center, Providence.
15 Apr 1910	Federal census. Statistics and names.
15 Apr 1915	State census. Statistics (Dubester, 56); names at Rhode Island State Records Center, Providence.

Date	Census
1 Jan 1920	Federal census. Statistics and names.
15 Apr 1925	State census. Statistics and names at Rhode Island State Records Center, Providence.
1 Apr 1930	Federal census. Statistics; names not available until 2002.
Jan 1936	State census. Statistics (Dubester, 57); names at Rhode Island State Records Center, Providence.
1 Apr 1940	Federal census. Statistics; names not available until 2012.
1 Apr 1950	Federal census. Statistics; names not available until 2022.
1 Apr 1960	Federal census. Statistics; names not available until 2032.
1 Apr 1970	Federal census. Statistics; names not available until 2042.
1 Apr 1980	Federal census. Statistics; names not available until 2052.
1 Apr 1990	Federal census. Statistics; names not available until 2062.

Sources

Bartlett, John R., ed. *Census of the Inhabitants of the Colony of Rhode Island and Providence Plantations Taken by Order of the General Assembly in the Year 1774.* Providence, 1858.

Chamberlain, Mildred M., comp. *Rhode Island 1777 Military Census.* Baltimore: Genealogical Publishing Co., 1985.

Dubester, Henry J. *State Censuses: An Annotated Bibliography of Censuses of Population Taken after the Year 1790 by States and Territories of the United States.* 1948. Reprint. New York: Burt Franklin, 1969.

Greene, Evarts Boutell, and Virginia D. Harrington. *American Population before the Federal Census of 1790.* New York: Columbia University Press, 1932.

Holbrook, Jay Mack. *Rhode Island 1782 Census.* Oxford, Mass.: Holbrook Research Institute, 1979.

Lainhart, Ann S. *State Census Records.* [Baltimore]: Genealogical Publishing Co., 1992.

Rhode Island. *Records of the Colony of Rhode Island and Providence Plantations, in New England.* 10 vols. Edited by John Russell Bartlett. Providence, 1856–1865. Cited as R.I. Recs.

Wells, Robert V. *Population of the British Colonies in America before 1776: A Survey of Census Data.* Princeton, N.J.: Princeton University Press, 1975.

Census Outline
Maps for Rhode Island

Colonial Census 1708

Colonial Census 1730

Colonial Census
1748–1749

Colonial, State, and Federal
Censuses 1755–1860

State and Federal
Censuses 1865–1960

Federal Censuses
1970–1990

Bibliography

Adams, James Truslow. *Founding of New England.* Boston: Atlantic Monthly Press, 1921.

Allis, Frederick S., Jr., ed. *William Bingham's Maine Lands, 1790–1820.* Publications of the Colonial Society of Massachusetts, vols. 36–37. Boston, 1954.

Andrews, Charles M. *Colonial Period of American History.* 4 vols. New Haven: Yale University Press, 1934–1938.

Arnold, Samuel Greene. *History of the State of Rhode Island and Providence Plantations.* 4th ed. 2 vols. Providence, 1899.

Atlas of the State of Maine, Including Statistics and Descriptions of Its History, Educational System, Geology, Railroads, Natural Resources, Summer Resorts, and Manufacturing Interests, Compiled and Drawn from Official Plans and Actual Surveys. Houlton, Me.: George N. Colby and Co., 1884.

Atlas of Washington County, Maine: Compiled, Drawn and Published from Official Plans and Actual Surveys. Houlton and Machias, Me., 1881. Reprint. Cherryfield, Me.: Narraguagus Historical Society, 1978.

Attwood, Stanley Bearce. *Length and Breadth of Maine.* 1946. Reprint. Maine Studies, no. 96. Orono: University of Maine at Orono, 1973.

Barber, John Warner. *Historical Collections, Being a General Collection of Interesting Facts, Traditions, Biographical Sketches, Anecdotes, Etc., Relating to the History and Antiquities of Every Town in Massachusetts, with Geographical Descriptions.* Worcester, Mass., 1841.

Barnes, Viola Florence. *Dominion of New England: A Study in British Colonial Policy.* New Haven: Yale University Press, 1923.

Bartlett, John R., ed. *Census of the Inhabitants of the Colony of Rhode Island and Providence Plantations Taken by Order of the General Assembly in the Year 1774.* Providence, 1858.

Bartlett, Ralph Sylvester. *History of York County, Maine, and A Rambling Narrative about the Town of Eliot and Its Mother-Town Old Kittery, with Personal Reminiscences: An Address Delivered by Ralph Sylvester Bartlett at Exercises Held in Eliot, Maine, August 29, 1936, in Commemoration of the 300th Anniversary of the Founding of York County in the Province of Maine.* [Boston: Jerome Press], 1938.

Bayles, Richard M., ed. *History of Newport County, Rhode Island, from the Year 1638 to the Year 1887, Including the Settlement of its Towns, and Their Subsequent Progress.* New York, 1888.

Bayles, Richard M., ed. *History of Providence County, Rhode Island.* 2 vols. New York, 1891.

Beers, Frederick W. *Atlas of Worcester County, Massachusetts, from Actual Surveys.* New York, 1870.

Beers, Frederick W. *Old Maps of Rural Cumberland County, Maine, in 1871.* Fryeburg, Me.: Saco Valley Printing, 1979.

Benton, J. H., Jr. *Early Census Making in Massachusetts, 1643–1765, with a Reproduction of the Lost Census of 1765 (Recently Found) and Documents Relating Thereto, Now First Collected and Published.* Boston: Charles E. Goodspeed, 1905.

Bickford, Christopher P. "Lost Connecticut Census of 1762 Found." *Connecticut Historical Society Bulletin* 44 (1979): 33–43.

Bingham, Harold J. *History of Connecticut.* 4 vols. New York: Lewis Historical Publishing Co., 1962.

Blodget, William. *New and Correct Map of Connecticut, One of the United States of North America, from Actual Survey.* Middletown, Conn., 1792.

Bowen, Clarence Winthrop. *Boundary Disputes of Connecticut.* Boston, 1882.

Bowen, Clarence Winthrop. *History of Woodstock, Connecticut.* 8 vols. Norwood, Mass.: Plimpton Press, 1926–1943.

Bradford, William. *Of Plymouth Plantation, 1620–1647.* Edited by Samuel Eliot Morison. New York: Alfred A. Knopf, 1953.

Brown, Richard D. *Massachusetts: A Bicentennial History.* New York: W. W. Norton and Co., 1978.

Burrage, Henry S. *Maine in the Northeastern Boundary Controversy.* Portland, 1919.

Cady, John Hutchins. *Rhode Island Boundaries, 1636–1936.* Providence: Rhode Island Tercentenary Commission, 1936.

Cappon, Lester J., Barbara Bartz Petchenik, and John Hamilton Long, eds. *Atlas of Early American History: The Revolutionary Era, 1760–1790.* Princeton, N.J.: Princeton University Press, 1976. Section on boundaries is thoroughly documented.

Carleton, Osgood. *Map of the District of Maine, Massachusetts, Compiled from Actual Surveys Made by Order of the General Court and under the Inspection of Agents of Their Appointment.* Boston, 1802.

Carpenter, Esther Bernon. "Conflict of Colonial Authorities in Narragansett." In *South County Studies*, 268–273. Boston, 1924.

Chace, J., Jr. *Map of Waldo County, Maine.* Portland and Philadelphia, 1859.

Chadbourne, Ava Harriet. *Maine Place Names and the Peopling of Its Towns.* Portland: Bond Wheelwright Co., 1955.

Chamberlain, Mildred M., comp. *Rhode Island 1777 Military Census.* Baltimore: Genealogical Publishing Co., 1985.

Child, Hamilton, comp. *Gazetteer of Berkshire County, Massachusetts, 1725–1885.* Syracuse, N.Y., 1885.

Clark, Charles E. *Eastern Frontier: The Settlement of Northern New England, 1610–1763.* New York: Alfred A. Knopf, 1970.

Clark, Charles E. *Maine: A Bicentennial History.* New York: W. W. Norton and Co., 1977.

Conference between the Commissaries of Massachusetts-Bay and the Commissaries of New-York; at New Haven in the Colony of Connecticut, 1767. Boston, 1768. Journal of the boundary negotiations.

Connecticut. *Public Acts.* Hartford, 1650–1971. Cited as Conn. Pub. Acts.

Connecticut. *Public Records of the Colony of Connecticut.* Vols. 1–3 edited by J. H. Trumbull; vols. 4–15 edited by C. J. Hoadly. Hartford, 1850–1890. Cited as Conn. Col. Recs.

Connecticut. *Public Records of the State of Connecticut.* Vols. 1–3 edited by C. J. Hoadly; vols. 4–8 edited by Leonard Woods Labaree; vols. 9–10 edited by Albert E. Van Dusen; vol. 11 edited by Christopher Collier; vol. 12 edited by Dorothy M. Lipson. Hartford, 1894–. Cited as Conn. St. Recs.

Connecticut. *Special Acts.* Hartford, 1789–1971. Cited as Conn. Spec. Acts.

Connecticut: A Bibliography of Its History. Edited by Roger Parks. Bibliographies of New England History, vol. 6. Hanover, N.H.: University Press of New England, 1986.

Cook, Louis A., ed. *History of Norfolk County, Massachusetts, 1622–1918.* 2 vols. New York and Chicago: S. J. Clarke Publishing Co., 1918.

Craven, Wesley Frank. *Colonies in Transition, 1660–1713.* New York: Harper and Row, 1968.

Cushing, John D., comp. *Bibliography of the Laws and Resolves of the Massachusetts Bay, 1642–1780.* Wilmington, Del.: Michael Glazer, 1984.

Daniels, Bruce C. *Connecticut Town: Growth and Development, 1635–1790.* Middletown, Conn.: Wesleyan University Press, 1979.

Daniels, Bruce C., ed. *Town and County: Essays on the Structure of Local Government in the American Colonies.* Middletown, Conn.: Wesleyan University Press, 1978

Davis, Charlotte Pease, comp. *Directory of Massachusetts Place Names: Current and Obsolete Counties, Cities, Towns, Sections or Villages, Early Names.* [Lexington, Mass.]: Massachusetts Daughters of the American Revolution, 1987.

Dexter, Franklin B. "History of Connecticut, as Illustrated by the Names of Her Towns." *Proceedings of the American Antiquarian Society*, new ser., 3 (Oct. 1884–Apr. 1885): 421–448.

Dexter, Lincoln A., comp. *Maps of Early Massachusetts: Pre-History through the Seventeenth Century.* Rev. ed. Brookfield, Mass.: Lincoln A. Dexter, 1984.

Doolittle, Amos. *Connecticut from the Best Authorities* [map]. [Philadelphia, 1795].

Drake, Samuel Adams. *History of Middlesex County, Massachusetts, Containing Carefully Prepared Histories of Every City and Town in the County, by Well-Known Writers, and a General History of the County from the Earliest to the Present Time.* 2 vols. Boston, 1880.

Dubester, Henry J. *State Censuses: An Annotated Bibliography of Censuses of Population Taken after the Year 1790 by States and Territories of the United States.* 1948. Reprint. New York: Burt Franklin, 1969. The standard guide for its subject.

Eno, Joel N. "Expansion of Massachusetts—Chronological—Based on the Official Records." *Americana* 24 (1930): 28–40.

Eno, Joel N. "Expansion of Rhode Island—Chronological—Based on Official Records." *Americana* 24 (1930): 515–526.

Faeth, Henry J. *Connecticut County: A Description of its Organization, Function and Relationship with Other Governmental Units.* Rev. ed., edited by Patricia Stuart. Storrs, Conn.: Institute of Public Service, University of Connecticut, 1954.

Fairlie, John A. *Local Government in Counties, Towns and Villages.* New York: Century Co., 1906.

Farnham, Mary Frances, comp. *Farnham Papers, 1603–1688.* Vols. 7 and 8 of *Documentary History of the State of Maine. Collections of the Maine Historical Society*, 2d ser. Portland, 1901–1902. These documents are concerned chiefly with territorial changes.

Federal Writers' Project, Massachusetts. *Massachusetts: A Guide to Its Places and People.* Boston: Houghton Mifflin Co., 1937.

Felt, Joseph B. "Population of Massachusetts." *Collections of the American Statistical Association* 1, pt. 2 (1845): 121–216. Only volume published; issued in 3 parts in 1843, 1845, and 1847.

Flick, Alexander C., ed. *History of the State of New York.* 10 vols. New York: Columbia University Press, 1933–1937.

Fox, Dixon Ryan. *Yankees and Yorkers.* New York: New York University Press, 1940.

Gannett, Henry. *Geographic Dictionary of Massachusetts.* Department of the Interior, U. S. Geological Survey, Bulletin no. 116. Washington, D.C., 1894. Reprint. Baltimore: Genealogical Publishing Co., 1978.

Gay, William B., comp. *Gazetteer of Hampshire County, Massachusetts, 1654–1887.* 2 vols. in 1. Syracuse, N.Y., [1886].

Gipson, Lawrence Henry. *British Empire before the American Revolution.* 15 vols. Caldwell, Idaho, and New York: Caxton Printers and Alfred A. Knopf, 1936–1970.

Greene, Evarts Boutell, and Virginia D. Harrington. *American Population before the Federal Census of 1790.* New York: Columbia University Press, 1932.

Greenleaf, Moses. *Map Exhibiting the Principal Original Grants and Sales of Lands in the State of Maine.* Portland, 1829.

Greenleaf, Moses. *Map of the Inhabited Part of the State of Maine, Exhibiting the Progress of Its Settlement since the Year 1778, the Representative Districts since the Year 1820, and the Population and Valuation of Taxable Property in Each District at the Year 1820.* Portland, 1829.

Hale, Richard Walden, Jr. "Forgotten Maine Boundary Commission." *Proceedings of the Massachusetts Historical Society*, 3d ser., 71 (1959): 147–155.

Harris, Caleb. *Map of the State of Rhode Island.* 1795. Reprint. Providence: Rhode Island Historical Society, 1969.

Hart, Albert Bushnell, ed. *Commonwealth History of Massachusetts, Colony, Province, and State.* 5 vols. New York: States History Co., 1927–1930.

Harwood, Pliny LeRoy. *History of Eastern Connecticut Embracing the Counties of Tolland, Windham, Middlesex and New London.* 3 vols. Chicago and New Haven: Pioneer Historical Publishing Co., 1931–1932.

Hatch, Louis Clinton, ed. *Maine: A History.* Centennial ed. 5 vols. New York: American Historical Society, 1919.

Hayward, John. *Gazetteer of Massachusetts, Containing Descriptions of All the Counties, Towns, and Districts in the Commonwealth; Also, of Its Principal Mountains, Rivers, Capes, Bays, Harbors, Islands, and Fashionable Resorts: to Which Are Added Statistical Accounts of Its Agriculture, Commerce and Manufacture, with a Great Variety of Other Useful Information.* Rev. ed. Boston, 1849.

Historical Records Survey, Connecticut. *Newington.* Vol. 17 of *Hartford County.* Inventory of the Town and City Archives of Connecticut, series 2. New Haven: Connecticut Historical Records Survey, 1939.

Historical Records Survey, Connecticut. *Weston.* Vol. 21 of *Fairfield County.* Inventory of the Town and City Archives of Connecticut, series 1. New Haven: Connecticut Historical Records Survey, 1940.

Historical Records Survey, Maine. *Counties, Cities, Towns and Plantations of Maine: A Handbook of Incorporations, Dissolutions, and Boundary Changes.* Portland: Maine Historical Records Survey, 1940. Reprint. Augusta: Maine State Archives, [1980].

Historical Records Survey, Massachusetts. *Essex County (Salem).* Inventory of the County Archives of Massachusetts, no. 5. Boston: Massachusetts Historical Records Survey, 1937.

Historical Records Survey, Rhode Island. *Guide to the Public Vital Statistics Records, Births, Marriages, Deaths in the State of Rhode Island and Providence Plantations, Containing Chronologies of the Legislation Relating to or Affecting the Records Together with an Outline of the Civic Divisions of the State.* Providence: Rhode Island Historical Records Survey, 1941.

History of Cumberland County, Maine, with Illustrations and Biographical Sketches of Its Prominent Men and Pioneers. Philadelphia, 1880.

History of Litchfield County, Connecticut, with Illustrations and Biographical Sketches of Its Prominent Men and Pioneers. Philadelphia, 1881.

History of Penobscot County, Maine, with Illustrations and Biographical Sketches. Cleveland, 1882.

History of the Connecticut Valley in Massachusetts, with Illustrations and Biographical Sketches of Some of Its Prominent Men and Pioneers. 2 vols. Philadelphia, 1879.

Holbrook, Jay Mack. *Rhode Island 1782 Census.* Oxford, Mass.: Holbrook Research Institute, 1979.

Holland, Josiah Gilbert. *History of Western Massachusetts: The Counties of Hampden, Hampshire, Franklin, and Berkshire: Embracing an Outline, or General History, of the Section, an Account of Its Scientific Aspects and Leading Interests, and Separate Histories of Its One Hundred Towns.* 2 vols. Springfield, Mass., 1855.

Hooker, Roland Mather. *Boundaries of Connecticut.* Tercentenary Commission of the State of Connecticut, Committee on Historical Publications, Pamphlet 11. New Haven: Yale University Press, 1933.

Hough, Franklin B. "Papers Relating to Pemaquid and Parts Adjacent to the Present State of Maine, Known as Cornwall County When under the Colony of New-York, Compiled from Official Records in the Office of the Secretary of State at Albany, N.Y." 1856. Reprint. *Collections of the Maine Historical Society* [1st ser.] 5 (1857): 1–138.

Hough, Franklin B. *Papers Relating to the Island of Nantucket with Documents Relating to the Original Settlement of That Island, Martha's Vineyard, and Other Islands Adjacent, Known as Dukes County While Under the Colony of New York.* Albany, 1856.

Hough, Franklin B. "Pemaquid in Its Relations to Our Colonial History." *Collections of the Maine Historical Society* [1st ser.] 7 (1876): 127–164.

Hughes, Arthur H., and Morse L. Allen. *Connecticut Place Names.* [Hartford]: Connecticut Historical Society, 1976.

Hurd, Duane Hamilton, comp. *History of Bristol County, Massachusetts, with Biographical Sketches of Many of Its Pioneers and Prominent Men.* Philadelphia, 1883.

Hurd, Duane Hamilton, comp. *History of New London County, Connecticut, with Biographical Sketches of Many of Its Pioneers and Prominent Men.* Philadelphia, 1882.

Hurd, Duane Hamilton, comp. *History of Plymouth County, Massachusetts, with Biographical Sketches of Many of Its Pioneers and Prominent Men.* Philadelphia, 1884.

Hurd, Duane Hamilton, comp. *History of Worcester County, Massachusetts, with Biographical Sketches of Many of Its Pioneers and Prominent Men.* 2 vols. Philadelphia, 1889.

Hutchinson, Thomas. *History of the Colony and Province of Massachusetts-Bay.* Edited by Lawrence Shaw Mayo. 3 vols. Cambridge: Harvard University Press, 1936.

International Boundary Commission, United States and Canada. *Joint Report upon the Survey and Demarcation of the Boundary between the United States and Canada from the Source of the St. Croix River to the St. Lawrence River.* Washington, D.C.: Government Printing Office, 1925.

James, Sydney V. *Colonial Rhode Island: A History.* New York: Charles Scribner's Sons, 1975.

Jenness, John Scribner. *Isles of the Shoals: An Historical Sketch.* New York, 1873.

Jodziewicz, Thomas Walter. "Dual Localism in Seventeenth-Century Connecticut: Relations between the General Court and the Towns, 1636–1691." Ph.D. diss., College of William and Mary, 1974. Ann Arbor, Mich.: University Microfilms, 1974.

Johnston, Alexander. *Connecticut: A Study of a Commonwealth-Democracy.* Boston and New York, 1887.

Kane, Joseph Nathan. *American Counties: Origins of Names, Dates of Creation and Organization, Area, Population, Historical Data, and Published Sources.* 3d ed. Metuchen, N.J.: Scarecrow Press, 1972.

Kaufman, Martin, John W. Ifkovic, and Joseph Carvalho III, eds. *Guide to the History of Massachusetts.* New York: Greenwood Press, 1988.

Kemp, Thomas Jay. *Connecticut Researcher's Handbook.* Gale Genealogy and Local History Series, vol. 12. Detroit: Gale Research Co., 1981.

Klamkin, Marian. *Watertown Then and Now.* Derby, Conn.: Bacon Printing Co., 1976.

Lainhart, Ann S. *State Census Records.* [Baltimore]: Genealogical Publishing Co., 1992.

Lay, George Cowles. "Famous Boundary Dispute between Rhode Island and Massachusetts." *Journal of American History* 7 (1913): 911–918.

Levenson, Rosaline. *County Government in Connecticut: Its History and Demise.* Storrs, Conn.: University of Connecticut, 1966.

Long, John H. "A Case Study in Utilizing Computer Technology: The Atlas of Historical County Boundaries." *Perspectives: American Historical Association Newsletter* 30, no. 3 (March 1992): 16–17. Describes how computers have been employed in the making of this atlas.

McLoughlin, William G. *Rhode Island: A Bicentennial History.* New York: W. W. Norton and Co., 1978.

Maine. *Laws of the State of Maine.* Augusta, 1840–. Until the 1970s, the title pages of these laws read, "Acts and Resolves." Starting in 1842, "Public Laws" and "Private and Special Laws" constitute separate sections in every volume, each section having its own chapter numbers and, until 1907, its own pagination. Cited as Me. Laws.

Maine. *Private and Special Acts of the State of Maine.* Augusta, 1820–1839. Cited as Me. Priv. Acts.

Maine. *Public Acts of the State of Maine.* Augusta, 1820–1839. Cited as Me. Pub. Acts.

Maine. Governor. Proclamation, 9 May 1838. Secretary of State Manuscripts. Miscellaneous Records, 2:99–100. Maine State Library, Augusta. Cited as Me. Gov. Proc.

Maine Historical Society. *Province and Court Records of Maine.* 6 vols. Portland: Maine Historical Society, 1928–1975.

Map of Maine, New Hampshire and Vermont, Compiled from the Latest Authorities. Philadelphia: A. Finley, [1826].

Map of Maine, New Hampshire and Vermont, Compiled from the Latest Authorities. Philadelphia: S. Augustus Mitchell, 1847. This map is nearly identical to the 1852 version (below).

Map of Maine, New Hampshire and Vermont, Compiled from the Latest Authorities. Philadelphia: S. Augustus Mitchell, 1852. This map is nearly identical to the 1847 version (above).

Map of Maine, New Hampshire and Vermont, from the Most Authentic Sources. Hartford: H. F. Sumner and Co., 1834.

Map of the State of Rhode Island and Providence Plantations. Philadelphia: D. G. Beers and Co., 1871.

Massachusetts. *Acts and Resolves of Massachusetts.* Boston, 1781–. Cited as Mass. Acts.

Massachusetts. *Acts and Resolves, Public and Private, of the Province of Massachusetts Bay, to Which Are Prefixed the Charters of the Province, with Historical Explanatory Notes, and Appendix.* 21 vols. Boston, 1869–1922. Cited as Mass. Col. Acts.

Massachusetts. *Charters and General Laws of the Colony and Province of Massachusetts Bay, Carefully Collected from the Publick Records and Ancient Printed Books, to Which is Added an Appendix, Tending to Explain the Spirit, Progress, and History of the Jurisprudence of the State, Especially in a Moral and Political View.* Boston, 1814.

Massachusetts. *Records of the Governor and Company of the Massachusetts Bay in New England.* Edited by Nathaniel B. Shurtleff. 5 vols. in 6. Boston, 1853–1854. Cited as Mass. Recs.

Massachusetts. Bureau of Statistics. *Decennial Census, 1915.* Boston, 1918.

Massachusetts. Court of Assistants. *Records of the Court of Assistants of the Colony of the Massachusetts Bay, 1630–1692.* 3 vols. Boston: Suffolk County, 1901–1928.

Massachusetts. Secretary of the Commonwealth. *Historical Data Relating to Counties, Cities, and Towns in Massachusetts.* 1966. Reprint. Clearwater, Fla.: Leonard M. Smith, Jr., 1975. Cited as Mass. Sec. Comm.

Morison, Elizabeth Forbes, and Elting E. Morison. *New Hampshire: A Bicentennial History.* New York: W. W. Norton and Co., 1976.

Morris, Gerald E., and Richard D. Kelly, Jr., eds. *Maine Bicentennial Atlas: An Historical Survey.* Portland: Maine Historical Society, 1976.

Nason, Elias. *Gazetteer of the State of Massachusetts, with Numerous Illustrations on Wood and Steel.* Boston, 1878.

Nelson, John. *Worcester County: A Narrative History.* 3 vols. New York: American Historical Society, 1934.

New Hampshire. *Laws of New Hampshire, Including Public and Private Acts and Resolves [1680–1835].* 10 vols. Concord, 1904–1922. Cited as N.H. Early Laws.

New Hampshire. *Provincial and State Papers.* Vols. 1–10 edited by Nathaniel Bouton; vols. 11–18 edited by Isaac W. Hammond; vols. 19–31 edited by Albert Stillman Batchellor; vols. 32–33 edited by Henry Harrison Metcalf; vols. 34–40 edited by Otis G. Hammond. Concord, 1867–1943. Cited as N.H. State Papers.

New Plymouth Colony. *Book of the General Laws of the Inhabitants of the Jurisdiction of New-Plimouth, Collected Out of the Records of the General Court, and Lately Revised, and with Some Emendations and Additions, Established and Disposed into Such Order as They May Readily Conduce to General Use and Benefit.* Boston, 1672. Cited as Ply. Laws.

New Plymouth Colony. *Records of the Colony of New Plymouth in New England.* Vols. 1–8 edited by Nathaniel B. Shurtleff; vols. 9–12 edited by David Pulsifer. Boston, 1855–1861.

New York. Commissioners of Statutory Revision. *Colonial Laws of New York from the Year 1664 to the Revolution, Including the Charters of the Duke of York, the Commissions and Instructions to Colonial Governors, the Duke's Laws, the Laws of the Dongan and Leisler Assemblies, the Charters of Albany and New York, and the Acts of the Colonial Legislatures from 1691 to 1775, Inclusive.* Report to the Assembly no. 107, 1894. 5 vols. Albany, 1894–1896. Cited as N.Y. Col. Laws.

Noble, John. "Incident in 1731 in the Long Dispute of Massachusetts and Rhode Island over their Boundary Line." *Proceedings of the Massachusetts Historical Society*, 2d ser., 19 (1906): 20–34.

O'Callaghan, E. B., comp. *Documentary History of the State of New York.* 4 vols. Albany, 1850–1851.

Old Maps of Androscoggin County, Maine, in 1873. Fryeburg, Me.: Saco Valley Printing, 1983.

Old Maps of Kennebec County, Maine, in 1879. Fryeburg, Me.: Saco Valley Printing, 1983.

Old Maps of Northeastern Essex County, Massachusetts, in 1884. Fryeburg, Me.: Saco Valley Printing, 1982.

Old Maps of Southern Somerset County, Maine, in 1883. Fryeburg, Me.: Saco Valley Printing, 1989.

Old Maps of York County, Maine, in 1872. Fryeburg, Me.: Saco Valley Printing, 1980.

Onuf, Peter S. *Origins of the Federal Republic: Jurisdictional Controversies in the United States, 1775–1787.* Philadelphia: University of Pennsylvania Press, 1983.

Palfrey, John Gorham. *History of New England.* 5 vols. Boston, 1882–1890.

Parry, Clive, ed. *Consolidated Treaty Series.* 231 vols. Dobbs Ferry, N.Y.: Oceana Publications, 1969–1981.

Paullin, Charles O. *Atlas of the Historical Geography of the United States.* Edited by John K. Wright. Washington, D.C., and New York: Carnegie Institution of Washington and American Geographical Society of New York, 1932. Excellent section on international and interstate boundary disputes.

Pease, John C., and John M. Niles. *Gazetteer of the States of Connecticut and Rhode-Island, Written with Care and Impartiality, from Original and Authentic Materials.* Hartford, Conn., 1819.

Perry, Charles M. "Southwest Corner of the Shawomet Purchase." *Rhode Island History* 10 (1951): 65–68, 80–85.

Pope, Franklin Leonard. *Western Boundary of Massachusetts: A Study of Indian and Colonial History.* Pittsfield, Mass., 1886.

Potter, Elisha R., Jr. *Early History of Narragansett.* Collections of the Rhode Island Historical Society, vol. 3. Providence, 1835.

Pratt, Daniel J., comp. *Report of the Regents of the University on the Boundaries of the State of New York.* N.Y. Sen. Doc. no. 108, 1873, and N.Y. Sen. Doc. no. 61, 1877. 2 vols. Albany, 1874–1884.

Preston, Richard Arthur. *Gorges of Plymouth Fort: A Life of Sir Ferdinando Gorges, Captain of Plymouth Fort, Governor of New England, and Lord of the Province of Maine.* Toronto: University of Toronto Press, 1953.

Pruitt, Bettye Hobbs, ed. *Massachusetts Tax Valuation List of 1771.* Boston: G. K. Hall, 1978.

Reid, John G. *Acadia, Maine, and New Scotland: Marginal Colonies in the Seventeenth Century.* Toronto: University of Toronto Press, 1981.

Reid, John G. *Maine, Charles II and Massachusetts: Governmental Relationships in Early Northern New England.* Maine Historical Society Research Series, no. 1. Portland, 1977.

Rhode Island. *Acts and Resolves of Rhode Island and Providence Plantations.* Providence, 1776–. Cited as R.I. Acts & Resolves.

Rhode Island. *Records of the Colony of Rhode Island and Providence Plantations, in New England.* 10 vols. Edited by John Russell Bartlett. Providence, 1856–1865. Coverage extends beyond independence to 1792. Cited as R.I. Recs.

Ring, Elizabeth, comp. *Maine Bibliographies: A Bibliographical Guide.* Portland: Maine Historical Society, 1973.

Ritchie, Robert C. *Duke's Province: A Study of New York Politics and Society, 1664–1691.* Chapel Hill: University of North Carolina Press, 1977.

Roth, David M. *Connecticut: A Bicentennial History.* New York: W. W. Norton and Co., 1979.

Russ, William A. *How Pennsylvania Acquired Its Present Boundaries.* Pennsylvania Historical Association, Pennsylvania History Studies, no. 8. University Park: Pennsylvania State University, 1966.

Schwarz, Philip J. *Jarring Interests: New York's Boundary Makers, 1664–1776.* Albany: State University of New York Press, 1979.

Sellers, Helen Earle. *Connecticut Town Origins: Their Names, Boundaries, Early Histories and First Families.* Chester, Conn.: Pequot Press, n.d.

Shepard, Odell. *Connecticut, Past and Present.* New York: Alfred A. Knopf, 1939.

Shortt, Adam, and Arthur G. Doughty, eds. *Documents Relating to the Constitutional History of Canada.* Vol. 1, *1759–1791.* Canadian Archives, Sessional Paper no. 18. Ottawa, 1907. Contains the full text of King George III's Proclamation of 1763, including boundary descriptions.

Sinko, Peggy Tuck. *Guide to Local and Family History at the Newberry Library.* Salt Lake City: Ancestry Publishing, 1987.

Skillin, Glenn B., ed. "Vermont-Massachusetts Boundary." *Vermont History* 30 (1962): 63–65.

Smith, Edgar Crosby. *Moses Greenleaf, Maine's First Map-Maker: A Biography, with Letters, Unpublished Manuscripts, and a Reprint of Mr. Greenleaf's Rare Paper on Indian Place-Names; also a Bibliography of the Maps of Maine.* Bangor, Me.: The De Burians, 1902.

Smith, Jonathan. "Massachusetts and New Hampshire Boundary Line Controversy, 1693–1740." *Proceedings of the Massachusetts Historical Society*, 3d ser., 43 (1909–1910): 77–88.

Spofford, Jeremiah. *Gazetteer of Massachusetts: Containing a General View of the State, with a Historical Sketch of the Principal Events from Its Settlement to the Present Time, and Notices of the Several Towns Alphabetically Arranged.* Newburyport, Mass., 1828.

Spofford, Jeremiah. *Historical and Statistical Gazetteer of Massachusetts, with Sketches of the Principal Events from Its Settlement, a Catalogue of Prominent Characters, and Historical and Statistical Notices of the Several Cities and Towns, Alphabetically Arranged, with a New Map of the State.* Haverhill, Mass., 1860.

Stephenson, Richard W., comp. *Land Ownership Maps: A Checklist of Nineteenth Century United States County Maps in the Library of Congress.* Washington, D.C.: Library of Congress, 1967. Most of the maps listed here have been reproduced on microfiche by the Library of Congress.

Susquehannah Company Papers. Vols. 1–4 edited by Julian P. Boyd; vols. 5–11 edited by Robert J. Taylor. Wilkes Barre, Pa., and Ithaca, N.Y.: Wyoming Historical and Geological Society, 1930–1971.

Swindler, William F., ed. *Sources and Documents of United States Constitutions.* 10 vols. Dobbs Ferry, N.Y.: Oceana Publications, 1973–1979. The most complete and up-to-date compilation for the states.

Taylor, Robert J. *Colonial Connecticut: A History.* Millwood, N.Y.: KTO Press, 1979.

Temple, Josiah H. *History of the Town of Palmer, Massachusetts, Early Known as the Elbow Tract, Including Records of the Plantation, District, and Town, 1716–1889.* Palmer, Mass., 1889.

Territorial Papers of the United States. Vols. 1–26 edited by Clarence E. Carter; vols. 27–28 edited by John P. Bloom. Washington, D.C.: Government Printing Office, 1934–1975. Cited as *Terr. Papers U.S.*

Thompson, Edmund Burke. *Maps of Connecticut before the Year 1800: A Descriptive List.* Windham, Conn.: Hawthorn House, 1940.

Thompson, Edmund Burke. *Maps of Connecticut for the Years of Industrial Revolution, 1801–1860: A Descriptive List.* Windham, Conn.: Hawthorn House, 1942.

Thorndale, William, and William Dollarhide. *Map Guide to the U.S. Federal Censuses, 1790–1920.* Baltimore: Genealogical Publishing Co., 1987. An atlas of well-designed county outline maps for each state, accompanied by a bibliography and an explanation of methodology.

Thornton, J. Wingate. "Ancient Pemaquid: An Historical Review." *Collections of the Maine Historical Society* [1st ser.] 5 (1857): 139–305.

[Tracy, Cyrus M., et al.] *Standard History of Essex County, Massachusetts, Embracing a History of the County from Its First Settlement to the Present Time, with a History and Description of Its Towns and Cities.* Boston, 1878.

Trumbull, James H. *Indian Names of Places, Etc., in and on the Borders of Connecticut, with Interpretations of Some of Them.* Hartford, 1881.

Trumbull, James H., ed. *Memorial History of Hartford County, Connecticut, 1633–1884.* 2 vols. Boston, 1886.

Ullman, Edward L. "Historical Geography of the Eastern Boundary of Rhode Island." *Research Studies of the State College of Washington* 4, no. 2 (1936): 67–87.

United States. *Statutes at Large of the United States of America, 1789–1873.* 17 vols. Boston: Little, Brown, 1845–1874. Cited as U.S. Stat.

Upham, George B. "'Great River Naumkeek': Once the Southern Boundary of New Hampshire." *Granite Monthly* 52 (May 1920): 193–201.

Van Zandt, Franklin K. *Boundaries of the United States and the Several States.* Geological Survey Professional Paper 909. Washington, D.C.: Government Printing Office, 1976. The standard compilation for its subject.

Varney, George J. *Brief History of Maine.* Portland, 1888.

Walling, Henry Francis. *Old Maps of Oxford County, Maine, in 1858.* Fryeburg, Me.: Saco Valley Printing, 1972.

Walling, Henry Francis. *Topographical Map of Hancock County, Maine, from Actual Surveys.* New York, 1860.

Walling, Henry Francis. *Topographical Map of the County of Penobscot, Maine.* New York, 1859.

Walling, Henry Francis, and Ormando Willis Gray, comps. *Official Topographical Atlas of Massachusetts.* Boston, 1871.

Washburn, Emory. *Sketches of the Judicial History of Massachusetts from 1630 to the Revolution in 1776.* Boston, 1840.

Wells, Robert V. *Population of the British Colonies in America before 1776: A Survey of Census Data.* Princeton, N.J.: Princeton University Press, 1975.

Willard, Josiah. *Census of Newington, Connecticut, Taken According to Households in 1776.* Edited by Edwin Stanley Welles. Hartford: Frederic B. Hartranft, 1909.

Williamson, William D. *History of the State of Maine, from Its First Discovery, A.D. 1602, to the Separation, A.D. 1820.* 2 vols. Hallowell, Me., 1832.

Winsor, Justin, ed. *Memorial History of Boston, Including Suffolk County, Massachusetts, 1630–1880.* 4 vols. Boston, 1880–1886.

Witherell, Eugene E. *Map of the Colony of Rhode Island and Providence Plantations, 1636–1740.* [Providence: Rhode Island Historical Society], 1925.

York County, Maine. Register of Deeds. *York Deeds [1642–1737].* 18 vols. in 19. Vols. 1–4 edited by H. W. Richardson; vols. 5–6 edited by W. M. Sargent; vols. 7–11 edited by L. B. Chapman. Portland et al., 1887–1910.

HOW TO USE THIS ATLAS

These excerpts from the CONSOLIDATED CHRONOLOGY and the INDIVIDUAL COUNTY CHRONOLOGIES demonstrate the depiction, both textual and cartographic, of county boundary changes and the relationship between these two sections of the atlas.

In addition to the Consolidated Chronology of State and County Boundaries and Individual County Chronologies, Maps, and Areas, the atlas includes the following:

Table of County Creations / Table of Censuses / Census Outline Maps / Bibliography

CONSOLIDATED CHRONOLOGY includes, in chronological order, all boundary changes reported for the state and its counties. Changes for more than one county may appear under one date. Historical sources of information are given in parentheses for every event; more detailed information about sources can be found in the bibliography at the back of the atlas.

Events from the CONSOLIDATED CHRONOLOGY correspond to the events listed in the INDIVIDUAL COUNTY CHRONOLOGY table. These events for Covington are illustrated by maps 4, 5, and 6.

21 January 1824

COVINGTON gained all of BAINBRIDGE; BAINBRIDGE eliminated. (Miss. Laws 1823–1824, 7th sess., ch. 26/p. 35)

JACKSON gained from HANCOCK. (Miss. Laws 1823–1824, 7th sess., ch. 36/pp. 44–45)

23 January 1824

SIMPSON created from COPIAH. (Miss. Laws 1823–1824, 7th sess., ch. 72, sec. 1/p. 87)

1 February 1825

COVINGTON gained from LAWRENCE and WAYNE. Part of COVINGTON's gain from LAWRENCE was unintended; MARION had been authorized to gain from LAWRENCE, but local officials and residents treated the area as part of the territory transferred to COVINGTON. (Miss. Laws 1825, 8th sess., ch. 22/p. 48)

2 February 1825

PIKE gained from LAWRENCE. (Miss. Laws 1825, 8th sess., ch. 33/p. 78)

3 February 1825

PERRY gained from HANCOCK. (Miss. Laws 1825, 8th sess., ch. 43/p. 99)

24 January 1826

JONES created from COVINGTON and WAYNE. (Miss. Laws 1826, 9th sess., p. 59)

4 February 1829

Non-county area (unceded Indian territory) divided into six regions which were attached to: MADISON, MONROE, RANKIN and SIMPSON jointly, WASHINGTON, WAYNE, and YAZOO. (Miss. Laws 1829, 12th sess., ch. 77, secs. 1–2/pp. 81–82)

5 February 1829

MADISON gained from HINDS. (Miss. Laws 1829, 12th sess., ch. 19/p. 17)

30 January 1830

LOWNDES created from MONROE and non-county area attached to MONROE. (Miss. Laws 1830, 13th sess., ch. 14, sec. 1/p. 18)

Part of non-county area detached from RANKIN and SIMPSON, attached to COVINGTON; parts of non-county areas detached from WAYNE and from RANKIN and SIMPSON, attached to JONES. (Miss. Laws 1830, 13th sess., ch. 43/p. 46)